"This book contains all of the things you should know if you are venturing into the filmmaking business and all the things you wish you had known if you're already in the 'Biz.'"
— Tom Ara, Esq., Film and Television Lawyer

"I've read half of Steves book as I only have one good eye. I had somebody read the other half into my one good ear ... Steve has captured the essence of our profession. He has as tight a grip on it as the oil cartels have on our collective nuts." — Chris Bearde, Producer
The Gong Show, Sonny & Cher

"To understand, how to behave on and off set working in film and television from now until 2050, study this book daily. After 2050, renegotiate! Buy this book and, with it, a bit of his hard earned wisdom. Learn from the best or forever be at their mercy."
— Carl Bressler, Talent Manager

"A unique view from the eye of the s***storm. Strapped to the helm, Steve hangs on. I know he has kept me from falling overboard many times." — Chris Donovan, Producer/Director
Golden Globes, Spirit Awards

" ... a rare practical guide to the ins and outs of producing utilizing a series of page turning essays. It is a must for every young filmmaker and student alike." — Steve Gerbson, Producer/Director, Educator

"Becoming a producer in Hollywood is like trying to drive up the freeway off ramp in rush hour. Steve's book will tell you how to avoid a head-on collisions and by end of it, you'll be driving like a stunt man. " — Laura Gregory, Producer

" ... smart filmmakers should use this book to get to their career destination quickly ... an insightful and entertaining view of da biz written by a man who has been in the trenches for many years."
— Bobby Logan, Writer/Director
Repossessed, F Troop

"If you really wanna be a producer in Hollywood or anywhere else in the world, stop talking about it and read Steve's book.
— Sean McNamara, Producer/Director
Robosapien, Bratz: The Movie, Even Stevens, That's So Raven

"It is funny, concise and on the mark. This will be a welcome addition to the world of budding producers. I will use it, I am sure, as a text-book."
— Lee Miller, Producer, Director

"It's like doing lunch with an uncle who's giving advice and sharing his wisdom. And we can all use an uncle in the biz!"
— George Rizkallah, Post Production Producer
The Product Factory

" ... even before I finished it I couldn't wait to give a copy to a young aspiring filmmaker who had recently asked me "So how exactly do I break into the business?"
— Tom Ropelewski, Independent Screenwriter/ TV producer

"This book should be required reading for every producer wannabe. It is truly a fascinating look inside the world of TV and Film."
— Scott Satin, TV Network Writer/ Producer

"After reading SO YOU WANNA BE A PRODUCER you can go right on to your PHD in film producing, the actual experience."
— Fred Sidewater, veteran Industry Executive

"A must read for anyone daring to come to Hollywood."
— Mitch Stein, Talent Agent

So You Wanna Be a Producer?

HOLLYWOOD

Adventures of a Migrant Film Worker

So You Wanna Be a Producer?

HOLLYWOOD

Adventures of a Migrant Film Worker

Steve Ecclesine

MENABREA BOOKS * 2008

SO YOU WANNA BE A PRODUCER?

Visit **www.soyouwanttobeaproducer.com**

ISBN 978-190235-37-3
First Menabrea Books edition July, 2008
Menabrea Books is an imprint of Babbage Press

Babbage Press
8939 Canby Avenue
Northridge, CA 91325

www.babbagepress.com

Printed in the United States of America

BOOK ONE

SO YOU WANNA BE A PRODUCER?

Table of Contents

BOOK TWO

ADVENTURES OF
A MIGRANT FILM WORKER

Table of Contents

So You Wanna Be a Producer?

BOOK ONE

INTRODUCTION

Most people believe being a movie or TV producer is a glamorous, high paying job where you sit by the pool, martini in hand, barking out orders all day surrounded by hot and cold running blondes — a myth that probably began as an inside joke during Hollywood's Golden Age. Ironically, today's producers often portray themselves as shallow, conniving, egomaniacal, thieving bastards who will do anything to see their name up in lights while chasing the almighty dollar. The truth lies somewhere between these two extremes.

Although there are several biographies about famous producers, very few will tell anyone who is interested what it's really like to be a producer or how to become one. *So You Wanna Be A Producer?* (*SYWB*) attempts to bridge the gap between perception and reality in a series of easy to digest essays.

So, where's the fire? What really goes on behind the scenes? Who are these men and women responsible for erecting all of those celluloid pyramids and how'd they get there? Contrary to popular belief,

93.5% of the people who work in Showbiz are not rich or famous. They are the "little people" who get thanked from the podium by an actor or actress tearfully clutching his or her gold statue. They are hard-working folks with partners in life and bills to pay. They are the crazy glue that holds this crazy business together. I know because I'm one of them.

Like *The Boy Scout Handbook, SYWB* is a survivor's guide for those innocents who have been hooked by the fame and fortune bug and happily volunteer to jump into this shark tank. As a 22 year-old Emerson College film school graduate who fell off the proverbial turnip truck, I'd tell anyone who'd listen that there'd be one of them gold statues on my mantel within five years or I'd do everyone a favor and jump off the Hollywood Sign. It's thirty-five years later and I'm still here, still learning my craft, still statue-less with no plans to jump off of anything except the diving board of the pool in the backyard I look forward to someday having.

During my career producing over 700 TV shows and a dozen movies, it often feels like I've been hired to referee the never-ending match between the *show* and *business* factions. *SYWB* maneuvers the reader through this enormously attractive minefield that has claimed far too many victims. Most of the failed wannabes can be attributed to ignorance of the rules of a game that on the surface doesn't appear to have any. Many seekers self-destruct because of myopic egos and self-inflicted wounds. There's a plethora of Showbiz magazines and books celebrating the careers of the famous and the infamous that have somehow managed to temporarily reach the top. There are scholarly books that relate various techniques how to become an actor, director, director of photography or writer but they conveniently skip over one of the hardest jobs: how to be a producer. *SYWB* addresses how to get a foot in the door, what skills one needs to have, and how to stick around long enough to actually have a career.

Reading this book is an easy way of getting prepared for the nasty curveballs Showbiz throws at you. It's not enough to show up and say, "I want it so bad I can taste it!" You have to earn it. Blind ambition without direction is a formula for failure. A lot of unnec-essary heartache and wasted time can be avoided by knowing the score. Maps to stars' homes are readily available in L.A. but how to land in one of those mansions still remains a big mystery.

The *SYWB* essays are not meant to be read in one sitting. For maximum enjoyment, my suggestion is to pick out a couple of topics of interest, read them, turn off the light and get some sleep. Pick up the book a few days later in between meals and read a couple more. Like an intricate quilt, each essay is a small piece of the overall picture. It's a non-linear approach to the subject matter where I throw a lot of pitches and you hit the ones you like. A few stories at a time will work best until finished. Then, hopefully, the cumulative effect will provide a much greater understanding and appreciation for who and what a producer is.

We producers train ourselves to hold a problem up to the light and examine it from many angles. If you have a real interest in becoming a producer, you'll have to figure out a lot of things for yourself, as there is no Showbiz manual to refer to. There are, however, several hard learned lessons contained in this book that you can hopefully benefit from in the future.

Who you know, being in the right place at the right time and having some inherent talent qualifies you for "getting lucky." It is difficult to explain to sane people in the real world that you've decided to dedicate your life to a business where success is deter-mined by lottery. "If handled properly" being the operative phrase, I've seen mediocre talent hit the heights and some of the most talented people prematurely jettisoned from the landscape. Hooking up with good people is the quickest elevator to the top. But how do you do that? How do you create lightning in a bottle or catch a comet by the tail?

Special Effects is one answer. Reading *So You Wanna Be A Producer?* is another. This is my chance to put something back in the kitty and improve the readers' chances for survival and success in a business they love, but one that doesn't always love them back.

CHAPTER 1

THERE'S NO BUSINESS LIKE SHOWBIZ

HOORAY FOR HOLLYWOOD

Hey, you! It's exciting being in Show Business. Tired of the same old humdrum existence served up in thirty and forty year installments offered up by the outside world? Step right up and win a prize because almost everyone has a shot at fame, fortune and fun! We're talking celluloid immortality here. If you're not interested, quit rubbernecking and keep moving along with the rest of the unwashed masses. Plenty of other fish in the sea. You, Sir (or Madam), you look like an intelligent person. (Hah!) All that is required is for you to invest your youthful energy, your hard earned money (if you have any) and that charming naiveté that still believes in magic and miracles. *HURRY!* There's gonna be some *ACTION!* and *GLAMORE GALORE*! You don't want to miss this chance of a lifetime because opportunities like these don't grow on trees!

And, hey, you can't beat those perks! Looking at all the beautiful scenery in front of the camera will keep you young forever! Did I mention the big bucks? Who wouldn't like to see their name on a paycheck followed by six or seven zeroes at least once before they die? No? Don't know what I'm talking about? Then keep moving. Don't know why I'm wasting my time with the likes of you. Step inside the big tent and let Dame Fortune have her way with you! She will seduce you into believing this grand illusion is not only fantastically real but also easily achievable. Don't be shy! You'll think you died and went to heaven. C'mon now, sing along, "There's No Business Like Show Business." If you don't know the words, just hum along.

When you think about this unofficial Showbiz national anthem, what sounds like an upbeat ditty with a catchy refrain is secretly a warning to all of the normal, sane people who populate the real world. "Stay away if you want to live a life that makes sense!" I was four years old in 1954 when Ethel Merman originally belted out this rousing Irving Berlin classic. In the interim, a couple other million folk like me have been suckered into the vortex of the entertainment world because of it.

It's been thirty plus years since I fell into this upside down world. Instead of being fleeced out of what I started with and booted out the exit door like so many others, I somehow figured out how to hang around. In evaluating the game from inside the belly of the beast, the only common denominators between those who make it and those who don't are the words, "perseverance" and "getting lucky." The flip side of these banners should read, "Sheer, blind, stupidity!"

Working with some of the most powerful producers in Show Business and some of the worst, (not mutually exclusive) I have experienced many hard-learned lessons about life, love, people, fame and fortune. Is the world a better place because some people like to put on funny hats and dance around in the spotlights? Are hours of pleasure and the lifting of the human spirit from its everyday yoke worth a few of your hard earned dollars? Only you can be the judge. One thing for sure, the world would be a duller place without us.

We are practitioners of the ancient art of folly, masters of illusion. We create powerful images that burn indelible holes in the old memory banks. We have mastered the art of being able to reach inside most people's control panel and make them laugh or cry, calm them down or rev 'em up. The sights and sounds we manufacture jump over the conscious brain, past the barricades people use to protect themselves from everyday life and laser right into the old subconscious. We produce multi-media jigsaw puzzles that dance before your eyes, invade your heart and influence your brain in unfathomable ways. Entertainment is a narcotic and once exposed to, it's hard to ignore and fairly easy to get addicted to.

It's a business where the end product never gets used up. You buy a loaf of bread, you eat it, and it's gone. You buy a car; it carries you from here to there for a few years before the built-in obsolescence kicks in. You make a movie or TV series and if it's really good, with the help of new technology, you can keep selling it over and over again from now until the end of time without ever using it up. If the world survives, *I Love Lucy* will still be delighting audiences in the 25th Century.

2006 was one of the best years ever at the domestic box office. The 500 TV channel universe is on the verge of happening. New technology is propelling this business forward at a dizzying pace. DVD sales and rentals — a technology that didn't exist ten years ago — out-grossed the domestic theatrical box office $22 Billion to $9.4 Billion. Internet broadcasting, VOD (video on demand), cell phone broadcasting are only the latest ways to milk the willing audience out of their spare change.

The most recent Coopers & Lybrand report estimates the worldwide media business will exceed *one trillion dollars* by 2009. It's an exciting time to be in Showbiz. More outlets require more storytellers to produce cheaper, better and faster. With the latest innovations, cheaper and faster are easy. Better is the greatest challenge for all of us fortunate enough to be operating behind the celluloid curtain.

There are layers upon layers of different realities in Hollywood. Having started at the bottom of the pile, on a few occasions I've enjoyed breathing the rarefied air at the top working for Sam Raimi, Orson Welles, Sam Arkoff, Roger Corman, John Landis, Rob Reiner. If big numbers in the bank account are how you keep score, then I haven't yet enjoyed the breakout hit that secures the home in Bel Aire. I have, however, had a wide variety of adventures along the way. It is in the trying and succeeding where others wouldn't dare to tread that I've enjoyed myself the most. Mundane and ordinary projects hold little appeal for me. Playing it safe isn't in my DNA.

Hooray for Hollywood! It's an amazing playground where just about anything can and does happen on a regular basis. So grab some popcorn and a drink, prop your feet up and hope you enjoy the show.

THE CIRCUS LIFE

While driving around L.A. on any given day, you will often notice a caravan of parked white production trucks that have sprung to life overnight and suddenly seem to be everywhere. Known in the industry as, "The Circus", it is seemingly protected by a force field, a couple of bored looking motorcycle cops and tough–looking security guards. This is a small, portable, self-sustaining army that has departed the safety of the studio walls because something unique was needed from the outside world that couldn't be easily duplicated. All of the participants are usually smiling, drinking coffee, munching craft service like there's no tomorrow. Today is special because a little piece of it will be recorded for posterity.

In this temporary home away from home, some scene of a movie, TV show, commercial or rock video will be captured on film, video or Hi-Def for the world to see. If it's a big movie, they'll be lucky to boil down the day's efforts into a minute or two of usable footage. If it's a TV show or Movie of the Week, they'll end up with five or eight minutes of cinematic gold.

It's no wonder somebody from the grip crew or set dressing department is sprawled out on the tailgate catching some rays. They're exhausted. In reality, they probably got up at 5 a.m. to shower and get to this location by the 6 a.m. crew call. They have to unpack the trucks, unwrap a mile or so of cable to get the lights and cameras in position for the day's work that will be lucky to get underway by 8 a.m.. They have to hook up all the other trucks to their own separate generator. They'll eat at noon, keep shooting until 6 or 7 p.m., re-pack the trucks in an hour and then drive home for about an hour of civility with their better half, kiss the kids goodnight before they hit the wall and crash into bed. The alarm clock goes off at 5 a.m. the next morning and they get up to do it all over again. And they wouldn't have it any other way because these are the lucky ones whose job it is to help create a world of make-believe that the outside world can't seem to get enough of.

The Circus is parked here because some location has proven to be irresistible to the powers that be that decide such things. It is deemed cheaper to spend the extra dough today on cops, permits, location fees, fire marshals, parking fees, extra drivers, extra trucks, overtime, noisy neighbors, nearby traffic, etc., etc. than staying onstage and building the equivalent. When the entire production is already burning through $50,000–$100,000 a day, what's another $15,000?

The set dressing, camera, lights and grip trucks belch out enormous amounts of gear onto the sidewalk. On a sound stage, there is a big space waiting to accommodate the beehive of activity. Out on location, all kinds of adjustments have to be made. Improvisation is the order of the day for the crew. A few entrances have to be breached to accomplish the task at hand. I've had pianos hoisted up to third story windows where we had to take out windows and doors to gain access. Once needed a flying car to land atop a twelve story building in downtown L.A. That required a very big crane.

Leaving the comfort zone inside the studio walls is a logistical challenge that would make any military tactician proud. A thousand details must be successfully dealt with in order to pull off the day. The actual physical shooting is the easy part. It's getting there, setting up, and pulling it all down at the end of the day that is the bitch. But you wouldn't know it to look at it. Everyone inside the bubble seems to be traveling in slow motion. I used to wonder why so many people were required to make a movie or TV show. Somewhere between 70–150 people are organized into small platoons who all have their marching orders. The crew never all works at the same time. They attack in waves until the location has been properly invaded and prepared for the actors to arrive and deliver their pearls in front of the cameras. Then the army disengages, having conquered the locale. All the extra bodies that have been hanging around are suddenly thrown into the fray so that the dreaded double-double overtime (after 12 or 14 hours) can be avoided.

In the beginning of the day, nothing less than perfection is acceptable. Discussions take place ad nauseum about the best angles to shoot from or whether throwing a fifteenth or twentieth light into the picture is going to improve the composition. Often, divine inspiration suddenly seizes the director that will cost a lot of money. The producer might be the only person who can point out the obvious that, "Yes, it's a great idea but we don't have the time or the budget to properly execute it and you don't want us to do something half-assed that you're going to be putting your name on, so let's just stick with the original game plan for the day, okay?" If, however, the director is one of the Golden 100, we may need to repaint a wall or knock it out altogether, stop traffic on the freeway outside or tranquilize the barking dog next door. Can we re-route the air traffic because it keeps ruining our takes? The plan of the day has to be flexible enough to roll with the punches because they're definitely coming.

The Location Manager watches out for the wooden floors or expensive coffee tables that the gear will inevitably scratch so we won't have to pay for the repairs. By the end of each day, the attitude of the crew has changed 180 degrees from the leisurely pace of the morning. It's become, "Screw it! Say the lines right. Pray the first A.D. says the words, "martini shot" (meaning the last shot of the day), check the camera gate to make sure no hairs or dust have crept into the lens frame, thus ruining the shot, and causing us to shoot another take because we all just want to go home!"

As a young man, I would pull over to the side of the road whenever I encountered The Circus. I'd meander over and pick somebody out who was sitting around and ask, "What'cha shooting?" They would answer with the name of some project and I'd nod as if I knew what it was all about.

I remember being drawn like a moth to the klieg lights one night in downtown L.A. to discover a crew shooting the pilot for *Toma*, a prime time cop show featuring Robert Blake with a talking parrot on his shoulder. (This was prior to his own troubles with the law, back when Bobby was about to resurrect his career for the umpteenth time.) I ventured past the invisible boundary of The Circus perimeter over to the tailgate of a truck where an old man was sitting, rooting around in his toolbox and struck up a conversation.

"And what do you do?" I asked.

"I'm the special effects supervisor."

"Uh huh. You mean like *Star Wars* spaceship stuff?"

"No, that's visual effects. I'm in charge of physical effects; gunshots, exploding windows, bullet hits. Things like that."

"Uh huh. Have you worked on any shows I might have heard of?"

He paused for a moment and sized up the gangly youth with the inquiring mind before plunging ahead.

"Yep. I was the Special Effects Supervisor on *Gone With The Wind* and *How The West Was Won*."

"You're kidding me!"

Nope and he proceeded to reel off ten other famous films I had either seen or was aware of. I was blown away. What was the Special

Effects Supervisor from *Gone With The Wind* doing in a downtown parking lot sitting on the back of a tailgate shooting a TV pilot in the middle of the night?

Now I know. He was just making a living doing something he loved. The Circus is in town and we've all run away from the real world to join it. Wouldn't have it any other way.

LUCKY SEVEN

Taking an idea and translating it into money in your bank account is the closest thing to true alchemy there is. Individuals from the following Lucky Seven professions must be present in order to get most shows off the ground; writer, producer, executive producer, director, actors, editor and distributor. As opposed to being a painter or novelist, Showbiz is a collaborative medium. Every individual personality in the mix alters the finished product in some way. There are multi-taskers in Showbiz who wear many hats but nobody can do them all well. Once in a great while there is a happy confluence of events where the right people find themselves working on the right project at the right time. *Casablanca, Citizen Kane, The Godfather, Dirty Harry, Ben Hur,* and a few hundred others that turned out truly great. The whole production becomes greater than the sum of its parts. Critics love it and the cash register sings from here to eternity. Gold plated statues bearing their names materialize during the many televised self-congratulatory ceremonies that Hollywood is famous for.

Nobody hits a home run every time at bat. More often than not, one of the key elements is the wrong person in the wrong place at the wrong time. The vast majority of shows aren't as great as they might have been. They're good, just okay or don't really live up to their potential which are all polite ways of saying, "It didn't turn out like we hoped it would." Nobody intentionally sets out to make a bad movie or TV show and yet, some people spend their whole careers creating entertaining mediocrity and live happily ever after in their Bel Aire mansions or castles in France. They couldn't care less — just spell the name right on the checks. As H.L. Menken once cracked, "Nobody ever went broke underestimating the intelligence of the American public."

And just as critically acclaimed box office smashes or hit TV shows periodically arrive on the scene, at the other end of the spectrum, there are a hundred failed TV pilots and several high-profile missteps each year (*Gigli, Ishtar, Heaven's Gate, Pluto Nash, Judge Dredd* to name but a few.) These 'epics' would normally be taken out with the trash to little fanfare except they often involve people of sterling reputations and cost tens of millions of dollars. These expensive duds are sent up the flagpole in the hopes of salvaging some recompense from what everyone on the inside quickly realizes is a bankrupt enterprise. The critics have a field day trying to outmatch each other in savaging the corpse. The finished product quickly joins a mountain of failed enterprises buried in Hollywood's backyard, often providing an unintended definition to the genre known as, "disaster pictures." By the time the audience gets to vote, the Lucky Seven have earned a few more dollars and moved onto their next project.

80% of all networks TV shows that are fortunate enough to make it onto the prime time schedule don't survive the first lap around the track. This cruel fate after a pitch has been bought by a group of highly paid network executives whose job it seems is to guess wrong most of the time. After they embrace an idea, the next step is to craft a great script (often re-written by a committee) and if all the right pieces fall into place, a TV pilot gets produced. Then Market Research jumps in and picks out a handful proclaiming, "Bingo! Looks like we have a winner!" I produced the 90-minute pilot of *Mantis* for Sam Raimi/Universal/Fox TV about the first black superhero on TV. It did a 24 share. The subsequent one-hour TV series got picked up for twelve episodes and quietly died because it couldn't sustain the rigors of trying to consistently pump out half a good movie in under two weeks. ABC yanked another series I produced for Sony TV, *Push*, a one-hour drama about a high-pressure collegiate athletic program after only three episodes. Unfortunately for all concerned, the best show was last episode we produced that nobody ever saw. Sometimes a show takes a little patience to work out the kinks.

In most sitcoms, the laugh track continues to guffaw at unfunny punch lines in an attempt to tickle our funny bones and convince us that we're missing some genuine comedic jewels. This all underscores the fact that producing a successful episodic TV series is one of the hardest jobs in all of Showbiz.

For every failure, there is a three-foot stack of data from Market Research providing "plausible deniability" for the decision makers who were toiling under the delusion that a well-defined segment of the audience was supposed to show up for this or that new show. "Hey, it was in the wrong time slot! Hey, the public relations and ad campaign sucked and nobody knew it was on! Hey, it's not our fault the lead characters hate each other and have no chemistry together! Hey, it's that darn fickle audiences' fault!" In any other business, the execs responsible for making these decisions would be pushed off the roof. In Showbiz, if you guess right 20% of the time, you're a hero because the winners will generate gobs of money and that pays for all the other mistakes made each year by the Executive Branch and then some.

Every project results in success, failure or something in between. Now that the parameters of this enterprise have been established, let's look at the individual job descriptions of the Lucky Seven who are the essential ingredients in bringing any idea to fruition.

WRITERS

A great writer is the closest thing to being god in Hollywood. They create new worlds populated by amazing characters doing memorable things. Their original vision overcomes the normal reservations we all have against new people and ideas. As the audience, we let perfect strangers reach into our emotional fuse boxes, tickle our fancy, make us laugh or cry, depress the hell out of us, ache with desire or inspire us to change our lives completely. Great movie writers put catchy phrases into actors' mouths that people the world over will remember. Others specialize in plot twists and turns that keep the audience on the edge of their seats. Some are known as "script doctors" who get paid a kings ransom for a few weeks work as they amp up the action or sharpen the witty dialogue of a script about to go into production. In TV land, the Head Writers are known as "show runners." The head writers are usually great collaborators who get a team of fellow writers to agree on an approach and consistently churn out above average scripts. There are a handful of individual savants who get their fingerprints on every word spoken by every character. Most writers simply enjoy telling a good story and getting a paycheck. Once in awhile, if they're responsible for creating a hit TV show, it's a very big paycheck.

Most projects start with a dreamer who enjoys the gift of verbally painting pictures. An idea gets crafted into a pitch. A pitch usually consists of a one sentence concept like any *TV Guide* log line. If the notion is responded favorably to, additional elements are explained in ten sentences or less. That's enough for an executive to digest and determine whether the idea is something the giant corporation they're working for would be interested in. Every idea you or I divine is a great idea. Unfortunately, most of them come to naught. But hope springs eternal as an average of 800 ideas; treatments, outlines or scripts are registered *each week* with the Writers Guild of America in order to protect the writer from future intellectual property theft (for a $20 registration fee.) To put this in perspective, this translates into twenty to forty thousand new scripts or ideas floating around Hollywood at any given time looking for a home, not to mention the old scripts and ideas still floating around Hollywood from previous years. If you can picture Showbiz as the egg and millions of spermazoid ideas banging on the door hoping to get in, you'll have a pretty good visual of what it's really like.

The most amazing thing is that this is a totally subjective business and potential is always in the eye of the beholder. If someone in a position of power takes a shine to a writer or a script, their work immediately has cache and they temporarily become a "hot ticket." The writer isn't any better or worse than they were before they became a "hot ticket", it's just the perception of their work has changed. If handled properly, one great success can be milked for the rest of one's life. Their ideas and opinions are sought after as opposed to being ignored and trampled underfoot. Their agents get to charge a tidy sum for all future efforts. That is, until the audience weighs in on a few of their not-so-great ideas and they are perceived to have "cooled off."

It is an awesome responsibility being a writer. An idea has fallen out of your head, is translated into words on paper that others will read and pass judgment on. Usually, after family and friends have had a look, the next person you want to show it to is a Producer.

PRODUCERS

"Remember, nothing happens until somebody sells something" is an old sales adage. Producers come in all sizes and shapes but are primarily glorified salesmen. You can't go to college and get a degree in Producing. Traditionally, producers are individuals with strong opinions and enthusiastic ideas that they enjoy sharing with anyone who will listen. A producer is someone who wraps an arm around your shoulder and points you toward a rosy tomorrow while they are picking your pocket with their free hand. The great ones have the gift of gab and know what makes people tick. They take a writers' story and slant each pitch to suit the listener. The bad ones take credit for every good idea and are quick to make excuses when things don't work out as planned.

Producers can be divided into three categories: the schmoozing producer, the line producer and the creative producer. *The Schmoozing Producer* is a professional idea wrangler apparently much in demand at hoity-toity social functions, charity events and grand openings. They somehow manage to hang around with rich, powerful, famous people and inveigle them to invest time, talent and/ or money in their project. They drink their liquor, laugh at their jokes and do whatever it takes to service their latest and greatest idea. Once they have cobbled together a package on paper, this script with that director and those stars, they go into pitch mode and hit the studios and production companies looking for money. With the average studio film taking five years to reach the screen, the Schmoozing Producer gets to do this several times with each project as key elements get busy or fall away. Their work is traditionally on speculation so they need to be able to afford to keep several projects alive simultaneously. Why do they do it? If successful, the Schmoozing Producer wins their name up in lights, a healthy slice of the back end profits and a chance to get rich and famous themselves. Schmoozing Producers traditionally don't know which end of the camera to look through but they provide a very important service in getting things going.

The "nuts and bolts" or *Line Producer* is a glorified master sergeant that understands the needs and wants of the army. He or she becomes the architect who creates the blueprint as to how to best achieve the assignment within the time and money parameters. Budgets, schedules, weather forecasts, the plan is constantly adapted to accommodate the myriad of daily changes. The Line Producer is responsible when things don't work because someone must be blamed. God forbid the Schmoozing Producer has sold somebody a bill of goods, taken their big fees up front (before production begins) along with the rest of the above the line talent (writers, director, actors) and there's simply not enough money left over for the Line Producer to fully realize the production. Usually the Line Producer is the rock upon which the house gets built. A weakness here is magnified throughout the project. He or she is traditionally the pragmatist in a world of dreamers, the adult overseeing the kids in the sandbox.

The Creative Producer (who is often the Line Producer) is the interpreter. He or she has to keep all the pieces of this jigsaw puzzle in alignment. As the keeper of the big picture, the creative producer is the strategist, the orchestra conductor who attempts to produce as close as possible the story that was originally sold. They are responsible for recruiting the talent both in front of and behind the camera. This is a critical component to the overall success of the enterprise. Without a good person in the driver's seat, you are speeding along a dark highway with your lights off and eyes closed meaning that sooner rather than later, something bad is going to happen.

Once the game plan has been divined, and before the Producer(s) can do their thing, an "Angel" must be found.

EXECUTIVE PRODUCERS, AKA ANGELS

Angels are people who fund ideas. The reason why Angels are drawn like moths to the flame of Showbiz is because every once in a while, things go right and some new enterprise becomes a gusher. A fleet of armored cars is required to accompany the latest deposit. The printing presses have to work overtime. There is no greater feeling than taking a chance on something that just keeps spitting out money.

There are many people who talk the talk about financing movies but don't really walk the walk. Meaning, there are a lot of deluded hangers-on trying to convince you that they have the means to make your dreams come true. The bottom line is that every production, sooner or later needs to climb into bed with one (or more) financier. The cost of the money is usually steep but they provide "the green juice" without which any shiny new idea is just that, a shiny new idea. Inside the walls, the bean counters guard the studio treasury and have the ability to "green light" a project. Outside the studio gates, where the independent filmmakers live, Angels invest in ideas all the time. Since they risk the dough, they usually carve out the lion's share of the back-end profits for themselves. It is the understood law of the jungle.

Independent Angels can be divided into three camps: the dilettantes, the gamblers and the non-gamblers. *The Dilettantes* have more money than they could ever spend in a lifetime and primarily live to have fun. They enjoy the company of bright, entertaining, famous, beautiful people who traditionally gravitate toward money. Financial advisors, business managers, accountants, lawyers, wives, girlfriends, and hangers-on of every stripe usually surround moneyed people. In spite of every counsel to the contrary, they'll write the check when they feel like it. There's always the hope for a gain, but more often it's the fear of a loss that gets them to sign up for a deal. Their ego would be deflated if the next *Star Wars, Seinfeld* or *Little Miss Sunshine* slipped through their fingers.

The best kind of Angel is a *Gambler* who bet on themselves and won big. Often, it's the sheer audacious nature of the risk that turns them on. They are usually colorful characters that enjoy the spotlight, being in the eye of the storm. They aren't afraid to lose their investment because there is a sense that the coffers will be replenished by the next gamble if this one doesn't work out. Huge appetites and egos are traditionally at work here. They play to win. They are keen observers of life or they don't get to stick around the high stakes poker tables very long. These Angels travel in rarefied air and it is every filmmakers dream to secure one of these kingmakers for a pal.

The lions share of would-be Angels fall into the *Non-Gambler* category. They have the money. They need to invest it in something safe. Showbiz, by definition, isn't a safe investment and at the end of the day, most deals with non-gamblers fall apart once the true risk has been defined. If they continue to play, they hedge their bets by making sure there are other investors involved because they are afraid of being the only chump holding the bag at the end of the day.

They rely on pre-sale agreements and any other collateral they can get their hands on to mitigate potential losses and only then will they risk their money and only for a short period of time. If you're not talking about a guaranteed two or three to one return on investment (ROI), get out of here. There are no guarantees in Showbiz.

Once the money leaves their hands, anything can go wrong. That's why so much power is given to the one person who is ultimately responsible for translating two dimensional words on paper into a three dimensional production, for it is on his or her head that the majority of the blame or the accolades will fall. He or she is the team quarterback, otherwise known as the Director.

DIRECTORS

In the movie business, the director calls the shots. Actors need to be told how to interpret their lines in order to best tell the story. Some directors become well-versed in camera angles, filters, lenses, lighting and film stock and let the actors do their thing. Others simply leave the technical details to a good Director of Photography and concentrate on the performances. Some do both very well. Some do neither very well. The director is primarily there to steer the cast and crew through the days work in creating a few more pieces of the great linear jigsaw puzzle known as making films. All of these pieces get glued together in the editing room and hopefully, when taken as a whole, prove pleasing to the eye of the beholder and profitable to the investor(s).

Directing is a subjective undertaking. Five different directors could be given the same script and budget and return with five very different movies. They would have hired different casts and key crew members, found different locations and used different motifs, special effects and editing techniques to tell their story. The Cecil B. DeMille martinet of yesteryear in beret, jodhpurs and riding crop has been replaced by a kid in a baseball cap with a viewfinder. Somebody has to be in charge down on the film set, and usually it's the director.

During most productions, there are daily compromises that need to be made. What parts of the shared vision need to be adjusted in order to achieve today's goals? The bigger the director and the more money to work with, the more likelihood that they will get their way no matter the cost. David Lean kept a crew on hold for six months waiting for the big climactic storm in Ireland for *Ryan's Daughter*. James Cameron went $100 million over budget on *Titanic*. Peter Jackson spent over $200 million on *King Kong*. As Orson Welles once said, "Directing movies is the best toy train set a kid could ever have."

The TV director is an entirely different animal. Some of them are brilliant but will never get their chance to direct a big movie. Some are nothing more than glorified traffic cops telling the actors where to stand, say their lines and keep moving because they have three to four times as much work to get in the can each day as a movie director. It's a high paying factory job. Shoot the master, close ups, matching over the shoulder shots and let's go to the next scene. They set the pace marching through four to ten pages a day, a rhythm gets established and twenty to forty camera setups later, everybody gets to go home.

Once typecast as a music video director, action director or situation comedy director, it is very difficult to break out of that label and convince somebody to take a chance on you in some other genre. No matter which arena the director works in, their success depends entirely on their ability to handle the Actors.

ACTORS

Actors often appear to be luminous vessels that channel voices from other worlds. The truly great ones are chameleons capable of making you forget who they really are underneath that makeup as they interpret a new world through their eyes. They choose from a wide range of emotions to best tell the story. Richard Burton, standing backstage before going on as Hamlet would announce, "Tonight, I'm going to make them laugh" or "Tonight, I'm going to make them cry." With the same words and same stage blocking, he had such great command of his craft that he was able to achieve the desired results.

Stepping back and looking objectively at someone who is, or wants to be an actor or actress, you might wonder what happened to them. Most people shy away from the spotlight and don't want to be the center of attention. Actors crave it. There are many reasons why people want to become actors. Some are born exhibitionists. Some are petrified of the task but never feel more alive than when they are in front of an audience. Somewhere along the line, many of them sang a song, learned a poem, or told a joke and the audience applauded, even if it was only Mom. It felt really, really good and so they try to recreate that experience for the rest of their lives. It's kind of an arrested state of development where a person stands up on a soapbox for the entire world to see and says, "Look at me. Aren't I special?".

Acting on the screen is quite different than acting on stage. In a film, there are few opportunities for actors to go off on long soliloquies and demonstrate their range of abilities. The eyes, the nuanced look, the body posture, and the tremor in the voice convey so much. With their image projected thirty to sixty feet high, the camera peers into the windows of their soul and sees them for who they really are.

As with any of the crafts, there are a few great practitioners at any given time, several good ones, and a slew of hacks and wannabes. By acquiring the services of one or two superstars, you automatically have a "go" picture at any of the major studios. Superstars are some of the most powerful people in Hollywood. These chosen few can "open a film," meaning they have a built-in legion of fans that will go see anything they're in. Sooner or later their popularity wanes. They either figure out ways to reinvent themselves and become "hot" again or they retire. A lot depends on if they make sound business investments during their heyday and only really work when they feel like it or need another transfusion. Some won't go quietly when their time in the sun is up and they become a shadow of their former selves who hang around in bit parts and cameos.

Stars are often miscast to the detriment of the project because they happen to be available or affordable. So many films these days are "deal films" where the green light is given if you can get one of these five stars to commit. Never mind that by hiring this person to play that role will totally destroy the credibility of the undertaking. Miscasting is one of the quickest routes to failure of any project and short-circuiting a career. Because most of the key roles in any project are a result of serendipity, sometimes the producer gets lucky and the right people are cast in the right roles and everybody hits the jackpot. And every once in a great while, a new star is born.

There is a whole subset of famous A- and B-list actors who hover near the top hoping for a big breakthrough role that will temporarily make them a star. Some of them get their shot, but most of them do not. Behind them is an army of wannabe famous actors toiling in the wings. It is a brutal existence where talent is plentiful and rejection is commonplace.

And at the end of the day, when that big emotional scene is completed and the film or TV actor goes home, the footage gets turned over to a magician in a dark room who has a machine that transforms the mundane into acceptable, good into great, and great into gold. They are known as Editors.

EDITORS

The Editor's creative contribution to the cause is easy to overlook. It's a most unglamorous job that occurs away from the bright lights and big magnifying glass in the sky. Long after the limos have pulled away from the Wrap Party carrying their precious cargo, the editor(s) can be found in the wee hours of the morning trying to resuscitate a dead body, prevent something from dying or polishing up a jewel in order to meet yet another deadline.

Editing is an art form that is taken for granted by the public. Somebody had to glue this story together. Just as with all of the other aforementioned crafts, there are artists and mechanics. The artist brings their personality and experience to the project and can make it sing. The mechanic can take the exact same footage and produce something perfunctory. On the scale of creative contributions to the cause, editors are vastly underpaid. Whereas the writers, producers, actors and directors bask in the glory and rake in the dough, the great editors toil away in relative anonymity making a comfortable living.

Editing is the absolute best training ground for anyone interested in becoming a writer, producer, or director because it's the only place you get to watch the mistakes a hundred times. The audience usually sees a show once or twice. They have little or no appreciation for the myriad of decisions that have gone into the postproduction effort. When the audience walks out, it all boils down to; "It stinks" or "It's great!" These four little words ultimately determine a show's fate.

No matter the size of the project, a small group of worker-bees have to toil in the editing room(s) for weeks, months (years?) to recut a project, always shaping, polishing, trying to give it a sense of style while figuring out how to best tell the story. Editors help design the visual effects that have become so important in today's entertainment. Their compatriots help create the opening titles, oversee the layering in of 50–100+ audio tracks for the audio mix, integrate the musical score and in general provide the final filter that is the difference between a memorable or forgettable production.

After Market Research comes back with their evaluation of a project prior to the public airing, the editor sometimes gets to disassemble the show and start all over again. The editor's job is to take all the pieces that are tossed under their door everyday (dailies) and deliver a finished product with the best possible chance for survival in the marketplace.

If there is an unsung hero in the Lucky Seven, it would have to be the editor. And once the editor is finished with their work, everything, all the hopes and dreams come down to the ultimate salesman, the Distributor.

DISTRIBUTORS

New technology continues to divine new ways to suck money out of the audience's deep pockets. Distributors take your baby into the marketplace and sell it the best way they can. They perform a very necessary function that is 10% of the overall effort as they rake in approximately 40% of the income stream. There are marketing expenses, overhead costs and multiple sets of books to keep that make it increasingly difficult for the true profit participants to collect their rightful share of the back end. It's a big wonderful game of jiggery-pokery and everyone soon learns it's the price one pays in order to play in the Reel World.

Things in the accounting department have gotten a lot better since the Fortune 500 companies took over Hollywood but most independent distributors should be made to wear eye patches and have pistols sticking from their waistbands so you know who you're dealing with. If you only have one little picture in the marketplace, you can expect to be shorn like a sheep. They'll leave you alive so that you can grow another coat. If your first offering does poorly it's, "Thanks for coming. Have a nice life. Don't let the revolving door hit you in the ass!" However if your first film does really well, then the independent distributors probably won't get a second chance at you because more than likely, you'll have graduated to the big leagues.

Sometimes an independent distributor hits it big and gets to print money all day long. (*Rocky, The Passion of the Christ, My Big Fat Greek Wedding, The Blair Witch Project, Friday the 13th, Little*

Miss Sunshine.) Sometimes it's a salvage operation where they attempt to extract every last cent from the audience with clever, often misleading, ad campaigns before everyone finds out that this one didn't work; *Blair Witch 2, Flushed Away, Around the World in 80 Days, The Master Gunfighter, Daredevil, White Castle, The Life Aquatic* to name a few .

The film distributor has to invest money in the prints and advertising campaign. It's the repetitious thirty or sixty second TV spot that drives 70% of the audience into the theaters. Movie trailers, print ads, radio spots, the Internet and miscellaneous publicity comprise 30% of why people go see this film instead of that one. Strategically placing those ads multiple times in front of the target audience has become a science. The Distributor determines how much money to spend on advertising, the quality of the TV trailers, when a film is released, the number of theaters, etc. Your fate is in their hands. They can take an average picture and sell the hell out of it. They can also take a great picture and ruin it with a poorly handled ad campaign.

In TV, the distributor (or syndicator) serves three primary functions; launching a new show, re-selling a show that is already a big hit (*Jeopardy, Wheel of Fortune, The X-Files*) or helping the producer find the deficit financing (the difference between the network licensing fee and the cost of production) by pre-selling some of the foreign territories, home video, or cable TV rights. When a TV pilot stinks or a new show is yanked after a few airings, it is generally consigned to the trash heap, taken as a write-off and hopefully never seen again.

TV is low stakes poker when compared to the high cost of making and distributing a studio feature film. However, the rewards can be spectacular, especially when you consider that the income derived from twenty years of *The People's Court* has out-grossed *Gone With The Wind*, it kind of puts things in perspective. The distributors determine the best way to make the most money from each project. They must be respected, feared and watched like a hawk if you happen to be an independent filmmaker with a stake in the outcome.

SUMMARY

The Lucky Seven need to play their part in the making of any project. You cannot succeed without them. There are several other important contributors in the making of any professional production. From the Director of Photography (DP) to the Production Designer (PD), each department head influences the finished project. The real trick any producer faces is choosing well. You are the divining rod. You have to learn to listen to that little voice in your gut that says this person, not that one. A lot of times you'll have no choice. One or more of the Lucky Seven have been chosen for you and you have to make the best of the situation. Each project takes on a life of its' own. You just have to position your surfboard in the right place to catch the wave, hang on for dear life and hope for a good ride instead of a wipeout.

Being an independent filmmaker is exhilarating. It's the equivalent of arriving in town in the Old West with a lot of talent and something to prove. Anything can and will happen. For every person who becomes a legend, there are a thousand dreamers buried out back in Boot Hill. It is very, very scary to subscribe your life to an industry where success is predicated on getting lucky. "It's a crapshoot" covers it in a catchphrase.

The wonderful thing is you'll never know if you have what it takes unless you give it a go.

WHAT IS A PRODUCER?

What is a producer?
A Producer acts as the interpreter between any idea and reality.

The goal of any production is to create a tangible asset that entertains its intended audience. A Producer understands what the finished project should look like and has to figure out how to get there without killing anyone.

Producing is a lot like being the orchestra conductor. He/ she knows what the music is supposed to sound like, makes sure the best people are in the right place with good instruments and that they have the rehearsal time to properly prepare. Any successful project is a collaboration of many talented people. The Producer's main asset is to be a great communicator who loves to share their vision. You have to spread the load out because nobody can do it all.

How do you get to be a producer?

The quickest way to become a producer is to own a property or have a story idea that somebody really wants to fund. You simply insist on getting a producer credit, which is easily granted because titles are cheap. An alternate route is to have business cards printed up and declare yourself to be a producer. Then you have to go out and find someone who wants to fund an idea or property that you, the producer, control.

The easiest way to the producer chair is to be related to or marry into a Showbiz family. The next best way is to come to the party with a lot of money where suddenly you'll have a whole bunch of new friends who will be happy to call you a producer and help you spend it.

Everyone else has to earn it the old fashioned way, through hard work and perseverance. There are a myriad of totally different genres to choose from; sports, soap operas, dramas, comedies, action, sci-fi, fishing, poker, reality, talk shows, news magazines, horror, family, etc. Which one turns you on helps define your goals. Next, you eat, sleep and drink in as much knowledge about your chosen career path as possible. You identify the people whose work you admire and learn everything about them. Next you try to get a job as an intern on a show in an area of interest and see if this is really what you want to do with your life. There's a very high washout rate once people get a taste of how difficult it really is to achieve a career in Showbiz since there are so many other people who want what you want and you're at the end of the line. I am living proof that it is possible for an outsider to become a real producer.

When starting from scratch:

1. Pick a medium — film or TV (remember that there's 10 times as much work in TV)

2. Pick a genre that you love and would like to be working in ten years from now.

3. Research who the leaders are in that particular genre.

4. Find out how they began their careers because most of them didn't start at the top.

5. Learn the basics: budgeting, scheduling, the history of the genre so you can at least talk the talk.

6. If you can afford to, get an intern job with a production company working in the genre.

7. Try to interview with people who are where you want to be. Many interns end up with jobs once the people inside the company get used to having them around.

8. Soak up as much info as possible once you're in the door.

9. Find a good idea and develop it to the best of your (or your friends abilities). Script, budget, schedule. Start pitching it to friends and relatives until you can tell the story in one sentence. [Embellish with ten sentences and either someone on the other side of the desk will respond favorably or they won't.]

10. When someone responds favorably, tell them that you will help out in any way but want a producorial title in some capacity and then hang on for dear life.

What role do you play in a production in relation to everyone else that is involved?

The producer is a leader. Somebody has to be in charge of any successful enterprise. The producer is responsible for helping the people who own the project to realize what is in their heads as best they can. The producer is also responsible to the people who are financing the project to make sure that the production comes in on time and hopefully under budget. The producer is responsible for setting the pace and establishing an environment where everyone involved can do their best work The producer answers the tough questions and usually makes decisions that nobody else wants to make.

How do you begin a new show?

Preparation is the key. Try to answer all the questions in your head before they arise. There will always be surprises along the way and not all of them are pleasant but if the basic game plan is solid, you can usually reach the finish line intact. Personally, I take a deep breath before jumping into a new show and hope that the whole experience will be more rewarding than all of the hard work and investment of blood, sweat, time and energy that will be required. I choose my shows carefully because *you become known by what you produce.* This is also true for any of the other Showbiz crafts.

What are the steps needed to put together a production?

Find a great project, put together a viable schedule and budget, and get pre-production monies paid up front so invaluable time isn't wasted. A project isn't real until someone is spending some money. When production gets the final green light and a big chunk of money needs to be spent in a short amount of time, hire the best people for key positions, (Director, Director of Photography, Production Designer, 1st AD, etc.) Find a good casting director because their contribution is critical. Next, go location scouting where a lot of practical and logistical problems materialize as you figure out interesting ways to overcome the sheer logistical problems. Then you take endless production meetings with the department heads so that most of the big questions get answered in advance of the time when everyone is under the guns. Great preparation is the key to success. Once the show actually commences shooting, the Producer begins to concentrate on post-production. It all works if you have enough money to do it right the first time. The key is good communication and employing a positive attitude.

Are you currently working on any shows?

Like every independent producer, you are always preparing for multiple projects because you never know which ones are going to survive the cut. You don't put all your eggs in one basket because more often than not, things don't quite work out the way you want them to. I am preparing to produce several different TV shows and a couple of movies ... always.

What education do you need to prepare for production?

The good news is Show Business is one of those rare industries that doesn't really require a college diploma. If you're fortunate enough to go to college and want to get into Showbiz, get an education in Psychology, English Literature, History or Economics, something you can make a living at if, and when, filmmaking doesn't work out. People who take four years of filmmaking and then washout of the industry don't really have anything to fall back on. These other subjects will also broaden your knowledge about the real world. Filmmakers draw upon real world stories, newspaper headlines and become very good at fictionalizing things. Become a sponge when you're lucky enough to get a job on a show. Drink in as much knowledge as possible because everything sooner or later will come in handy.

How Much Does Art Cost?

There is no standard answer to this question as evaluation, much like beauty, is in the eye of the beholder. Making films and TV shows is an art form that was born in the Twentieth Century. Every project is a world unto itself. The experts can look at a treatment, a script or package deal for a film or TV show and make an educated guess what the marketplace will yield. At best, like a good baseball hitter, they guess right thirty percent of the time.

If it's a TV show, will it be scheduled in a good time slot, on a hot or cold network? Will it be pre-empted by world events and lost in the shuffle? All of these things have a direct bearing on the project's ultimate success. As with every other kind of artistic endeavor, once a product is delivered to the marketplace, everything else is outside of their control.

A movie producer figures out what a project is going to cost, raises the money, gets it produced and then waits. You need to have a divining rod when selecting projects, as it will be six months to two years before the audience finally gets to see it. Will today's "hot topic" still be relevant? Will the critics be kind or take pot shots at it? Will it be properly promoted in an increasingly crowded field? With a theatrical movie, it's a one shot deal: all the eggs in one opening weekend basket. There's a quick hook waiting for a film that doesn't perform as expected.

Execs yank a new TV series off the air after two or three episodes if it doesn't immediately attract the anticipated audience. Back in the old days, a show was on the schedule for an entire season of 26-39 episodes until people got used to it and knew where and when to look for it. *All In The Family* and *Seinfeld* are only two examples of mega-hit series that wouldn't have made it in today's hair trigger climate. Sometimes a TV show deserves a second, third and fourth chance until the actors settle into their roles and the writers find their voices.

On a daily basis during the actual production period, the producer gets to referee the ongoing battle between the Show vs. the Business. Sometimes the producer decides in favor of art over commerce and fights with the studio/financier for a little more time and money to make something better. Then there is the prick bastard producer hired by the studio to ride herd over a group of profligate kids who pulls the plug just as a climactic moment is about to be shot and doesn't really care about anything other than the bottom line. The director yells at you because he or she didn't get all the coverage they needed to complete the scene. The creative producer diplomatically points out that if they had been better at clock management or hadn't screwed around on a particular scene earlier in the day or were unwilling to compromise their creative vision, they would've finished within the agreed upon time frame and gotten the day's work in the can.

When big egos are involved and you don't own or happen to be related to someone who owns the studio, the producer becomes the referee who tries to call a fair game. You know going into the enterprise that it's going to be rough going and there's a good chance you will be a casualty. When it's a big time feature film director, fugetaboutit. They have the power to pretty much do whatever they want, the budget be damned. They often operate under the Eric Von Stroheim philosophy of not-so-secretly wanting to bankrupt any company that is myopic enough to hire them. The business be damned because they are only interested in making art.

If you have gone a little bit over budget, the financiers grumble but all is forgiven if the audience loves the show. If the show doesn't find its intended audience and the producer brought it in under budget, they want to know, "Why didn't you spend the damn money and make it better?" If the show turns out poorly *and* went terribly over budget, the not-so-subtle message is get out of here and don't darken our doorway again. One way or another, if things go wrong it is usually the producer's fault. They are the most convenient scapegoat and someone must be blamed.

Art is an amazing game. Nobody's right and nobody's wrong and everyone has an opinion. One man's junk is another man's fortune. What somebody is willing to pay for something isn't always an accurate reflection of what it's really worth. The perceived value or the previous success of the evaluator is often what drives the marketplace.

The audience doesn't know how much the average movie-of-the-week or TV show costs, nor should they care. It doesn't matter to them that the star had pneumonia, bad weather washed away the sets or the director was going through a messy divorce and had a drinking problem. These are the producer's problem. All that matters at the end of the day is did the project live up to its promise? Was the audience satisfied? You'll certainly never find out by thinking about it. Sooner or later, somebody has to take the plunge and commit to financing this risky art form.

There are only two ways to win with any project — at the box office or attracting critical acclaim and the two rarely coincide. *Titanic* was originally budgeted at $100 million. There was much howling and gnashing of teeth when the film approached the $200 million mark. The critics and naysayers had their knives out. The pundits and rumor-mongers had a field day about the impending disaster. Leo who? Kate what? Where are the big stars? Not since *Heaven's Gate* had a studio been so hornswoggled. It was a debacle akin to "Seward's Folly", the purchase of Alaska for $19 million, and look how they both turned out.

To date, *Titanic* has grossed over $2 Billion, the biggest film gross in the history of the cinema. Who knew? Certainly not the so-called experts. Each studio would love to have one of those projects impact its bottom line every year and be more than happy to go through the birth pains. That's if the return on investment (ROI) could be guaranteed. Just because you spend big money on a project doesn't guarantee it's going to work. A great opening weekend doesn't always mean the studio will ever see a profit on a particular film. If it doesn't have "legs", if it doesn't stay in the theaters very long because the word of mouth has killed it, a mega budget film can go down in flames just like a an ultra low budget film. The audience doesn't really care how much it cost – only if it lived up to it's billing.

Every year a couple of small independent films break out of the pack and fly in the face of conventional wisdom. The following films, and many more, were produced outside of the studio system *for budgets less than $2,000,000*. Some have won Academy Awards.

Some have spawned film sequels or successful TV series. An independent producer had an idea or found a script they fell in love with, raised the money and without the oversight committee watering down the premise, went off and produced a little gem of a movie. Next, they had to find a distributor with some guts who was willing to spend money on a speculative venture call the P&A fund (prints and advertising). The average film print costs under $1500. The lion's share of the P&A money goes for buying thirty and sixty second TV spots and a couple of ads in the trade papers to let everyone know that the movie exists.

Once in the marketplace word of mouth, the absolute best form of advertising, kicked in and the audiences lined up around the block to see these micro-budget movies. These films not only proved to be very profitable but also launched the careers of many big stars and directors:

Halloween	*Rocky*
Friday the 13th	*Enter the Dragon*
Texas Chainsaw Massacre	*Easy Rider*
The Evil Dead	*Mean Streets*
Napoleon Dynamite	*Night of the Living Dead*
Nightmare on Elm Street	*American Graffiti*
The Full Monty	*Dirty Dancing*
The Great Santini	*The Groove Tube*
Eraserhead	*Blood Simple*
Good Guys Wear Black	*Strictly Ballroom*
Pieces of April	*Slingblade*
Tadpole	*Porky's*
The Blair Witch Project	*Whale Rider*

With the healthy profits involved with a successful small film, you would think the studios would set up an extremely low budget film production division to make a handful of these little gems a year. They don't and probably never will because the aforementioned films didn't fit the formula divined by Studio Market Research. Little films represent pure risk because they don't involve well-defined commodities whose potential in the marketplace can be pre-determined. "Hell, we could lose our shirt on this one!" As the average studio film now costs over $60 million, a micro budget division could take thirty swings at the ball each year and one home run would pay for everything.

Big canvas or little canvas, the audience doesn't know about any formulas. They just want to get their money's worth. In this big guessing game, a producer has to figure out what art is worth long before the audience weighs in with their opinion at the box office.

THE PRODUCER CREDIT

There has been a proliferation of producing credits in the opening titles of any TV show or movie. They seem to invent new interpolations all the time. It must be very confusing to an outside observer because if you look at an old studio picture from the 1920's to the 1960's, you'll see one or two credits with the title "Producer". Where did all these other people come from in the last twenty years and what do they really do?

There actually is an explanation for the cornucopia of producer titles. A few are earned but most are awarded or rewarded for being in the right place at the right time. You chatted up the right person at the right cocktail party and made a critical connection that helped get this or that project off the ground and suddenly you're an Associate Producer. As they say, "Success has many fathers and failure is an orphan." Just in case something really works, everybody and their mother wants their name affiliated with it. It gives them cache as they look for their next job because almost everyone in Hollywood is always looking for their next job.

Because it differs slightly on every show, unless you're inside the bowels of a production, it is difficult to know who is really responsible for what but in general:

Executive Producer – usually finds the money and is the deal closer. They are silver-tongued devils that are already rich or have rich, famous, powerful friends.

Co-Executive Producer- often a great "opener" or a person who is very friendly with the money but can't close the deal or they'd get the aforementioned credit.

Producer – A consummate salesman who is usually pals with the Executive Producer who has access to the funding. Most of the time, the producer finds the project, creates a package that attracts the prerequisite talent that makes it a safer bet.

"Producer" (in name only) Nowadays these are often business managers or important people's representatives who negotiate for the credit and demand compensation for not really doing much of anything other than chaperoning their client to the party. It's a little mystifying to the outside world but the people working on the show know who the real producer is and who the "Producer(s)" are.

Co-Producer – the glue that often holds the show together and does a lot of the crap work that the producer doesn't want to. Sometimes it's just a fancy title for a friend of somebody important.

Supervising Producer – a TV credit meaning "Head Writer".

Line Producer — responsible for the budget, schedule, crew, equipment and generally making things work. Think smart master sergeant that translates the dream into a bottom line, provides a viable game plan and knows how to reach the finish line.

Associate Producer – a reward for detail-oriented people training to be a producer. As often as not, it's a gift title for a friend of somebody important in any of the above titles.

Assistant Producer – sometimes a glorified secretary, often the Producer's right hand that keeps communication channels open and solves smaller problems before they become big problems between warring factions helping to quell the myriad of little fires that break out along the way.

37

Executive in charge of Production – the go-between the Producer and the production company that is funding the project. A watch-dog that rings the alarm bells when things are going south.

A couple of new Producer credits have probably been invented since this was written but these are the important ones. Once again, only those inside each production really know who deserved what credit. The proliferation of titles is terribly confusing and it only took a couple of years to sort out who was doing what to whom.

METEORIC SHOWERS

It's amazing how hot new stars, tyro writers, and genius neophyte directors just seem to plop full-born onto the landscape. Managers, agents and publicity machines churn these people out, heralding their arrival like a cinematic Second Coming. You'd think we'd tire of the ongoing ballyhoo about this or that fabulous undiscovered talent but we don't. "Hey, what if they're right this time? I don't want to miss the boat!"

Different studios and/or big time producers get caught up in the hype and the next thing you know, some unknown actor or actress gets a three-picture deal at Paramount and is guaranteed a boatload of money. For what? For showing up? We all showed up and most of us have the cleat marks on our backs to prove it. Buying into the bullshit is understandable because there's nothing a good salesman enjoys more than another good salesman. As Phil Hendry, the genius radio funnyman said, "You can fool some of the people all of the time, and those are the ones you have to concentrate on."

After a couple thousand "can't miss" future leading young men and any young female who happens to arrive in a big film playing against an aging male movie star, most of whom are destined for the "future star scrap heap", there still seems to be a voracious appetite for unproven talent. They have what I call, "drive-thru careers." They're consumed for breakfast, pass through the system during lunch and then are just as easily forgotten by dinnertime. They came, they generated a boatload of money (or more than likely were cheated out of a boatload of money) and now they're gone.

They didn't understand the rules of engagement in Hollywood — lots of engagements (with the resulting euphoric intercourse) but very few actual weddings. These shooting stars deliver the tantalizing appetizers but aren't invited to stick around for the main course. If they're responsible for producing a hit "something-or-other" that generates a lot of money, their fair share of the spoils is usually deflected into somebody else's pocket. This falls under the, "paying ones dues" category.

I had a talented writer friend who went to court clutching a full-page ad in *Variety* that boasted a huge box office number on a low budget film that he wrote. He had a piece of the back end and wanted to know where his money was. You could almost see the judge shaking his head, calling my friend up to the bench and saying, "It's Hollywood, kid. Nothing is as it appears to be." He ended up on the wrong side of the disappearing profits ledger and quit the business heartbroken.

There have always been one hit wunderkinds in Showbiz. You record a song that everyone in the country is humming (i.e. *"You Light Up My Life"*) and then the next wave crashes down and wipes out traces that you were ever there. Some hotshot director from the hinterlands sweeps into town and wants to turn the establishment on its' ear. "Hey, Spielberg did it, why not me?"

A couple of times in a generation somebody arrives that breaks out of the box and defies all the rules. As long as they have the touch and can consistently generate oodles of cash, the sharks will follow them anywhere. The world is their oyster. When things cool down, as they always do, we can only hope that they salted away a few bucks for the coming rainy days.

What most of these bright lights haven't been told is that they're running a marathon as opposed to a hundred yard dash. The beatings, heartache, disappointments continue throughout your career.

As you look back on a body of work you helped create, there will be wonderful highs and terrible lows along the way. You made a bunch of money, watched it piddle away and then the cycle began again. The trick is how to get out of your gerbil cage and enjoy the beautiful scenery passing by. "Top off my glass and throw another shrimp on the bar-b!"

Unless you are born into it or have gotten extremely lucky to be traveling in that rarefied air where you are paid handsomely to fail upwards (quick, name Bruce Willis' or Sylvester Stallone's last three films), what you have in store is more heartache and disappointments, lots of near misses and also-rans. Why do people stick around? "It's a fascination with shiny objects", says the moth about the flame. Or maybe it could be wondering about that mysterious fate that stirs the pot, calls the shots, and picks the winners. As long as we stay at the tables and play, there is always the chance that we'll be in the right place at the right time with the right project when the fickle finger of fate points in our direction.

There's only one sane answer: everyone in showbiz has Lotto fever.

THE PRODUCER'S LOT

With few exceptions, they don't teach Producing in film schools. Once you understand what the job entails, who would really want to be one? "Nobody," is the correct answer. Most film and mass communication schools dazzle the younger generation by promoting glamorous careers in Showbiz as directors, writers and DP's but for the most part, they stay away from heart attack central aka "producing" where everyday the slightest slip-up can knock the best-laid plans off the tracks.

Once a game plan, budget and schedule have been agreed upon, and the project is given the green light, the producer's job is to expect the unexpected. Not something you can really teach in any school. You often feel like a lone sentry out on the front lines. You know the enemy is going to make a run at you but don't know what form it's going to take. Often it's the people who hired you who can be found playing in the ammo dump with their new Bic lighters. Yours is the first neck they will chop off if anything goes really awry because someone must be blamed and obviously it can't be their fault.

The true test of your producorial abilities is to figure out how to recover from the latest screw-up before a) anybody notices, b) you cost the production company more money than the gaffe is already going to cost, c) anyone looks more closely and sees a very panicked person behind the calm façade who is madly scrambling to put Old Humpty back together again. Band aids, spit, smoke and mirrors, subterfuge, robbing Peter to pay Paul while leaving poor Peter bleeding from several orifices by the side of the road and knowing you are going to have to return sometime soon and get another transfusion are all unwritten talents required for the job of producing. If you can't tell someone you love a bald-faced lie, look for a different job on the team.

The producer's greatest asset is experience. You learn to recognize a torpedo, a kick or a punch from a mile away and you have to figure out how to duck the blow. It's the little things that kill the production schedule. 90% of everything that goes wrong on a production happens because somebody forgot to tell somebody something in time to be able to do something about it.

In that respect, it's a lot like life. It's the little things that fall between the cracks that prove most irritating. Everyday during production there is a "Waterloo moment". Some unexpected piece of business that ends up costing the production company a very expensive hour or two of overtime at the end of the day. This has a domino effect on the entire production and must be avoided at all costs.

The Producer's next greatest asset is prayer. It is that silent communication with God that says, "I know my ass is exposed in a hundred different ways but I'd really appreciate it if my trip across the high wire today was an uneventful one."

Once, I simultaneously produced two totally different TV pilots fraught with danger in two different cities. One was a one-hour martial arts drama, *Black Sash* for the WB (now the CW) shot in San Diego full of motorcycle chases, stunts and fight scenes. One was a new sport, *Slamball* for Spike TV, six one hour shows featuring full contact basketball with players jumping on trampolines and performing spectacular crashes five feet above the court shot in LA.

Two different worlds had to be created from scratch. It is very tiring holding one's breath for two weeks, hoping that nobody gets hurt and that we'd all make it to the finish line in one piece. When post-production was completed, their respective networks picked them both up.

I took a much-needed vacation and vowed not to do that again.

CHAPTER 2

STAYING ALIVE

University of Hard Knocks

There is an apocryphal story about the fellow who follows the elephants around all day at the circus with a shovel who someone asks if he ever thought about another line of work, "What, and give up show business?" Showbiz ain't for the faint of heart. If you're looking for a comfy ride to the top of the fame and fortune mountain, my advice is leave now, enjoy the show from the balcony and thank me later.

If you're not willing to get your hands dirty and pay the admission fee to get into the game, there are plenty of people out there who will. They say a little bit of knowledge is a dangerous thing. Film schools around the U.S. are belching out 30,000 kids a year with degrees in Mass Communication. There are probably twice that numbers who can't afford college who have decided that Showbiz is the ticket out of a dull and predictable life. This translates roughly into 2,000 people a week who will literally do anything it takes to give it a go. Why? Because Showbiz offers an adventure that regular folk ("noncoms" as *Variety* calls outsiders) only dream about. In Hollywood, the only businesses that will never go bankrupt are those taking actors headshots and Xeroxing scripts. Unlike most other industries, a sheepskin on the wall is not a prerequisite for success in Showbiz, unless it happens to be from Harvard, Yale, Stanford Business or Law Schools.

A couple of times a year, the magic wand descends on a few virtual unknowns who are momentarily plucked from anonymity and touted as the next great thing. As the public relations machine goes into overdrive, their work gets noticed but after some initial success, very few actually learn how to stick around long enough to make a career out of it. Don't believe me? Go on the Internet and look up the hot, new directors, stars, writers, and singers from five, ten, twenty years ago and see how many of them are still working in "the big show." And these were the people who were dubbed, "can't miss" by those in the know. What chance do us mere mortals have? I, for one, was certainly hoping it would be easier catching an escalator to the top but thirty plus years of effort on this never-ending stairway has taught me otherwise.

The collective mindset in Showbiz is like panning for gold, "Keep 'em coming." Every once in a while, a true gem materializes that has the ability to generate a ton of money and create a body of work, i.e. Matt Damon, Kevin Smith, Brett Ratner, Mark Wahlberg. Most of the other "can't miss" candidates get held up to the light, shine for a moment, make somebody some money and then are discarded on the used star heap out back. Nothing personal. Business as usual.

For those not fortunate enough to be related to someone in the game and/ or possessing some spectacular talent(s), there is a five-year unofficial "paying ones dues" fistfight in the foyer. As with doctors, politicians and jet pilots, Showbiz boasts an extremely high washout rate. Think of it as an extended Pledge Week to a very fickle fraternity or sorority that you desperately want to join but doesn't need your admission fee. If you make the cut and survive this first lap around the track, then, hopefully you've made a few good friends and learned enough to hang around. Oh, and Mom and Dad should be forewarned that more transfusions of capital will be required when jr's career hits one of the inevitable dry patches. On second thought, maybe it's best not to tell them yet.

If you are already attending or are thinking about going to film school, seriously consider getting a minor in Accounting, Business, Psychology or Teaching, so you'll have something to fall back on in case you aren't one of the fortunate few who get picked out of the chorus line. If you want to be a producer, writer, actor or director, take a trip around the world and live a little after graduation so that if, and when, you get your turn at the microphone, you will have something distinctively unique to say. If the primary reason for wanting a career in Showbiz is that you've digested tons of video games, TV shows, movies, comic books and pop culture, then the best you can produce will be regurgitated clichés. You've got to have something original to say in order to get noticed. If you're primarily interested in getting famous, rich and powerful, get in line. The line begins somewhere around Des Moines.

Nobody is telling the next wave of dreamers that there aren't many job openings within the status quo. Most people like to plod along the beaten path looking for a crack in the façade as the entre-preneurs blaze new trails in cyberspace and create original program-ming for the direct-to-DVD marketplace. New technology con-tinuously demands less expensive storytelling. Once a proven moneymaker emerges, the big boys will swoop in with the mega-bucks and marketing muscle and turn the fledgling enterprise into a gusher.

As a film school graduate, I believed that opportunities abounded and anyone could make it in Showbiz. When it finally dawned on me that it was pretty much a closed game, restricted for those who could afford to play in it, I guess I was too stubborn or too proud to throw in the towel. If "Getting Knocked On One's

Butt" were a category in the *Guinness Book*, I'd at least have gotten an honorable mention by now. I wasn't about to dust off my dignity and return to the real world with my tail between my legs. Hell, I had a degree in Mass Communication and was going to succeed in LaLa land if it killed me! If going headfirst through my windshield and bouncing off the other guys windshield while taking film cans to a sound editing company didn't kill me, nothing would.

A friend once remarked, "If Show Business were easy, everyone would be doing it." To a wide-eyed noncombatant looking at this fishbowl from the outside, it really does looks like a fun way to make a quick fortune. "Hey, I've got a camera and some film. Let's make a movie!" What could be more seductive than hanging around smart, beautiful, sexy, famous people running around in their underwear (or less) playing pretend and being paid a king's ransom?

Hollywood is like a tall skyscraper populated by layers upon layers of salespeople. In order to get ahead, you quickly find out that you have to sell yourself first and your latest screenplay or great new idea second. This is a business built upon subjective opinions and most execs are loath to make a decision until they have to because ... what if they're wrong? No exec wants to return to the unemployment line. It's far safer to be a consensus builder than a decision maker.

And then there are those rich, crazy, powerful people who, like drunk drivers weaving through traffic, aren't playing by the same rules. They go where they want to go, do what they want to do, and are surrounded by a phalanx of fawning sycophants who kiss their ass and act as a buffer zone between them and the outside world. Some of them like to play games and screw around with people's heads because they can. Tens of millions of dollars flow through their hands and they can make or break careers. It's nothing personal. If they see something they want, they'll step on their best friends throat to get it. If you are going to be successful in Showbiz, you will get to see some of these 800-pound gorillas up close. Upon encountering these mercurial beasts, you just try to avoid getting squashed.

As you attempt to flog your great American screenplay, know that every studio owns the rights to a myriad of books and scripts that they've already spent a fortune on that probably will never be produced. It takes a long time to find the right combination of people in front of and behind the camera before the studio decides to take the plunge. Big films come together and fall apart all the time long before they get the green light. It's not unusual for a studio to spend a couple million on the rights and employ several highly paid writers to take different passes on a project before they decide whether or not to make it. On the surface, it seems like a tremendous waste of time and money perpetuated by people who can't make a decision. It explains, in part, why films that should have been made for $20 million cost three times as much and often take several years to make.

In comparing notes with my contemporaries, I'm a lucky bastard because I've been unemployed about a third of my career. Their scorecard reads more like fifty-fifty meaning 50% of the time found them in-between-projects (aka unemployed.) That doesn't mean they were sitting in front of the tube waiting for the phone to ring. You're out taking meetings, going to screenings, just trying to keep the circulation going until somebody gives you a call and throws you a lifeline. When it finally comes, there's usually good news and bad news! The good news is you got the job. The bad news is that you've got the job.

As a producer, this means that you've opened your big mouth, finally gotten somebody to take a chance on you and now you have to go out and pull off a modern day miracle — produce a TV show or movie within some impossible time and money parameters, often with a couple of crazy people both in front of and/ or behind the camera. Oh, and one more thing — make sure it turns out great. And if not great, than really good. And if the fates conspire against you, then pretty good. And if all hell breaks loose, you better hope to get that leaky ship back to port in one piece.

I have taken all of the aforementioned journeys and lived to tell the tale. It's been an adventure full of the highest highs and the lowest lows, and in retrospect, although I thought I would have already conquered the mountain by now, in a way I'm happy that I haven't yet reached the summit or peaked too early. It's been an amazing trip thusfar and I have no idea where or when it will end.

One thing I can vouch for, it's easy to lose one's self at the University of Hard Knocks.

How to Get In the Room

One of the most important pieces of advice contained in these pages is that there is absolutely no substitute for quality face time. If you are a newcomer, armed only with your brief resume and a lot of ambition, you have to figure out a way to get in the room with someone who can help you. Until that moment, no matter if they've talked to you or some go-between on the phone, you don't really exist. You're not a real person until you get in the room.

Somebody in power has to look you in the eye before they decide whether or not to lift a finger to help you. Until you've made it onto the "A-Team" roster where the great paying jobs are chasing after you, your carefully prepared resume is just a piece of paper that either landed in the wastebasket or made it into a resume binder in the back room.

So, how do you get in the room? Numero Uno is to learn as much about the decision maker as possible. You can pull up their name and credits on imdb.com (international movie data base.) Rent their movies or TV shows or anything that they have been responsible for. Look for any connection, no matter how far-fetched. You can't forget that the decision makers are always under siege. A myriad of already established people are after them all the time, hoping to get a little bit of their attention. If you have a mutual friend, a distant relative, went to the same college, wrote a great comedy script, found out that the person you want to meet was once a lifeguard, shares the same middle name, likes the same baseball or football teams, almost anything will work.

The decision maker tends to hire the same people over and over because it's easier than taking a chance on somebody new. The challenge anyone faces is to break into their reverie and get them to pay attention to you. These are people who are always supposed to be looking for wonderfully talented people but rarely take a chance on them. They need to be courted through phone calls, letters, resumes, and exposed to your best work.

If you don't have a direct line into the head honcho, the next most important person you need to impress is the decision makers' right hand person. You do everything you can to enlist their assistance in reaching the person you need to meet. Every decision-maker has at least one great assistant. You can usually get their name from an Internet search or the secretary answering the company phone. They are terrific conduits and their contribution is too often overlooked. They usually enjoy the attention and you should try to develop a rapport, make them laugh, send them flowers, anything that acknowledges their position because you desperately need their help. They are usually the keeper of the boss's calendar and can make things happen if they take a shine to you. If handled properly, they'll put a demo reel or resume in front of the boss and nudge them to take a look. They'll find an opening on the calendar, let you know where the boss will be dining or a convenient place you might be able to "accidentally" bump into the big cheese.

When you finally get in the room, you have to figure out a way to mention the tenuous connection, if any, and you better have a great story to tell. The best thing you can do is somehow remind the person of themselves when they were starting out way back when they were in need of a break. If you wear your earnestness on your sleeve and somehow reassure the boss that you won't let them down if they decide to help, you're a thousand percent more likely to get a job than someone who just sends a letter, resume or calls once in awhile.

This is a business built upon facades and chutzpah (brass balls). If you got 'em, use 'em. If you don't have a set, find them. An acquaintance called up a bunch of *machers* (big shots) and said he was writing a book about the people responsible for creating the cable TV business. He got interviews with most of them and after each interview; he started talking about his ideas. He figured correctly that people with big egos like to talk about themselves. I don't know that he ever got around to actually writing the book but he ended up selling a couple TV shows.

For the most part, your career doesn't really begin until you've figured out how to get inside the walls. The trick is learning what separates balls from obnoxious, myopic behavior. Calling every day for weeks on end is a surefire way to get ignored. You can't ever forget that this is a courtship dance. You need friends in high places. Often, they don't have anything going on at that moment but maybe one of their friends does. When the boss recommends you to the next person, it's the best kind of introduction.

When you get your chance in the room, it all boils down to chemistry. Sometimes you're in the right place at the right time with the right person and sometimes one of these elements is missing. You have to get as many interviews as possible before the law of averages catches up to you. As I've said elsewhere, you can't lose them all!

If you've already accomplished a few things and you want to move up the ladder to the next level, all of the above advice still applies.

When to Push & When to Pull

A rich persons' bathtub is overflowing. A plumber is called. He walks in, assesses the situation, walks over to the pipes and whacks it with a wrench. Problem solved. He turns to the owner and says, "That'll be $500." The owner says, "For what? It took all of five minutes." The plumber replies, "It's $10 for hitting the pipe and $490 for knowing where to hit it."

There is no great Showbiz manual that explains what to do in every situation. Knowing when to push and when to pull can't be taught in a classroom. No two situations are exactly alike. To each job you bring a healthy dose of common sense, an understanding of what has worked in the past for you and when things look their bleakest, there is always the power of prayer. Also, never underestimate the value of cheap theatrics. Getting angry once in a while often works wonders in getting the engine going again.

Anytime you take a risk, there's an inherent opportunity for failure to rear its ugly face. Being a real producer is learning how to control chaos. It's understanding the big picture and not letting the little details derail the process. There's a mountain to climb and there's no sense tripping over the pebbles encountered along the way. As a Producer, the primary job is to surround yourself with the best people the budget can afford. Next, you have to separate what the heads of the various departments really need versus what they want because everybody always wants more than the budget can afford. No department head wants to be singled out for doing less than a stellar job. They usually want extra help, more prep time, more equipment just in case the plan changes. That's because the plan always changes. Self-preservation is a healthy attitude to have but most people will do anything to avoid the embarrassment of getting yelled at in front of everyone else.

The producer is responsible for creating a battle plan and making sure it works. Funnily enough, one of the hardest tasks is communicating the plan to everybody on the team. Sounds simple but it isn't. You always have to be ready for "Uncle Charley." In baseball parlance, "Uncle Charley" is the curveball. If you don't learn to hit the curveball, the word gets around very quickly and your days in the big leagues are numbered. Everyday during production, curve balls are thrown at the producer. It's often something you couldn't possibly plan for like; a sudden torrential downpour ruining your shooting schedule, an actor arriving late and/ or drunk, the flight path at the local airport suddenly changing so everything takes off overhead, an incessantly barking dog, quarreling neighbors, people flashing mirrors in your camera lens in the middle of a take.

Throughout any production you have to watch everything like a hawk. I am at my most vigilant when everything seems to be running smoothly. It always feels like the calm before the storm. You give the production team a nudge now and then, occasionally providing a pep talk. Some days it feels like you're running a very expensive babysitting program for pampered ADD kids. You have to coddle petulant actors or cajole temperamental directors into doing something they don't want to. Early on, it's important to establish a rapport with the director and stars because the relationship will usually be tested over the course of the production. In the ongoing struggle between art and commerce, there is a natural distrust between a director and producer. In a business of subjective opinions, time and budget constraints, clashing egos, conflicts and compromises become inevitable. Like any relationship worth having, it's how you handle adversity that defines your character and determines whether you get to stick around and make it work.

Myopia is a big problem in any business. Not seeing the forest for the trees is a formula for disaster. If you like yelling at people and aren't a Sacred Cow, the word gets out real quick and you'll find yourself sitting in your underwear watching daytime TV wondering what happened to your career. This is a high-paying pressure cooker full of anxious people. If you can't disguise how you really feel and have to publicly get things off your chest, it will be duly noted. Don't be surprised when you aren't included on the next roster.

You have to pick your battles. I don't believe in bleeding over the same ground twice. The Producer should be equipped with a bullwhip and chair. They keep things moving down the chosen path. There are a hundred horses wanting to pull the wagon in their own direction. Somebody has to be in charge. How you crack the whip, when to crack it and whom you crack it at is an art form unto itself. There is no optimum time, place or target as each situation dictates your choices. You just have to be prepared to use the whip and they have to know you mean business.

Filmmaking is a collaborative effort. You must be open to new ideas because they come from all different sources. You have to be ready to change course in a heartbeat in order to take advantage of an opportunity. I once pointed a director towards the most spectacular sunset I'd ever seen and asked him to stage the scene he was about to shoot in that direction. He grudgingly flipped the camera around and it was one of the more memorable shots in the movie, but he was unhappy because *he* hadn't envisioned it that way.

No school or book learning is going prepare you for the myriad of problems that will arise. Common sense and experience are your best guides of knowing when to push and when to pull.

OUTSIDE THE BOX

Most people are so busy in their everyday lives that they don't make quality time to ever put things in perspective. "Thinking outside the box" really translates into any thinking that takes place outside of the pine box awaiting us at the end of the line. We are running from meeting to meeting, jabbering into our phones, watching movies and TV, reading scripts, books, magazines, newspapers, the Internet, amusing ourselves in any number of ways, worrying about the next job and paying the bills, eating, talking, sleeping. As Yogi Berra, the famous New York Yankees catcher replied when asked what he was thinking in the batter's box, "Who has time to think?"

Inside the box means the status quo. In Showbiz, the box would be your local movie screen or TV set. These boxes have length and width. The storytellers' job is to create depth. Anybody can buy a camera and take pictures but try making a living doing it. The truth is nobody really wants to suffer through your photo albums or home movies besides your immediate family. They are not interesting narrative journeys with beginnings, middles and ends. They are little personal reality shows that capture the moments of our lives. If the home movies feature a friend or loved one (or a pet) falling down, making a big mess or getting hit in the privates by a foreign object, you can send them to *America's Funniest Home Videos*. Otherwise, they should only be seen by loved ones and only once in a great while.

Speaking of exposing film, I visited the AFM (American Film Market) and saw a bunch of posters and trailers for the upcoming slate of indie films from all over the world. It was a lot of the same old, same old. Wannabe *Matrix*-like flicks that were produced for a fraction of the original movie with spectacular slow-mo martial arts leaps, kicks and punches, swarthy looking bad guys, scantily clad women in jeopardy, fancy cars, big explosions, many featuring B, C and D grade American actors vacationing in some foreign country. This, of course, is a gross exaggeration and it's unfair to lump in a lot of interesting little jewels that were also in evidence but those will have to make their way through the celluloid jungle (distribution maze) via somebody spending some marketing money and most importantly, positive word of mouth.

As filmmakers, it's our job to not only keep abreast of the latest developments but to be able to project ahead a year or two as to what the audience might be interested in. What's a good story that hasn't been told lately? What's an interesting way to re-tell an old story? i.e. Boz Luhrman's *Romeo and Juliet*. What do I want to see my name on besides a big fat paycheck?

New technology is rapidly changing the entire economic picture both in production and the way our stories get distributed, i.e. video on demand, (VOD), video streaming via the Internet and cell phones to name a few. The audience requires a steady diet of new, improved, better stories. If you don't happen to be one of the powers that be, your job is to think up cheaper, faster ways of telling your stories. We need to find the time in our busy lives for some quality thinking. Otherwise, it isn't the boogey man but the status quo steamroller that's gonna get you.

You have to be open to new ideas. You have to see what the competition is doing and figure out how you might fit in. Inspiration and opportunity surround us all the time. A million people can read a great story in a magazine or newspaper. Several thousand say to themselves, "This would make a great movie or TV show." It takes a creative producer or writer to acquire the rights and transform it into box office gold.

It's what we do for a living — thinking outside the box!

LOTTO FEVER

A career in Showbiz is one big gamble and we're all betting on ourselves. Everybody in Hollywood has lotto fever. We all think we've got the winning ticket and it's only a matter of time before our number is called. The real truth is that you have to pay your bills or your days at the gambling tables are numbered. Nobody will officially ask you to leave thus making room for the next sucker. It's understood that you'll know when your time is up.

You need to have a positive attitude that emanates from some inner wellspring of self-confidence. Everyday you wake up and say, "Today is the day I've been waiting for my whole life. I believe I am the right person in the right place with the right answers. Today they are going to recognize my brilliance because today I'm going to get lucky." Either you'll get the phone call and have that great meeting that will change your life … or you won't. You just have to hope it happens before they trip over your body jammed in a doorway someplace.

As W.C. Fields said about quitting drinking, "It's easy. Why, I've done it a thousand times!" It's easy to look in the mirror and say, "I give up. I can't, I won't take it anymore." If you say it often enough, you'll save yourself a lot of heartache and hit the exit door. Once you leave the Big Top, it gets harder to get back inside. I've retired twice from Show Business. I figure the third time will be the charmer.

Until you somehow figure out a way to demonstrate your talents and become invaluable, Showbiz unfortunately treats you like an interchangeable cog in the wheel. If you can't or won't do something, you are quickly reminded that there are a thousand other people waiting right outside who are willing to take your place in a heartbeat.

Like a pyramid chart, there's the Golden 100 up at the top (writers, producers, directors, actors) who have made the corporate overseers so much goddamn money that they can pretty much do what they want to. They are surrounded by a thousand front linemen whose job it is to prevent them from failing. These are corporate execs, attorneys, managers, agents, accountants, hairdressers, friends and relatives who have access to the Golden 100. Beyond them are the ten thousand middle management execs that can't really green light anything. If they like something, they can send it upstairs for closer inspection but their primary job is to keep the looky-loos and interlopers out while they are panning for gold. They are the Showbizness buffer zone. It's musical execution chairs in this outer perimeter. When the music stops, they're lucky to be holding onto their jobs. If one of the middle management execs proves to have a divining rod and guesses right more often than not, they ascend to the inner circle because hardly anybody guesses right most of the time.

Beyond them, at the bottom of the pyramid, is where the unwashed herd moves around blindly, searching for a way into the game. This is where most people start. This is where most will end up.

If you go back and study the roots of the current Golden 100, most of them began at the bottom. It's not like they were anointed at birth and given the kingdom of Viacom or Sony to run. It is the reason we're here. And just like the lottery, there is no rhyme or reason because every once in awhile, the magic wand descends from the clouds and one of the unknowns is plucked from anonymity. They have either displayed some enormous talent that someone has decided they can wring a few dollars out of or they happen to be in the right place at the right time with the right skill set. There are ways of improving your chances but sooner or later it all boils down to knowing the score and getting lucky.

Have you bought your ticket? If so, I hope you win.

GETTING WITH THE PROGRAM

During the early part of your career, the dues paying phase, you have to work very hard for little or no money. As you move up the ladder, you get paid more to work less. Doesn't make any sense but somehow that's what the program calls for. They will spend up to $100,000 a day to produce 3-5 good minutes of usable film in a 12-hour period. Unless it involves some big stunt or complicated camera move, it's hard to work that slowly.

And the absolute best-paid, A-team of players go even slower working behind the banner of "perfection." This gang is lucky to get a good minute or two of usable Kodak Moments in the can by the end of a very expensive production day. Do they go home at night and tell their spouses, "Another tough day in the salt mine? Take thirty two was a beauty!"

You can't really blame the crew members because they take their cues from the people in charge. It apparently takes a lot of cooks in the kitchen to make a decision about anything and everything. It takes a lot of time changing your mind before changing it back again. Read somewhere that Stanley Kubrick shot 87 takes of Jack Nicholson crossing the street in *The Shining*. Always wondered what the instructions were for take 86 — "This time take three steps, look left, hop on one foot avoiding the crack in the road, take your hand out of your pocket and wave at somebody, spin around and have a that crazy glint in your eye." Nobody had the power or the chutzpah to say to the sacred cow, "Stop already! We got the four seconds that we need in the can. Let's move on."

Once visited a producer friend's set to watch a big film being shot. They took all morning for the master shot and then the famous Director sat down in his chair and closed his eyes. Everyone settled in while the "genius" was deciding what to do next. The crew shuffled around, visited the craft service table and waited. After a half hour snooze with everyone remaining respectfully quiet, Herr Director woke up with a start and said, "Let's punch in for coverage." Then the army jumped to it like nothing out of the ordinary had happened.

Nobody can afford to risk incurring the wrath of the golden geese. The truth is that it's amazing that the studios produce anything truly great anymore. It's kind of a happy accident, as it doesn't appear to be consciously part of the plan. They are busy crafting deals for the highest paid talent while consistently aiming at the lowest common denominator of the market researched target audience.

Is it any wonder that they produce such a high failure rate? They can't fathom why the audience didn't turn out to see their latest 'deal movie.' It wasn't really a movie. It was a great deal, skillfully negotiated where everyone got the proper billing (above the title, below the title, all paid ads, etc., etc. ad nauseum) and they were all paid way too much up front because that's what the AAA decided upon (Agents, Accountants, Attorneys.) Got to keep those quotes up and god forbid somebody takes a pay cut to make a great little movie.

Long before there is any food on the table, the back end gets carved up like an imaginary Thanksgiving turkey. It's almost as if they're bored with the process by the time it gets around to actually making the film. Let's focus on the Wrap Party and logos for the t-shirts and crew jackets. Let's concentrate on the marketing campaign. Anything but the fact that we're supposed to perform the miracle of transforming a mediocre script and some patchwork quilt of available actors into box office gold.

At the end of the line, some lucky Producer gets the $1.98 that's left over to actually make the movie while having to hit some unrealistic delivery date because all of the lead-time has been eaten up by people talking and negotiating the deals. *But hey,* this is how things work inside the walls. You want in on the gravy train, you gots to get with the program.

SQUARE PEGS, ROUND HOLES

It's hard to put your finger on it. There's this feeling deep inside that you have to contend with from time to time. You're not wanted. You don't belong. It is reinforced on a weekly basis by the lack of people banging down your door, vying for your services. It is subtle as it is blatant. Other people get the nod ahead of you because of any number of intangible things. You know you can deliver the goods no matter how difficult the challenge if just given the opportunity to perform.

It's hard to break out of the pack and distinguish yourself to the powers that be. You have to contend with living off the orts and watch your peers or newcomers given chances that had you been given, would be your golden opportunity to prove to the big boys that you have what it takes.

It's not that you haven't paid your dues, learned your craft and earned a chance. It's that you didn't know the right people at the right time that could champion your cause and drop your name at the crucial moment in the right meeting. You often meet the right people later on who are impressed by the great job you deliver. They say they wished they had known you earlier when this or that project was falling apart and how you would've been the perfect fit. Doesn't really help you now but it's nice to know. And maybe when they get their next at bat, your name will be closer to the top of the list.

You wrack your brains going through a mental checklist of the steps to be taken in order to secure future work. The reality is that it all boils down to who you know, right place, right time, getting lucky. Having talent, being a hard worker and a good person are of secondary importance. They of course determine whether you get to stick around when the opportunity does materialize but they are not the primary considerations in the beginning.

There isn't anything wrong with you that a great opportunity won't fix in a hurry. That's the good news and the bad news. Those opportunities are few and far between because a couple of the players in front of you have to drop dead, get arrested or screw up royally before they are removed from the active roster. It feels like one of those interminable lines down at the DMV and just when you reach the counter, they say sorry, you've been standing in the wrong line and what you're looking for is in that line. There's nobody to ask because Information sent you here in the first place.

You have to make your own chances. You look at the problem of getting gainful employment from a hundred different angles. You aren't content to sit around, waiting for the phone to ring. You have to make things happen for yourself because nobody else can do it better. You take meetings, arrange lunches, devise plans to get yourself in front of "the right people" or friends of the right people.

You have to learn how to be a survivor, washed up on the shores of Showbiz. A landscape littered with broken hulks and shiny palaces of those who came before you. You were not invited to the banquet. Nobody knocked on your door at some tender young age (like in pro sports) and said we must have you in our business as soon as possible and here's a couple of million as a signing bonus. It doesn't quite work that way.

Your job is to figure out a way into the banquet hall. Then you have to ditch the waiters costume and figure out how to blend in with the guests. Then you have to position yourself near the most important people in the room and say a few witty, original things to get their attention. And then you have to jump up on the piano, grab the microphone and start singing a passionate love song to the most beautiful girl in the room so that she falls madly in love with you and daddy pays you off to leave her alone but ... I digress.

Sorry about that. Don't know what got into me. It's just the daydreams of a square peg that would have fit so nicely into that round hole. Wasn't meant to be that easy.

CHAPTER 3

TELEVISION

PRODUCING FOR TV

There is a fork in the road facing everyone traveling into Showbiz territory. The road sign reads, "Movies" or "TV". You have to make a decision which one attracts you the most. If you have all the money you need to make the journey, movies are the way to go. Since the average movie takes five years to get produced, that's the ticket for people who have time on their hands and a good chunk of money in the bank.

If, however, dad and mom forgot to give you a million or two to get started with and you're forced by circumstances beyond your control to have to earn a living, there happens to be a hundred times more work in TV as there is in feature films. There are four major networks, two minor ones in free TV land, two major pay cable networks, a dozen mini-majors and what appears to be a thousand emerging minor cable channels. All of these have a 24/7/365 mandate to keep something on the air vs. the 150 films produced by the major Hollywood studios each year.

To put things in perspective, 150 movies played back to back would fill up one network's prime time schedule (1 movie per night) for five months. What about the other half of the year? What about the other hundred networks out there? If you need to make a living and really wannabe a producer, TV is the way to go.

Producing for TV is of the same genus as making movies but a completely different animal. Both require creating an interesting story to be delivered to the masses in as pretty a package as possible. Both deal with time and budget constraints but in TV, everything moves much faster, the budgets are smaller, the schedules impossible, and the axe falls more quickly if you or your show aren't up to the task of attracting a large enough segment of the audience to justify the ongoing investment. TV is filmmaking on speed, fueled by espresso coffee and craft service. (Craft Service is a smorgasbord of tasty food situated near the set at all times that will cause you to pack on a few extra pounds in a hurry if you're not careful.)

Network TV executives are under tremendous pressure to come up with the next big hit. One breakout show can prop up a network's schedule for an entire season. Each of the emerging cable networks have targeted a different segment of the viewing audience; teens, kids, women, blacks, Hispanics, gays, history buffs, travelers, sports nuts, etc. Each network is looking for their signature show that is different from everything else on the tube that raises their visibility and keeps people watching and/or paying their monthly cable bills. *The Sopranos, Heroes, Rome, Deadwood, The Shield, Extreme Makeover, Desperate Housewives, Ugly Betty, The Office, Queer Eye, Nip and Tuck* are some of the most recent crop that have made it into the winner's circle.

This pressure on network execs to find the next hit filters down to the producers who pass it along to the troops whose task it is to help create half a movie in eight to ten production days or shoot a half-hour sitcom once a week in front of a live studio audience. If a newly hatched star doesn't get in sync with the program, the producer not so subtly reminds him or her that there is a line of people hoping they screw up royally who are waiting around the block ready, willing and able to take their place in a heartbeat.

There is a lot less money to work with in TV than most films. TV execs require that you produce what would ordinarily be a $30 million movie for one-tenth the price. As always, the key to everything is great preparation. And if there isn't enough time or money, then good prep will suffice. And if there is even less time and money, then you have to be quick on your feet and shoot well from the hip or risk being buried alive. Producing for TV is all about learning how to juggle — cast, crews, schedules, budgets, locations, logistics and equipment. Like that guy juggling the chainsaws, you have to get good at it quickly or lose an appendage and wash out of the program.

The next question becomes, can you be great at it?

In all of TV there are less than two hundred people at any given time who are capable of physically producing A-level material. Half of them are working and the other half are looking for their next gig. Once you've gotten out of the music video, commercial, infomercial, fishing show, talk show, reality genre, documentaries and kid show trenches, there are a limited number of opportunities at the top of the game to strut your stuff. One can make a very good living in those different categories producing something a lot of folk enjoy. But for those who quest for them gold statues, the last climb up to the podium is a pretty steep one.

One interesting aspect about Showbiz is how the movie industry treats TV like it's their minor leagues. They come along and cherry-pick the new stars both in front of and behind the cameras and run them up the flagpole to see if anyone salutes. Occasionally, a couple of them easily make the jump from the little screen to the big screen. Most don't stick. If you check out the prime time lineup, there's many an actor who started off on the big screen and after a lull in their career, retreat to the steady paycheck offered by the TV networks who are always hungry for a new show featuring familiar faces. It keeps the actor's careers alive as they figure out how to reinvent themselves for future success on the big screen.

Lately there has been a trend for big time film producers to dabble in TV. They are initially surprised by the rapid pace and relatively small size of the initial paycheck but the back end profits for a hit TV show that lasts long enough to become syndicated can be enormous so they continue to want to play. The TV execs love them because they can brag that this or that new show is from the producer of this or that big movie. It helps in the initial marketing campaign but if you don't consistently satisfy that hungry audience who after a short while don't really care about pedigree, their shows will be quickly consigned to the trash heap out back. Some film producers have been very successful but most lick their wounds and return to the big boys sandbox where there's lots more time and money to play with.

Producing for TV isn't for the faint of heart. It is a major league pressure cooker and if you have a character flaw, it will be magnified a hundred times for all to see. But, if you can keep your head while all around are losing theirs and don't care if they're blaming you, there's a good chance you have the right stuff to make a go of it.

TV Pilot vs. TV Series

Upon arriving at the Pearly Gates, St. Peter offers Joe a choice of whether he wants to spend eternity in Heaven or Hell but first he wants to show a promo tape about what each has to offer.

The Heaven video features an angelic choir, beautiful people dressed in shiny robes gliding quietly through a neighborhood of beautifully manicured lawns and mansions. The Hell video is a loud, raucous party, non-stop orgy of flesh, booze and rock and roll. Joe chooses Hell.

St. Peter ushers him to an elevator, hits the down button, and waves goodbye. Upon arriving in Hell, Joe is confronted by an entirely different scene. 120-degree temperatures in the shade, half-starved and naked people chained together, breaking rocks all day long. Joe manages to sneak away and reaches a phone where he calls St. Peter. "How could this possibly happen? Hell is nothing like the tape you showed me."

St. Peter smiles and says, "Oh, that was the pilot."

There is usually a great disparity between the promise of the TV pilot and any episode of the resulting TV series. TV pilots traditionally require twice as much money, prep and post-production time than the subsequent episodes. Hence, the producers throw in everything but the kitchen sink to make their pilots sing. If the pilot doesn't get picked up, then all the money, time and effort goes down the drain. There is no market for dead pilots and there are thousands of them locked away in vaults never to be seen again representing hundreds of millions of dollars.

There are a myriad of reasons why this TV pilot gets picked up and those others don't. The winner often features a great original idea that is derivative of some old successful series, great casting, sharp writing and excellent direction. The losers usually lack one or more of the aforementioned elements. Perfectly good pilots get produced but there aren't any available time slots on the very network that paid for them. Too often, there is a lack of chemistry between the principal cast members who are hastily assembled and thrown together in some improbable situation. A pilot's fate is often determined by what is on the rival networks. "Hey, they have a flying car show! We need a flying car show!"

In the Major Network Brass Ring department, if a series gets a pickup, producing the subsequent episodes requires setting up a very expensive sausage factory. A small army of very talented people gets hired to produce a one-hour, prime time dramatic TV show with an average cost over $2.5 million in 8–10 days. The post-production on each show will take an additional 3–5 weeks. A half hour, four camera TV sitcom traditionally takes a week to shoot and costs over $1 million. The networks will order anywhere from 6–13 episodes of a new show. That way if it fails to attract the intended audience, they can yank it off the schedule after a few airings and not have invested too much money. A series that gets picked up for an entire season will usually produce between 22 and 26 episodes per year.

The grand slam home run is to land in a choice time slot on a hot network with a great lead-in show whose audience will stick around and give the new show the benefit of the doubt. Somebody in the new cast often becomes an overnight sensation and suddenly the network has a bona fide hit on their hands. "Eureka, let's start printing money!"

As a rule of thumb, the major TV networks traditionally fund 75% of the production costs as a licensing fee. This entitles it to two showings over a twelve-month period. The financing studio, or producer who owns the property, is responsible for coming up with the deficit shortfall. They either have deep pockets and can write the check themselves or they have to sell off different pieces of the future back-end revenue streams in order to raise the money.

There is obviously a great deal of pressure on the producer(s) by the financing studio and network executives as producing a winner means tens, possibly hundreds of millions to the corporate bottom line. One hit covers a multitude of mistakes and helps keep the machine well oiled. It often makes the difference in how a network is perceived by the audience, the advertisers as well as the Wall Street investors.

Here's the calendar for a typical network primetime, one-hour, action adventure or dramatic TV pilot:

1. June–September — pitch the idea to the network

2. October – having heard all of the pitches, the network options the project and commissions a pilot script to be written.

3. December – the writer(s) deliver the script before the Christmas holidays so the execs can take along on their skiing trips.

4. January – the network execs return from their skiing trips and decide which pilots get the coveted "green-lights".

5. February – a mad scramble for choice directors, stars, supporting cast and the best crew members. The 100 pilots being shot all vie for key people from the same talent pool. It gets very crazy and the talent agents have a field day.

6. March – shoot the dramatic pilots in 10–14 days. Editing begins immediately.

7. April – Finish editing of each dramatic pilot includes opening titles, sound effects, original music, sound mixing, visual effects, color correcting so that the show maximizes its chances for survival. A lot of sitcoms get produced in April because they take time less time to shoot and edit.

8. May – deliver all the pilots in the first week so the networks can begin an intensive market research effort. Over a two-week period, target audiences are recruited in several cities across America to screen the pilots and provide tons of feedback.

9. Mid-May — the word comes down from the mountaintop that these new series are getting a pick-up and going on the air in September. Some of the really good ones that don't make the initial cut are designated as mid-season replacements and will be ready to air in January or sooner if some of the first crop of new shows get a quick hook in the fall.

The lucky producer(s) who have been given the green light have to shift gears into series mode, as things get really crazy. 20 new shows get to compete with the 40–50 returning shows for writers, directors, actors, etc.

Mid-May- mid-June — line up the writing staff and start pitching storylines around.

Mid-June–mid July — start writing madly, lining up directors for the upcoming shows and hiring the rest of the key crew people.

Mid-July — production begins – The sausage factory needs to produce a new show every 8–10 days.

September (or more likely October) — the new shows premiere and have a couple of episodes to demonstrate that they deserve to continue to be on the schedule and get picked up for the balance of the season.

Some don't make it past the third show before being yanked off the air and permanently consigned to the vaults. All the market research was for naught. Turns out the audience hated the "can't miss" concept and stayed away in droves. Possibly another similarly themed show made the cut on a competing network and the critics loved it. Possibly the new show was scheduled up against a well-established hit series and got totally ignored. Possibly nobody knew where the new show was on the schedule because they kept switching time slots and the network didn't promote it properly.

The audience knows from nothing. They come home after a hard day in the salt mines, put their feet up with a beverage of choice in one hand and the remote control in the other, ready to change the channels in a heartbeat if what they're seeing doesn't grab their attention. They'd be absolutely amazed if they only knew how hard it is to get each one of those notions on the air.

TAKE A CHANCE

The Pay Cable TV networks have a year round development department. HBO is the leader of the pack when it comes to innovative programming. They consistently spend much more money than their major network rivals to produce shows that you can't find anywhere else. Because they derive their principal income from people willing to pay a monthly fee, they are not subject to the same constraints that the advertisers and the Federal Communications Commission (FCC) puts on their Network counterparts. HBO's philosophy is to produce totally different shows for very specific segments of the paying audience. The crowd that tunes in for *The Sopranos* is different than that for *Big Love* or *Six Feet Under*. ($20 per month times twenty million homes is a lot of cabbage.)

There are usually a hundred other networks that come bundled as part of a basic cable package. The subscriber can cherry pick the networks that they have an interest in. HBO isn't the only one making money. The Disney Cable Channel is the most profitable arm of the Walt Disney Company. With an average annual budget of $200 million, it will take in $1.5 Billion of revenue. They have a totally different target audience than HBO but their goals are the same; keep their core audience satisfied with TV shows and original movies (*High School Musical*) that they can't get elsewhere.

The major broadcast Networks have to water down their content by always aiming for the largest possible audience while offending the fewest number of people. They crank out over a hundred pilots each year. Dramas, situation comedies, reality shows that all need to be delivered by May 1st. It's like television's version of salmon spawning season where creation is unleashed and hope springs eternal.

Back in the old days, a network president made the ultimate decision about what shows made it on the air and how long they lasted. Today, Market Research usually dictates the Network Fall TV lineups because the executive branch seems afraid to make any decisions by themselves. It doesn't really matter that together they ultimately guess wrong 80% of the time because the income thrown off by a winning TV series will cover a multitude of mistakes.

Believing there is an audience willing and wanting to see this or that idea is the crux of any enterprise in Showbiz. "If you produce it, they will come", being the underlying philosophy. An opportunity is perceived. Time, energy and money get invested which results in either success or failure. Mostly failure as history tells us that nine out of ten new businesses fail in the first year, which is in keeping with the Network Programmers batting average. Why should they be any better than the national average? Just because they went to some Ivy League school and are making six or seven figures, they're certainly not guaranteed to be better guessers. It's simply a very expensive crapshoot.

In various TV executive offices you'll find 4'x 8' versions of the entire major network schedule laid out on a Monday thru Sunday multi colored strip board. The Execs are supposed to stare at this for hours every day and divine the mysteries of the universe. The real objective is to save their jobs by figuring out how to attract the fickle public's eyeballs.

Let's get that monkey who picks stocks down on Wall Street at the beginning of each year by throwing darts at blown up copies of the newspaper stock page. The stockbrokers keep track of the monkeys' picks throughout the year versus their own and the monkey usually wins. It's time to fly that ape out to LaLa land first class, ply him with liquor, have a limo waiting and whisk him away to the inner sanctum of any of the Showbiz conglomerates; the scheduling room. This modern day War Room is where the multi-billion dollar TV horse race is laid out.

So in walks the chimp. Give him a handful of darts and point him towards the wall where the cover pages of all the pilot scripts are posted. Maybe there's artwork for the potential *TV Guide* covers for each of the new series that have been picked up for the New Fall Season. The monkey randomly throws his darts. The Executive branch holds it's collective breath. They could keep track during the rest of the year to see which ones make it and which ones meet an early demise. (Maybe extra points are awarded for any *TV Guide* covers the monkey licks.)

They should ...but wouldn't dare. What if he made a monkey out of them? How would the so-called experts be able to look themselves in the mirror? How could they continue to justify those big salaries? They would quickly derive the best solution, "Let's kill the monkey!"

It is from the trying and failing that learning results, right? The sign of an intelligent person is someone who doesn't make the same mistake twice. The sign of a creative person is someone who just keeps making new ones. As a creative executive, the biggest question becomes whether can you stick around long enough in any one job to "weather the storm" and achieve the success that the law of averages dictates.

A friend on the inside at Fox once told me that each episode of *The X-Files* was worth approximately $25 million to the corporate bottom line. This show had an average budget of $2.5 million per show. You do the math. If possible, they'd have kept producing new episodes until Scully's hair turned grey and her teeth fell out. Who knew? Who could've predicted that a little show would save an upstart network, help define its audience and earn over a billion dollars for the parent company?

Where's that damn monkey?

THE PLAY'S THE THING

People are fascinated by construction and destruction. Build some star up, enjoy him or her in a couple of movies or TV shows and like a child's shiny new toy, they usually end up being thrown on the pile as the audience looks around for something newer and shinier to play with. Been in rich kids playroom lately or attended a five year olds birthday party? Talk about a disposable culture.

Everyone is asked to suspend their disbelief every time they turn on the tube and watch their favorite TV series. Nobody really lives in those well-lit pristine houses with a canned laugh track accompanying their every grimace. Sure, our heroes may momentarily be in danger but everyone knows they will survive to fight another day or it's goodbye show. Most people take succor and comfort in passively watching TV because it's like a commuter train ride. It's the same sights and sounds every day, the same commercials appearing on different TV stations, the same re-runs shown forever in syndication, the same repetition of aping successful formats. Same old, same old.

The interchangeable news people and the blurring of the lines between truth and fiction have turned the nightly local news into just another form of sitcom. News departments, especially out in Los Angeles, have decided to lower their standards in order to compete with the Jerry Springer mentality and ratings. Most men admire the feminine form as much as the next guy but setting up cameras for the nightly report from some sleazy strip club should not be classified as "news." And as the field reporters stand at the scene of the latest tragedy or get rained on by falling ash or torrential downpours, their stories ought to be introduced in a daily segment titled, "the voyeuristic report for people safely ensconced in their homes that are interested in events that befell less fortunate people today" ... but that title won't fit on the marquee.

Part of the audiences' huge response to "Reality TV" is that each program isn't being delivered as an individually wrapped, sanitized piece of processed cheese with a predictable ending. The audience is fascinated with the unpredictable nature of things that more closely resembles the life they are experiencing. Live sports are such a huge draw on TV because anything can happen. It's a shame that most of the televised contests are now filled with athletes passing by landscapes littered with billboards and logos. It distracts from their efforts but helps pay their enormous fees. When rooting for my pro teams I always pray, "I hope our millionaires beat their millionaires."

True success in TV should not be measured by how many eyeballs get attracted to the latest contrived "reality'" shows: *Bachelor, The Apprentice, Who wants to Marry a Millionaire? Fear Factor, Who Wants to be a Playmate?* Instead of pandering to the lowest common denominator, the quest should be to raise the sights and create programming that enriches our lives and elevates our souls to a higher plane of thinking. (That thought and a dollar won't buy a good cup of java these days.)

There are some enlightened production executives at the networks and studios. But unfortunately they are in the minority. Their not-so-enlightened counterparts send in a shockingly bad script into my operating room and say they're willing to throw millions at it. When I look up into the peanut gallery and ask if they, who are empowered to make such decisions, are really serious? They say, "Absolutely, this is the one." After checking the bank account and realizing that the rent is due, I jump in and give them the best looking corpse that could possibly be made from this fodder. When it fails to attract an audience, they are temporarily vexed before blindly moving onto their next project. "Well, that didn't work. Let's try something else!"

Either they're oblivious or don't really care. They happily repeat the same mistake several times a year. They hang out the laundry in seven-minute segments between the commercial breaks for the brain-dead segment of the audience. For many executives, the most important decision of their day is, "Where do we eat lunch?" — which they will keep asking each other until the expense account is taken away and they're out on the sidewalk looking for their next job.

It's disheartening and yet, every once in awhile, that happy confluence of bright minds meeting up in the right place at the right time produces a blazing meteor that illuminates a mediocre land-scape. This breath of fresh air startles the audience. It's like coming around a familiar corner and encountering unexpected fireworks. We're momentarily elated by the effort. "It's alive. Hope springs eternal!"

The chance to be proud of our work for more than having over-come the production challenges is what every producer strives for. The powers-that-be need to dig in their heels and look for unique, wonderfully original creative ideas, nourish them, protect them as they get ushered into this world. I've had the good fortune to oversee some pretty cool entertainment that has proven to be worth the time invested by all involved, especially the viewer.

Since it's all the luck of the draw, I am eternally grateful. For the other shows I produced that should never be seen by humans again, mea culpa.

CHANGING LANDSCAPE

In the final analysis of Showbiz data, what does it really matter who's Number One? It only affects a few people's paychecks if their network, their movie studio, their TV show is temporarily number one (or number five or number 50) this year. This used to be private information kept locked away but nowadays, the local newscasters in Cleveland or Oshkosh bandy about the weekend box office reports as if they were important.

Is somebody in Peoria really supposed to care that NBC won the November sweeps or what the top five grossing films of the week were? It's just so much blather that we inundate the public with in the hopes that we can make them care. It was long ago established that Big Box Office doesn't = Good Movie. It usually means the Big Hype Machine is still doing its job.

Inside the beast, we have gotten so caught up with the opening weekend box office and who's number one that quality storytelling takes a back seat. Movies are louder, flashier, more amped-up than ever before but it seems our collective humanity has been cheapened in the process. The audience has become part of the market research flow charts that usually determines which projects the bean counters green-light. We have become a Pavlovian society that claps and yells louder when the scoreboard tells us to and spends money when they ring the bell.

The so-called experts are always surprised when another mish-mosh film filled with high priced talent tanks on opening weekend. They scratch their heads when eight out of ten new TV shows don't make it to the second season. Since failure is so prevalent in our business, there are a million acceptable excuses why things didn't work out: "Bad weather, crappy time slot, lousy promotion, world events overshadowed us." Then there's the old chestnut that, "too many TV shows that look alike premiered this fall and we got lost in the shuffle." Nobody says, "It was a mediocre idea that not surprisingly translated into a bad show."

It is very difficult to get out in front of the wave with something new and original. If something works, rest assured that there will be several clones competing next season on the other networks. Although nobody sets out to fail, especially in such a public forum, most execs figure out a way to avoid being tarred by the brush of failure if they want to keep their high paying jobs.

In Showbiz, the only constant is change. Adapt or die or, worse yet, be rendered obsolete which is akin to being buried alive. It's a tricky business to thrive in. You have to keep one eye on the horizon of where you want to be in five years, and one eye on the foreground so that you don't step into a sinkhole that has suddenly materialized underfoot. Quick, "Who's on First?"

THE BIG GAME

Super Bowl Sunday is Christmas in Vegas. The media blitzkrieg hopes to attract a half a billion people all over the world who will be glued to their TV sets watching the single biggest sporting event of the calendar year. It's a rotten shame when a team from a major media center city like New York or L.A. isn't playing. (Will L.A. ever get another NFL team?) Lately we've had to settle for upstarts from Indianapolis, Boston and North Carolina. Huh? Who? What happened to the Lions, and Giants and Bears, oh my? Since he announced his most recent retirement, we won't get to watch grim-faced Bill Parcells, aka "the Miracle Worker", stalking the sidelines like a constipated hungry bear. The Super Bowl would have been the perfect ending to his Cinderella story in Dallas.

The powers that be would like to see the Giants, Eagles, Redskins, Steelers or 'Niners in the big game but no such luck. No stories about the over-the-hill gang of juvenile delinquents from Oakland this year. I'm particularly happy we won't be subjected to any Warren Sapps' or Tyrell Owens' cavorting in our faces all afternoon. As far as they're concerned, the 25 TV cameras are all there to record their every emotional tirade and gesture for posterity as they ham it up and play to the back row of the stadium.

Make no bones about it; this is theater in the round taken to the max. Madison Avenue will pump in fresh oxygen in the form of million dollar commercials to keep us awake that they paid a scant $2.6m per thirty-second ad for the airtime. They're all trying so hard to be memorable and so few of them make the grade. By the time the evening news arrives, the expensive ads (and often the game) will be fused together like a pile of steaming manure that you stepped in that needs deleting from the bottom of your brainpan.

Last year it was the Colts and the Bears, eh? This year it was the undefeated Patriots who got upset by the Giants. Most people who watched the big game would be loathe to name three players and a coach from either team. It doesn't really matter. It is irrelevant who wins the physical game. Besides the advertisers, it mostly matters to the people betting *several billion dollars* on the game, half of who will walk away winners and half losers. Vegas Sports Books and the bookies of the world take a handling fee on every transaction so they're happy because tens of millions have already landed in their bank accounts regardless of the outcome.

Like the Christmas Holidays of my youth, the early Super Bowls were exciting and packed with drama. Now it all comes down to a blizzard of corporate sponsorship and last minute field goal, usually by a kicker with an unpronounceable name. You'll need to flip the channel and watch Australian football if you want to watch manly men being manly, no padding, and no zebras with whistles throwing flags after every play. These guys smash into each other like it's war! They spit out bloody teeth, ignore the broken jaw and keep playing. In comparison American football looks like a damned ballet class. Oh no, I think little Jimmy fell down and skinned his knee! Bring out the stretcher.

The old Plains Indian tribes played lacrosse matches for days and the losing team was killed. In more modern times, Afghani tribesmen played polo using somebody's head as the ball. C'mon, let's up the stakes! Maybe there's a reality show or at least a pay-per-view event in our future where death plays its part. (See *The 10th Victim*) If we ever wanted to really clean up the national debt in one afternoon, we'd televise a pay-per-view tournament featuring our state's Death Row inmates against your states Death Row inmates! The winners get commuted to life imprisonment and the losers get fried on live TV. Oh, what bloody fun!

Super Bowl afternoon will usually find a gazillion people plunked down in front of the tube watching the spectacle because it's always fun watching millionaires bang heads. But the morning after, nothing will have changed and we'll still have to get up and figure out a way to pay our bills.

(Anybody who thinks the pay-per-view death match idea is a winner, have your state's Attorney General call my State's Attorney General.)

What a Big Game it all is!

CHAPTER 4

THE MOVIES

PRODUCING MOVIES

Of all the professions in the world, producing movies has got to be one of the most difficult arenas in which to succeed. If you look back at the entire hundred-year history of filmmaking, there are fewer than one thousand people who have actually produced more than ten hit movies. What are the odds that you're going to become one of them? Not very good. If you really had your heart set on being a big time movie producer and this splash of reality is discouraging, put down this book and go have a nice life. If you're the type of person who is a natural born leader and, regardless of the odds, believes that dreams can come true and they can happen to you, then step right up and let's see if you can win a prize.

There is no surefire way to become a successful film producer other than to learn your craft, pick your projects well, become involved with good people and get lucky as all get out. Contrary to popular opinion, throwing a ton of money at a great idea or a best selling novel, attracting big stars both in front of and behind the camera, marketing the hell out of the finished product often results in a big pile of manure. How could this be true? Easy. It happens a couple of times a year. Every year. The audience quickly hears the negative buzz about the latest bomb and stays away in droves. A popular showbiz sobriquet, "Alan Smithee," has been used on several occasions when a big name talent wishes their name to be removed from the credits of yet another stinker. (Hard to do when you're the star of the film.)

We all grow up watching the "flickers" filled with fantastic imagery and famous people in amazing stories. What kid doesn't like to play pretend? Everyone has their childhood favorites who they want to emulate. Inspired by Jimmy Cagney, Edward G. Robinson, Hopalong Cassidy and Roy Rogers, my specialty was getting into mock gunfights and taking spectacular death dives. Tales of derring-do filled my head and helped shape the images of the life I wanted to someday have. Dream the impossible dream and all that jazz.

It was only later while attending college, floundering around, looking for a path to channel myself into that it suddenly dawned on me that there were people who actually got famous and were well paid to create these make-believe worlds. Like so many others before me, I jumped right in without looking. "Eureka! Go West, young man. Thar's gold in them thar hills!" Those little gold statues named Oscar handed out in someplace called Hollywood claimed another victim.

Emerson College, a small film school in Boston, was where I took eighteen film courses in two years. When the time came for our class to produce its senior film project, all of the choice jobs got grabbed and the only slot left that nobody else wanted was being the producer. So I won the consolation prize. This little bend in the road dictated my life's course as I discovered that I enjoyed taking responsibility for the small army of dedicated classmates who were required to bring an idea to life. (We adapted an Ernest Hemingway short story, "A Clean, Well-Lighted Place.")

A real producer learns how to deal with a wide variety of talented folk in front of and behind the camera. He or she needs to know the names of different kinds of equipment, has to master budgeting, scheduling, and post-production. Like any good car mechanic, they have to understand how all the pieces fit together and best work in productive harmony. These skills don't happen overnight. Great producers are few and far between. It's one of those professions where you learn by trial and error, many trials and lots of errors.

Real artists fall in love with an idea, person, place or thing and decide this is something that they want to paint, write or sing about in order to show off and share with others. The best way film producers have to tell their story is to translate it into a movie. One of the most fascinating aspects of being a producer is somehow accommodating the fact that filmmaking is a totally subjective business and that success is predicated on getting lucky. Nobody's right, nobody's wrong and everyone has an opinion. What one person divines in their brainpan might be the next billion-dollar idea or could turn out to be a total waste of time and money. In movies, because there's no guarantee of a "sure thing", nobody really knows until the audience votes. Up until then, it's best guesstimates all around.

There are a thousand little missteps along the way that can ruin any film production and prevent it from realizing its full potential. Everything can go absolutely perfectly – right story, right cast, right director, right producer, great weather, beautiful scenery, enough money to do the job properly only to find that the ad campaign sucks, the film arrives in the crowded marketplace at the same time another similarly themed movie steals it's thunder, some world event coincides with your premiere that gets everyone's attention and suddenly your very good movie is overlooked and consigned to the DVD shelves down at the local video store.

You can't ever forget that there are a lot of other people out there trying to scale this same mountain. A big, star-studded extravaganza with studio marketing muscle behind it i.e. *Around The World in 80 Days* has the same chance of finding an audience as a little independent jewel that breaks out of the film festival/Art House circuit and becomes an Academy Award winning big hit i.e. *Little Miss Sunshine*. The audience doesn't care what a film costs to make. They are just looking for a little piece of entertainment to enjoy before returning to the real world.

If you have a nose for talent, employ a divining rod when it comes to picking good stories, are at peace with yourself in a chaotic environment and are luckier than most of the people you know, then maybe, just maybe you have what it takes to run in this horse race. Know that there are people in front of you who have been to the winner's circle before that most of the people with the money will bet on before they bet on a dark horse candidate. You can learn as much from their mistakes as their victories. Because this is a totally collaborative medium, very few projects reach the finish line as they were originally envisioned. It is a rare breed of individual that rises to the challenge, has the ability to steer the ship through the obstacle course of entropy that awaits every production and figures out how to win against lifelong odds.

One must learn to enjoy the ride as it happens because it can be the most fun you'll ever know in this lifetime.

MASTERS OF MANIPULATION

A stranger walks in off the street, pays for a ticket and sits down in a dark room with other strangers to watch still other strangers cavort up there on the silver screen. Every week tens of millions of people around the world do this. Don't they have something better to do with their time? Yes. Is there something else they'd rather do with their time? Not really. Lots of people simply love going to the movies.

For most folk, everyday life becomes fairly predictable. It's one of the main reasons people enjoy being surprised in the relative safety, comfort and anonymity of the cinematic experience. They love the plot twists and turns, the latest thrills and spills, if we're really good at our jobs, they empathize with our heroes and heroines, temporarily suspend their disbelief and actually root for them to succeed. Sometimes, it's a life-altering experience.

We have become masters of manipulation. The music builds as the lone survivor of an impossibly difficult journey walks down the dusty road towards the old homestead. The long-suffering spouse looks out the window, her eyes widen in recognition and she runs to embrace the conquering hero. We get a lump in our throats. Just like coming home after another hard day at work, right? Sure it is.

It's a dark and stormy night and something wicked this way comes. An innocent (or three) is thrust in the path of evil and we fear for their safety. Out of the dark, a hand shoots out and lands on someone's shoulder. Adrenaline races through our body. They turn the corner or open a creaky door as we're silently yelling at them not to — only to find their favorite cat (aunt, butler, missing boyfriend) in some horrifically gruesome position. We jump out of our seats faster than Pavlov's dog.

A plain-faced comedian does or says something so blatantly stupid that we can't help but crack up. There is no cinematic experience more cathartic than to be in a room with a couple of hundred people who all burst out laughing at the same sight gag. It's like getting an instant tune up discovering that we are still in sync with all these other strangers. Laughter is Drano for the soul. Big laughs cause endorphin chemicals to be released into our body as we are enveloped in a feeling of wellbeing.

A boy cradles his best friends (fathers', mothers', sisters', dogs') dead or broken body and looks up into camera with tear-filled eyes and vows revenge to the heavens. We've all been wronged somewhere along the line and want to see the bastard who did this get their comeuppance. It doesn't really matter to us if the actors involved in this memorable moment ever speak to each other again or send each other Christmas cards because this tearful scene has been captured for posterity and will stir audiences for years to come.

The audience is right there with the actors riding shotgun. We want the same things they want, the power over their own destiny, the righting of wrongs, finding a soul mate, going on great adventures, etc. That's the beauty of what we do for a living. When we do it well, millions of people are transported to another time and place, made to care about people they will never know and enjoy sights and sounds they might never ever otherwise experience.

Unfortunately, too many of these collective cinematic collaborations turn out like cubist artwork. Seen by few, understood and appreciated by fewer. We can't ever forget we're dealing with a mass audience out there. Old, young, stupid, smart, black, white, yellow, brown, rich, poor, ugly, beautiful, caring and uncaring, they turn to us, depend on us, to help put this world in perspective for them. It's an awesome responsibility and so few of us consistently get to do it well.

Pandering to the lowest common denominator in search of the quickest return on investment is the myopic corporate credo. Too many filmmakers simply acquiesce or have been forced by the committee to embrace the underlying "built-in obsolescence" philosophy of our disposable culture. "Cheaper goods at higher prices!" It is how the corporations make their living out there in the real world. Since they moved into Hollywood and bought up the old studios, why should mass entertainment be any different?

It is the difference between fine dining that you'll always remember and a quick trip to the drive-thru. It's the difference between a great painting hanging in a museum for a few centuries and a calendar on the wall from Earl's Tires. When we, life's storytellers, get our chances, part of our task is to elevate the audiences' sights and encourage them to shoot for the stars. Get them out of that market-research comfort zone and make them think, care and feel for those strangers up there on the silver screen. We should always try to rediscover where the edge is and take it one step farther.

It has long been demonstrated that we actually have the ability to influence peoples' attitudes about how they think, what they buy, and even how they feel about all kinds of strangers they encounter once they emerge from that darkened room (womb?) We create new ways for folk to look at and interpret this world we all live in. If our images are continuously filled with hate and disrespect for our fellow man, we have no right to be surprised when we reap a crop of violent, anti-social types. We have to fight the myopic vision that is blindly in pursuit of profits and figure out better ways, less harmful ways to tell our stories.

We have the power to influence not only what people want, how they talk and what they wear, but also to plant little ideas in their fertile imaginations that can sometimes become very important ideas. We allow the audience to plug into a dream state while they are awake. Powerful sights and sounds jump over the natural boundaries everyone has erected to protect themselves. Music can reach into our souls and excite us, inflame us, scare us, ennoble us. When combined with startlingly beautiful imagery, the experience can stir us like nothing else in the world.

We play with people's heads. Unfortunately, these days, too many of the decision makers just think it's a cool way to make big money and meet chicks.

ANTICIPATION

We spend every day of our lives in various stages of anticipation. What are we going to eat? Who are we going to meet? How far can we push the rock up the hill today? Some things are much more enjoyable to contemplate than others. One of my favorite events occurs when a few souls take their seats as the lights dim. The bad music with the syrupy-voiced DJ is finally over. Hungry mouths throughout the room can be heard munching on sweet and salty empty calories like there's no tomorrow.

The slide show billboards are replaced on the silver screen by the Pre-Show Countdown featuring ads to join the army and be all you can be or buy a subscription to this newspaper or how to purchase on-line movie ticket services for morons. The ads go away about ten seconds before you wanna scream.

Previews of Coming Attractions arrive in the nick of time and just keep coming. Eight or nine different upcoming films are promoted in 90-second heart pounding, gut-wrenching trailers. You mentally put a couple on your future theater-going list, one or two more go on the "I'll wait for the DVD" list and the rest can be trashed and burned or turned into guitar picks for all you care. You saw enough of the film in 90 seconds to know this one ain't for you. You can't help wonder who would pay to see this or that one? More importantly, who in their right mind spent millions to make this or that one and why? The answer is too disturbing to dwell on. Save it for later when a bottle of spirits is handy.

And in case you'd forgotten, at least once or twice during the cinematic onslaught you are exhorted to patronize the theater snack bar by dancing candy bars and smiling Coke cups. In most movie theaters, it's the profits made from the snack bar that keep the doors open and the lights on. More than anything else, it's the fresh popcorn that gets the old saliva percolating. The smell envelops you like a nostalgic reminder from your youth. You ignore the fact that you have just survived fifteen minutes of a non-stop commercial onslaught that you paid to see because everybody knows the damn movie actually starts fifteen to twenty minutes after its advertised time!

The anticipation of a particular film is often more enjoyable than the actual film-going experience, but hope never diminishes that something surprising or special might be in the offing. Maybe, just maybe, this one will live up to it's billing. Maybe it'll even be better than expected! The theater goes dark and suddenly you're five or ten years old again, waiting, hoping, praying to be transported to another time and place. You are ready to go on the adventure if the filmmakers have done their job correctly. Total mind meld. It doesn't get any better than that!

The corporate mother ships' logo lights up the screen accompanied by a symphonic fanfare. Four, five, six different production entities take credit in the opening titles and finally, finally, after all the hoopla and hype that lured you in, the filmmaker (or more likely the committee of filmmakers/ businessmen/ marketeers) gets to show you what it's all about. It's Showtime! *El momento de verdad!* All the chips are out on the betting line and they're going for broke.

Millions upon millions of dollars have been spent on the production, millions more to lure you in. Thousands of talented men and women hours are exhibited in every moving picture art gallery. Tens of thousands of details and decisions have been made in this uniquely collaborative effort. A year or two of hard work, hopes and dreams have been transformed into ten or twelve reels of film that contain yet another linear jigsaw puzzle designed primarily to separate you from a little of your hard earned money in return for a hopefully enjoyable respite of entertaining make-believe. Twenty-four flickering images per second either take you away on a magical journey ... or you've got a 100 minute ride through somebody else's Purgatory or Hell.

At the end of the movie, it all boils down to four words. "It's great!" or "It stunk". This translates into word of mouth, helps determine the all important opening weekend box office numbers and the fate of the filmmakers immediate future.

Any film that makes it to the local theater is a miracle. Any TV series that gets on the air, good, bad or indifferent, is a Herculean task. It is there in that darkened room, on that screen of length and width where the storyteller has ventured out on a limb to be judged by their peers. The best and the brightest will see their work along with the illiterati, the great-unwashed masses, and everyone will come down of one side or another – "It's great!" or "It stunk!"

Anticipation and deliverance. That's what it's all about. And every once in a great while, like a harmonic convergence, there's a perfect blend of story, style and substance, all the planets lining up just so. Right stars, right story, right director, right DP and composer, right ad campaign, right time to release the film. Only happens a couple of times a year, but it's enough to keep hope alive that your next movie-going experience will ring your chimes and keep you coming back for more.

APOLITICALLY CORRECT

There should be a billboard on Sunset Boulevard reading:
ANTAGONISTS NEEDED!
The sad fact of the matter is that Hollywood is running out of bad guys. The cinematic language is being truncated. We are losing entire groups and races of people who can no longer be made fun of or be the antagonists without stirring up some controversy or outraging some new anti-defamation league. People from every ethnic persuasion will soon be on cinema's endangered species list.

Within our lifetime we've seen Hispanics, Italians, African Americans, Jews, Irish, Hillbillies, homosexuals, Japanese, Arabs, mentally handicapped, and obese people hire lawyers and make the corporations who run Hollywood aware of their displeasure. No more calling anyone: "spics, wops, niggers, kikes, micks, boonies, gaybirds, slant eyes, towel heads, morons, or lard-asses." They've all formed groups who protest loudly whenever any of their members are portrayed in an unflattering light. (In the case of the lard-asses, it's always unflattering light.) It doesn't matter if the plot is historically accurate. It just makes this group or that look bad and stirs up old controversies. "Does it have to be Japanese pilots who bomb Pearl Harbor?"

Producers are so afraid of being politically correct that they are seriously running out of buffoons to poke fun at and bad guys to hate.

We're lucky that aliens, ghosts and monsters haven't banded together to form a union or there would nothing left to propel our stories forward. "Darth Vader wants you to join him in a crusade against stereotyping fictional bad guys! Hey, not all of us are out-of-control egomaniacs who want to take over the world every goddamned week! Not all of us are mutant cretins seeking revenge upon those who have rejected us because we're not pretty. Can't we all just get along?"

No. It doesn't matter if we ever achieve a completely scrubbed and hygienically sealed, politically correct world. Some people will still call each other names. Some people will still get high and do stupid things they regret the next morning. Some people will still fight, hurt and kill others because they couldn't control the demons within. Some groups will still oppress their weaker neighbors. Some people will hate each other because it's easier than taking the time and trying to understand them. Some governments will still want to grab something their neighbors have for some trumped up reason and don't care who they have to kill to get it. Some cultures are naturally belligerent. Their talking to each other about the weather sounds like a nasty argument to our ears. All people are different and the differences should be celebrated.

But seriously folks, we need some new foils. C'mon, don't you want to see your name up in lights? You know what they say – there is no such thing as bad publicity just as long as they spell your name right. If you are in a group that hasn't yet been attacked or persecuted, please step forward. We'll get the word out to the appropriate producers and rectify the situation, pronto.

THE BIG PUZZLE

As a sickly kid, I learned a lot about life by doing jigsaw puzzles. Putting together a thousand piece jigsaw puzzle is a daunting task. I quickly got good at defining the hard edges that frame the puzzle. It was fun and took a lot of patience sorting everything by colors, figuring out which funny pieces belonged together and watching the picture slowly came to life. In many ways it's terrific training for becoming a producer. Painstaking attention to detail without ever losing sight of what the finished project is supposed to look like.

When asked what you've been up to lately, it's sobering to hand somebody a single videotape or DVD that encompasses the last six months (or year) of your life. The big question of course is, "Was it worth it?" Was the investment of time, energy, blood, sweat, toil and money justified? When you step back in the clear light of day and regain a little objectivity, was the finished product worth that piece of your life encased in plastic? It's hardly a black and white answer because everything is leading to something else, right? Hopefully bigger and better opportunities await you around the next corner.

Every year some talent or film sets the world on fire like an out of control meteor. Usually it's not what anyone planned. Dreamed about, yes! Planned, no. The right project arrives at the right time and everybody jumps on board. *My Big Fat Greek Wedding* came from passion and hunger. It was a small theater production in L.A. that got it to the launching pad. As a movie, there were no big writers or stars, (other than the Exec Producers) and at $5 million, no big up front dollars. Everyone bet on the back end. At $220 mil domestic box office, it's one of the most successful indie movies ever made.

It makes you wonder about the system that didn't spawn but spurned this project, wanted nothing to do with it. You'd think the flaw would be corrected and every major studio would set up low budget or ultra low budget film divisions searching for the next great little movie. In a business that is built upon taking advantage of creative people, you'd think it would have dawned on some bright president of some big company (other than Roger Corman) to say, "Wait a minute! There *are* people out there living in our backyard who know how to produce quality stories for a fraction of what we're paying. Let's exploit them!"

The answer is hard to believe but they can't. It's not allowed. They invoke the David Putnam Rule. David Putnam, the brilliant producer of *Chariots of Fire* and many other films took over Columbia Studios way back in the eighties and announced, "No movie over $10 million dollars! Curtail the perks and let's tell really good stories inexpensively." Inside of a year, the rest of the boys in the club mugged him and had his head on a pike. A small warning shot across the bow of anyone else who tries something that enlightened.

If you make a good quality project for a minor amount of money, what do you need the big stars, the high priced producers, writers and directors for? Wait, what do you need all of the big salaried execs that guess wrong most of the time for? What about all those perks and golden parachutes they keep handing out to each other like lollipops? Market research? Overhead fees? Stop right there, mister! You're questioning the validity of the status quo. They would have to admit that for the most part, they're not very good at their jobs. Hey, a blind man with a shotgun is going to hit the side of the barn once in awhile.

Besides, if you did away with the expensive façade, there would be no need for the standard 40 page definition of Net Profits, no place to hide the money from the real profit participants that a successful film or TV series earns. No way to pay for all of the mistakes that were made over the rest of the year with the profits of a handful of the really big winners. Blasphemer! Heretic! Take that guy out and shoot him and please tell the chef I'd like my fillet mignon a little more well done this time.

Why doesn't some enlightened mind cop to it? Ignore the status quo up and install a different paradigm? It's because when Sam Goldwyn, the last of the original moguls died in 1964, the triple A (accountants, attorneys, agents) rushed into the void. They analyzed how the moguls built the business from scratch and devised a formula that would approximate their success. Every year the magic wand has to descend on a dozen writers, producers, directors and stars and they are dubbed "hot stuff, bet on them, can't miss!" The fact that they guess wrong most of the time and the hot stuff cools down and disappears doesn't deter them because the couple of strands of spaghetti that stick to the wall will more than pay for the ones that don't.

They say, "Hey, nobody went to see my movie!" when they should be saying, "Hey, nobody went to see my deal!" It was a great deal. I got a lot of money and so did all the boyos up front leaving $1.98 to make the film. Don't they know how little I really worked and how much I pocketed? I just don't understand that fickle public. Three or four of these bad deals, uh movies, and my career is going to be over. Let's face it; most of the lollipops disappear above the line. Hmm ...The puzzle is figuring out how to get one of those jobs that provides you with one of them golden parachutes that should just about cover your expenses for the rest of your life.

CHAPTER 5

THE INTERNET

The Big Little Picture

I'm afraid the Internet is going to eradicate attribution, copyrights and royalties altogether. The horse is out of the barn and running around wildly. Things that have stopped the video version of Napster thusfar are the lack of computer storage space, quality of picture and download time. The MPAA and their techno wizards are trying to devise a viable defense against the horde of hackers who are licking their chops like hungry wolves at a sheep convention as they gaze not only at the old media libraries, but any new film release as fair game. The minute the security boys announce the latest anti-piracy measures, the Oklahoma land rush is on to see which hacker can break the code the fastest. It's a badge of honor in their world.

While this thrust and parry rages in cyberspace, how does this affect you and me? It's yet to be determined in this age of trickle down economics but the old business model is going to have to change. At the high end of the spectrum, you have the major studios that cumulatively average producing 150 movies a year. Under twenty are the designated, "tent pole pictures" that prop up the entire enterprise. The blockbusters will hopefully help pull all the other studio boxcars through the worldwide distribution maze. If you want blockbuster Q, you must also buy movies X, Y and Z. If blockbuster Q doesn't hit the heights, they then pin all their hopes on the next big engine coming down the tracks. It's high stakes poker up there in the rarefied air but this Internet threat has them in a tizzy.

What if several million people avoided paying to see the next big picture and could instead grab it off the Net, sometimes even prior to its theatrical release, and watch it on a postcard sized screen for free? It's already happening on a small scale but soon enough it will be available to all. The ethically challenged will have no qualms about blatantly stealing someone else's work. They believe it's their birthright to go where they want to go and take what they want to take. Once several million people avoid the $10 entry fee, we're looking at hundreds of millions, if not billions of dollars, not making it back to the studio coffers. This puts a dent in their ability to fund the $150–$200 million dollar blockbusters because there is a hole in the battleship and it's taking on water. If the blockbusters go down, it leaves movies X, Y and Z to fend for themselves and maybe they're not so good a bet as they once were.

During America's Civil War, Abe Lincoln's story about the hotel owner trying to rent out rooms in the front half of the building while the back half is on fire seems apropos to the threat posed by the Internet to the status quo. The "pigs-at-the-trough" above-the-line mentality of the writers, directors, actors, producers, where a few people make way too much money up front is going to have to change if they are going to be able to afford to keep making the big pictures. And the big boys have to make the big pictures or their world collapses. The above the line talent that eats up 60–70% of the budget is going to have to scale back it's voracious appetite if the machine is going to survive. It won't happen until one of the majors threatens to go belly up after choosing a couple of high-priced stinkers in a row. Then there will be a meeting in a back room someplace like the Polo Lounge where the boyos finally agree to finally rein in the above the line talent.

Here's a novel solution; reintroduce the risk and reward cycle and honest accounting into the equation where everyone is incentivised to make better productions. As is, if you are the above the line talent being paid all the money up front, where is the incentive to do great work? Ego? Pride? Nobody sets out to make a bad $100 million dollar movie. Especially ones that could've cost less than half as much if the above-the-liners salaries were keeping pace with inflation instead of trying to catch up with the latest Enron boys. The only reason they are being paid all that money up front in the first place is because of accounting obfuscation and the incestuous relationships at the top of the food chain.

The Internet is still going to put a huge dent in the returns until they figure out a way to track every download and put tens of thousands of pirates in jail (which ain't gonna happen.) If a former big tent pole picture costs half as much to produce, it will hit paydirt a lot quicker and take the sting out of the piracy losses until the technology boys can figure out how to stop the leaky dam from busting wide open. It's a long overdue market correction, but it will never happen unless a disaster strikes one of the six remaining majors. They're such diversified, monolithic, multinational corporations that they really don't need to keep the three sets of books like in the good old days.

Down at the other end of the spectrum, people who have figured out how to make things cheaper, better and faster will suddenly be in demand. Cheaper and faster are the easy parts – better is the real challenge. The Internet is going to become the principal outlet to the sea for the independents. Imagine a world where the artist can produce something and sell it directly to their audience without the middleman. It's the status quos' worst nightmare.

Several artists are at the forefront of the groundswell that will completely change the business paradigm and the balance of power in Hollywood. It's happening as you read this.

Wait'll Lucas or Speilberg officially release their next film over the Internet first. After they punch a hole in the wall, we'll watch as it all comes tumbling down.

COOKIES

When signing up for the Internet, I don't recall anybody mentioning that every time I logged on, some cyber-world Big Brother would be monitoring my activity. Everybody knows that each Internet user has chosen a different user name and password. What most people don't realize is that there is an additional identification code that is capable of tracing back all of your e-mail, every credit card purchase and website you visit. The tech wizards who invented this marvelous tool attached what is known as a "cookie" so they can keep tabs on what you're doing, when you're doing it, and how often you do it. They sorta slipped the idea of "cookies" by us while they dazzled us with an affordable future we all had to have in order to keep up with those mythical cyberspace Joneses.

It would've gotten more attention if they had called it a "User Identifying Tracking System." The conspiracy theorists and Civil Libertarians would've made a big stink, but like a Pork Bill surreptitiously added onto a piece of legislation sailing through Congress at the end of a legislative session that nobody is supposed to pay any attention to, "cookies" were pretty much ignored because everybody wanted the Internet to work and this tiny encroachment of our privacy was a small price to pay.

A "cookie", like its namesake, is a much easier concept to swallow. Makes it sound like we're all kids playing some kind of big game. Hey, whose got the milk to go along with them cookies? The real game is that somebody out there at HQ wants to know what you're buying, reading, viewing and listening to at all times of the day and night. Through automated banking and telephone payments, they're keeping track of how you spend your money and who you're talking to. Now, apparently, everybody has to have a cell phone that shoots pictures and plays video games. The ads make us think that we're all having one big party.

In reality, the noose tightens.

The rest of the world is slowly getting wired up. They have no idea what's in store for them. We're the guinea pigs. If it can be made to work here, the rest of the world doesn't stand a chance. "Why should we care?" you ask. The powers that be are slowly but surely putting together dossiers on each one of us that will create a complete profile full of personal information much more invasive than a TRW or any other credit check could ever dream about. Short of bugging our house and everyone around us to find out what we are talking about, they will have more info on us than anyone needs to know. Future employers and banking institutions will have access to your entire life from education and health records to what size underwear you buy and where you buy it.

When you decide to run for President or apply for a job, they'll be able to pull up what videos you've watched throughout your lifetime, what's your favorite kind of porn, what books you've checked out at the library, last visit to the proctologist, how many cavities you have, etc. etc. ad nauseum. Don't know about you but I'm not happy about my secret life being available to anyone willing to pay for it. Under the Homeland Security Act, they're probably consolidating all of that info on each of us right now. Maybe someone will take notice when they finally figure out how to breed us without all of our genetic defects. Sounds vaguely similar to an earlier plot we learned about in the middle of the last century emanating from Germany. Hmmm ...

All this info gathering would've made J. Edgar Hoover proud. Think what a guy like that could've done with all them cookies.

FASTER, CHEAPER, BETTER

New technology helps raise the bar of excellence as things get faster and cheaper to achieve. In order to appreciate the jet stream we're all currently in, one need only step back and look at the increasing number of ways we communicate with one another. Letters, tom-toms, smoke signals, reflected mirrors, pony express, telegrams, telephones, radios, films, television, fax machines, computers, pagers, the Internet, text messaging and now moving pictures on our pocket cell phones.

A technological communications revolution is sweeping across the world. Asia and Europe are hooked up in such a way that when you are out and about, (and being tracked by your cell phone's built-in GPS) you can now receive personalized text messages that provide discounts for items at nearby stores that you like to shop at. You can buy a ticket to a movie you want to see via text messaging, bring your cell phone to the theater and swipe it across a bar code reader like they have at the supermarket checkouts. The cost gets added to your monthly bill. Won't be long before you can just watch the newest movies on your little screen and avoid the hassle of finding a parking space down at the Cineplex. (As my optometrist happily said, "Everybody in the world is going to need glasses!")

Nanotechnology is going to be available to our kids and grand-kids that will hopefully have tiny computers flying around in their bloodstreams zapping cancer cells. It's going to be a *Fantastic Voyage* kind of world. People will soon be taking sightseeing tours to the edge of the stratosphere for a hefty fee, departing daily from s space station being built in New Mexico. We will probably be able to communicate with whomever we want to, whenever we want to, wherever we happen to be. And yet, what are they doing with all this gee-whiz-bang techno revolution? When you boil it all down, they're primarily using this amazing medium to sell somebody something. They're still trying to convince us to part with our hard earned cash (or use our digital credit data) to buy something, see something, or do something that we didn't otherwise necessarily need or want.

But hey, everybody has to buy something sooner or later, so we might as well put the new mediums to good use and point them in the right direction. No matter how you look at the proposition, it all comes back to convincing people that anything they're selling is a good investment of our time, energy and money. How to improve the quality of our lives and increase the number of choices for less money should be the quest.

That's where the storytellers come in. Spinning yarns, capturing people's imaginations, singing songs that resonate in the audience's soul. From hand shadows on a cave wall to holographic imagery in our living rooms, it's all about magic. Making up something from nothing. Creating the illusion in the mind's eye. Inspiring people to dream while awake and ask, "Why not?" We live in a world of infinite possibilities. It is time to carpe diem or as my father used to say, *Carpe Pecunium* — Seize the money!

It's what this crazy business is all about.

SOFTWARE, SOFTWARE, SOFTWARE

Billions are being spent hooking up the country to facilitate streaming video to our computers. The Internet is in the transition phase from being a text-based medium to becoming a visual medium.

After the initial bloom was off the rose, big financial hits in the economic community caused confidence in the Internet to take a dive. What did anyone expect? Average Joe computer guy builds a website without a sound business plan and suddenly millions of dollars are being thrown around, all façade, no beef! Welcome to Cyberland's version of the Oklahoma Land Rush! The Internet promised to be this communication gizmo that was going to save everyone a lot of time and money. The death of several high profile web companies that couldn't keep the hot air in the balloon much beyond their IPO date left a sour taste in the initial investors' mouths.

Well guess what? The Internet isn't going away, in part because it very economically provides its users with a tremendous amount of information. It also gives buyers and manufacturers the ultimate interactive capability — eliminating the need for the expensive middlemen known as the distributors and retailers. Just because many a blissful honeymoon went bust, the marriage between TV and the Internet is still on. The Internet is destined to become a uniquely different kind of moving picture portal and is positioned to take advantage of the audiences' voracious appetite for personalized programming.

An opportunity exists to become a producer of economically viable software. Creating a network of original programming that caters to the individual is the goal, while producing a library of titles that can be exploited in other mediums is the quest. The home run ball is to produce shows that can crossover from the Internet to cable, first run syndication and if truly successful, the Big Networks. The major suppliers can't produce original shows for this new medium because they can't afford to. The economic truth is that the TV networks can't keep paying big licensing fees for bad programs viewed by a dwindling audience. With the rise of cheaper reality programming, game shows and magazine shows, the networks are already producing shows they own but can't rerun or syndicate. The audience is continuing to find it's amusements elsewhere — the Internet could ultimately become the biggest winner in the eyeball sweepstakes.

Like any other TV outlet hoping to attract and keep enough people coming back for more, the problem becomes what to program? The rise of inexpensive digital video cameras has helped level the playing field. With the success of shows like *Cops, World's Craziest Car Chases* and *America's Funniest Home Videos*, a large chunk of the audience has become accustomed to less than spectacular Hollywood production values.

There is a treasure trove of interesting material ready to be tapped into from home via the Internet for a fraction of the cost:

What if you could follow your favorite musical group night after night on its cross-country tour?

What if you could discover a new comedian and follow him or her through the comedy club circuit?

What if you enjoyed a particular strip club in another city and wanted to peek in each night and check out the dancers?

What if you loved little theater and wanted to watch *Cabaret* in Kansas City, *Death of a Salesman* in Denver or an actor's workshop Off Broadway tonight?

What if you wanted to see your Alma Mater's Homecoming football game on Saturday afternoon that probably wasn't being broadcast on TV?

What if you wanted to tape your favorite pastor or rabbi back home as he delivers his weekly sermon and watch it when you get back from playing golf?

What if you wanted to check out certain specific traffic cameras before your morning commute?

What if you couldn't get enough of those police pursuits or cops on the job? A central switchboard could immediately switch around the country to the hot spots and bring the action home live to your living room.

What if you wanted to wake up and go to bed watching nature shots and soft music like they have at the end of the CBS *Sunday Morning* program?

What if you principally liked to watch Cheerleaders in action? There are all kinds of football and basketball games going on with all sizes and shapes of those spunky cheerleaders. The real game could become the picture in the box in the lower right hand corner or go away entirely.

What if you liked marching bands performing at halftime shows more than the halftime recap?

What if you wanted to attend fashion shoots featuring beautiful models strutting their stuff and changing their clothes in exotic settings?

What if you enjoyed watching people fish? From deep-sea marlin fishing to the angler in hip waders standing in the middle of a beautiful stream trying to pull in a big bass?

What if you were wondering how things were going in Paris, London, Moscow at this very moment as a roving band of camera people are always walking around, talking to strangers in the street and taping everything?

What it you couldn't get enough opera, jazz clubs, and adult entertainment clubs?

There is a flood of interesting material ready to be tapped into for a fraction of the cost.

All of the above and much, much more are probably being teed up as we speak. It's only a question of time and money. As the audience has demonstrated, they are willing to pay for their amenities if they are cheaper, better, faster. Amazon.Com, FedEx, MCI, Sprint, Costco, K Mart, Xerox, Sears and several other Fortune 500 companies were built into multi-billion dollar enterprises based upon this premise. The same will happen to the Internet if given half the chance.

Almost anyone with a cell phone camera and a little vision can overnight become a producer. We're really not all that far away from all of the above becoming a reality.

DON'T BOGART THAT NET, MY FRIEND

I have a confession to make: I've become an Internet junkie and don't think I'm alone.

Sometimes you feel like you're chasing a rabbit down a hole. You plunk down in your seat merely to find out what the weather will be today or how your favorite team fared last night and the next thing you know, you're branching into all kinds of uncharted Wikipedia territory that you never had an interest in before. After filling your head with a dazzling display of visual imagery and terse text, you look around and another hour has clicked off the clock. It's downright addictive.

We've all heard about carpel-tunnel syndrome for people who spend endless hours at their jobs in front of a computer terminal. Your wrists get funky. Your fingers wear down to the nubs. It's easy to foresee a day when most of Americans will suffer from it because of the allure of the Internet.

Wait 'til they install that last mile technology and/or increase broadband tenfold so that all those still photos become animated and then look out. That information highway will become a million lanes wide, all screeching to a halt in front of your eyeballs. Let's just jump to the next level and get those computer chips planted in our heads now. Don't know about you but I'd love to know how to play the piano without all those boring years of practice.

There will be fistfights in every family foyer over who gets to sit in front of the terminal and for how long. The TV networks don't stand a chance when our choices become infinite. Don't know if you've been channel surfing lately in cable TV land but they mostly feel like one long commercial occasionally interrupted by original programming. The holy trinity, Corporate America, Madison Avenue and Silicon Valley, are taking us apart piece by piece and then putting us back together again the way they want us to be – placid, functioning zombies, programmed to buy, buy, buy! Once we, the guinea pig generation, have been figured out, the rest of the world will get permanently hooked up and it'll be all over but the consuming.

We're on the cusp of the next phase of our total absorption and capitulation. It is called VOD (Video on Demand) where we will all get to watch what we want, whenever we want, wherever we are on the delivery platform of our choosing as long as our credit cards hold up. When combined with an infinite number of Internet streaming sources, why would anyone go back to the tube? TV will become what the Model T Ford was to today's Formula One racecars.

We are heading towards a tailor-made world of our own creation. Make no mistake about it, the advertisers are zeroing in on your brain, figuring out what makes us tick. Using the database of encrypted pages that we are all filling out as we qualify for this contest or that free giveaway, they are knocking us down and tagging us like they're on some big media safari. You'll be sitting at your terminal downstairs getting bombarded with new car commercials and better equity home loan rates, while little Jimmy upstairs will be watching the same program getting hit with Dockers jeans commercials and discount coupons for the local amusement park.

It's creeping up on us incrementally. Think about those children in the early stages of the Industrial Revolution who were hooked up to clunky machines in noisy environments, spending endless hours of toil and trouble becoming human automatons. We've all seen their hollowed expressions and forlorn looks as they stared into the cameras for all eternity to see. If your spouse were to snap your picture the next time you were sitting in front of the computer screen, you would see the same vacant stare, the dullness behind the eyes of a person hooked up to our modern day opium den - The Net.

We are those children of yesteryear but we have a brand new master. Pull your head out of the LCD screen and smell the roses. There is a technological revolution taking place that is conquering our hearts, minds and pocketbooks one gigabyte at a time. It's well underway, nobody seems to care and there's nothing we can do to stop it. Here in LaLa land, we're the experts at creating fodder to hang out during the entertainment breaks between the commercial islands. When the computers are programmed with reasoning and discreet logic, it's all over.

Reminds me of a story I heard about a big time TV writer/producer. Somebody pitched him an idea about a kidnapping and he said, "Wait right there." He turned to his computer, typed in the word "kidnapping" and said, "Let's go to lunch. The script should be ready by the time we get back." He had apparently programmed every show he was ever responsible for into a database and the computer was able to sift through it all, combine it with the principal characters of his new show and put it back together. Oh, some story editor probably had to clean up subplot B and C and come up with some witty dialogue but it's scary just to contemplate — especially if you happen to be a writer. The media has always been at the forefront in shaping the future by interpreting the present. We have abdicated almost all original thought to the people writing the programming. The Internet is going to become more pervasive than we can even imagine. World domination is the goal. Can cyber-cannibalism be far off?

One thing the media has always done well is clone itself. A successful TV show spawns four others before the first rerun hits the air. Most of them fail. No real explanation for the big hit other than right time, right place and pure luck. Formulas are divined and we, the lazy audience, fall into familiar viewing patterns. Advertisers count on us to show up in droves for this show and not that show. The electronic Internet database they are building for each one of us is their ticket to the future. We are data. What we think, eat and talk about in chat rooms is more data. That data is deemed to be invaluable to the would-be sponsors of the world.

Sometimes I will be mainlining on the information highway and look up to discover my better half hovering in the doorway. Try as hard as I might to ignore her, I'll glance up and she's shooting me daggers. There is that silent communication that says, "Get up. Get out. Get your own damn breakfast! I need to check something out right now and you're in the way." It's nothing personal. She just needs her fix.

CHAPTER 6

MONEY

Producing a Budget

Once an idea, treatment, book, or screenplay is selected as a possibility to be translated into a visual medium, the first question the prospective investor usually asks is, "How much is this sucker going to cost?" Transforming a script into a viable budget is an art form.

The schmoozing producer, who is often responsible for finding the money, usually makes up a number they think the traffic will bear. Next they hire (or prevail upon) a creative producer or production manager (UPM) to actually put together a budget and schedule. It is their job to know how much everything traditionally costs and identify the variables in order to get their arms around a project and put a price tag on it. The first pass or two at any budget is a best guesstimate so that everyone understands which ballpark they're playing in.

The initial budget becomes a living, breathing, ever-changing organism adapted to fit the ever-changing circumstances. The projected bottom line is the starting point. Before the first frame of film is shot, it is not unusual to put together fifteen to twenty budget versions of a single project. Once the major decisions get made, the budget reflects all of the hard costs the project is likely to incur. After these have been totaled, the next arena becomes aesthetic decisions where every item in the budget is influenced by the bottom line.

One of the first things to figure out is how many shooting days will be required to adequately tackle the project. Is it a walking and talking show or one full of stunts, explosions and visual effects? The next big category is identifying the number of different locations called for in the script, which eventually determines whether the project is primarily a stage show with sets (more controllable) or a location show. The easiest kind of show is obviously to stay on one stage or one location throughout the entire production, i.e. a soap opera or TV sitcom where everything happens in the home base set with one or two swing sets per episode.

Every day away from the stage/warehouse/home base usually requires permits, extra security, set dressing, lighting, pre-rigging preparation crews, crew parking (up to 200 spaces including the work trucks), policemen with motorcycles if the shot involves picture cars in traffic, restoration fees to return the locations to the condition that the production found them in, paying off neighbors, temporary relocation fees if the owners of the location are displaced for more than a day, additional Teamster drivers, additional trucks, minivans, generators, etc., etc. (adding approximately $10–20,000 per day to the bottom line.) To rent someone's property is a separate location fee negotiation, traditionally handled by the Location Manager. Renting a mansion in Beverly Hills can cost $10–25,000 per day. Shooting at a Southern California beach or State Park currently costs around $2,500. How many cast, crew people and extras will need to be fed each day?

One of the most important things to be figured out once pre-production commences is whether a lot of the scenes can be played in the same location thus minimizing the number of times the company has to move. Experience teaches the person putting the budget together to be conservative in their estimates as opposed to overly optimistic because everything costs more money and takes more time than originally anticipated. Once a bottom line number has been divined, nobody wants to go back to the financier on bended knee and say, "Please sir, our original guesstimates were off and now we need some more dough." It'll come but usually at the cost of a bigger piece of the back end profits.

The next task is to determine the number of crew people and what kind of equipment is needed. This is dictated by how complex each scene of the script is. Will the production be local where everyone gets to sleep in their own beds or does it need to be shot at a distant location where cast and crew travel, incurring extra housing and transportation costs? Shooting at night is harder than during the day because bigger lights, extra manpower and specialized equipment is usually required. Traditionally, night exteriors on location are the least productive and most expensive production time.

Until somebody puts pen to paper and divines a game plan, everybody is in the dark about a realistic bottom line. Sometimes the person putting the budget together is backing into a finite amount of money. Other times, the financiers just want to know how high is up. Ultimately, the bottom line influences all of the other categories including; camera, sound, props, set dressing, grip, electric, number of extras, transportation, set design, set construction, wardrobe, makeup, production staff, post production, music, insurance, publicity costs, etc, etc. A detailed movie budget will often exceed 40 pages of information. (See GENERIC BUDGET in the Appendix for an example.)

The creative producer draws upon all of his or her previous experiences to make educated guesses about all of these categories. If something out of the ordinary is required for a project, they'll call upon outside experts to put together a preliminary budget breakdown in their respective fields. These days, many films and TV shows require a variety of special effects. Each special effect shot has to be figured out how to best achieve. Is it a; simple superimposure, a computer generated animation (CGI) shot, a miniature, an animatronic puppet creature requiring puppeteers, practical special effects like bullet hits and explosions or some combination of all of the above? Are there a lot of similar types of shots (laser gunfire in *Star Wars*) or is each one totally different (the Death Star explodes)? Multiple uses of the same elements usually saves money. Once you've paid for the monster costume or built an expensive set, you can hopefully use it in a variety of ways.

Often the person putting the initial budget together has less than a week to make all of these decisions, usually without the director's input because he or she hasn't yet been hired. In preliminary budgets, a lump sum in various categories is used as a placeholder until more details become available.

The money boys like to play around with different scenarios. What if the project were to be shot in Australia, Canada, Mexico, Hong Kong? Each of these locales has different exchange rates, crew and equipment rates, airfares, etc. Most distant locations outside of California offer a variety of government incentives and rebates to produce shows in their backyards. They range from 10% to 40% of the final budget. California offers no incentives to local filmmakers, which is why a couple billion dollars of runaway production shoots elsewhere each year. By now, some distant locations have a deep talent pool to draw upon both in front of and behind the camera. Exotic locales often require bringing in almost everyone and all the equipment. A call to the local film commissioner's office helps determine who, what and how much is going to be available when you need it.

How much film to be budgeted for an average shooting day is determined by how many cameras will be rolling and what type of director is being considered for the project. On average, an hours worth of film gets exposed each day. This translates into 6,000 ft. of 35mm film that will eventually be boiled down to four to six usable minutes. This can easily go up to two or three hours of film being shot per day if the director tends to over-cover his or her scenes. Between the cost of the film stock, developing it at a film laboratory and transferring it to video (telecine), this all works out to about $1 per foot. That's an average of $6000 per day if it's 35mm film. 16mm costs about a third less than 35mm. If the project is to be shot on High Def or video, the daily cost is much less for the same amount of exposed footage (approximately $1000) because the negative is originating on video and only needs to be transferred to a usable format for the editing.

Whether 35mm film or Hi Def video, a typical camera package with two or three camera bodies and a compliment of lenses will cost approximately $9,000 per week. If the DP requires Panavision, the Rolls Royce of cameras with all the bells and whistles, the number goes up to $15,000–$25,000/week depending on the number of accoutrements. Top of the line productions will pay twice that much for the same gear because they can afford it. A Stedicam with a specialized camera operator will cost an extra $2000/day. This useful tool provides smooth gliding shots like people walking through the corridors on *E.R.* Whether to shoot on film or video is usually determined by the ultimate release plan for the project. Can this movie justify a theatrical distribution (spending millions more to market it) or will it be heading straight to TV or DVD/home video? Is it going to be a TV pilot or a low budget movie of the week destined for a cable network? These latter two choices often means that Hi Def will work just fine because the costs keep coming down and the people in Iowa can't tell the difference in the quality of the imagery.

An average sized movie or TV show lighting package costs $8,000–$10,000 per week. Big movies will spend twice that much and require more manpower and additional generators. There are lights you leave on stage because setting them up and taking them down can be expensive, and there is the location lighting package kept on the electrical truck. A specialized portable lighting truck (i.e. Musco) that can light up a football stadium will cost $2500 per night. Renting a big silent generator to power the lights costs approximately $1500 per week and can use an average of 30 gallons of gas per day. The size and number of generators is predicated on the amount of lights that will be required and the number of places that simultaneously require power.

The bottom line determines how much the heads of the different departments will cost. On a union project, the crew wages are prescribed by the IATSE basic agreement (BA) that represents the 14–18 different guilds. Their respective rate cards are predicated on the type of show and size of the budget. A union technician on a low budget show could earn $16 per hour. Performing the same job on a big budget movie would pay $10 more per hour.

Once all of the mechanical aspects of the project have been corralled, next up are the esoteric aspects. What kind of Director of Photography (DP) is desired? A meat and potatoes DP will cost $3,000–$4,000 a week. If this project requires an artiste who paints breathtaking pictures, they can earn ten times as much. Know that an artistic director and their DP usually require a lot of extra expensive equipment and like to surround themselves with highly paid assistants who tend to work at a slower pace because every shot has to be a Kodak moment. This usually means the number of shooting days will increase. The kind of music and how many recognizable tunes are often determined by what's left in the budget when post-production is finished.

All of these decisions become the Below The Line (BTL) hard costs. Next up are the Above The Line jobs (ATL.)

A writer of a cable TV movie will earn 1/3 of what a writer of a feature film earns, even if both scripts are very similar. In fact, the script may have originally been designed as a theatrical release and now it's only hope to ever see the light of day is as a direct-to-DVD movie. The writer has had to work just as hard but the ultimate budget and release format determines the size of their paycheck. The writer(s) usually get assigned a value (2–5% of the budget), the producers (5–10%) and the director (3–5%). When you've created a hundred budgets, the hard costs are relatively easy to determine. The next big hurdle is figuring out the level of actor(s) required in order to secure the financing. Does the project require a famous face or two for the DVD cover in order to get funded or is it a genre film (horror, teen comedy, family drama) that could work with a group of newcomers who cost far less? On a budget greater than $3m, the Screen Actor's Guild (SAG) minimum weekly scale is approximately $3000/week for 44 hours of work time. Will a famous face work for scale because they a) love the project, b) love the Director, c) owe somebody a favor? Or do they command a hundred times scale and demand a lot of other perks because they have an opening on their dance card and they're picking up some extra pin money before their next really big payday arrives? Each major star has their own extra-added attractions from drivers to chefs, makeup artists to bodyguards, size of dressing rooms to the size of their names and positioning in the opening titles.

When shooting on location, are the cast and key creative players, (producers, writers, director, actors) going to be housed in fancy hotel suites or at a Motel 6? Is the production serving catered meals every day or does everyone brown bag it? A thousand little details add up to the all-important bottom line. Every project can always cost more money. The big question the Executive Producers (EP) usually wants to know is how little can any project cost and still turn out something that is commercially viable.

The difference between what was originally budgeted to what the new bottom line becomes by hiring some key talent that everyone agrees is necessary to make the finished film more commercial is called "breakage."

Each production needs liability insurance to protect against somebody being injured on the job and/ or various kinds of property damage. Often Errors and Omission insurance is required that protects the production company from being sued for copyright infringement, slander or theft of the underlying intellectual property the script is based upon. Insurance traditionally costs 1.5% to 2% of the budget.

Studio pictures cover cost overruns internally. On most independent features, the financiers require a Completion Bond. This is an extra insurance policy in the event that something catastrophic happens during the course of production, i.e. the lead actor dies, the sets are blown away by a tornado, the film gets ruined in the lab and you have to re-shoot several scenes. All of these things would be covered by the Completion Bond Company that would have to write a check to fix the problem. They traditionally require a 10% contingency to be included in the budget as a buffer zone between the normal unexpected cost overruns before they have to dive into their own bank account. A Completion Bond usually costs 2% of the budget.

There are a range of percentages and fees enumerated above. Once the project actually gets funded, all of these are part of the producer's job to negotiate for the best deals. Some items will in actuality cost more than is budgeted and others will cost less. Since the initial budgets are best guesstimates to begin with, everyone knows that future budget revisions will be required as more hard facts emerge. In the meantime, the producer's best guesstimates will have to do in order to put a frame around any idea.

Every day during production is a house of cards where nothing goes exactly as planned. Was there enough money in the original budget to get the project from here to there? What went right and what went wrong are all lessons to be learned from that will help in producing any future budgets.

When all of the real costs are figured in, it's easy to see how a professional TV or film production can burn through $50,000–$100,000 per shooting day. Big movies will spend double that and not bat an eye. And if they happen to go over budget, there's always that studio ATM machine readily available. Independent producers traditionally are working without a safety net and necessity truly becomes the mother of invention.

It's all a matter of time, the size of the egos and thickness of the wallets of those involved. These critical decisions determine whether the production will travel first class or steerage. In the end, the challenge is to determine how to best tell the story for whatever the traffic will bear and reach the largest segment of the target audience.

PRODUCING A SHOOTING SCHEDULE

One of the most interesting and difficult challenges of any production is putting together a viable shooting schedule. This requires taking apart the script, scene-by-scene, and translating it into a schedule that everyone on the production team can work from. It is the equivalent of an architect's blueprint. A schedule is usually created before the budget. Both undergo several revisions before the show actually gets produced. Putting together the shooting schedule helps frame the time and money parameters of any given project. Like the budget, the initial shooting schedule is a best guesstimate until the director and key crew people have been hired, locations scouted and all of the other little details get taken into consideration.

First step - the script scenes need to be numbered. The easiest way to go; every time the location changes in a script, it becomes a new scene number. Each script page gets divided into eighths of pages. If a scene takes up half a page, it is 4/8 of a page long. If a scene is an establishing shot of a location, i.e. Ext. Hospital with a one-line description, it is assigned 1/8 of a page. Page counts help determine the length of time required to shoot each scene.

Page counts can be deceiving. A long scene of three pages might be an easy dialogue exchange between two people having a cup of coffee that takes two hours to shoot. An 1/8th of a page big stunt scene could take an entire day to produce. The director ultimately determines the importance of each scene in the project. The producer has to figure out how long each scene will take to shoot and how much they will cost.

Everybody does it their own way but I start with a yellow pad and set up various categories in order to get a broad brushstroke overview of the script before diving into a detailed production schedule.

The main categories include:

Locations — Exterior or interior, how many and where.

Sets — If enough scenes take place in the same locale and the budget allows, it is prudent to build (or rent) sets on a stage or in a warehouse. You "own" that space and don't have to deal with the myriad of problems encountered when shooting on location.

Principal Cast — How many scenes require the featured performers? Special Guest Stars?

Supporting Cast — Who are they and how often do they appear?

Bit Parts — How many cast characters appear in only one scene and have a line or two of dialogue?

Extras — Estimating the number of warm bodies in the background is often dictated by the size of the budget. Crowd scenes can be 20 people in a restaurant or 20,000 in a football stadium. These can be hired on a daily basis. For the bigger crowd scenes, stock footage, cardboard cutouts, inflatable extras or clever CGI computer tricks are often utilized.

Stunts — How many stunts are called for requiring how many warm bodies to do what? The more dangerous the stunt usually takes more time to produce and influences the Stunt Adjustments — a degree of difficulty bonus paid over and above their normal pay, i.e. falling off a 20 story building into an airbag pays much better than being involved in a traditional barroom brawl.

Vehicles — A list of all the vehicles that are called for. If it's a featured or hero car, is it used throughout the show or just appears once? Because of stunts, will multiple cars be required? Is it a contemporary project or a period piece requiring old cars, wagons, chariots, etc.?

ANIMALS — What kind? How many? Do they need to learn any specific tricks? The animal gets a daily fee and the trainer/ handler gets a fee. Exotic animals (anything other than a trained bird, cat or dog) usually require special transporting.

Special Effects — Explosions, guns, fire, smoke, water, breakable furniture, rain towers? All of these take additional time to set up and execute properly.

Visual Effects — CGI animation helps create big sets, spectacular locales, and greatly enhances action scenes.

Extra Added Attractions —This catch-all category covers anything other than the ordinary walking and talking scenes, i.e. sometimes a body double is required if the star doesn't want to do nudity, a big prop needs to be manufactured, a specialized lighting gag is called for, a platoon of parachuting Elvis impersonators, etc.

By going through this exercise, one can step back and look at what is required by a particular script. The next step is to lump together all of the scenes that potentially could take place in the same location. For example, if you have a script that calls for a trip to the hospital, if an exterior establishing shot is required it can be; a) a real hospital, b) any building exterior you are already shooting that could feature a new hospital sign out front, c) a Hospital Establishing Shot purchased from a stock footage film library. The interior of the hospital is often set up on stage if it's going to be used extensively or can be shot at a totally different location that can be dressed to look like a hospital room.

In Hollywood, there are a couple of independent stage facilities that have standing hospital sets, police stations, prisons, courtrooms, City Hall, suburban homes, etc. It's far cheaper to rent these than to actually go on location and/ or have to build them from scratch.

Once the scenes are numbered and the page counts determined, then each location gets subdivided into Exteriors or Interiors, Day or Night, who's in the scene, etc. The scheduler usually tries to minimize the number of times the whole production company has to move. Each company move during the middle of a very expensive shooting day is at least 1–3 hours of lost productivity. The producer ultimately tries to find locations near each other so the crew can move the camera and key equipment around so the work trucks stay in the same place all day. The entire workload then gets divided into a five or six day/ week shooting schedule.

Once the first schedule has been roughed in on a yellow pad and you have an overall sense of what is required to produce the project, then it's time to dive into much greater detail. Using one of the professional computerized scheduling programs, i.e. EP Movie Magic Scheduling, the script gets translated scene-by-scene into all of its parts. The computer program offers tremendous flexibility when you arrange the strips on the production board into a shooting schedule.

Any scheduler keeps the bottom line in mind. Does this proposed budget allow for a thirty-day shooting schedule or will the same work have to be completed in half that time? Who are the proposed directors and what are they used to? Once the project is underway and pre-production commences, the First Assistant Director (1st AD) is responsible for updating the shooting schedule and figuring out how to keep the train on the tracks.

A good shooting schedule is a necessary part of creating a viable budget. It also points out many of the problems each particular production will encounter. A good production schedule often causes the script to be rewritten so that it is made more producible within the financial parameters. In that respect alone, a good schedule is an invaluable tool.

MONEY = OXYGEN

In Showbiz, never has the Golden Rule been truer; "Them with the gold makes the rules." It requires massive amounts of dough and hot air to keep these giant Macy's Day balloons aloft. In essence, the worker bees are a bevy of talented blind amoebas holding down a spot on the roster helping to get a project from here to the finish line. We producers bump into walls and trip all over ourselves hatching plans and beating the bushes trying to find capital, raise it, and hold onto some of it as it passes through our hands. Everybody in Hollywood, and I do mean *everybody*, harbors a dream that requires funding.

In the case of writers, they need the least amount of dough to keep going. Besides affording a roof overhead and the other accoutrements of everyday life, let's look at their expenses in order to have a career in Showbiz. They require a typewriter or computer and a printer, a supply of ink and paper, a bottle of Jack Daniels, a carton of cigs or whatever they need to free their minds and create a steady stream of brilliant words. They don't require much space because they live in the realm of ideas and the lucky ones get paid to play god all day. The only other thing they need is a nice sports jacket, a pair of clean blue jeans and a car so they can take meetings and discuss their work with anyone willing to read their latest masterpiece.

Actors and comedians are the next cheapest to feed. They require most of the above plus a stage, a microphone and an audience, all of which is usually provided on somebody else's nickel. They need a couple more shirts and gas money to get to their next gig. There is the occasional face-lift, liposuction or hair-weave but that's for later on after they've made the cut and can deduct these expenses on their income taxes. They also dwell in the world of words, ideas and make-believe.

Composers need a piano, or a guitar, computer, boom box and some kind of mixing studio in order to show off what they can do. Sometimes it helps to include other people called "musicians" (not a prerequisite in the rap world.) If they are film composers, they need to put their music next to pictures and show the producer that they have a unique take on the emotional impact of the scenes they are underscoring. If they are song composers, they'll usually require someone who can sing.

Singer's need the aforementioned stage, spotlight, audience, plus musicians or, at the very least, a karaoke machine in order to show off their pipes. They need to get their teeth fixed, have a nice wardrobe and maybe spend some money on plastic surgery because other than a few enormously talented divas, there aren't that many homely chanteuses atop the music business. They keep the really talented bowsers locked up in recording studios and use artistic photos for their album covers.

Moving up the financial food chain, a TV or film director needs a place to shoot, actors, a crew, a camera, film stock or videotape at the very least. After capturing their point of view with some kind of recording device, they oversee the post-production with an editor who puts all the pieces together. When you get into the big leagues, a director has to find a situation that can afford $30k to $100k a day. It can get very expensive to show off what a director can do.

And then there is the schmoozing producer. All he (or she) needs is a cup of coffee at The Ivy or Dupar's, a cell phone, a business card, a good line of BS and arrange to be sitting across the table from the right person at the right time as he (or she) spins their yarn. If all is right in the heavens and somebody buys their story, he (or she) gets themselves a cushy job and a nice big payday. Then they have to find some schmuck to actually figure out a way to actually produce the piece of blarney they just sold.

Doesn't get much sweeter than that! "I'll take a chocolate donut to go."

THE BRATS ARE #1

It's almost laughable if it weren't so true. The primero target of the big corporations who own Hollywood are snot-nosed, pimply kids, many of whom wear pants with crotches down to their knees, an earring or three, maybe a "too" on their forearm or neck, a vacant look in their eyes and if you aren't rich and famous, a peer, food, video game or a good looking member of the opposite sex, fugeta-boutit.

These are the very kind of punks they keep out of fancy clubs and restaurants with a dress code. The executive branch wouldn't give them a second thought except for the fact that they often pay for those fancy clubs and restaurants. Corporate America just keeps dreaming up new ways to milk this crowd out of their lunch money.

The kid's collective lunch money amounts to almost $30 Billion a year in disposable income falling out of their pockets. That's serious money. It all started when we gave them quarters to pay for those noisy video games at the mall. Then we enabled them to become more anti-social by staying home with their new Play Stations that they had to have because everyone else had one. Lucky us! Each new game only cost $50 or $60. It kept them happy for hours on end and their eye-hand coordination/ kill ratio became spectacular. (Note to self – market bumper stickers that read, "My kid killed more aliens than your kid this week!")

They don't have jobs. They don't really appear to be motivated to ever really want to get jobs, certainly not dressed like that. The US Army is definitely interested in them as potential cannon fodder but Corporate America isn't out recruiting them other than to get their butts into those seats for another serving of mindless fun. What, if anything, are we preparing them for? Where did they get all this money? *We gave it to them* and are *still giving it to them*! They'll live off of us until we die and then where will they be? Living in our houses, eating our food and burning our furniture in the fireplace to keep warm.

It appears that the standard issue uniforms being passed out at window Number 5 are white t-shirts, wraparound sunglasses, bandanas, ill-fitting baggy pants with their bellies and/or underwear showing. Don't know if you've noticed but there seems to be some unwritten contest going on about who can show the most underwear before they feel a breeze or the need to hike up their pants.

When you stop and think about it, the Three Stooges profoundly influenced American culture during the latter half of the Twentieth Century. Moe Howard had his day in the 60's starting with the Beatles ripping off his trademark mop-top haircut. Then in the 70's, Larry Fine (and Art Garfunkle) set the standard as we celebrated *Hair* and a frizzy counterculture of stoned-out hippies. That generation subsequently traded in their beads and leather fringe jackets for three-piece suits and dinner at Spago's.

There was a lull in the action until the Curly Generation arrived in the 90's.

What could all these cue balls be thinking? I look pretty darn cute with this "do?" How do you like my new haircut? Nyuk, nyuck, nyuck? If you had gone to a desert island twenty years ago and returned to America, you'd wonder where all of these automaton, Jerry Mahoney look-alike robots came from. Lots of them have surly attitudes, funny accents or speak in some new slang language that should be called, "Youknow".

No, I don't know. Don't get it. Don't want to get it. I guess every older generation looks askance at the next crop coming up and shakes their heads wondering how quickly we are all going to hell in a hand basket. And yet somehow the cream always rises to the top. The smart, talented and ambitious ones emerge from the pack, set the pace and save the world.

Hopefully they'll get through this phase and grow their hair back. With what life has in store for them, they'll be losing it soon enough.

ONE QUESTION

Since money is a means of exchange that has a perceived value and allows people to keep score, I have one question and don't really know whom to ask: is there a finite or infinite amount of money in the world? It's a simple question with a myriad of answers. There are economists' answers. There are theoretical answers. There are practical answers but I doubt anyone really knows for sure.

New wealth is being created all the time. Is a corresponding amount of old wealth being buried in the back yard in order to keep the books balanced? Don't think so. The government, big business and the occasional stock market manipulator appear to be simply printing it up in the basement whenever they need some more. This takes the form of currency, Treasury notes, debentures, stock warranties and other pieces of paper that supposedly have a value.

In 1999, Enron petitioned the government for "mark to market" accounting. They won their argument and were allowed to announce future profits long before they were realized. They claimed a $63 million dollar profit that year from an oil pipeline that hadn't yet been built. Anybody see anything wrong with this picture?

By adopting these acceptable accounting methods, why can't you or I announce that one day we're going to be rich, borrow a bunch of money against our future potential earnings from complicitous banks with the assistance of the big eight accounting firms and the approval of the SEC or FDIC government 'watchdog agencies'? When the time comes to repay the bank, or our creditors, if we haven't yet hit the jackpot, we tell them to go away or better yet, loan us a whole bunch more money because we've dreamt up an even bigger, more outrageous scheme that they should all want to get in on. That way we could pay them back their original loan, plus interest and points of course, proving that we were good customers who just needed to go a little bit deeper into debt. This all sounds like a solid business plan, right? Unfortunately, it would be really scary to discover how many big companies subscribe to this particular method of financing.

Like a deer trapped in the headlights of the TV glare, WorldCom hiccups out a belated mea culpa. Seems they made another three billion dollar ($3,100,000,000) accounting mistake and warn that there might be few more surprises. So far that's about $7 billion in surprises if you're keeping track. Don't know about you but I get a serious talking to if a payment is late or the checkbook isn't balanced properly.

Don't really think I could look myself in the morning mirror knowing that I had in some way helped manufacture phony ten digit numbers that beefed up the annual report and suckered a ton of people to sink their life savings and pension funds into the biggest Ponzi scheme ever. Sure, they've been inflating movie box office numbers for years and a couple of Showbiz boyos have made their little contribution to the fleecing of America, but these guys on Wall Street, the big defense department contractors, our very own government makes Showbiz liars look like pikers. They seem to be saying, "You fellas just keep them amused while we back the armored car up to the treasury door. Pay no attention to the thieves behind the bigger curtain."

In Production, if a producer goes several thousand dollars over on a multi-million dollar budget, we get treated like we've committed a crime and taken food off of the execs table. Of course, if the show is a success then all is forgiven and you can return to the vineyard in the future. If it's a bomb, your name goes on the Mudd list and everybody in town knows you're a bum.

I have this reoccurring dream about producing a hit show and when it's my turn to step up to the cash register, the clerk looks up and says, "Sorry, we just ran out of money." Hope I'm wrong. I'll simply advise them to go back downstairs and print up some more.

ILL GOTTEN GAINS

The "grab" has always been part of human nature. Having contributed little or nothing back to their fellow man, there has always been a small, very rich vein of people who rode high on the hog from ill-gotten gains. They don't feel guilty about it. They're either;

a) smarter than everyone else, b) deserved it because somebody else in the family did all of the fleecing and they are simply repurposing the resources c) just trying to keep up the family tradition, or d) the suckers deserve what happens to 'em. Screw 'em if they can't take a joke.

The skullduggery often takes place in the back rooms of expensive watering holes, usually in the dark of night, away from prying eyes. A couple of the boyos sit around carving out the lion's share of some enterprise and sticking as much as they can carry in their pockets. History provides us with many examples. One of the most famous happened in old Mexico about five hundred years ago. "La Noche Triste" or "The Sad Night" was a truly audacious story of flat out greed and hubris.

Hernando Cortez, and his small contingent of Conquistadores, defeated the mighty Aztec warrior empire of tens of thousands. There had always been a legend about a white god who would one day arrive and destroy them. Never having seen horses before, the Aztecs thought that man and horse were joined together as one beast and their fate was sealed. At the end of the conquest, Cortez captured the Aztec leader, Montezuma, and insisted a large room be filled with golden tribute if they ever wanted to see their god/ king alive again. (see *Royal Hunt of the Sun* – Christopher Plummer in the lead.)

On The Sad Night, Cortez' men decided the jig was up, killed Montezuma and tried to make a run for it. Each man grabbed as much gold as they could carry and the greedy bastards met their fate trying to escape the wrath of the Aztec warriors at the bridges leading out of Mexico City. Most sunk to the bottom of the surrounding moat, clutching their golden treasure to their armored breastplates.

Ah, the good old days. Nowadays, a handful of Armani-clad corporate looters who've stolen billions and billions get arrested as they leave their multi-million dollar mansions or office buildings and the cops gently guide their heads into the back seat of the police cruisers, all for the benefit of the TV cameras. Justice is served, right? We spend millions more of taxpayers money and years of legal wrangling to ultimately hear them say, "Yeah, I stole a lot of money and I guess I shouldn't have done that."

When they acknowledge their wrongdoing, what they're really saying is, "Why are you persecuting me? I know a lot of other big pricks out there who stole a whole lot more than me and got away with it. I belong to a country club full of 'em. How come you're picking on me?"

They're smart people who rarely recall where they placed those millions and billions that disappeared down a hole, or more likely, into some Singapore or Swiss bank vortex never to be seen again. The few scapegoats or high profile poster boys who do get snared in the public headlights usually do under ten years in some Club Fed. When they are released, defrauded stockholders and bankrupt pensioners should be notified and maybe between the prison wall and the waiting limo, allowed to bring along a brick or a baseball bat and get in their licks before the boyos jet off into the sunset and live happily ever after. This gauntlet run would certainly give future crooks pause. Sometimes we're too civilized for our own good. Too many of our modern day, big time white collar criminals manage to dodge the bullet entirely by affording the right lawyers and having friends in high places.

Once had lunch with a studio accountant and naively asked how come all the profit participants in Hollywood have to fight for what they are contractually owed? Is it true about the three sets of books? He looked around, dropped his voice and said, "Let's just put it this way – the Producer never breaks even." The light went on and I tried to remember when was the last time I saw a Showbiz exec being led away in handcuffs for looting the treasury. I drew a blank. What kind of business is this where the studios buy splashy full color, self-congratulatory trade ads boasting of their latest huge success that when the profit participants go asking for their sliver of the pie are told that the production is actually deeply in debt back at the accountants' office?

Things don't add up and that's just the way they like it.

GENERIC BUDGET

In the Appendix you will find a detailed generic $4 million budget for a 35mm, full union cast and crew, 20 day shooting schedule, 90 minute horror film to be produced in New Mexico in 2008. It is a good starting point to define what things cost these days and understanding how production numbers work. This introduction to a professional budget is very important if you are seriously interested in becoming a Line or Creative Producer.

Necessity being the mother of invention, if the Line Producer had to shave $1 million or more from the budget, this same story could be told with a non-union crew, on High Def video in L.A. with reduced fees and fewer number of shooting days. A professional eye could tell the difference between the two finished films because one would look and feel less expensive. Chances are that most of the audience would never know.

Conversely, the same script could always be produced for ten times this budget. It would feature bigger name stars both in front of and behind the camera, more shooting days, cooler visual and special effects and more recognizable music. The principal difference would be that everyone involved would get paid a whole lot more. It wouldn't necessarily guarantee that the finished film would be more successful but it would definitely look and feel more expensive. Once again, most of the audience probably wouldn't notice the difference.

Any budget is based upon what the traffic will bear and the level of professionalism expected to be delivered.

This Generic Budget reflects a reasonable amount of money budgeted (25%) for the above the line (ATL) talent including the writer, director, producers and actors. Many projects are top-heavy as the ATL consumes 40–60% of the budget. With a top-heavy project, the bottom line usually has to increase because you can't suddenly reduce the number of shooting days in half and expect the same results.

This budget is based upon a 20-day production schedule (four consecutive five day weeks) that would require the production team to average four and a half to five minutes of usable finished footage per day. This project utilizes two 35mm film cameras, transferring the exposed film to video and delivering a digital beta video master. If the finished film was destined for projection on the silver screen as opposed to being delivered to a TV network or DVD distributor, instead of finishing on video, for about 2% more (approximately $80,000), this same movie could go the old fashioned route of negative cutting, answer printing, internegatives, optical sound tracks, etc. and delivered to the distributor as a 35mm, color timed master.

What's the difference? If the finished film is to get a big theatrical release (more than a thousand movie screens simultaneously) a film finish is the most economical way to go. If money is no object, then a digital intermediate (DI) gets created transferring the finished Hi Def video master back to a new 35mm negative, one frame at a time at 1080 lines of resolution per frame for the absolutely prettiest pictures. At $4 per frame, times 24 frames per second, times 60 seconds per minute, times a 90 minute film adds up pretty quickly. If the final movie is going straight to home video or TV and there's little or no chance it will ever be projected on the big screen, then a video master is the way to go.

This is a full union budget including:

Screen Actors Guild (SAG) — all actors, stunt people, stand-ins, extras, and voice over artists

Writer's Guild of America (WGA) — the writer(s)

Director's Guild of America (DGA) — the director, assistant directors, production manager

International Alliance of Theatrical Stage Employees (IATSE or IA crew members)

The Teamsters — transportation coordinators and captains, drivers, catering chefs, location manager(s) and casting directors.

Every production has to decide whether to shoot a show with a union cast and crew using the most experienced people, or trying to make it work with a non-union cast and crew primarily consisting of neophytes and ex-union members. A production company can decide which unions to sign up with. The IA and Teamsters usually come as a package deal. The IA and Teamsters enjoy flexing their muscles by pressuring non-union producers into signing contracts that usually pays the crew much higher wages. Not only does the producer have to abide by a whole subset of union rules but also they get to pay additional 14–22% payroll fringes of pension and health contributions into the union coffers. This usually requires taking a big bite out of the contingency or having to raise additional financing.

If a newcomer writes a script, to be directed by a newcomer, the production company has to decide whether or not to sign up with the WGA and DGA. If so, there will be higher wages to pay, all kinds of union rules, health and pension fringes of 13–15% of their member's payroll. These unions have pre-negotiated residuals once the finished project starts to generate income. Different tiers have been established for the myriad of different types of production, i.e. the daily or weekly rate card for a director's services working on a big theatrical movie is much different than a reality show segment director. In the accompanying budget, you will notice that the DGA fees are 60% of rate card scale. This is a break provided to producers of low budget feature films (under $3.5m excluding the contingency and Completion Bond fees) and TV shows. It keeps their membership employed and provides some relief to the bottom line.

If it's an under $1 million film, SAG allows it's members to work at greatly reduced up front fees. Once the finished project starts earning income, however, the actors will be made whole, which means making up the difference between what they were paid and what they should have been paid at SAG scale rates (or whatever was negotiated with the performers.)

The accompanying budget isn't particularly heavy in locations, stunts, special effects or visual effects (CGI). It doesn't require a 2nd unit (a smaller production unit that often specializes in action sequences) and lots of extra expensive equipment: cranes, helicopters, stedicams, shotmakers, fancy motor homes, etc. It allows for building sets in a warehouse facility (as opposed to a more costly soundproofed stage) and shooting on location for about half the show. There are extra costs allocated to pay for travel days, hotel, transportation and per diem for the key talent who need to be imported from L.A. in order to shoot the show in New Mexico. Per Diem is a daily bonus (a perk) paid out by the production company for extra food and other expenses the key talent might incur while away from home. The box or kit rentals are provided to key crew people as a bonus to rent their computers and other equipment the production would otherwise have to rent from outside vendors.

There are bound to be certain categories and jobs that the neophyte reader will wonder what they mean. There probably is a book out there that explains each budget line, what each person does on the crew, how many of each category are required, how they all fit together and how a budget is divined. That information is taught in a full semester down at good film schools for people who really want to know.

Heads of the various departments usually negotiate for wages above scale. Scale is the minimum hourly or weekly wage the unions require that their membership be paid for services rendered. If this were a higher budget, the union hourly wages would be increased as per the BA (the IA Basic Operating Agreement) and the crew size would undoubtedly increase. There are fixed costs like crew wages, payroll fringes, the price of film, cameras, truck rentals, etc. There are esoteric aspects that can always cost more like; principal actors, production designer, building sets versus going on location, visual effects, amounts of money to spend on music, location fees, etc.

Most of the information is self-evident to anyone who knows anything about the different crewmembers required to create a professional production. However, down at the bottom of the Generic Budget top sheet, you will notice three categories that require a little more explanation.

Agency Packaging Fee – 1%.

If a project is "packaged" by one of the major talent agencies, meaning they helped bring together the stars, writer(s), director and sometimes even the financing, the Agency will receive anywhere from 1 - 5% of the total budget or a flat fee predicated on how involved they are. With many independent films, the Producer puts all of these things together and no Agency Packaging Fee is paid.

Completion Bond – 2%

For most independently financed productions, the Completion Bond Guarantor is often required by the funding source as an additional insurance policy in case something totally unanticipated happens that jeopardizes the entire film in the middle of shooting. It is once again subject to a negotiation but the Completion Bond can run anywhere from 1.5 – 3% of the budget. Major studio productions don't require a completion bond because they have deep pockets if and when disaster strikes.

Contingency – 10%

Traditionally the Completion Bond Company and the funding source will require a chunk of money to be set aside on top of the agreed upon budget for the little and big surprises that await any production. This is rainy day, emergency money. Whatever contingency money is left over after production is completed is often used during post-production to enhance the finished project by paying for better music, more ornate titles and fancier visual effects. The Completion Bond company carefully monitors this reserve on a weekly basis because it is the only buffer between the production company and their pocketbook.

I debated whether to include a budget but since movies and prime time TV are such expensive undertakings, it is important for the interested reader to see what a professional budget looks like so they can wrap their brain around the myriad of details that await them. [See appendix]

CHAPTER 7

CREATIVITY

THE CREATIVE PRODUCER

If there's one thing a producer has to be, it's creative. It's part of the unwritten job description. The producer has to organize an enterprise that makes something out of nothing by turning an intangible idea into a tangible asset. The genesis of any production is the simple act of creation.

It looks a lot easier than it is. As the producer, you are the captain of the ship entrusted with tens of thousands, hundreds of thousands, tens of millions of dollars riding on the outcome. More often than not, like the early explorers, you are expected to set sail without enough provisions to comfortably get from here to there, without enough time to discover the best course and most importantly, without a great map of where you're going. To run this metaphor completely aground, your vessel is often a leaky ship with a motley crew, because you usually can't afford the best, and all that is expected of you is to achieve the task at hand and return the boat safely back to harbor without killing anyone along the way. And if anything goes right, the Financiers will take most of the credit and reap most of the profits. If it goes wrong, it is simply all your fault.

This includes acts of God, who happens to be your co-pilot on the journey. When an out of control, Santa Ana wind-blown fire races towards your set and the Fire Department requires your cast and crew to immediately evacuate forcing you to leave all of your trucks and gear behind wondering if they all burned up overnight, when the director is in the middle of a messy divorce and is unable to think straight or is coked up and standing on the studio roof threatening to jump, when your production manager is sexually harassing a female cast member, when the shopkeeper next door to where you are shooting decides to turn up his radio loudly thus ruining your audio takes until he is paid off, when the rich lady who rented you the mansion wants you to pay for a new marble floor in the foyer because someone lightly scratched the old one, when the prop man drives off with the hero jeep the night before, had a few drinks and doesn't remember where he left it, when the crew returns to their hotel rooms to discover that some of their possessions have been stolen (including the director's wallet while he was sleeping), when the lead actress arrives with bags under her eyes because she stayed up late partying, when an exploding door cuts your star's nose with the rest of the night's work to get through, when the stage facility bills you for phantom workers on their payroll, when the back door of a pickup truck full of your master tapes flies open while being driven to a vault for safekeeping (hah!) and twenty of your masters are strewn across Santa Monica Boulevard, when computer equipment gets stolen by disgruntled employees, or suddenly a reel of the edited film is "missing" until the editor gets a pay raise, when the call from the lab comes on Monday morning telling you there's been a shutter problem with the camera and your entire weekend's shooting has been ruined, when your film has been stolen and is being held for ransom, when any of the above happens, as they happened to me, although it's unfair, it is ultimately my fault because I wanted to be a producer.

Needless to say, none of the above situations get taught in film school. You just have to gird your loins each day and expect the unexpected. I am no different from any other working producer. As each new problem arises, you can't respond with an emotional tirade but instead have to present a calm façade, divine a clever solution and keep forging ahead. You live in the eye of a man-made hurricane and things won't get back on an even keel until all the energy (money) is spent.

The producer has to be able to think on his or her feet. They have to thrive in pressure situations. I have always envied my friends who only need a microphone, spotlight and an audience in order to show off their talents. I require a small army of fifty to two hundred souls and spend anywhere from $30,000–100,000 each day in order to show off what I do best.

In the final analysis, you can't send out a postcard with each DVD or run a banner across the bottom of the screen telling the audience about the difficulties you encountered during the production. The baby will be judged on its own merits. The creative producer is the person responsible for translating ideas into assets that will hopefully satisfy the intended audience and generate revenue for many years to come. For people who enjoy responsibility, it is one of the wildest rides available. I wouldn't have it any other way.

THE ALCHEMIST'S TASK

During a third of our life (while sleeping) we create a mirror world where we meet, greet, eat and do anything we want to, with whomever we want to. The other two thirds (our waking life) is spent trying to achieve the kind of random abandon we can only enjoy in our dreams. I've hired a variety of writers and actors who take booze and drugs to help re-create that gauzy dream state while awake.

(Hell, I might have tried it myself once or twice.) Making movies (and some TV shows) is the closest thing mankind (not necessarily kind men) has yet devised to approximate this collective dream state.

When you think about it, producing movies and TV is nothing short of modern day alchemy. Somebody gets an idea and conveys this vision to others via words, pictures, and story-telling and pretty soon a couple of dreamers are hooked. The idea gets polished up and the brain trust tries to figure out how to make a withdrawal from a corporate or personal bank account.

Orson Welles called movies, "ribbons of dreams". A whimsical phrase that doesn't convey how difficult it is to actually create something worthy of investing millions of dollars in. It begins with a story that tens of millions of people will hopefully want to see. At any given time in Hollywood, there are a hundred thousand of these whims, notions, ideas, treatments, books, or finished screenplays floating around in the ether, waiting for the stars to align themselves just so (literally and figuratively) before becoming a reality.

Now, if you stop right here and freeze the tableaux, this is Critical Junction Numero Uno, the first piece of alchemy. A dream, an idea, a story is about to get funded. A couple of dreamers carrying pieces of paper, a book, a comic book, maybe some artwork, have convinced sane, rational, hard-nosed businessmen to write a check. This runs contrary to normal Business World practices where collateral is put up for ransom before funding just in case a new idea turns out to be a stinker.

Moneymen take great comfort in touching buildings, kicking tires, sub-dividing the earth into small sections of dirt roped off with stakes in the ground. On Wall Street, aka Gambling Central, at the very least, they want little pieces of paper (stocks and bonds) or digital information that represent future potential earnings by a reliable corporate accounting firm with some kind of prospectus (the greatest paper pyramid Ponzi scheme ever invented and sanctioned by the government.) Tangible assets, even if they're not worth the paper they're written on, provide them with plausible deniability if, and when, things go south. "Look at who's involved! Look at this slick brochure! The print job alone cost a fortune! We wuz robbed!"

In Showbiz, it takes guts to sell thin air and get dreams funded. If you're an independent producer and don't have the connections to take the studio/ corporate route, you've got to find a gambler with money – "the golden as-yet-to-be-fleeced." There are only two reasons to write the check: hope for a gain and fear of a loss. More often than not, it's fear of a loss. Think about it; if you're in a position to write a five, six, seven, or eight figure check to fund an idea, you've already beaten the odds. Life is different for you than the majority of people on earth. You've got a pretty good nest egg, a comfy future planned out, nice digs, access to great food, rich friends, etc. If you take the gamble and it fails, if the project blows up in your face, if you lose the entire investment, chances are your basic lifestyle won't change that much and it'll make for an interesting story at the next cocktail party.

Most rational, hard-nosed business types don't step up to the betting line with their own life savings or the company assets on the line and hope that fate will be kind. They're taking a chance with excess money. If it disappears, they don't die. They might be looking for another job in the morning, but they don't die.

Why bet on a dream at all? Because the public has an increasingly voracious appetite for entertaining diversion and cumulatively, those scheckles can really add up at the end of the day. Everyone can always use a few more zeros in the old bank account. That's the "hope for a gain" part. Now in the "fear of a loss" department, the ego usually gets involved. The check often gets written because they don't want Harry, Bob or MaryJo to have the big success. It bothers them to no end that somebody else becomes the resident genius with the magic touch. They risk millions each year in the hopes that a couple of ideas will turn into gushers and they want to be the person who gets the credit, not Harry, Bob, or MaryJo.

So, it's incumbent upon us producers of the world to make our pitches really sing. They've got to break out of the pack of a hundred thousand and catch somebody's eye. Don't forget, Show Businessmen have lust, greed, envy, but they mostly rent passion from the storytellers. They supply the ignition switch and the launching platform; we supply the dreams that touch people's hearts and minds. We help create the words and images that burn indelible holes in the great collective unconscious out there. People make career decisions about their lives, how they feel about a subject, who they want to marry, how they want to look or what they want to eat based upon what we do for a living.

The moneymen are the acid test. If you can get the damn thing funded, you're in the hunt.

Lots of projects, very few openings because the Big Boys control all the major outlets to the sea. Unless you've got their marketing muscle behind you, your little dinghy will be swamped or totally ignored. Even though we know the odds are against us, that friends and loved ones won't survive the journey, every year a few lucky little films somehow make it to the theaters, find their audience and inspire the rest of us to keep dreaming, keep taking chances, keep telling stories that the Big Boys didn't want to tell, i.e. *Borat, My Big Fat Greek Wedding, Little Miss Sunshine, Strictly Ballroom, The Full Monty, Mad Max, Waking Ned Devine, Badlands, American Pie, Pulp Fiction, Nightmare on Elm Street, March of the Penguins,* and micro-budget *Supersize Me, Napoleon Dynamite, The Blair Witch Project, American Graffiti, Halloween, Easy Rider, Night of the Living Dead, Blood Simple, The Evil Dead, Texas Chainsaw Massacre, The Groove Tube, Mean Streets, Friday the 13th* etc.

The audience is willing to pay their hard-earned money to be temporarily diverted from their waking lives. Once smitten by the movies, they crave it. For a winning film, gobs of cash comes belching through the box office windows. In the trickle down theory of life, some of it actually lands in the filmmaker's pocket. You start with a good idea that keeps getting consumed but never used up. And if you've got a good lawyer, you keep getting paid for it.

If this isn't modern day alchemy, I don't know what is.

ON CREATIVITY

Everyone seems to have an endless supply of words that jump off our tongues with the greatest of ease. What separates us in Showbiz from most other people on the planet is that we live in the realm of ideas where anything is possible and make a living from our words. We employ ideas to convince others to spend a bunch of money so we can paint the moving pictures that help frame the world, make 'em laugh or cry, wow them or scare the bejeezus out of 'em, or maybe just help explain what the hell we're all doing here. Our words, music and pictures inspire our fellow mortals to do things they never thought possible. Go to the moon, fight countless wars, create miniature computers that travel through the bloodstream, sail around the world on rafts, in wooden ships or nuclear subs, search for the mouth of the Amazon, climb Mt. Kilimanjaro, ad infinitum. But one of the greatest mysteries we'll never really know for sure is the true source from where all these words come from.

Oh, scientists have identified the portion of the brain where speech emanates from, but methinks there is a curtain in your head behind which an army of tiny secretaries instantaneously ferrets through dictionaries, searching for the right words for you to say or write down. Maybe there's a Board of Directors sitting around a long table deciding how you should phrase everything who help decide what is politically apropos to fit the moment. Possibly there's a group of historians thumbing through the old memory banks looking for the right anecdote or clever quip to dazzle the audience with. Somebody in there decides when it's best for the personal revelation, the baring of one's soul, the perfect thing to say this very second that instantly becomes part of your permanent personal record. Once the words are spoken, they can't be taken back. Little words like, "I do," may take a lifetime to explain and cost a fortune along the way, but they can't be taken back.

Diving past our carefully erected facades, the trappings and wrappings, through the makeup, flesh, blood, bones, and grey matter, there is this wellspring of creativity where every idea, hankering, and supposition bubbles up from. It is the part of us that the scientists haven't been quite able to quantify, commonly known as "the soul." This is where the divine spark jump-started us into existence and where that spark will someday falter and quit each of us. This is the part that looks back at us in the mirror each day, eyeball to eyeball, no bullshit, and knows who we really are. We may be able to fool the world out there, but never that person in the mirror. As yesterday's victories and defeats are still fresh in mind, the mirror is the one place where our shortcomings are well known.

And as you look in that mirror, there it is - the elusive soul, the creator of all those words, hiding in plain sight for all the world to see. Quick, tuck it away before anyone else notices!

After a brief respite of sleep or that quiet moment of introspection, it all begins again. The engine warms up as we head out for another day filled with words. The brain is doing a million things simultaneously but in the communication department, the best it can manage is a steady parade of words, one at a time. They champion our cause. They get us where we want to go. Where do these damn things keep coming from? I'm sure we'll someday get to the bottom of it but in the meantime we continue on our journey, blissfully ignorant and taking them all for granted.

The real challenge everyone faces is to make every day above ground a great day and make every word count. It's who we are and how we define ourselves.

FINDING YOUR VOICE

The real life Coach Carter, of whom a movie was based, said that most people get up in the morning and don't have a clue why they're here or what they're going to do today. He has a very clear notion of his goal each day – *to bring honor to his family name.* With a goal such as this, it is easy to make decisions about your life. In fact, they seem to make themselves.

The quest to find your voice takes many forms: from art to music, writing to performing. This need to show the world that we are here, that we have something special we want to do or say is what stokes the engines and gets us going each day. Unfortunately, too many people who actually achieve the goal of getting to stand in front of the microphones forget that they need something original or of import to impart if they expect to stick around.

We are all in some way, shape or form searching for our outlet to the sea. I found mine in these short missives. Don't really know if the world has use for yet another memoir about life inside the belly of the beast, but if I can discourage a couple of young people from clogging up the freeways in L.A. and try to do something sane with their life, I will consider this effort a success. This is no life for sane people. After being blinded by the lights, camera, action and run over a few times, the realists stand up, dust off what's left of their dignity, and head for the exit sign, leaving behind us talented, masochistic dreamers.

Everyone knows what they're capable of. The repeated headfirst slamming into walls sort of defines the boundary lines. You can go here but don't even think about going there. It's like that old *Twilight Zone* episode where once you arrive in a small town, you're trapped inside some invisible barrier at the city limits. After investing our youth in Showbiz, we wake up one morning in middle age to realize it's too late to become brain surgeons and all the best desks down at the real estate office are taken.

Each of us knows what makes us happy. Working and paying the bills in this business is a major accomplishment but at the end of the day, it's not enough. Tapping into who you are and what you really want to say is the challenge. It's the only way to experience the highest of natural highs. Everyone has to divine their own best way to get there.

Ray Bradbury said, "If we listen to our intellect, we would never have a love affair. We would never have a friendship. We would never go into business, because we would be cynical. Well, that's nonsense. You have to jump off cliffs all the time and build your wings on the way down."

If history teaches us anything, success will come from a corner that we least expect and we need only to be prepared when it arrives. Success happens when preparation meets opportunity. In the meantime, we are happily building our wings on the way down and hope to find our voice before the ride is over.

DREAMING/SCHEMING

This pretty much sums up how we spend our time in Showbiz. You dream up an idea, divine a plan, run it up the flagpole and hope somebody who sees it or hears it is buying. This applies whether you're trying to sell a new TV show or trying to convince a certain someone that it's time to go to bed. We're human beings. Don't know how they do it in the rest of the animal kingdom, but dreaming and scheming is what we do.

Of all the different professions in the world that you could've (probably should've) selected, you decided upon something called Showbiz. Nobody is holding a gun to your head or forcing you to slave over the piano, take tap dancing lessons, write screenplays, stay up half the night doing budgets or paint the scenery. Most of us start somewhere else, i.e. psychologists, engineers, the armed forces, business majors, educators, etc. But sooner or later that Showbiz siren song keeps calling our name until we are sucked down this rabbit hole. Friends and loved ones pray that this is a passing fancy and that you will soon recover your senses. They pretty much shake their heads like you don't know what you're doing and are dooming yourself to a life of heartache and disappointment. As you reach the point of no return, you take one last look at the real world before happily leaping into the void.

Even though most people have never jumped out of an airplane, they've got a pretty good idea what it might feel like. The principle difference is that our trip down to earth takes weeks, months, and years. It's liberating to throw off the yoke that your parents and the world have prepared for you. It's exhilarating to enjoy the sights and sounds of this make-believe world where anything can and does happen. It's terrifying to see that ground approaching rapidly without knowing the outcome in advance. Like kamikaze pilots, no matter how hard they try to stop us, a few good people miraculously manage to get through the defenses each year and against all odds, make their voices heard.

Some people glide to the earth like they were born with wings. Most tumble head over heels, arms and legs akimbo. We check for damage, pull ourselves together, and try to find our place in this strange new world. Everything appears normal on the surface but upon closer examination, nothing is as it seems.

When something works out well that you are responsible for, it's amazing how fast the naysayers in your life will step in with, "I always knew you could do it", and an "atta boy" pat on the back. When something actually works, it's like a happy accident. It's certainly not by design because if success could be taught or easily duplicated, the people in charge would have a much higher batting average and would've figured out a better system to nourish talent, encourage innovation, and welcome creativity. Once upon a time there was this training ground called the Studio System that only worked well for about forty years but that model is no longer in vogue.

Today, the help-wanted billboard outside of most major studios and networks reads, "If your idea is really original and different, get out! If you've got an idea that looks and feels a lot like another idea that worked before, come up here to the head of the line, we're all ears."

Whether you like it or not, pure luck determines whether or not you and your project make the cut. There is a bottleneck of talented crazy people always trying to squeeze through the same rock polisher. The powers that be are the gatekeepers who are always on the lookout for the next golden goose. "Hey, Gene Rodenberry once blew his nose on this napkin. I think we can make a TV series out of this one!" There are the lucky few who found themselves standing in the right place at the right time when the door opened and closed very quickly admitting them to the club. If they have talent, they get to stick around. Imposters are quickly re-deposited on their keisters back on the sidewalk. That is, of course, unless they are related to someone important in the pecking order and then they get several more chances to fail upwards.

So we continue to dream and scheme our ways inside the walls of the mighty fortresses. Remember, if it were easy everyone would be doing it.

LOOKING FOR TRACTION

It's funny how certain words or phrases come into vogue and can be heard simultaneously in disparate conversations. A word that pinged the radar screen is "traction", as in trying to make some headway with one's career or on a project. The word itself implies forward momentum, which, for the independent producer, seems to be in short supply these days. It's like trying to climb a mountain of marbles, a slippery slope at best. It's why a word like, "traction", comes into vogue. It is difficult to get traction when the status quo appears to be mired in the mud. Don't see many great creative visionaries or original thinkers out there among Showbiz's elite officer ranks. Lots of businessmen who are great copycats, not many true risk takers. If something works, they clone it fifteen times until they've exhausted the basic concept.

Think about what a blind person must go through when they are placed in a brand new environment where they have to learn how to feel their way along in the dark. Is the next step going to yield an unpleasant surprise? Because no coherent body of decision makers or no one person is really in charge, and there is no manual to codify the rules, it appears that almost everyone at this high stakes poker game is afraid of being wrong.

Failure is organic to the process and it's usually the first step towards success.

Things gummed up in the executive suites make it very difficult for the individual to make any headway. Nobody wants to stick their necks out on the chopping block until they see a few other heads out there. You can't just ignore all the caution tape and go zooming past the blind people inching forward unless you can afford to absorb the loss. It leads to spectacular crashes. Ted Turner personally took a $60 million dollar bath on the Civil War epic, *Gods and Generals*. Hard to do when the original approved budget was $36 million. Don't care how rich you are, ouchcats, that's got to hurt! If not in the pocketbook, then at least the ego.

You can't move forward, can't afford to fall back. Where to go, what to do? The quest is security, a good job, a challenging project, something we can get our arms around and show the world that we can ride this pony.

Opportunities just keep slipping around like the elusive bar of soap that we can see and touch but holding onto it and not falling down on our butts is the trick. And in the end, the best opportunities usually land safely in the pockets of the big boys who already have the money to fund the dreams and control the various distribution outlets.

It's daunting, discouraging and simultaneously exhilarating out here inching along on the high wire. You have to get used to working without a net because you decided to bet on yourself. Not the system, not some corporation, just you. "What fools these mortals be!"

Every once in awhile, an innovative TV show or an independent film gets safely across the wire to that next little platform in the sky. The crowd cheers. Everyone is inspired to continue on. Reports of dry land ahead with solid footing have proven erroneous in the past. That doesn't dampen our attraction to the action as we all continue looking for traction.

ON WRITING

The quickest way to get to the director or producer's chair is to be a great writer. Sitting down in front of a blank screen and filling it up with words is easy. Learning the form and writing screenplays or short stories is relatively easy. Saying something uniquely original and entertaining, that's the hard part that so few do well.

My earliest memories are of my parents pounding away on their respective keyboards, his a Remington, hers an electric IBM Selectric, hammering out another short story or interview for some national publication. Just a couple of wordsmiths practicing their craft. They were total opposites in personality and approaches to life, but I can still see them sitting on a couch together on the front porch, reading each others work, laughing like school children, making editorial comments or suggesting better ways to approach a particular idea. They were each other's first sounding board and biggest fans. It was watching them from the doorway where I came to understand what love looks like, feels like. I almost hated to interrupt their reverie with some trivial thing like a skinned shin or a need for food.

This was something to shoot for in life: to find a partner who loves your brains, helps you selflessly whenever and however possible. To hear that pure burst of laughter fills all the voids of one's life. It echoes throughout the day and carries you along to that wonderful peaceful place where quality time really matters. We can whack our brains around with all kinds of booze and drugs but there is no better reward in life than making someone you love laugh. When it's right, it's the best kind of high and you try to recreate it as often as possible.

Something inside compels me to sit at a keyboard and let it fly. It's not a bad compulsion as far as compulsions go. If they took away the keyboard and all the writing instruments, I could be found scribbling notes on the sidewalk with chalk or printing messages on the sides of buildings with spray paint cans or worse (ala *Quill*). I awaken in the dark to discover a title or phrase sitting in my mind like a boulder deposited in the middle of my highway that cannot be avoided. It's a mental post-it note left behind by some subconscious writing muse. It must be the same for musical composers who hear snatches of a haunting melody that they turn into a song or a symphony. Ad copyrighters come up with the perfect catch phrase for this or that product while in the shower. For a painter, it's a blank canvas that dares to be invaded. For a sculptor, it's the statue in that big rock begging to be set free.

You reach for your instrument of choice and try to capture the essence of the notion by its tail before it retreats into the morass of the mind. Like footsteps in a blizzard, you retrace your steps and go as far as you can catch up to the idea and try to discover from whence it came. With a quick burst of creativity, you suddenly find yourself traveling through a porthole where a cascading waterfall of words, images, melodies await you. Out of a wisp of a notion, a whole idea is born. Some of these ideas merge with other ideas and pretty soon the mind is racing downriver faster than the fingers can type. For a writer, it's in the words, sentences, paragraphs, chapters, books, where whole stories and philosophies are born.

For me, it's as though there are a gaggle of people inside all struggling to get to the internal microphone and have their say. Some of the voices shout out snatches of phrases like it's a noisy press conference. I've had entire movies downloaded into my internal zip drive in one minute, beginnings, middle and ends but I usually can't find a pen in time before they disappear. Some ideas arrive full born in the inky darkness of night and scare the hell out of me. Others are discovered on my computer the next morning and I vaguely remember typing them up while I was sleeping.

Now that I've conquered it, I can admit that I was addicted to a related compulsion, Xeroxism. I just made lots of copies because I was convinced that sooner or later, I would be discovered or somebody would trip over my body of work and clamor for more. Copies needed to be readily available when they called. It's a better addiction and far cheaper than stopping at every bar on the way home and having a drink trying to obliterate the day.

My wife throws out most of the excess Xerox copies during the annual spring-cleaning. "Why do you need eight copies of this or that?" No good answer comes to mind and I imagine people yelling, "tree killer". Now I've become convinced that when a document is saved on the computer or floppy disc that it actually will be there when I need it. Can't really control the automatic writing any longer so I stopped trying.

In writing this book, it's all about re-writing, editing, pruning and trying to provide the reader with a small glimpse of what it's like to be a creative producer in a very tough business. Maybe I'll reach the heights I've always dreamed about. Maybe I won't. But this is the path I've chosen and I can only hope that my observations makes it a little easier for those who will follow in my shoes. (Size 11 EEE for those who might wonder about such things.)

CHAPTER 8

MANAGEMENT

The Business vs. The Show

There is a mutual distrust between the Show and Business arms of the octopus. Instead of it being a collaboration between different factions that desperately need each other, too often it devolves into an adversarial relationship. The Line Producer is often hired to referee the bout.

"No hitting below the belt. Let's have a good, clean fight."

Business: "You're going to spend too much of our money!"

Show: "You haven't given us enough to do a great job in the first place."

Business: "If you can guarantee us a hit, we'll give you more money."

Show : "If we could guarantee you a hit, we could borrow the money from an entertainment bank using our track record, all of the foreign distribution contracts and pre-sales agreements as collateral, rent your distribution system and keep the lion's share of the profits for ourselves."

Business: "So, what you're saying is that you don't know for sure that this is going to be a big hit."

Show: "We believe there will be a big enough audience for this project to justify the investment."

Business: "And you need our money to make this crazy idea happen?"

Show: "That's why we're here, hat in hand, asking as politely as we know how."

Business: "If this doesn't work…"

Show: "You'll have to give us more money to fix it in post that you should have given us in the first place. Otherwise, everything will go down the drain."

Business: "If that happens, I'm going to look stupid and I can't afford that."

Show: "When this works out, you'll be the hero who saves the day. Trust me."

Business: "I don't know. I'm afraid you're going to spend too much of our money!"

There's a lot of B/S dialogue at the heart of any Showbiz project because neither side ever knows for sure and everything boils down to luck and totally subjective decisions.

Unless you're dealing from a position of strength, like having produced a string of winners or are bringing half of the money to the table along with a great project, the producer has to deal with a wide range of wary executives in a wide range of scenarios. You have to respect the fact that your future dealings with the parent company depend on how you are perceived by the particular executive you are dealing with. You have to get out of your head and walk a mile in their shoes in order to truly appreciate their job and the pressures they're under. They need to be associated with box office or critical successes or it's only a matter of time before they get to play musical execution chairs up in the executive suites.

Some execs are as passionate and knowledgeable about the process and the projects as you are. Some are almost totally incompetent and you have to wonder who they are related to or whom they're sleeping with. Most fall somewhere in between these two extremes. They are often overwhelmed by having to play watchdog on too many projects and always border on being burned out. Most of these execs only have time for half meetings. You have an agenda for a meeting that covers XYZ. Their busy schedule, or constant phone interruptions, only allows you to cover X and half of Y before they run out of time. You've got to reschedule later to cover the balance. By then, other things will have changed and there will once again only be half the time for what you really need to talk about.

There's a lot of myopic thinking in the executive suites because many of them are holding onto their jobs for dear life and need good news to report to their superiors. Most execs are given a short window to strut their stuff, 12–18 months. Most projects take six months to a year to get off the ground so they've only got a couple of chances to prove themselves before the "honeymoon period" is over and/or this year's development budget is eaten up. Finding anyone who has held onto the same job with the same company for more than five years is a rarity.

These are the survivors. They range from Machiavellian princes to enlightened king-makers. They are responsible for spending millions to hundreds of millions of dollars and the corporate overseers expect a return on their investment. Somehow, a lot of mistakes get through the maze. Even a blind man with a shotgun hits the side of the barn once in awhile. You wonder what they were thinking (or drinking) when they green-lit this or that project. The only rational conclusion is that many of them don't really have any idea of what works and they're just guessing most of the time.

Usually it's a producer, or writer, or famous actor who comes to a pitch meeting, sells the exec a clever idea that gets sent upstairs to the handful of folk who actually make the decisions and somebody bought it, hook, *TV Guide* logline and sinker. At the other end of the spectrum comes the new or unknown producer with a great script, half the money, a product placement deal, a couple of recognizable faces attached, a budget, schedule and viable production game plan, artwork or even a video trailer. The exec will take a pass on the project because they've seen enough to know it won't fit in with this week's corporate agenda or it's so well developed, they can't readily get their fingerprints on it. Besides, they're only really comfortable dealing with producers they've dealt with in the past and any newcomer will have to pass through the "trial by fire" period.

Sometimes, as the producer with the great idea, when you're actually in the room, the executive will say something or give you a piece of corporate thinking that makes you revise your pitch on the fly. "Did I say washed up ballplayer who makes a deal with the devil? I meant to say it was a devilishly handsome dishwasher who wants to be a ballplayer." Always have a Plan B to fall back on. Go in with two different pitches completely convinced that they're going to buy something from you today. You'll often need to make adjustments to the pitch to suit the mood of the room. Is it before lunch and are they hungry? After lunch and they need a sugar fix? Is it at the end of a long day and they're tired? Are they just back from vacation and want to talk about their trip or how the Dodgers are doing? Is there some artwork or a movie poster on the wall that gives you a clue as to who they are and what they like? Yes, it's grasping at straws but reading the temperature of the room is an art unto itself.

It all pretty much comes down to chemistry. They have to be thinking, "Do I like this person? Do I want to allow them into my life for a very intense three months to two years? What will this person really be like once they're under the gun because right now, they're on their very best behavior trying to make a good impression?" It's so much easier dealing with people you already know or that friends of yours can vouch for instead of having to break in new ones.

The front line execs are part of the phalanx of people who surround the real decision makers. They have the power to kill an idea in the cradle. If they like it, they are encouraging but they can't really say "yes." All they can do is pass something up the ladder when they think they've struck gold and keep their fingers crossed that their boss agrees with them.

When you get in the room, never let them see you sweat. You must present a picture of complete confidence without seeming arrogant. Sink or swim. Feast or famine. Rain or shine. It's Business vs. the Show and the producer has to learn their lessons early because everyone is planning on sticking around for the long haul and this may be the start of a beautiful relationship.

SUITS

A producer calls up an executive one day and says they have the hottest script of all time and they're sending it over with the proviso that it be read overnight. They will want to speak with the executive first thing the following morning because this is going to sell quickly. The executive agrees. The script is sent. The next morning, no phone call.

After waiting patiently, the producer finally calls the executive around noon.

"Well, what did you think?"

"I don't know yet. I'm the only one who's read it."

In Showbiz, any member of the executive branch is commonly referred to as a "suit", whether they wear one or not. It's like an invisible line existing between officers and enlisted men. Most suits have no idea what they're asking producers to accomplish and wouldn't know which end of a camera to look through. Every wannabe suit that will one day be making decisions about which movies and shows to produce should be assigned to a project from its inception to its conclusion early in their careers. They would return to the executive ranks much richer for the experience. How could it hurt to learn about the production process so that they might really understand what it's like to toil in the belly of the beast?

Doctors in training have to spend a couple of seasons in the ER so they truly know what they're doing. Would-be lawyers have to clerk for a while in order to learn about the intricacies of the law. Somehow, pushing a mail cart inside the walls for a year or two, jockeying with the other wannabe sharks-in-training, doesn't appear on the surface to be the best way to separate the executive wheat from the chaff.

If the criteria for success in Suitland is how large of a sponge for information and how big of a fawning sycophant you are, then that possibly explains the resulting myopic decision making process that boasts a .200 batting average. This translates into approximately 20% of what the geniuses select to green light actually works. A random strand of spaghetti has a better chance of sticking to the wall than a thoroughly tested TV concept has of being picked up for a second season.

Imagine a building contractor sitting across from a banker trying to borrow money saying, "I know 80% of the houses I've built have fallen down but I've got this great idea for a totally new way to build them so can I please have a couple of million to try it again?" In Showbiz, a person who consistently hits 20% of the time is deemed to have "the touch." A bloody genius that will earn millions for the parent corporation and that, my friend, covers up a host of other mistakes. In any other business, a 20% guessing average would have you shown to the door if not the firing squad wall.

How can an industry tolerate such mediocrity? It's because the triple AAA, (agents, accountants, attorneys) who run the show are trained in risk avoidance. Let Market Research steer the ship. If they're wrong, the suit making the decision points to the three foot high stack of binders containing all kinds of reinforcing statistical data and answers, "How could I have known that this idea would fall flat on its' face? Look at the track record of all involved. This was a can't miss, slam dunk winner!"

In the end, they don't understand why nobody went to see their deal. It was such a great deal. Bob, Jack, Mary and Harry made a ton of money up front. The fact that only 50% of the budget (or less) was left for the real producer to actually make the picture or TV show doesn't really figure into the equation. That's the producer's problem.

When the dust settles, the money they wouldn't let you spend to do it right suddenly materializes in order to try and fix it in post-production. Everything would have been so much better if the two sides had joined forces to make a great project in the first place. Too often, the suits want you to shoot the budget, to hell with the project. If the number wasn't there in the approved budget guesstimate that more often than not was created in a void before all the facts were in, you have to plead your case to try to get a little more money to finish the project properly.

Both good and bad things happen during production, meaning some things will cost more than originally anticipated and others cost less. The producer focuses on maximizing the good and keeping the bleeding to a minimum. Of course, if you're starting with a mediocre idea or a poorly written script to begin with, the chances for success are already slim to none. The best that the producer can hope for is to get the lemon of a project over the finish line in one piece.

Suits traditionally wait for their bosses to determine which way the wind is blowing. It's one of the realities everybody has to deal with in LaLa land. It would definitely be easier if they actually knew what they were asking the producer to pull off and this truly became a collaborative exercise.

No matter what business you're in, not everything is going to work. Shakespeare, Einstein, Michelangelo had ideas that were duds. Nobody is right all the time. Unfortunately, the folk who make the decisions in Showbiz are not required to get down in the trenches, sully their suits and really learn how things work. It would make things a lot easier to communicate in the future between the two warring factions. Besides, they're missing most of the fun.

THE POWERS THAT BE

Always thought it would be nice if when you arrived in Southern California to make a go of it in Showbiz, that there was a highway checkpoint, a little desk at the airport or bus station where you took a number, signed in, wrote a short essay about yourself and what your dreams were. The Chamber of Commerce or Board of Tourism that sponsored this operation would be populated by ex-Busby Berkley showgirls who would save a ton and a half of heartache and wasted time by telling a certain percentage to return to where they came from. This washout procedure would be cruel but keep the waters from being muddied and the L.A. freeways from getting even more congested.

In the end, the washouts would thank us for not wasting two, five, ten, twenty years of their lives in a business that only harnesses up the lucky ones and uses us to build these great celluloid pyramids until we drop in our tracks. Oh, we all meet with some success during our journey, enough to keep us going for a while but the true power atop the pyramids remains concentrated in the hands of a lucky few.

These modern day wannabe Pharaohs are surrounded by a phalanx of security guards, assistants, advisors, lawyers, vice presidents, accountants, partners, shareholders, relatives, ad infinitum. The trappings of wealth and power have a tendency to warp the vision of the sanest among us. There are shiny new examples of the latest Wall Street fiasco or Washington debacle every week to support the theory that power corrupts and absolute power corrupts absolutely.

Even though we live in a "Me, first!" kind of world, have you ever wondered why so many bastards, bullies and bitches are very successful in Showbiz? Don't know about other industries but an inordinate number of them have elbowed their way to the top of our business.

Having worked for more than a few, I got to study them up close. They sit around in fancy watering holes laughing about the $50 they screwed somebody out of today as they order another $500 bottle of wine. Their bad manners and lashing out seems to be motivated by fear. "I'm going to smack you around, show you who's boss, keep you off balance because I don't need you or anyone else to get too close. You might tell the world I'm a frightened, no-talent, lucky bastard and once they find out, I'm DOA." It's not that the Emperor isn't wearing any clothes, it's that they're running a goddam nudist colony up there and enjoying every minute of it.

Step back and look at the portraits they paint of themselves for mass consumption; The E Channel, *Beverly Hills 90210, The O.C., Dynasty, Dallas, Wall Street, Peyton Place,* the supermarket tabloids. They all scream, "Look how screwed up, how miserable all of us are. You don't want to be rich because it's such a burden. We lie, cheat, backstab, go into rehab, screw around and steal because we're so unhappy."

It's such a hoot because everyday they are laughing their way to the bank. Life is good atop the pyramid and don't let anyone tell you otherwise.

Everyone reads about rich peoples grand parties, outrageous excesses and are bombarded by their decisions everyday on TV, in the newspapers, magazines, and everything playing down at the local movie cinemas. Because it costs so much to produce any of the above, rich people necessarily make these decisions. Although YouTube and the Internet are helping to level the playing field by making it accessible to everyone who can afford a camcorder and the monthly DSL fee, rich decision makers will never be on the endangered species list.

And so you continue on, pushing, pulling, turning over rocks, looking for omens and meaning in world fraught with peril. And every day when most of us feel like throwing in the towel, we should go back to our hope chest, pull out that little essay book that was filled in upon our arrival and remember why we came here.

We're not here to make the powers that be happy. We're here because we want to be and once upon a time we bet on ourselves. We're here because we know something about us that nobody gave us credit for that we're uniquely talented people who are hell-bent on writing our own history. The odds are daunting, the fresh lash marks still sting but the spirit inside will take us to our destiny. If we make it, great. If we make a few good friends and have some adventures along the way and come as close as we can to realizing our original dream as is humanly possible, great.

Regardless, it's important to stay in touch with that internal voice that got you this far because after all is said and done, it's the reason you're here and not out working at the DMV or the graveyard shift at some 7-11 store.

NOTHING PERSONAL

Anyone who has tried to succeed in Showbiz knows how hard it is to forge ahead in a business that doesn't care whether you live or die. It will take advantage when you hit upon a commercial idea and just as quickly ignore you when they have no further use of you. This sentiment was captured beautifully in the *Godfather* when the would-be drug importers tried to kill Don Corleone. "Nothing personal, just business as usual." This translated into, "We love the guy. Respect him. We just had to whack him because there was a buck to be made and he was in our way."

Today, our field of endeavor should really be called "Business Show" instead of the other way around. Back in the old days, the show took precedence. It was paramount to put on a good show, keep the customer satisfied and coming back for more. With the exception of a few great filmmakers, the lions' share of today's productions will ultimately become interesting placeholders in between TV commercial breaks.

The worldwide audience has a voracious appetite and there's a certain percentage who will pay to see anything. The question is whether the marketing magicians can weave their hypnotic spell and attract a big enough crowd on a film's opening weekend or watch the first few episodes of a new TV series to justify the enormous expenditure of time and money.

The marketeers must wake up in a cold sweat sometimes when they finally get to see the finished project and realize they have another dead dream to sell. After a series of drastic triage maneuvers in the editing room, some abomination arrives on their doorstep that vaguely resembles an idea that some executive bought six months or a year ago. They have to figure out a clever way to slap some lipstick on this pig, take it to market and try to wring every last nickel out of it before it disappears down the tubes.

When the next bomb arrives at the local theaters, word of mouth travels fast. People scatter in droves. Mediocre films often arrive at the multiplex by design to coincide with the release of a big blockbuster because people are primed to see something and can't get into the flick they came for. They've paid for a babysitter and have money burning a hole in their pocket. Watch their eyes sometimes as they're standing in line - celluloid junkies looking for their next fix.

So they grab a seat to anything else that is starting about the same time and suffer through the also-rans. The theater owners and distributors count on the fact that people rarely get so disgruntled that they ask for their money back at the box office. The marketing boys get a pat on the back Monday morning for having dodged another bullet as the Business of the Show must go on.

Talk about getting back to what Showbiz's Founding Fathers created, I had this dream that somebody makes a great film one day and didn't charge admission. Imagine empty theaters filling up faster than ever before because the admission price is FREE. At the end of the film, ushers are waiting with their collection plates. You are encouraged to pay what you feel is a fair amount on the way out.

If the film was truly great, made you laugh and cry, touched your heart, resonated in your soul, as only the great ones can, I truly believe many people, while still enthralled, would empty their wallets and feel good about it.

I'd be worried if heretics were still stoned to death.

THE FOUNDATION

You needn't be a student of Showbiz history to realize that most ideas, both large and small, fail to achieve their desired goals. Nobody ever wants to say a project failed because it was a piece of crap. Despite the millions spent on Market Research, they who make the decisions, the collective unconscious, (and some of them do appear to be functioning unconsciously), guess wrong more often than not. Myopic crystal ball gazers are calling the shots and it's impolitic to notice.

Great success is usually a happy accident and hence can't easily be duplicated. Showbiz is an inherently risky business that specializes in risk avoidance. It's a place where damage control "spin doctors" put a happy face on the latest debacle as hopes are dashed, millions wasted, careers flounder in some grey limbo and the people most responsible, the small gang who controls just about everything, shrugs their shoulders and say, "Well, that didn't work. What's next?" Some of them revel in how much money they waste. Oh, there are those who really care about their place in the hierarchy, want to be known as great philanthropists or humanitarians but too many who have reached the top, not unlike the great robber barons of yesteryear, and have amassed their fortunes by being able to run over Mom (or whoever is in their way) with the Mercedes and then hit them a second time just in case. They don't really care what anybody else thinks of them because their egos are gigantic and their emotional range goes from lust to greed to envy and back again.

They hire people who have passion. They don't understand what this "passion" thing is, but they'll take a chance with those fortunate few who have made it through the obstacle course without completely compromising their dignity and retained some of that original fire in their belly. The fire in the billionaires belly was initially quenched when the first couple million arrived in their bank accounts. From that point forward they'll rent other people's passion. They move people around the chessboard like Olympian Gods of yesteryear. This is the fortunate group that whenever they get a whim, an urge, they can make a call or have a little piece of plastic in their wallets that allows them to hit the local ATM for another fifty or hundred grand. They are the physical embodiment of the "Let them eat cake!" crowd. They, the ultimate powers that be, are known as the Status Quo.

To an independent-minded person, they clog and control all the outlets to the sea. Every once in a great while, a few mere mortals sneak past the sentries and get their turn at the game by sheer dint of personal charm or talent and they instantly become the stuff legends are made of. The kingmakers then use these rare success stories to fuel the fires and condescendingly say, "See! You too can become rich and powerful if you just do what we say, dance to our tune and keep your nose to the grindstone!" Ha! When your time pulling the plow is up, and as you and your body of work are tossed on the funeral pyre, they won't give two seconds to think back on the years of toil and dedication, the enormous perseverance, the beatings you've taken. Pawns on the chessboard. "Ooh, too bad! Tough luck old chap! You got old and forgot to get rich along the way? Better luck next lifetime!"

I say fuck that. That's the way things are. Doesn't mean that's the way they'll always be. There is a new technological wind blowing and change is in the air. The independents, the people who actually know how to make great looking shows for less money, their day is coming. The system can't continue to support the big bloated slices of mediocrity it has been dishing up to the public. Although the

Billionaire's Boys Club heavily invests in the boyos who have learned how to defy gravity and fail upwards, they are taking a second look at the layers of bureaucracy and wonder if all the redundancy is necessary. How did the Moguls or original TV execs do it in the old days? What I want to know is how did Cecil B. DeMille produce *The Ten Commandments* without cell phones, pagers, e-mail, faxes, Xerox machines, computers, satellite uplinks, TV's, radios, walkie-talkies, air conditioning, union grievance committees, etc, etc.? How did anybody get anything accomplished before all these mechanical devices came along to make our lives easier?

By the sheer force of their personality. They pulled together a talented group of fellow artists and craftsman who took advantage of the system of their day and made stories that will stand the test of time. This should be the goal of any producer in Show Business. Never lose sight of the goal. You have to make a living in the mean-time but ultimately you'll want what every other producer wants; autonomy to tell the kind of stories you want to, work with whom-ever you want to and to reap the benefits that are rightfully yours instead of watching them go to pay for other's mistakes. And hope-fully, you will leave behind a body of work that you're proud to have your name on.

It's not easy but nothing in life worth doing usually is. Try to have some fun every day if at all possible. Hell knows, they do!

SOME PEOPLE

Some people procrastinate as a way of life. In Showbiz, it's like permanently being in development hell where nobody makes a definitive decision. After some initial positive response to an idea you've pitched, your project crawls up the food chain at a snails pace. Slow roasting over the spit. A large majority of Showbiz's exec-utive film branch should be shown *Napoleon Dynamite, Slingblade, Easy Rider, Friday the 13th, El Mariachi, Nightmare on Elm Street,* (each produced for under a million dollars) and marched to the rooftop and pushed off.

What are they doing? It's so far out of whack it reminds you of Iraq. Nobody seems to be in charge. Nothing seems to get accomplished. Two steps forward, one step sideways and one step backward appear to be the marching orders.

Where the hell are this generation's David O. Selznicks', Stanley Kramers', Harry Cohns', Alfred Hitchcocks', Billy Wilders', Jack Warners', Richard Zanucks', Louis B. Mayers', and George Cukors'? These guys saw the future and made it happen. Since Lew Wasserman departed to the big screening room in the sky, it seems like most of the lions in the zoo have either died or been declawed. They've been replaced by a breed of Armani-clad corporate suits who specialize in taking lunch, taking fabulous vacations and moving paper from the In box to the Out box. They probably prefer their cheese in individually wrapped slices, preferably untouched by humans.

I went into a major studio to discuss a direct-to-DVD movie project and the VP in Charge of Production was scratching his head because the script was 20 pages too long, They were trying to save some money and didn't know what to do. I wanted to yell, "Have some balls. Risk offending the sacred cows of creativity. Somebody has to take a stand and smack their hands on the way to the cookie jar instead of bitching about them being obese later on and wondering how this could have happened."

Instead, I offered a one word solution, "scissors." Simply tell the writer or the producer to either cut out the redundant, superfluous, expensive little scenes that don't propel the story forward or you'll do it for them. "Oh, but they're emotionally attached to this or that scene. They really want to see the hero do this or that and we really need the big Act Three payoff that takes place at a nuclear reactor." I answered with, "Bullshit!" This particular project is a cable TV movie and/ or direct-to-DVD sequel that will be watched by adolescent males who say they like Sci Fi and Horror, but the real reason for 98% of the purchases will be because a nubile young female alien walks around naked for most of the movie, killing the poor unfortunate men who want to "mate" with her. This isn't like brain surgery or going off to discover a cure for cancer.

Start with the DVD cover artwork and good story synopsis and work backward from there. I asked, "Will you lose one sale because you don't really go to the nuclear reactor at the end of the movie?" I don't think so. When you want to make a $50 million dollar movie for $5 million, something has got to go. Make the cuts, trim back the scope so that it's producible and understand that the lion's share of the success for this particular film will depend upon casting the uninhibited hot female alien. She doesn't even have to be that good of an actress. God knows, there are plenty of candidates to choose from!

It's so basic. It's what the old studio bosses would have done in a heartbeat. Nobody in the executive branch wants to be solely responsible for making a mistake or be perceived as "anti-creative". It's politically incorrect. Someone's sensibilities might be offended. Can a lawsuit be far away? Some people in positions of power aren't cut out for making hard decisions. It's not their nature. They are consensus builders and great cheerleaders, but at the end of the day they'll let somebody else say "yes" or "no." Their job is to separate the various ideas they hear into possibilities that might work for their target audience from those that don't fit their current business strategy that changed dramatically over the past weekend thanks to the Monday morning box office results.

Sometimes you come out of a meeting shaking your head, wondering if anybody knows anything for sure. You feel like these execs are placeholders until the real execs finally arrive. It's always interesting to come back six months later and see how many of them are still holding down their jobs.

When Sony bought MGM, a few of the top execs got to cash in their golden parachutes but most everybody else simply got a pat on the back for a job not-so-well done and a boot in the butt out the door, clutching their pink slips after years of dedicated service and wondering what happened.

SACRED COWS

Every production has at least one Sacred Cow whose opinion is more important than yours. They are usually an Executive Producer, Producer, Director or Star. Sometimes there are several Sacred Cows on one production and the crew often gets a ringside seat to "Clash of the Egos." In most businesses when there is a problem, you fix it first and dole out the blame later. In Show Business, usually a culprit must first be blamed for the problem, have their noses rubbed in it by a Sacred Cow and only afterwards is the problem dealt with. Often, a sacrificial lamb must be offered up because the official party line is, "Sacred Cows never cause problems or make mistakes." If a Sacred Cow wants to plop down in the middle of the road, we simply divert the traffic around them. They are usually in a position to have you hired or fired, so people walk on eggshells, trying to make sure they stay happy.

When Jack Kent Cook, an NFL and NHL hockey team owner, changed his mind about the team jerseys and was asked about it after a lot of money and time was spent, he replied, "A foolish consistency is the province of small minds." They, the powers that be, the Sacred Cows, change their minds all the time. Sometimes they're bored and screw around just to see if they can liven things up by provoking a fight. Sometimes they think that causing problems and getting sparks to fly down on the set is the best way to get something original and exciting up on the screen. Sometimes they're in over their heads, hoping that nobody notices and think they can bluff their way through. They procrastinate until the last second or flip flop around whichever way the wind is blowing. They'll keep running everyone around in circles until the time, money or patience runs out. Why? Because they can.

The only constant in Show Business is change. If you don't roll with the punches well, start looking for another line of work. Uptight, autocratic, anal-retentive a-holes are drummed out of the service early. Unless, of course, they happen to be one of the afore-mentioned Sacred Cows, in which case their every whim is catered to. There aren't enough hours in the day to make a Sacred Cow happy for long. Oftentimes, it is to the detriment of the project, i.e. casting a no-talent girlfriend or relative in the lead. But who's going to tell the Sacred Cow that they don't have any taste or not to write the check? The answer is nobody. Everybody wants to work. And sometimes, once in a blue moon, a project that started out with low expectations (*Star Wars*) turns into a huge success. Right time, right place, fantastic editing, great visual effects and a powerful music score can often ameliorate a myriad of mistakes.

And then there are some genuine Sacred Cows who have truly earned their position by being right most of the time. They have an internal divining rod plugged into the public zeitgeist that figures out a year or two in advance yet another way to get more millions from the unwashed masses who will happily part with a little of their hard earned money for a momentary respite from their lives. These Sacred Cows are that rare breed that actually knows what they like, knows how to achieve it, and when something doesn't work the first time (which it rarely does), they can be counted on to help you figure out the best way to fix it.

If you are to achieve any kind of success in Showbiz, there is nothing you can do to avoid the Sacred Cows. If you value your job, you have to learn how to address their concerns in such a way that doesn't jeopardize the whole production, because they are often their own worst enemy. You have to quickly figure out who they are, what makes them tick and how to keep them happy. Take it from me, when you can no longer look at yourself in the morning mirror because you've become a fawning sycophant, it's time to find a different job.

You can never forget that no matter how any project turns out, the Sacred Cows will retain their status and often become a reference for your next project. Since nothing is permanent in Showbiz, every job you get is merely an audition for your next job. You've got to be very careful when dealing with Sacred Cows. If you're lucky enough to hook up with one of the great ones, hold on for dear life, watch them carefully, and learn all you can because they are indeed few and far between.

CHAPTER 9

PROBLEM SOLVING

MAKING ORDER OUT OF CHAOS

For people afflicted with the producing bug, making order out of chaos is one of the principal themes of their lives. The job is to tell good stories using art, music, words, and images while interpreting human emotions into something millions of people can instantly recognize and respond to. At 24 frames per second or 1080 lines of video resolution, we literally and figuratively connect the dots and try to breathe life into an idea for others to see, hear, touch, and feel.

In the beginning, almost everyone in Showbiz is a stranger in a strange land. Not only do we have to figure out everything for ourselves, but, once we do, the audience out there depends on us to help make sense out of it for them. We are travel guides in a world of random atoms colliding who provide the sign posts at the intersections that people's lives lead them to everyday; "Go here! Do this! Eat that! Look like this! Use this great new product! Read that book! See this movie!" Carney barkers to the masses.

Layer in a string section during an emotional moment in a film or TV show where we hopefully have gotten the audience to identify with one or more of the main characters and invariably there's a lump in the throat or a tear in the eye. Put an object like a banana peel in harms way and eventually a victim will land on their keister and be rewarded with howls of laughter. Our audience is more predictably responsive than Pavlov's dog.

You can get so caught up in staying ahead of the steamroller that it's often hard to keep things in perspective. Many people live their whole lives without figuring out what they're doing here. They roll around in their personal pinball machines, going hither and yon, never really accomplishing anything of importance before it's Game Over. Their epitaphs should read,

> "Here lies another well-trained consumer who ate, slept, prayed, wept, bought, sold and did as told!"

Part of our job in entertaining the masses is to also show them different ways of relating to each other, looking at the world through a different pair of eyes, hopefully inspiring some of them to elevate their sights and try to exceed their reach. Isn't that what great art is supposed to do? The storyteller's challenge is to make them laugh and cry. Wow them! Dazzle them! Surprise them! When it's working, you get paid well to provide this unique service. Some of our brethren are also well paid to turn out mindless drivel, but that's a whole 'nother story.

There is enough mass confusion out there already that you need not add to it. There aren't enough hours in the day to do everything you want to so you need to use the this precious time wisely. Dreamers are building new celluloid pyramids all the time. Everyone in Showbiz is merely looking for their outlet to the sea.

After arriving kicking and screaming, you hopefully will leave this world a better place than the yucky mess you originally found it. And if you're really good and lucky, maybe you'll get our name on a couple of productions that people will be touched by and remember fondly for many years to come.

It's a daunting task to provide meaning and inspiration while creatively reiterating some of the important things in life. The great storytellers of the world remind the audience what love looks like and how to care about their fellow man. We get to hold up the mirror that enables the viewer to reflect on who we are as individuals and as a society. And if we're really good, while we entertain them, we might even get a chance to point them in the right direction so their tomorrow is actually better than today.

Although it might appear to be on the surface, Showbiz ain't all about sex, drugs and rock and roll.

THE INSTITUTE OF FAILURE

Q. How does one make a small fortune in Show Business?
A. Start with a large fortune.

After the bank of flashbulbs go off and the glittering hoopla of the multitude of self-congratulatory award shows temporarily blinds everyone to the reality of the situation, when your vision returns, you are left to contemplate a Showbiz landscape littered with failures. Like the aftermath of some great battlefield, there are a lot of dead projects and careers scattered all over the place. Some show signs of life but most of 'em are kaput. For every person still moving there are five hundred, (five thousand, ten thousand?) people who've tried and failed to get a toe-hold in Hollywood. There are millions who would've liked to have given it a go, but early on they were sucked back into the real world.

With so many public failures so readily available and before they get buried in the back yard, there ought to be a Showbiz post mortem (cinetopsy?) where these misguided adventures can be examined for common denominators so that something relevant might be gleaned. That way, the mistakes of the past wouldn't keep re-appearing in next years *TV Guide* Fall Preview issue, destined once again for failure. A database could be created and cross-indexed in a variety of categories. TV shows about certain topics, starring certain actors, written by certain writers, produced by certain companies would win the "Snowball's Chance In Hell" rating. This could happen *before* the wheelbarrow full of money got spent.

Criteria could be devised for feature films regarding certain topics with certain people involved in key positions that are almost sure to be doomed to failure. An old friend, Sam Arkoff, President of AIP, who produced over 20 movies a year for 25 years, always did a little market research before producing each film. His partner, Jim Nicholson, and Sam shared an executive bathroom. In the morning, they would arrive at the urinals at the same time and Jim, who was a drinking man, would have come up with a couple of titles the night before – *I Was A Teenage Werewolf, Beach Blanket Bingo, The Beast With A Million Eyes, Earth Vs. The Spider, How To Make A Monster,* etc.

Sam would call in the Art Dept and get them working on the poster art. When the next crop was ready, a half dozen new posters would get sent to their branch managers around the country, who would then approach the local theater owners and ask them which films did they want to play in their theaters? Sam and Jim would look at the feedback and say, "Well, I guess we ought to get scripts written for the winners and make 'em." AIP made money in 24 of it 25 years of existence. Sam and Jim were Exec Producers on over 200 Roger Corman Films and started filmmakers like Francis Coppola, Martin Scorsese, Robert DeNiro, Dennis Hopper and hundreds of others. What did they know? They were the kings of the B-Pictures. They were the first to target the teenage audience while their peers were making *Quo Vadis, How To Succeed In Business Without Really Trying* and *Valley Of The Dolls.*

You would think somebody might have learned something about how not to pick losing propositions. Then again, it's how Las Vegas, Race Tracks and State lotteries generate over $500 *billion* in revenue each year. At $140 *billion* of combined revenue, the TV, film and music industries seriously lag behind.

Some of us will go our entire careers without graduating from The Institute of Failure. Don't know about you but I've got a space on the wall waiting for my diploma.

ANATOMY OF A STRIKE!

Every couple of years in Show Business, war drums are heard in the distance. As they approach, both sides announce how they are being screwed out of something they think they deserve and how they're not going to take it anymore. "Nobody should have to slave away under these intolerable conditions or unreasonable demands. The pie continues to grow and it's an insult that we have to live with the scraps! Where's ours? We deserve more, more, more! You can't function without_____(fill in the appropriate union; DGA, WGA, SAG, AFTRA, IA, TEAMSTERS, NABET, etc) and you're nothing without us!"

As the battle lines are drawn, the independent producers and below-the-line crewmembers are small potatoes in the big game and can only watch helplessly from the sidelines. No pleading, cajoling, weeping, wailing or gnashing of teeth is going to prevent this man-made collision course from happening. No Senators to call or letters to the editor will alter the outcome. The impact of its inevitability is felt several months in advance. This is a family squabble that eventually will be settled in the back room by the big boys in a bare-knuckle, no holds barred match, involving high priced lawyers charging thousands and thousands of dollars an hour.

As the strike deadline approaches, the opening salvo is usually the AMPTP (Alliance of Motion Picture & Television Producers), representing the multi-billion dollar international mega conglomerates, pleading poverty. They need a rollback in wages or a reduction of pension contributions or some other such concession that was gained by the last strike. "Can't we all just go back to 1972?" The guild(s) or union(s) get up in arms and say, "No f*#@ing way!" They walk out of the negotiations calling each other names, pissing and moaning that they're not going to take any more of this shite.

The elected union reps, who started out as members of the rank and file, have recently returned from their expense account holidays where they strategized the best way to re-skin the cat. They have decided it's time to draw a line in the sand and go fight for the little guy. They thump their chests and address their constituents as though they're idjits. Strike placards are stapled together. The troops are riled up and told that solidarity is the only answer. "If we all stand shoulder to shoulder in the face of our overseer and show them how united we are, they'll have to cave in and acquiesce to our demands!" What the noisy picketers don't want to know is the real overseers dwell in far off places, living the good life and don't really care. "Labor strife, you say? Pass the Champaign and call me when it's over."

The various union representatives are left to tilt at windmills and make as much noise as possible. They have to stir up the hornets' nest every couple of years in order to justify their jobs and avoid losing those accompanying perks. It's amazing how fast a person adjusts to a high-on-the-hog POV. It's nice to travel about with an expense account, taking lunch at fancy places and talking about how the Big Man is screwing the little guy and now is the time to make them pay. Heaven forbid the reps ever get voted out of office and have to return to being a member of the rank and file on the assembly line again.

So they roust the troops out of their innate complacency to picket, use bullhorns to yell at each other, eat sandwiches, march around shouting slogans for the TV news crew, use sunscreen and talk about the injustice of it all. Maybe a few punches get thrown, a window or two is broken to show they really mean business this time, lawsuits filed, etc. A friend related how Lew Wasserman, then the president of Universal, would sit in his window at the Black Tower watching the picketers with binoculars at the front gates and took down the names of the more boisterous ones for future reference.

All of the unions are battling with the studios for more _____ (money, a bigger piece of the back-end pie, job security, fixing the credits, better health care, etc.) Right on cue, the studio PR machine swings into action. "We can't give up anything else because _____ (the piracy issue, Internet, runaway production) is killing us. Hey, we have to keep ourselves alive first because if you kill the golden goose, we all die. Contrary to what we're reporting to our share-holders at the annual meeting in some fancy resort, we're really feeling the pinch and will possibly have to cut back on production or maybe even shut down altogether. Oh, and please don't notice that we're outsourcing a bunch of your jobs to Third World countries where labor is cheaper and plentiful. It's this lousy economy."

So after all the saber rattling and posturing, after the noisy pick-eters have quieted down and the siege has taken its toll on both sides, the concession that was initially sought by the AMPTP is quietly dropped. A small sliver of the expanding pie is given to the strikers. Both sides declare a face-saving victory and the town theo-retically goes back to work. A little dignity has been lost by both parties as they forget about all the nasty invective that was recently hurled around, dust themselves off, straighten out their expensive suits, and let's all be pals again.

After weeks or months of high-priced lawyers extracting every pound of flesh from their respective clients, these mortal enemies can often be found playing golf together, laughing all the way to the first tee. The rank and file have no choice but to swallow their bile, grumble a bit amongst themselves but are thankful to have the Sword of Damocles removed from overhead. Now, they can get back to work and try to figure out how to make up for two to six months of lost wages. Using the strike as an excuse, the studios traditionally tighten their belts, get rid of some of the deadwood occupying the corporate offices, and continue on their merry way.

It's all such a myopic exercise. The big corporations have played a magicians slight-of-hand trick on all the participants, as they've done with so many of the other industries they control. Why pay somebody $30 an hour and place all these limitations on abusive working conditions, when you can pay someone 30 cents a day in some foreign country and do whatever you want? It's a slum land-lord, sweatshop mentality. Take it or leave it. We don't really care. Plenty more where you came from!

As it applies to Showbiz, they are training our replacements in Canada, Australia, New Zealand, South Africa, Romania, Russia, etc. They blithely ignore the fact that while they were giving themselves and much of the above the line talent an 800% pay raise over the last 20 years, that the below the line folk have barely kept ahead of the inflation steamroller. "That's their problem. They should hire bigger prick lawyers next time."

Huge egos demand huge salaries up front because it's the best way of keeping score. You can't blame them because if they don't get it up front, there's a very good chance that the "monkey points" (aka back end profit participation) will evaporate in the bean counting department. It's hard to believe that the hit TV show *Frasier* has grossed $1.5 *billion* and somehow is still $200 million dollars in the red according to the studio accounting department. The profit participants with "juice" have been amply rewarded but lesser downs on the food chain were given a sob story and told to sue if they expect any kind of legally deserved compensation.

The great shame is that it doesn't have to continue this way. Let's take a page from the sports industry and elect a Showbiz Commis-sioner who mediates the problems long before they become strikes. An annual summit could be held where the leaders of the industry get everybody on one side of the table, labor and management, and the Commish's job would be to remind them that there's plenty of money to go around in the business of entertaining the masses. If we could discard the "divide and conquer" mentality and instead partner up and share the risks and rewards fairly, the whole army could be maintained without labor strife and together the next "Golden Age of Hollywood" would be ushered in.

The studios and key principals will still earn the most money, but it will be a more equitable division of profits honestly accounted for all to see.

A fellow can dream, can't he?

As we are busily entertaining ourselves to death, the scientific and engineering communities are having trouble recruiting from the younger generation. Why? Because the bright young candidates have decided to become business majors, doctors or lawyers. They want to cash in on their brains and own bigger houses. I don't recall there ever having been a hit TV show or movie about a happy scientist or an engineer (ignoring, of course, The Absent Minded Professor.). Because of the successful launch of the first Chinese astronauts, it is estimated that the Chinese will be able to harness up to one hundred million (100,000,000) brains into their scientific and engineering community.

Think about that for a moment. Think about it for one more beat in terms of what this will mean to the balance of power in the world. It's time to brush up on your Mandarin.

TO BE A MARK

If you close your eyes in a darkened room with the TV on, flashes of different colored light can be seen through your eyelids. They dance around on your face like little blue-hued demons wearing masks meant to cajole you, entice you into doing something when you open your eyes and return to the real world.

"Buy this! See That! Come here! Think this way!" Subliminal messages implanted in our brains like post-hypnotic suggestions. If you are hit with the same message a hundred times, a thousand times, the next time you drive past a McDonalds or a Nissan dealership, there is a an electrical connection in the brainpan that immediately asks, "Aren't I hungry?" or "Don't I need a shiny new car?" The knee jerk answer is always, "yes." The only other question is, "Do I have the money to pay for it?" Some people don't have the willpower to even ask the question. They simply stop whatever they're doing and go buy something they don't really need. A certain percentage of people can't really help themselves, which is, of course, what the Madison Avenue boys are counting on.

It's called "impulse buying." Let's call it by it's real name — "brainwashing." Everyone is subjected to a daily regiment of TV and radio ads, banner ads on bus benches, large billboards, slick magazine or newspaper ads. There's a gaggle of smiling, good-looking people selling you this or that. And let's not forget the blue-hued demons. Like a freeway rumble in the background, we get used to the noise and try our best to ignore the ever-present interruptions of our favorite radio or TV shows. The saturation bombing is ever-present, always working hard to get even a small percentage of the audience's attention.

Some people hate to be challenged, don't want to fight. They will go out of their way to avoid a confrontation. If a salesman flags them down, they must stop, listen and buy something just to placate the insistent or friendly individual before heading off to their original destination. They wake up later, look at the shiny new object in their hand or their bulging waistline and wonder what happened. They call it, "buyers remorse." Most people won't return the object because they don't want the hassle. Won't go back to the box office and ask for a refund because they were lured into a movie under false pretenses. We came, we bought something we didn't really want and went on with our lives.

We seek out self-serve stores without the incumbent annoying used car-like attendant, who obviously couldn't care less if you live or die. They have been trained to pleasantly ask, "May I help you?" I want to say, "If I need any help, I'll ask for it but in the meantime, stay the f*#@ out of my face" but I politely say, "Just looking," and their eyes roll up in the back of their heads as they return to whatever they were doing. It's no wonder Internet shopping is booming.

Some people with the impulse buying affliction hit the fast food drive-thru window and upon hearing a happy, pre-taped computer voice announcing the latest special on the menu, usually involving enough food to feed a small army, end up buying a 14 piece bucket of chicken when all they wanted was a drumstick and something to wash it down with. And we wonder why a ton of our fellow Americans qualify as "obese." Stop wondering. "It was just such a good bargain, I couldn't resist. I saved more money buying something than not buying it!" We're all such helpless children susceptible to the charms of the ubiquitous blue-hued demons. It's a wonder anyone can resist the siren song at all.

The Carney folk (carnival workers) call non-Carney people, "marks." We are all marks in a way. We're all suckers for something. It can range from buying that candy bar or sensational magazine while standing in the checkout line to acquiring ten or twelve wheelbarrows at Saturday morning garage sales. "Hey, they were cheap and you never know when you're going to need a good wheelbarrow!"

We are helpless until we stop, look ourselves in the mirror and ask, "Who am I? What do I really want? Why am I doing this? Am I here to be tethered to a machine in some cubicle in order to earn a paycheck so I can afford to eat, sleep, fornicate, eliminate waste products, ("shit" is such an ugly word), put in a couple hours a day as another statistical pair of eyeballs glued to the computer or boob tube as the dancing blue-hued demons paint brand new images on the never-ending blank canvas of our minds? Is this why I'm here? To be a mark?"

The unfortunate answer for most people is, "yes". The quest is to carve out some quality thinking time, quality creative time, and quality sharing time with significant others. Our lives are measured in seconds, minutes, hours, days, weeks and years. I sometimes feel like some invisible tailor is working on my inseam preparing me for my own funeral. I want to tell him to get the f*#@ out of my space. It's not time yet.

We all need to figure out how to shut out the clutter and squeeze out a few more "me minutes" everyday. Since going headfirst through the windshield of my car and bouncing off the other guy's windshield one rainy afternoon in Laurel Canyon thirty plus years ago, I discovered that every day is a gift. What do I want to do before I'm all used up? What changes can I make to improve the quality of my life? Eating, thinking and speaking are the three most important functions that I actually have any control over. Sorry for the priorities but if you don't eat, after awhile there won't be any thinking or things to talk about. Besides, what goes into your mouth and what comes out of it primarily defines who we are.

So us marks need to prioritize our time. We have to pull ourselves out of the gerbil cage and try to get some perspective on what is happening in our lives. How do we avoid becoming just another Madison Avenue pre-programmed automaton? The challenge is what we do with what's left of our time that makes us happy. Beware the blue-hued demons my fellow marks. They are the electronically produced parasites that are persistently trying to invade our control centers and grab hold of the wheel. Otherwise you'll wake up twenty to forty pounds overweight and driving a shiny new car you can't afford and never knew you wanted.

In Between Films

One could get used to a career of not having a real job. Independent filmmakers spend much of their lives with time on their hands. What's a creative, dynamic individual whose mind is racing 90 miles an hour to do? As a producer in between projects, there are no deadlines to meet, no heart attack central, no standing army waiting for their marching orders, no gang of people awaiting your arrival knowing that now they have to look like they're actually working. Out on many a set, people have mastered the art of stretching six hours of hard work into about twelve or thirteen hours when things are moving slowly. This is usually the result of endless discussions by the people in charge as they finally decide how to best tell the story.

The fact of the matter is there is usually a lot of time to kill in between setups as the core group makes up its mind what to do next. The core group is usually comprised of the Director, DP and 1st AD, not necessarily in that order. They are the floor generals who have studied the script and are supposed to have thought about how to tackle each scene. In many cases, they're looking at the script like it's ancient Sanskrit and they haven't a clue how to decipher. "How about something like this ... " is heard far too often down on the set. A lot of time, I'm the one saying it because I realize the brain trust has hit a blind spot.

Everyday down on the set there is what I like to call, "A Waterloo moment". It is the moment when something very simple suddenly becomes very complex. It's a particular shot or scene that requires a lot of re-thinking, plotting and time wasting that should have been pre-thought out and discussed as opposed to when the meter is running at $5,000 an hour. I usually have to keep my hands in my pockets in order to keep from strangling someone. The shot that takes hours to conceive and thousands of dollars to achieve will usually make it on screen for a couple of seconds. That is if it even survives the cutting room floor. Will the shot in question make a difference to the overall success of the scene, the act or the show? Usually not.

Saying these things to the brain trust in the middle of their collective brain fart usually is met with daggers. "Can't you see we're making *Art!!??*" No, I see a couple of people fumbling around because one or more didn't do their homework. They hate it when the Producer is hanging around when it happens. They hate the fact that they've been discovered. They hate the fact that the Producer might be right. I'll politely suggest an alternate way to attack their dilemma and get the shot in the can, make the days work. Having directed a couple hundred TV shows, I understand the mechanics of what is required. I politely dig in my heels, make sure it gets done so we can get the show on the road. We'll schedule the screaming match in my office for later.

By then, everyone's usually too depleted to want to fight and they just want to go home. I usually have a sign on my door that reads, "12 hours=5 minutes." We have mastered the art of wasting time and making it look like we're working hard to the untrained eye. If and when we were to ever get in and out in less than ten hours, like many of the great filmmakers of yesteryear, production could really be a lot of fun for all concerned.

When I am in-between-projects, I miss the smell of coffee and bagels in the morning. At the beginning of each day, the world is ripe with possibilities. The weather is cooperating. It's a beautiful day for a ballgame. All the requested equipment and crew are waiting to be used. Makeup, hair and wardrobe put the actors through "The Works" in an efficacious manner. The crew is raring to go fueled up on coffee and pastries, and the actors hopefully know their lines. There's excitement in the air. The average $50,000–$100,000 daily expenditure will eventually translate into two to seven minutes of usable film. The Line Producer's goal is completing the day's work on the call sheet with some panache and avoiding major overtime (OT) at all costs.

Hell, everything could go as planned today. Hah! That's like watching a perfect game at the ballpark. That happens when 27 batters in a row in a nine inning game all make outs. As the other team attacks our pitcher and when their first hitter reaches base I silently say, "There goes the perfect game". After the first hit, I say, "There goes the no-hitter". After the first run is scored I say, "There goes the shutout". And then we hold on for dear life and hope I don't have to say, "There goes the old ballgame."

A perfect game is about as rare as having Black show up 27 times in a row at the roulette wheel or scratching the lottery ticket to discover you've won more than you've invested. Doesn't happen very often but hope springs eternal.

At the beginning of each day we're shooting *Gone With The Wind*. By the end of the day, when everyone is tired and fed up and just wants to be back home with family and friends, we're shooting any Roger Corman movie (the maestro of low budget fare.) We want the day, the procrastination, the endless discussions by the brain trust and the 1st AD to call for the martini shot which means the day is just about over. As the producer, you basically helm a twelve hour, never-ending meeting where everyone needs a piece of your time, a decision, a signature, a confab, an opinion on a myriad of subjects.

I miss being on call all the time down at crisis central but one could get used to this life of being in-between films. Strolling down to the corner for a paper and a cup of java knowing that there are always a variety of war rooms out there in LaLa land where people are tearing their hair out and looking for someone to blame for the latest debacle ... If only there weren't those annoying bills to pay.

WHAT A WORLD, WHAT A WORLD!

Hard to believe but back in the day, old fashioned people thought that running off to the world of Show Business was akin to becoming a prostitute and falling into the deepest abyss of living hell on earth. Oh sure, on the surface, it looked like everyone was having fun but just behind the façade, drugs, illicit sex with anything still breathing, the seven deadly sins, and worse were commonplace everyday occurrences.

Whether we like it or not, we all get tarred by the same brush that paints our business in an unsavory light. Just to keep things in perspective, let's take a look at some of our competition out there and see how they're faring.

The Sports Business is populated by talented but often greedy, petulant children. Spoiled brat behavior is rewarded by national headlines and multi-million dollar contracts. With few exceptions, the various players unions and billionaire owners pay lip service to the fans. They couldn't care less if they're playing in front of an empty house as long as the TV contracts keep picking up the tab as they gouge each other in the wallet. The players and owners seem hell-bent on discovering the maximum amount of money that can be extracted from a public that likes to watch grown men and women play games. The only question is who goes bankrupt first?

The Politicos seem like another bunch of rich privileged kids who piss on each other in public and go have drinks with each other and laugh about everything afterwards. All the finger pointing, posturing and baby kissing would be okay if they didn't have the power to spend more of our unborn grandchildren's money and have our fellow citizens killed all over the world. On the surface, it seems like the electoral process is an adequate checks and balance but the entrenched power is the principal constant behind-the-scenes. The boyos in the foreground too often resemble the marionettes they happen to be. Most of us have already made up our minds about any upcoming Presidential election. Isn't there a better use for the Billion dollars that will be spent on advertising? Of course, in their world, a billion dollars is like a little confetti being tossed around because they can afford it. After all, it isn't their money. Hey, who really gives a damn about having one more lousy Stealth Bomber?

The Wall Street Gang are yet another bunch of cheeky bastards. It's not enough that money was originally created as a source of barter. "I'll give you this piece of metal or paper in return for those goods and services." Originally paper money was redeemable at the local bank for gold or silver. Those days are long gone. The Feds would probably be hard pressed to cover 1/2 the currency that's out there if anyone ever really asked. All this is rendered laughable by the printing presses working overtime down in Wall Street's basement knocking out pieces of paper that are essentially worthless and selling them to a gullible public. Ordinary money for goods and services wasn't good enough. Without taking any vote that I'm aware of, this group of boyos imposed another layer of financial burdens on all of us whether we're players or not called "IPO's, futures, warranties, debentures, stocks and bonds". This other funny money game was all done, of course, with the complete blessing and turning of a blind eye by the Politicos because they happen to finance their campaigns.

A famous TV personality went to jail for saving $50,000 because she sold stocks based upon some inside info. She gets made an example of because she's a pushy broad. What about the thousands of thieves in their three piece suits who are stealing the treasury blind? Does anybody truly believe that no stockbroker who is handling an IPO doesn't happen to mention something to a friend or three at the next poker game or cocktail party they attend? Most people are honest but a small percentage of unethical types don't mind profiting from the goodwill of others. Nothing personal. What about the sanctioned corporate profiteers who steal hundreds of millions (billions?) from all of us in the form of increased surcharges, outrageous insurance premiums and interest rates? This gang of thieves strolls down to the bank enjoying the fruits of their crimes — nothing short of unmitigated chutzpah and nobody really seems to give a shit.

The Politicos and members of the Securities and Exchange Commission (SEC), who are supposed to be watching the Wall Street boyos, instead take corporate jets to far flung junkets and see nothing wrong with accepting a few perks that go hand in hand with this watchdog business. Did somebody say, "The fix is in!?"

Currently it's the Energy boy's turn to see how much they can squeeze out of our wallets before we yell too loudly. We sit back as exploitive oil companies gouge us at the pump using trumped up shortages and disruptions to their business while they enjoy record profits and hope the masses can't/ won't read the Business Section of the newspaper. Haven't heard any of the Politicos step up to the microphone and address the fact that one day the Towel-heads won't be sitting on that ocean of oil anymore and the balance of power will once again shift. Nobody seems to be taking the long view and coming up with long-range solutions to the global warming problems we and our grandkids will soon be facing. Anybody heard those three dirty words, "alternative energy sources?" Solar, wind, hydro? Guess not. They're too busy giving tax breaks to Hummer owners and other large corporations with offshore accounts.

What about the proliferation of bible-thumping TV Evangelical Ministers with strange hairdos who claim to have a direct pipeline to God that you too can access for a small fee? It is particularly disturbing to see 'onstage miracles' being eaten up by the rubes in the audience. Business is so booming that individual letters no longer get read on TV. A minister with the worst comb over ever lays his hands on a stack of letters three feet high and prays over them asking God to take care of this group request and by the way, keep those checks coming in. It would seem to the untrained mind that everybody gets what they want. You part with something green in your wallet and the TV minister announces that you're all better. I wish God had better aim with a spare thunderbolt or tornado. Maybe it would help clean up the televangelical industry if a religious TV station's transmitter was struck by lightning or a tent revival suddenly disappeared in a funnel cloud.

Hotline Psychics and Astrologers reading your future from prepared scripts are yet another way to separate you from your money. Lets produce a reality show where we take a bunch of Psychics down to the racetrack and see who ends up winning the most dough. The losers get fired out of cannons with no safety nets awaiting them. It's just another racket with a long line of losers trying to phone in.

Hey, don't mean to ruin anybody's day but Pro Wrestling is fixed. It's why sports books in Vegas don't make bets on 'the contests'. I happen to be an aficionado of this form of theater that panders to the lowest common denominator. Two big bruisers stage one helluva fight and somebody might actually get hurt? It's better than having a ringside seat to a train wreck. What does it really matter anymore?

It's like the wrongdoers enjoy taking turns dosi-doing in the spotlight saying, "Look what bad boys and girls we've been! We're laughing all the way to the bank!" As each new scandal erupts, the old one disappears to the back pages. Out of sight, out of mind. Somebody will write a book ripped from today's headlines that nobody will read and who really cares?

On the overall scheme of things, being in Showbiz isn't the worst thing in the world. At least it looks like we're having some fun. A lousy ten million tickets sold to a tiny fraction of the world population, translates into $100 million at the box office. "It's easy, step right up. Hit the target audience and win a prize!"

What a world, what a world!

CHAPTER 10

LESSONS OF A LIFE LIVED IN HOLLYWOOD

ALL THAT GLITTERS

A lot of people choose to travel in life's slow lane. They tow the line, chugging along doing the speed limit, trying to get through the day without rocking the boat or being noticed. At every fork in the road, they take the path of least resistance and glide along under the radar. They never raise their voices or toot their own horns. Somewhere along the line they have, "Go along to get along" tattooed on their souls.

And then there are people in Showbiz. We have chosen to tromp on the accelerator looking to discover how fast this baby can go! This is a lifetime quest to determine how high is up? What's next after we climb this mountain? Contrary to certain religious beliefs, this may be the one and only E-ticket we're ever going to get so we better damn well enjoy each spin of the globe.

It is a study in opposites attracting. Everyone reading *People* magazine or watching through the fishbowl filter of *Entertainment Tonight* or *Extra, Extra* must think a busload of ADD kids has overturned and are running wild in the candy store. Looks like we're hardly working while being paid a king's ransom and having way too much fun! At least this is the image presented to those traveling in the slow lane. The truth of the matter is far less glamorous. Most of us inside the fishbowl are dedicated, hard working pros who hope to be proud of the work we do when we're lucky enough to find it. This is the part that they don't see. Must never see.

There really is no advantage in shattering the illusion. If they ever knew how hard it is pursuing this dream, they'd be laughing at us instead of dreaming about being amongst us. What we want is their stability but we just aren't willing to have the mind-numbing tedious life to get it. We are hell-bent on winning life's Trifecta: to work on projects we want to, with people we want to, and get paid what we ought to.

We voluntarily got suckered into this vortex, seduced by the lights, the glamour, and the promises. Nobody put a gun in our ribs and said, "Stick around, you won't believe what happens next!" We have missed numerous exit signs that would have taken us back to the real world. Nobody really prepared us for the slow roasting over the spit. Hah! It was in the fine print on page 27. Forgot to read the manual? Tough luck – there is no manual.

The twists and turns that our career takes often feels like trying to pick up that elusive bar of soap in the shower. We look terribly foolish doing it and we're certainly in the right position for our daily bout with our opponent. One big problem is that we love pirouetting on thin ice, waiting for it to crack beneath us to see if we still have enough speed to reach safety without drowning or getting wet. Can't really help ourselves because we're simply action junkies looking for our next fix.

Anybody who hasn't written at least one acceptance speech while cradling that imaginary gold statue can now leave the building. I wonder what deceased funnyman Sam Kinnison might've said at that moment? ... It would've been worth the price of admission.

How to Make a Living in Hollywood

As with any industry, how a newcomer gets started is simply the first of many hurdles they need to overcome. A lot depends on what you bring to the party. Are you beginning from a position of strength, i.e. with a bankroll that could choke a horse, relatives in high places, and/or a sheepskin from a prestigious college? In the beginning, if any one of these situations are true, then you have a great advantage over everyone else who shares the dream of becoming a producer or having a career in Hollywood because you get to start the climb halfway up the mountain. Although nepotism happens in other businesses, in Hollywood, who you know at the start of the competition far outweighs talent, raw ambition and determination. It's unfair but it's a fact of life.

Ultimately though, Showbiz is a meritocracy. No matter where you begin in the food chain, you have to prove your worth. How do you do that if you're starting from the back of the pack? You simply out-hustle and outshine everyone else. You go far beyond the extra mile and learn as much as you can about your chosen profession. You must develop survivor skills in the jungle or die. The jungle will not adapt to you until you have mastered your craft and emerged on the other side as a consistent winner. What this really means is that opportunities come to you instead of you having to go out looking for them. It is only then that you have any real semblance of control over your future.

Like keeping an eye on the rearview mirror for cops when you're driving too fast, it's important to also keep an eye on the horizon as to where you want to go. The goals shift as your career evolves. In the beginning, you dream of picking up one of them gold statues.

Later on you realize that the chances of that ever really happening are pretty slim. It's important to learn how other producers, directors, writers or actors managed to win the big prize. Some of them started from the halfway mark but most of them started from scratch. They persevered and somehow got themselves in a position to get lucky.

The phrase, "getting lucky", is used throughout this book. In separating the careers of those who make it from those who don't, it usually can be attributed to a series of chance encounters, lucky breaks, and ones ability to not only recognize an opportunity when it arrives but to maximize the impact that it has on their future. A positive, "Never-say-die, I'll-do-anything!" attitude is also very helpful. Meeting the right people, learning what the competition is doing and keeping your eyes and ears open are critical. You need to make friends with anyone who has landed on these shores because you can't do it alone. Everybody is striving to find his or her place at the banquet table.

There is no single path to enlightenment or advancement. I'm always looking to learn from those who have succeeded in conquering this mountain. I'm still hoping to create a body of work that qualifies as great so I will be remembered as having had a career in Showbiz.

Where there's a will there's a way. Upon first glance, the studio fortresses seem impenetrable. Upon closer inspection, much like our porous national borders, there are a myriad of ways to get inside.

LEAP OF FAITH

Unless your game plan includes buying your way into the game, you will only be successful if somebody takes a chance on you. Besides the hard work and raw talent, there have to be a few pivotal people along the way who see something in you and take that crucial leap of faith. In the beginning, you are like an orphan on Showbiz's doorstep. Your personal charm and blind ambition are not enough. Somewhere along the line, somebody in a position of power needs to have an inexplicable, unquantifiable, positive chemical reaction to you. More often than not their thinking is, "Hey, somebody has to do the actual work — it might as well be you."

You soon discover that your next job is merely an audition for the job after that. It has always been and will always be this way until you end up in an executives chair, write the great American screenplay, marry the boss's daughter, or somehow take that ride on the A-team train to securityville and have "f*#@ you money" in the bank. (This means you don't have to take any old job you don't want to because you have enough dough to get by for a while.) It's either that or exit stage right. Your big break usually happens when somebody else's ship is sinking and they suddenly need someone to bail them out.

It's easy for an executive to look at a resume full of great credits and know that they're making a safe decision. It's a whole 'nother ballgame to give an untried commodity a chance to run with the ball and possibly fail. If you trace back the roots of most success stories in Showbiz, there was a guardian angel or two who made the difference. The angels are usually long gone by the time big success is achieved. Their job is done. It's as though they arrived in your path, steered you into this or that doorway and disappeared. Very few get taken along for the ride to the top. It's okay. I have played both parts; as the willing receiver and happy giver of big breaks.

You become part of a flow of energy that is passing through our lives. It's a great responsibility to help people on their journeys as you have been assisted on yours. Every once in awhile somebody surprises you with a, "thank you," but so few have the time or good manners to remember that I no longer take it personally. They're on their way and you're just another stone in the river they're crossing.

I always felt people giving me a break were just bending to the inevitability of my future success. I have gotten better about saying, "thank you" because I now understand the burden of responsibility that goes along with any job recommendation. When, and if, a person you recommend for a job is less than great, the powers-that-be quickly let you know about it and happily remind you how "your friend" screwed up.

You're allowed to stick around because you didn't disappoint when you got your chance. The person who took the leap of faith with you was satisfied that his or her judgment was still sound. In a business where "risk avoidance" is tattooed inside the eyelids of most executives, you were selected from the long line of hopefuls clamoring to get noticed.

In the meantime, you have to keep putting one foot in front of the other. It's the right chemistry, the mysterious X-factor that has gotten you this far. You wake up every morning believing you're one phone call away from getting your next big break and someday soon, you'll be right. A friend once told me his secret, "You can't lose 'em all." Believe it or not, that thought has gotten me through some particularly bleak moments.

Or as Wayne Gretzky said, "You miss 100% of the shots you don't take."

RELEVANCE

Having some sensible or logical connection with something else.

Because it contains the words "sensible" and "logical", there is a flaw in this definition as it applies to Showbiz. There is very little that is sensible or logical about this business. You go to bed thinking you have a deal with somebody, only to wake up the next morning to find out it's either evaporated or you're suddenly being sued.

Somebody who was about to invest in your great idea got cold feet or was read the riot act by their cadre of risk avoidance advisors (lawyers, accountants, business managers, spouses, etc.) If the peanut gallery never advocates investing in anything other than blue chip, four star, guaranteed returns, then they can only be accused of protecting their client's best interest.

Every industry has it's own jargon. What sane person would knowingly subscribe themselves to a business where "great" means "okay", "yes" means "maybe", and "sweetheart" is a snide remark?

There is only so much book knowledge that can be taught in film schools. You gotta dive in and get beaten up a few times before it sinks in that all is not as it appears at first blush. There are technical aspects to master and myriad examples of how other people climbed the Showbiz mountain of success. How they became successful is only half the story. Sooner or later "drive" and "being relevant" became their trump cards.

Showbiz attracts a lot of dilettantes who don't want to work in dad's business back in the real world. After a few years of kicking around and burning through a small fortune, dad's business is usually happy to give Jr. his VP stripes now that playtime is over. That is, of course, unless dad owns a studio in which case, playtime continues.

The biggest task the rest of us cogs-in-the-wheel have is to be is positive and remain relevant. We need to keep up with the latest technical innovations and learn more interesting ways to tell our stories. We have to constantly re-invent ourselves in order to stay one step ahead of the youth steamroller. Every year a tsunami of 20-30,000 young would-be moguls arrive on the scene clutching their newly minted sheepskins as though they are magic talismans to ward off evil spirits (good luck with that!) A third of them hit Hollywood. A third hit NY. A third stick closer to home. They all toil under the delusion that they actually know something that will allow them to succeed. They all love Showbiz and have to learn enough to pay their bills and survive. Next, they have to get lucky and can convince someone in a position of power of their worth.

Fortified with a burning ambition to fulfill their destiny, the youth brigade will work twice as hard, know half as much and get paid next to nothing. They ignore the fact that there are talented people with gold statues on the mantles who can't find work primarily because they are no longer deemed relevant. Their old-fashioned values and story-telling techniques are out of step with the voracious and somewhat capricious demands of the MTV flash, cash and trash generation. As a young Dennis Hopper is reputed to have said to Billy Wilder after the initial success of *Easy Rider*, "We will bury you, old man!"

Even though it's an aging group of decision makers, they remain relevant by figuring out how to keep them kids hooked up to the vacuum cleaner that sucks a couple hundred bucks out of their pockets every year in return for some mindless fun. This core group of decision makers is always surprised to learn that older people (their contemporaries) are still alive and will respond with their wallets when a good story somehow makes it through the corporate rock polisher. Besides, we've got more disposable income than those brats.

In the final analysis, it's good to have relatives in high places but it's more important to be relevant.

SUCCESS!

Everybody in Showbiz simply wants to control his or her own destiny. This lofty goal is reserved for a thimbleful of fortunate people who achieve superstar status in front of and behind the cameras. They get treated phenomenally well and some of them actually seem to enjoy it. Everybody else is a worker bee. Some have fancy titles, fat paychecks, convenient parking spaces and good-looking secretaries but if you ask most of them, they'd rather be doing something other than what they are doing.

People get typecast in life. An invisible bar code gets slapped on your forehead and that's how you are perceived. It's understandable because there are so many people who are good at so many things. The powers that be have to categorize the herd in order to channel the flow of humanity and keep things organized. Everyday this blind horde attempts to storm the gates of the major studios and networks madly trying to get inside in a very civilized way. What do they want? To ransack the place, take over and wreck these carefully erected multi-billion dollar facades? Nope. There's the group of actors that desperately needs to get their mugs in front of the camera. Most of the others just want a job in the mailroom or to pitch their ideas and hope whoever is listening can actually help them realize their dreams.

Got a newsflash for the new arrivees, the game is rigged! Don't know if you ever had the experience as a kid at a carnival boardwalk where a game looked so easy to win some cute toy or prize, and then had some huckster sucker you out of $5 or $10 of your hard earned nickels and dimes as you got close but no cigar. "Aw, too bad! Better luck next time. You ran out of money? You got your thrill, now get out of here kid, you bother me." In Showbiz, 80% of the seats on the bus were taken before you were born. Somebody dies, somebody screws up and they throw a bone out into the crowd and watch them fight over it. Some lucky person, through the sheer force of their charisma, undeniable talent or ruthless cunning gets to sit on the bus for a short ride. After delivering their best shot, if they don't quickly make themselves (or somebody on the bus) a lot of money, most are deposited at the next stop. "Nothing personal, kid. Now go away, you bother me."

The big money and real power in this world is reserved by and for those who already have it. If you can live off the orts, you get to hang around and do their bidding. You speak up and scream how unfair and your name goes on that non-existent blacklist - "Trouble-maker! Do not hire." Meanwhile the gang in power plays musical execution chairs. They get into the club and fail upwards. The bigger they screw up, it seems, the more invaluable they become.

There actually are a small group of executives who can tell you what's wrong with your project and how to improve it, but most of them don't really know what they should know. The incompetent ones say, "Something's wrong and just go fix it until you make me happy." It's purely subjective. They don't really know if something will work until Market Research or the audience votes. The medical equivalent would be a brain surgeon holding a knife in the middle of an operation and saying, "Hmm, let's see what happens if I do this!"

Occasionally an atomic bomb goes off in their backyard and temporarily disrupts the status quo. Usually this is enabled by some technological breakthrough that happened while they were sleeping. *The Blair Witch Project* phenomenon wouldn't have happened without the Internet. Artisan had 40 marketing tie-ins with various sponsors before the film was ever released. A $35,000 amateurish, grainy black and white movie was marketed primarily through the Internet, hit a home run and raked in over $250,000,000 worldwide. No stars, no name director, no carefully crafted deal created by the powers that be. These spectacular results totally fly in the face of conventional wisdom. As William Goldman so brilliantly points out in his book, "Adventures in the Screen Trade", those who are supposed to know, don't.

What was the status quo response to *The Blair Witch Project*? Instead of setting up low budget film divisions searching for other small jewels that can be inexpensively produced and marketed, they optioned the franchise from the original creators, made a bad, expensive sequel with totally different people (more seasoned professionals), killed the franchise and buried it in the back yard. Why? Well, what happens to that multi-billion dollar façade if a couple of kids with cameras can go off and make a film that becomes the single most profitable horror feature film ever made? More importantly, what happens when the last mile technology is completed and everyone's computer becomes a bootleg movie theater or the major way that the kids get their entertainment?

There is a crack in the façade. When the artists, filmmakers or music talent can bypass the established distribution systems and deliver their product directly to the consumer and get paid for it, things will have to change. Don't know if you've noticed but it seems they've slowed down that last mile technology until they can figure out how to control the revenue stream. The horse was about to bolt from the barn. It eventually will, but different mega-corporations (Ma Bell, Microsoft, Google, Yahoo) will control the flow.

In the meantime, here's the best formula for a successful project that I know of:

1 great script, best selling novel, comic book, or idea = 10% chance for success

1 great script, best selling novel, comic book, or idea, a realistic budget & shooting schedule = 15% chance for success

1 great script, best selling novel, comic book, or idea, a realistic budget & shooting schedule + a viable Producer and/or director = 25% chance for success

1 great script, best selling novel, comic book, or idea, a realistic budget & shooting schedule + a viable Producer and/or director + 1 big name star or two = 40% chance for success

1 great script, best selling novel, comic book, or idea, a realistic budget & shooting schedule + a viable Producer and/or director + 1 big name star or two + financing = 60% chance for success

1 great script, best selling novel, comic book, or idea, a realistic budget & shooting schedule + a viable Producer and/or director + 1 big name star or two + financing + an excellent crew, luck with the weather, a great editor and music composer = 75% chance for success

1 great script, best selling novel, comic book, or idea, a realistic budget & shooting schedule + a viable Producer and/or director + 1 big name star or two + financing + an excellent crew, luck with the weather, a great editor and music composer + a good marketing

campaign (and/ or landing a great TV time slot) = 90% chance for success

1 great script, best selling novel, comic book, or idea, a realistic budget & shooting schedule + a viable Producer and/or director + 1 big name star or two + financing + an excellent crew, luck with the weather, a great editor and music composer + a good marketing campaign (and/ or landing a great TV time slot) and having the audience respond favorably = 100% chance for success

Actually getting paid what you're worth in the marketplace happens after you have a couple of successes under your belt. My personal definition of success in Showbiz is, "I'm being yelled at by a better class of people!"

CREDIBILITY

In the beginning of any Showbiz enterprise, two or more parties get together and decide that they want to make a deal. An idea has been pitched and somebody on the other side of the table sees its merit. The buyer usually runs the idea up the flagpole within their organization including partners, the sales force, the would-be financiers to see if their judgment is still sound. The acid test more often than not is the spouse and kids back home.

If everyone (or at least the majority) agrees that this is a commercially viable idea that will be worth the time, energy, and capital investment then the next part of the dance begins. This usually involves Business Affairs, lawyers, agents, contracts, and partners all getting involved. It often resembles haggling in a mid-eastern bazaar, as both sides want to make the best deal for themselves and yet not become too vociferous during this phase as to scare the other party off.

I've seen a wide variety of perfectly good deals go south because the negotiating phase was mishandled. Somebody got greedy and thought they deserved a much bigger piece of the back end than they were rightfully entitled to. When they were negotiating a fair deal, their vituporous (and often litigious) nature was revealed and subsequently one of the parties got a shaky leg and decided that life was too short to have to put up with this shite. I've seen deals never get off the ground when it is discovered that one of the participants had a particularly difficult agent or attorney. They'd rather walk away from the deal than having to negotiate with this or that particular pit viper.

Oftentimes, the best deal is unfair, slanted in favor of the folk with the money. They invented a phrase that justifies their position. They want to know what the other parties' "skin in the game" is. This translates roughly into what pound of flesh or piece of genitalia is on the line if everything should go south. The financiers will lose their investment. What will the person with the idea lose? Losing face is not the equivalent of losing money. Hence the disproportionate deal is usually in favor of the money boys. Of course they discount the years of hard work spent polishing your craft and the ability to recognize a very commercial idea from the mountain of potentially mediocre ideas that are always floating around out there. As far as the money boys are concerned, good ideas are a dime a dozen and if this one doesn't stick, they'll always be others to glom onto.

The standard fair deal in Showbiz for an independent movie would be that the financiers are in the first recoupment position from all revenue streams until they are made whole (usually with some interest for the use of the money — up to 20%) and then the financial and creative parties split everything else that comes in 50/50.

Much to the chagrin of several business affairs people, I have had the following inserted into my contracts, "In the event of any disputes between the parties, with an agreed upon witness in attendance, a coin will be tossed with one party calling heads or tails while the coin is airborne and prior to it landing on the ground. Both parties agree in advance to abide by the outcome of the coin toss and what it represents." This saves a lot of wrangling and keeps the legal bills in check.

In the meantime, the credibility of both parties is what is at stake. Are they acting in good faith, wanting to reach a fair deal that is good for both parties or is it simply a one-way street. "I put up the money, you do all the work and I walk away with the lion's share of the profits!" The best kind of deal is between honorable people who say what they're going to do and do what they say in a timely way. No hidden agenda. No knife in the back the minute your back is turned. Honest and straightforward is totally disarming in Showbiz because it is such a novel approach. Sometimes conniving people mistake goodness and kindness as a weakness to be taken advantage of as they wipe their feet on your welcome mat. The greedy ones identify themselves early on in the proceedings because they can't help themselves – it's who they are.

Best to steer clear of them if at all possible. Their word, handshake deal and credibility ain't worth the oral agreement it's written on.

FOLLOW YOUR STAR

There's a small voice inside that whispers in our ear from time to time suggesting what we should do next. Sometimes it's a shout if we haven't been paying enough attention. Life is all about making choices and how we spend the time that we have been given. It's important to remember that this life won't be around forever. We can only procrastinate so long before the jig is up. Then it's our final broadcast. Over and out. *El finito*. The End.

Battling for a place on the Showbiz roster is a daunting task. Once you've made it, learning how to stay in the big leagues is a whole different ballgame. Succeeding in achieving your wildest dreams doesn't only happen in the movies. If you were to sit down and have a candid conversation with any of the real shakers and movers in any business, they would tell you just that – that they followed a voice inside and got very, very lucky to be in the right place at the right time.

Unlike royal lineage, success in Showbiz is not a birthright. The history of the industry is rife with stories of rich and powerful people's offspring who had every door opened and were ushered in at the top before managing to screw up their chances in any number of ways. They were on the "25 Year Descent Plan." That's about how long it takes to run through the money, burn every bridge and outlast all the favors and good will created by the famous or powerful parental unit. Sometimes it happens much more quickly. People in the know shake their heads and say, "What a shame." Collin Powell hit the nail on the head when he noted that one of the biggest problems in America today is that we've lost the "concept of shame". Some people aren't the least bit concerned to be publicly humiliated. If you don't believe it, watch any episode of *Jerry Springer* or most of the so-called "reality" shows.

It all goes back to the choices we make. If you're lucky enough to arrive in some position of power or influence in this world, you can open the door for your family and friends, but they're the ones who will ultimately have to make something out of it or squander the opportunity. On the flip side, however, the quickest elevator ride to the top of the heap is hooking up with somebody who is connected and has ambition, good taste and integrity. Like finding a good marriage partner, you hold on for dear life because it's going to be a bumpy ride. These winners are going to get their at-bats in the big leagues and if they do well, they'll be sticking around for a long time so they're very good people to know.

You have to look in the mirror every once in awhile and take stock. How am I doing? Am I happy? Am I where I want to be? And if not yet, what steps can be taken to get you there more quickly, because you haven't got all day. The sooner you launch your boat, the quicker you find out if you've got what it takes. One thing is for sure, nothing works out exactly the way you think it will. There are changes and compromises that will need to be made all along the way. The question often becomes how much of your integrity are you willing to sacrifice in order to get what you want?

In this crazy business the magic wand hits a few relative unknowns (more often than not, unknown relatives) on the head each year. Their success exceeds their wildest dreams and they hopefully can find a way to live happily ever after. That's what happens to the protagonists in fairy tales, why not you or me? The odds are against this happening to you or me or anybody we know. This doesn't prevent us from adjusting our sights and enjoying the ride while it's happening. You get to meet and befriend an enormously talented and colorful cast of characters. If you're lucky, you get your name on a couple of shows that everyone sees and hopefully enjoys. No matter what, a career in Showbiz is still better than digging ditches and working as a cashier out there in the real world.

AFTERWORD

Putting this book together has been a much bigger task than I ever imagined. My main reason for doing it is to share some insight and relate a few adventures that have happened to me so that others can learn from my mistakes. A lot of time and money gets wasted by the executive branch that doesn't want to take responsibility for guessing wrong. Because there is no such thing as a sure-fire hit in Showbiz, everyone is mostly guessing all the time. In the end, it's all about having a clear understanding of what you want to accomplish, realizing what your limitations are, making good choices, and improving your chances of getting lucky.

You've got to learn to listen to that little voice inside that says go here, do this. Always try to exceed the expectations of anyone smart enough to hire you. Treat them the way you wish to be treated if your places were suddenly reversed. If you are successful, one day somebody else will be the applicant knocking on your door. Help them out if you possibly can and make a deposit in the good karma fund. Take every advantage to advance your career without appearing too needy or greedy. There are definitely things you can do to improve your chances. I hope reading this book proves to be one of them.

This is my locker room speech if they put microphones under the writer's nose when their book is finally finished. Peace and good wishes on your journey.

BOOK TWO

HOLLYWOOD

Adventures of a Migrant Film Worker

PREFACE

The writer of this book has worn a producer's hat for most of his thirty plus years in show business. By necessity, he worked his way up through the industry, mastering film and television production both as a creative enterprise and an innovative business. Very often the marriage between the show elements and the demands of the business makes most productions a fight to the finish. Far less frequently, this marriage of opposites produces something remarkable and lasting, and that is what this producer lives for.

INTRODUCTION

Adventures of a Migrant Film Worker (*MFW*) comprises some stories and wry observations from my life-long love affair with Hollywood's film and television industry.

So You Wanna be a Producer? is a helpful guide acquired from hard-won experience and offered up to anyone looking for practical information about sustaining a career as a working producer. Both titles seem to need each other as traveling companions, much like two drunks holding each other up as they move down the street.

This two-books-in-one are a collection of essays, most of them written while I served as president of a Hollywood networking organization called The Exchange. Our group met every month for almost five years at the CBS Radford commissary in Studio City. Membership grew to 250 industry veterans from across the show business spectrum. As head cat wrangler for this organization of so many eclectic talents, I found a loyal audience for a series of short essays known as "Steve's Midnight Howls," written as much to amuse myself as to stir up ideas and provoke conversation within the group.

The subject of each essay depended on which demon possessed me in the middle of any particular night. Averaging more than one missive a week, the "Howls" found an appreciative and encouraging audience, and I recall more than one person mentioning something about a book. So here it is.

This is my best explanation for a certain amount of redundancy and why these stories are all over the place. The difficult task was to corral the essays into chapters that share a common thread in order to make a more cohesive whole. Moreover, a book about the entertainment industry should be, well, entertaining and, as such, the author strives to entertain and inform anyone contemplating making a go of it in the challenging, always changing, and very entertaining world of show business.

— Steve Ecclesine

CHAPTER 1

THE LAY OF THE LAND

THE BIG PICTURE

Any person who really wants to be a producer needs the gift of overview. This is the ability to step back and see the forest for the trees and to be able to figure out the optimum path one needs to take in order to transform an idea on paper into a tangible asset. Producing is learning how to best achieve the goal within the agreed upon time and budget parameters that results in the fewest number of disgruntled folk left in the rearview mirror once the project is delivered. There are very few useful books that provide any practical information on this subject. Most of this type of education is experienced at the School of Hard Knocks. Hopefully, this book will steer a few readers away from some of the quicksand pits that I have inadvertently fallen into during my education in Showbiz.

My credo: There are a thousand ways to climb the mountain resulting in nine hundred and ninety four dead bodies along the way. There are six ways that work and I am fortunate to know one of them. If you've got a better way, I'm all ears. If not, then get out of my way or give me a hand.

Being responsible for spending a couple hundred million dollars of other people's money (OPM) while producing over 700 TV shows, commercials, rock videos and a dozen movies, I've avoided more than my share of near-fatal collisions and learned a few things along the way. On most shows, there are several people who enjoy a variety of fancy producer titles but, ultimately, the day-to-day responsibilities devolve onto the shoulders of the real producer. This person's job is to break down a project into all of its parts and then put it back together again so that in the end it most closely resembles the project that was originally intended.

No matter what you think of any TV show or movie, some dedicated producer(s) sweated bullets to get each and every one of those babies born. Whether it's an Oscar-winning film or an infomercial, the producer(s) had to figure out a budget, shooting schedule, hire the on-camera talent, the behind-the-scenes crew, rent equipment, oversee the editing, and make thousands of decisions along the way. The best producers understand how to motivate people and get them to do their best work. It helps to have an excellent memory, an appreciation for details, and a great eye for talent, because the producer always needs a lot of help along the way. With few exceptions, producing any kind of show is a collaborative art. Its outcome depends on attracting the best affordable talent both in front of and behind the camera and devising a couple of game plans how to reach the finish line - because the best plan doesn't usually quite work out as hoped for.

Unless you happen to be one of the fortunate few in Showbiz who are currently "hot" or happen to have long-term contracts working inside the studio walls, working as an independent producer is seasonal by nature and tenuous at best. When work finally arrives, it feels like riding a bucking bronco twelve hours a day. You arrive home bone-tired and weary, recharge the batteries, and return to do it all over again the next day. However, when all the pistons are firing, when everyone is doing what they're supposed to, when the machine is functioning properly and you're consistently turning out a great product, it is a truly joyful experience. If you make it to the big leagues, you're responsible for helping to transform an idea or words on a page into something that millions of people all over the world will see, respond to, and hopefully enjoy for years to come.

I've lived a life of extremes. Feast or famine. Great luck followed by horrible luck followed by great luck. My first job in Hollywood was as an assistant film editor on a Roger and Gene Corman low budget black exploitation movie. I then got lucky and began a 2-1/2 year stint as Orson Welles' film editor where I learned about Hollywood's heyday from someone who actually made history. Herman J. Mankiewicz, the primary writer of *Citizen Kane*, once remarked as Orson walked by, "There, but for the grace of God, goes God."

Orson was a fascinating, self-invented creature. He had become world famous in his early twenties and said he used to carry his fame around "like a ball and chain." He also remarked that, "Gluttony is not a secret vice." He certainly proved it at 6'1" and almost 500 lbs. He was mercurial and pretty much had his way with the world. I was just a lucky kid who got to hang around and watch the genius at work. Orson could be demeaning and indifferent. And just when I was going to tell him where he could shove that legend, he would wrap his meaty arm around my shoulder and sincerely say, "Have I told you lately what a good job you're doing?" We figured out how to make it work and I learned from one of the best that ever was.

At the other end of the artistic spectrum, I was also fortunate to befriend Samuel Z. Arkoff, legendary co-founder with James Nicholson of American International Pictures (AIP). Sam, who billed himself as a simple Iowa farm boy, was full of stories about the good old days. From the 1950's through the 80's, AIP produced over

500 "B" movies; *I Was A Teenage Werewolf, Dr. Phibes, Little Shop of Horrors, The She Creature, How To Build A Monster, Beach Blanket Bingo, The Amityville Horror, Dressed To Kill* to name a few. Sam was a very smart cat who was the first to zero in on the teenage audience that needed somewhere to go on Friday and Saturday nights. Twenty years later, all the other major studios discovered that the young crowd had become their primary target for most new movies and TV shows.

In the late '70's, I was fortunate to produce 540 half hour tax shelter TV shows in a three-year period for doctors, lawyers and airline pilots looking for a 7-1 tax write-off. In 1986-87, I Executive Produced the TV series *Airwolf* for Universal in Vancouver B.C., a place that soon became Hollywood North and home to billions of dollars of runaway production. In my nomadic experience, I've subsequently produced film and TV series for HBO, WB, ABC, CBS and NBC, Fox, Castlerock, Disney, Sony and Universal.

Flying by the seat of one's pants in Hollywood used to be the order of the day. Everything has changed as multi-national conglomerates whose existence is dictated by the all-important bottom line currently own the major studios. As an independent producer, you quickly learn out on the high wire without a net and how to make it safely to the other side ... or you don't.

Fate is a cruel mistress. Thwarted ambition is the order of the day, as almost everybody in Showbiz would rather have some other job. The big time music video producer or highly paid commercial producer wants to be taken seriously as a long form storyteller and work in TV. The successful TV producers keep trying to prove themselves worthy of a shot to produce feature films. Movie producers want to run a studio so they can control their destiny. The studio execs all want to produce or direct or write and show everyone how bloody creative they are. It's a vicious cycle and very easy to lose oneself in the process.

In Showbiz, the only constant is change. If you are a shy, wilting lily type and don't roll well with the punches, you're probably not going to make it. Too many people miss great opportunities because they're busy stumbling over pebbles and lose sight of the mountain they thought they could climb. As with everything in life, it's very easy to accommodate success. It's learning how to deal with adversity that determines your character and ultimate fate.

Any would-be producers have to learn the mechanical skills involved with filmmaking like budgeting, scheduling, writing, directing, editing — all of which are addressed elsewhere in this book. What's difficult to learn is how to convince a truculent star to leave his trailer for a fight in a mud hole when the icy wind is howling and the crew is heading into double overtime. There's no class that teaches you what to say to a director high on coke who is waving a pistol around at the end of a fourteen-hour day and scaring people. (Get close enough to grab the gun from the side. Don't stand in front of a gun if you can help it.) How to get a barking dog to shut up in a neighbors yard while you're trying to film is a neat trick — keep feeding it peanut butter sandwiches.

Having experienced all of these adventures and many more and learning a few things along the way, I am happy to share so that you can avoid these problems in the future. Something else they don't teach in film school is that Showbiz is teeming with failure. But when it does work, one successful film or TV series can generate more money than the gross national product (GNP) of several small South American countries *And it's all cash!* That kind of success pays for a lot of mistakes and keeps the big machines well oiled.

What other industry takes complete unknowns, makes them TV or movie stars, and pays them better than the leaders of the free world?

As for the gift of overview, what's important is to keep your eye on the prize while surrounded by chaos. A great producer thrives under these circumstances. It's when they feel most alive because the responsibility falls directly on their shoulders. How the enterprise makes it to the other side of the high wire is based directly upon their ability to communicate the vision, inspire the cast and crew to exceed their limitations and deliver something that surpasses every-one's expectations.

It's good to know where you want to go. It's better to be able to get there in one piece and live to fight another day.

A Man Behind the Curtain

I don't think anybody starts out wanting to be a great producer. The audience has scant idea of what a producer really does and in spite of the growing number of film schools around the world, one of the most important subjects they don't really focus on is how to become a producer. Almost everyone in these schools fantasizes about being "creative". Producing is often deemed to be a job that is non-creative and perfunctory at best. Film students primarily see themselves becoming famous directors or writers and/ or somehow getting their mugs in front of the camera. When it came time for the final senior film project at Emerson College in 1972, all the good slots were quickly snapped up and the only job left for me was to organize the effort by becoming the producer. Turned out I enjoyed over-seeing the short film thus setting the table for what followed.

Unknowingly, during my childhood, I had had an invaluable head start in becoming a producer. Being the middle of eight kids meant that I already had a lot of experience in the art of compro-mise and getting what I needed without alienating the rest of the brood.

A producing career in Show Business was akin to the trips I took as often as possible to the Fun House at the local amusement park when I was a kid. In the entranceway, there was hall of mirrors that distorts your carefully crafted view of reality. This was followed by a hazardous trek across an undulating bridge where the bottom dropped out and you had to hold onto the railing for dear life. Next you had to run through a giant wooden tube turned on its side that was always churning. If you weren't careful, any spare change would fly out of your pockets and the other kids would grab it. The squeals of laughter mixed with adolescent screams of terror in the background added to the surreal ambiance.

When you finally emerged from the tube, in the middle of the Fun House, on a slightly raised platform, was the piece de resistance; a large (40' diameter) convex spinning wheel packed with excited kids and daring adults, all with wild looks in their eyes, faces flushed with anticipation. As the wheel began turning faster, bodies on the outer edges quickly yielded to gravity and spun off onto the matted floor, arms and legs akimbo. Thinking back on this exciting experience, because of the many scrapes and flesh burns, it was a class action lawsuit waiting to happen.

If you happened to be one of the lucky ones near the middle of the fast spinning wheel and positioned yourself to withstand the increasing centrifugal force, you enjoyed watching pals and strangers flying off like rag dolls. You temporarily reveled in your moment of triumph until some unseen hand pressed a button and an electrical charge ran up through the screws your body was touching, shocking your butt and hands. You taught yourself to withstand the pain or you too went flying. As the wheel finally slowed down, you'd wave to your pals and take a triumphant spin around the universe. It was one of the great thrills of my young life.

I spent my hard-earned paperboy money to get into the Fun House because you could stay as long as you liked. All the other rides had a time limit. You stood in line for the Dragon Coaster or the Tilt-o-Whirl, they temporarily spun or jerked you around for a couple of minutes and then it was over. The Fun House was a half-day adventure and turned out to be an invaluable experience that helped prepare me for a life in Show Business; there were no rules, no rhyme or reason, and once experienced, nothing would ever be the same.

As kids, we were brought up in a world that made sense. You finished sixth grade, hair sprouting in strange places on your body, autumn followed by winter, and you got a new wardrobe as you forged ahead on life's journey into seventh grade. If you studied hard and avoided your teacher's wrath (ah, the good ole' days when the nuns had ESP and absolutely knew who didn't do their homework) everything fell into place, heaven and hell, cause and effect, rhyme and reason. When you finished High School you were expected to go off to college and get a good paying institutional job at 3M, Mutual of Omaha or the Civil Service and become a productive member of society. After changing careers a few times you would eventually find the right partner and settle in for the long haul with one wife and 2.3 kids. (Anybody else ever wonder about the .3 kids?)

You blink your eyes three times and 25 or 30 of your most productive years whiz by. The plan was always to set yourself up so that you could enjoy the "Golden Years", surrounded by loving family and friends until they bundle you up one last time for the trip into the hereafter or wherever the journey really ends.

Me, I'm a died-in-the-wool independent TV and Film Producer, one of the people toiling behind the curtain, and all bets are off.

In the Beginning

My first real job in show business set the direction my life was to take. The largest independently owned theater chain in New England was looking for an assistant booker. While all of my friends and fellow film school graduates rushed off to conquer the production world, I was curious about the business side of Showbiz. How did the money work? Who got paid how much for doing what?

When I would ask visiting guest lecturers at our film school about the money trail, they all seemed to laugh and shrug like, "We don't want to dampen your enthusiasm, kid. You'll find out soon enough." The more I asked, the more obfuscated the truth became and that, of course, made it all the more intriguing. What was everyone not saying and why?

So I got all dressed up for my first Showbiz job interview and met the head film booker of the largest theater chain in New England. George was a wonderfully gregarious walking encyclopedia of film history who ended up hiring me on the spot. On my second day, the Sicilian who ran the place handed me four sheets of paper that held the box office numbers from the previous night's grosses of the 180 theaters they operated. He says, "You're a college boy. Take it down by a hundred." I asked for some clarification. "Take each of these numbers down by a hundred dollars."

I dutifully sat down at my new desk and somewhere in the middle of the second page I came to the startling revelation that by under-reporting the box office grosses, these guys were stealing $100 from the distributors and filmmakers from each theater. That amounted to $18,000 in cash disappearing every night without a trace (and this was 1972 when money went a lot farther.) My mind raced ahead; $126,000 a week, half a million a month or $6 million a year, *ALL CASH*, not being reported anywhere. Stealing! Totally illegal. The law put petty crooks in jail for years for a liquor store robbery. My God, I had fallen in with a den of thieves!

All I had wanted to learn was how the money at the box office got distributed so that cinema gods like Orson Welles, David O. Selznik, George Cukor, John Ford, John Schlesinger, Francois Truffaut, Cecil B. Demille, David Lean could finance their dreams. Upon discovering this sanctioned prevarication, my altar boy/ Boy Scout sensibilities started yelling at me to flee as quickly as possible, but the always curious me decided to stick around a little while and see what else was going on. Hey, I wasn't doing the stealing. I was just following orders.

With that much cash moving under the table, presents were being bought for mistresses, weekend vacations to exotic places, brand new fancy cars were being driven by the help. All of these adults were working hard and seemed very happy. There was electricity in the air. It was exciting being in Showbiz! This theater chain ran the gamut from black exploitation theaters in downtown urban centers to gay art houses out on Cape Cod, from multiplexes in the suburbs to drive-ins out in the boondocks.

Once a month I took an envelope full of cash to "Cousin Louie", a pudgy guy in a backstreet warehouse who sat around in a wife-beater t-shirt amidst huge bags of popcorn and boxes of candy destined for the theater concession stands. I learned the Mob supplied most of the major amusement arenas throughout New England at that time. It turned out that if you didn't buy your candy from them, somehow your films were not delivered in a timely way to your theater. A not-so-subtle form of extortion! Totally illegal. "Run boy, run!" the voice inside yelled. Not yet. There was more to learn.

My bosses were always in trouble with a couple of the distributors for not paying their bills on time. They collected the cash from the box office and would use it to buy houses or build new theaters. When the distributor finally had a big film that they really needed, they finally had to cough up some of the money they legally owed for last year's movies (often paying fifty cents on the dollar owed.) It was very sophisticated horse-trading. God help you if you were a distributor who didn't have a blockbuster film in the pipeline, tough luck. TAC. Try and collect! Highway robbery! Totally illegal.

Now, you have to stop the story right there and ask the question: if these guys were such thieves, why didn't the various distributors cut them off and just do business with the more honorable theater chains? Turned out the competition was more or less operating in a similar fashion.

Mom and Pop theater owners didn't stand a chance when it came to booking the best films. The practice of "block booking" is illegal. This is where the little guy is blocked from getting any of the big movies by the big guys who carve up the territory and decide who gets what big picture in which theaters. Early on I was asked to come in one Saturday morning and bring coffee and bagels to the conference room. I stood in the doorway listening as the five major theater owners in New England were saying, "Okay you can have

The Godfather in Providence Rhode Island but I get it in Hartford, Connecticut." Eliminate the competition. Organized block booking. Totally illegal.

This was a multi-faceted entertainment enterprise. Besides the theater chain, these guys operated their own distribution company under another name. They financed $300,000 horror films, exploited them throughout New England and then sub-distributed them across the country. *The Hills Have Eyes, Last House on the Left.* They really hit the jackpot with *Friday the 13th* - that was picked up by Paramount and generated untold millions spawning several sequels and a TV series.

My favorite part of this story occurred twice a year when one of the two Armenian partners returned from Cannes or MIPCOM with a new film under his arm. He had bought the North American rights for $30,000 to some slasher picture that had cost a couple million to make over in Spain or Germany. The films got dubbed into English in Italy for $10,000 and four prints would be shipped over.

The in-house distribution/marketing guys would screen the films and had to come up with an ad campaign. They might decide to call it, *Asylum Erotica,* bearing the slogan, "The day the inmates took over the asylum!" They would create some artwork, in this case a scantily clad woman lying in a pool of blood, slap a new title card on the head of the picture, (my job since I was a college boy who had graduated from film school), and they would ship the four prints out to the hinterlands – Pawtucket, Rhode Island, Springfield, Massachusetts, Bennington, Vermont and Bar Harbor, Maine. They would buy a small ad in the local newspaper on the movie page and wait to see if anyone showed up.

If the film dropped dead at the box office, they'd bring the prints back, re-christen it, *Twitch of the Death Nerve* and send it back out to the same four theaters two weeks later. This version would have a gal in a sexy nurse's outfit taking tickets as you passed through a final warning station that announced this was your last chance to get your money back. New ad campaign. New title card. Same exact movie. It dropped dead.

On the third try, they called it, *Mark of the Devil* and provided a vomit bag with new artwork, some hard candy to suck on, and cotton balls to put in your ears so you wouldn't have to listen to your neighbors screaming. They would ship it off to the same four theaters two weeks later and for some inexplicable reason, there would be lines around the block.

They immediately got fifty more prints made up and bicycled them throughout New England. American Independent Pictures (AIP) or some other distributor would take them out across the rest of the country. By the end of the tour, the film would have grossed between $10m and $20m. I was amazed and came to the realization that I had to get out to L.A. and see how the production side worked because this was it! I'd found my calling. Any business where grown ups get to play pretend and make tons of money is where I wanted to be.

Things didn't exactly work out as planned, or to paraphrase Willy the Shake, "Twas many a twist betwixt the cup and lip."

IN THE BEGINNING
PART II: FROM THERE TO HERE

Before you start something, you never really know for sure what the best angle of approach is going to be. In my case, swimming upstream with all of my contemporaries in search of a career in Showbiz, editing became the doorway to my future. It was actually chosen for me by the head of the Emerson film school way back in the dark ages of the 1970's. Some local do-gooders had shot a bunch of 16mm film about cleaning up the their beloved Boston Harbor and they needed an inexpensive editor to put it all together.

I was selected to sit at the school Moviola (old fashioned upright editing machine) in the evenings and weekends with a cellist from the Boston Pops Symphony, who was probably all of thirty years old. He had dreamt up this project for a group called, Save Our Shores, and gotten a few rich people to throw in a few bucks. I tried to figure out how to best tell their story with the footage that we had. The result was a ten-minute film. There was a lovely party down at a fancy restaurant one evening to premiere the finished movie. This was the first time the film was projected on a big screen. I had only seen it on a half-a- postcard-sized Moviola editing screen. It was there that I noticed a couple of the aerial shots of Boston Harbor were upside down. Nobody else seemed to mind and at night's end, I was presented with a gold painted lobster claw statue mounted on a spindle as a token of their appreciation.

Right after graduation, I went to work for a large New England theater chain as an assistant booker. When my boss found out that I had some editing skills, I was put to work on an entirely different kind of project. Once upon a time, all of the states had individual film censor departments that decided what the local citizenry could or could not see. By the time I arrived on the scene, only Maryland and Massachusetts still had functioning organizations to protect the locals from the filth that Hollywood and those damn foreign film-makers were producing.

A magical name, Boston. Isn't that where they burned witches? If you were young or a semi-curious person who enjoyed prurient things, advertising "Banned in Boston" on a movie or book was like screaming, "Come and get it!" Hell, way back in the stone age times of the late 1960's, *I Am Curious Yellow*, a soft core foreign "art film" showing naked people humping, outraged the moral sensibilities of the nation. The end of Western Civilization! A lot of people in Boston got frostbite standing in line in the dead of winter when that film was released. It was ironic but by becoming, "Banned In Boston", a film automatically had cache throughout the rest of the country and usually gave the film much higher visibility. In reality, the Massachusetts Censorship Board still had the authority to call in the cops and confiscate every print of any film they deemed morally reprehensible. The prints were either destroyed or locked away, and prints cost money.

This particular theater chain of 180 screens happened to own a couple of gay "art" theaters. Almost all of the films they got from California and Europe required some trimming or they risked being taken away and burned in a fiery furnace of righteous indignation. The head booker for the theater chain was a real character and screamingly gay. He took me under his wing, and delighted in embarrassing me thanks to what I suppose at the time was my charming naiveté.

And so I periodically found myself sitting in a dark empty theater with a flashlight watching gay porno films. Whenever the actual naughty parts arrived, (I'll leave this to the readers imagination) I would aim the flashlight at the projection booth and the projectionist would place a piece of paper at the spot in the take-up reel. When the deed was done, I'd flash him again for another marker. After the screening, I'd take the reel containing the offensive material back to the office and edit out from here to there. My gay boss would usually arrive at the editing room to watch the exorcism and squeal with delight at what those bad boys in Hollywood were up to. We were the only two people in Massachusetts to be subjected to this toxic celluloid material.

I got married the weekend before starting this job. Film school had introduced me to the great masters and how to appreciate the cinematic language in all of its glory. I had acquired editing skills but nothing had prepared me for this part of my first professional job. I was repulsively fascinated by the crudeness of these "art" films. There was no real plot to speak of and the 'actors' all appeared to have been picked up earlier that day on Santa Monica Boulevard. After a while, I noticed that the so-called acting was non-existent and the sex just seemed repetitive. Nobody looked like they were really having any fun.

I'd splice up the material and have to keep track of the trims, because the prints had to be reconstituted before they were shipped back to wherever they came from. The Massachusetts audiences missed the really juicy parts but presumably enjoyed the rest of the show. I vividly remember asking a talented advertising executive why he stayed in Boston and he responded that he was content being a big fish in a little pond. That offhand remark, as much as anything else, propelled me to take off for Hollywood to see if I could become a big fish in the big pond. It's what got me from there to here.

IN THE BEGINNING
PART III: THE CELLULOID ADDICTION

My addiction to film began as a kid. A local New York Channel 9 TV program bearing the name, "The Million Dollar Movie", played the same movie each night for an entire week from 7 to 9 pm. Talk about reruns. They also played the same film again on Saturday and Sunday afternoons. I remember seeing *King Kong* six times one week and was permanently hooked on the flickers. Whenever possible, I could be found at a double feature on the Saturday afternoons of my childhood.

The previews of coming attractions were usually worth the price of admission. The trailers were for the adult features in the evening. The theater owners knew exactly what they were doing to a packed house of underage, screaming, and high testosterone kids when they showed half-dressed women being chased in the woods and epic scenes of Roman orgies and blood. They were grooming their next audience. You probably remember seeing the sensationalistic movie trailers from the 50's and 60's where sizzling adjectives slashed boldly across the screen to some pounding music and the voice of God commanding you to come and see shocking and sensationalistic stories.

During my first job out of college as an assistant booker, I sat alone in an empty theater and screened three indie movies a day, 10–15 a week. Since I was "the kid" on the staff, I would identify which ones were good for the drive-ins, which ones were possible fodder for the Saturday morning kiddie matinees and which ones should never be seen by human beings again. I always loved movies and now I was getting paid to watch them. All was right with the heavens.

So it was one winter's night, standing in the theater chain offices in Boston where I was working, when the opportunity of a lifetime presented itself. I had a chance to speak to the New England branch manager of Paramount Pictures, who was trying to collect some money from my thieving bosses. I waited for their shouting to die down and as he was packing up to leave, I told him of my burning desire to go to California and make movies. He was an old guy (probably all of 45) who later became the head honcho at WB distribution. He said the magic words, "Go to Hollywood and look up my son-in-law who is running the L.A. Paramount office, he'll give you a job." And based upon that fateful utterance, I went home, told my wife our life had changed and we were moving to Californ-i-a because there was a job waiting for me at Paramount.

No contract. No letter of introduction. Nothing but a promise and a handshake was all I needed to pack all our worldly belongings, including a small collie prone to carsickness, into a Saab 96V (about the size of an old VW bug) and drive 3000 miles in six days. It was, "Look out world, here we come!" Thinking back on it, I can only shake my head and laugh about how young and naïve I was. Hatchlings. Coming from good stock but totally unprepared for the Reel World.

It took two months to get an appointment with the son-in-law who said, "Sorry kid, I couldn't get my own son a job." Despite the fact that I later found out his kid already had a job in the front office, (probably my job) it didn't matter. As I so painfully recall, it was no fun going out to the car and telling the waiting wife that things hadn't quite worked out as planned. My mind raced to come up with a new plan. I blurted out, "Give me five years and if we haven't put a dent in the battleship, we'll go back to the real world with no regrets and live happily ever after." Hah!

In my heart, I knew this was the place I was supposed to be. The introduction to Daily Variety taught me the strange new language of "ankling in for confabs." It was great to be part of the biz, looking for work everyday, getting doors slammed in my face and just-missed opportunities. I often spent afternoons at a double feature with a box of popcorn and a few hours to kill, once again caught up in a waking dream state. Whenever I go to a movie, I'm temporarily transformed into the young me so full of hope and promise, watching those flickering images, being told yet another fantastic story and all is right with the world again.

Some things never change.

GET A JOB!

It all started innocently enough. My older sister, Kim, in assessing the financial mess I had made of my life chasing rainbows in Hollywood, uttered three fateful words that changed everything forever, "Get a job!" I replied, "What, and give up show business?"

I had promised my wife and now newborn son that if I hadn't found my place at the banquet table in the first five years that we would leave Lala land forever. The deadline was rapidly approaching. I'm sure most of you are aware that financially treading water gets old quickly.

A few years earlier, I had begun my nascent Hollywood career as an assistant editor on a couple of Corman Brothers "kill whitey" flicks back in the 70's. The experience caused me to retire from show business for the first time. For the next year and a half I became proficient at selling tape recorders and Xerox toner over the phone to nuns around the country. As fate would have it, an opportunity to be Orson Welles's film editor arrived and I jumped at it. This low paying stint lasted off and on for 2-1/2 years. This story is a book unto itself as I learned never to be in awe of famous people again. They have to put their pants on one leg at a time like you and me. They just happened to get lucky. I've subsequently known enough extremely talented people who didn't get lucky to appreciate the situation.

After this gig ended, I hung around our little bungalow on Western Avenue and Hollywood Blvd, waiting for the phone to ring. I used to say that we lived within shooting distance of the St. Francis Hotel because on the night we were bringing our baby home from the hospital, we weren't allowed in the neighborhood because of the sniper on the roof of the nearby St. Francis hotel who was randomly firing at anything moving. Anytime a filmmaker wanted to shoot a scene in some red light, sleazy neighborhood, they would park their trucks out in front of our house. Although I was within touching distance of show business, nothing was working out for me (*quel surprise!*)

After listening to my sister, I put the big brass ring dreams on hold, picked up the Sunday want ads because it was time to hitch up to somebody else's plow and start making a living again. There's always a plethora of salesmen job openings in the want ads but this one was unusual. The innocuous two-line ad in the middle of the page read "TV production company looking for salesmen." It hit me like a kick in the head.

By now, I'd pretty much learned the hard way that Showbiz is a closed game. It takes care of its own. The Executive Branch plays musical execution chairs and shuffles around so much that it's hard to tell the players without a program. If you happen to be in a position of power and need somebody to do something, you mention it aloud and chances are somebody knows somebody or has an unemployed relative who can fill the bill. There are several thousand hangers-on of every stripe who are trying to breach the walls at any given time. If an employer is truly looking for new warm bodies, they merely post an ad in the trades (*Variety, Hollywood Reporter*) and the vacuum is quickly filled with a plethora of applicants who will do just about anything for the gig.

That's why the ad in the *L.A. Times* of a TV production company looking for salesmen was so incongruous.

I applied along with 300 other people and was one of fifteen selected to sell a product that they didn't tell us about right away. This TV production company occupied very impressive digs on an entire floor of a Century City office building. This experience taught me not to judge a company based upon its facade. My new Fearless Leader was a former white minister whose African American congregation had been in Watts. He sincerely believed a dead Supreme Court Justice was speaking him to in his dreams. In hindsight, I probably should have moved on right there but I've always had a weak spot for crazy people in unusual circumstances.

The spectral jurist had revealed that a very abusive tax shelter loophole involving movies and the record industry was about to be closed by the IRS but in doing so, the Feds would omit the word "videotape" — which at the time was a recent technical development — and a new loophole would be created. (I know I'm dating myself but fortunately I was married at the time.)

So the boss had a slick prospectus written up, a legal opinion prepared, and this freshly minted sales force hit the ground running the very next day after the IRS ruling in October of '76. We were the first kids on the block with a shiny new tax shelter and the formerly thriving mountebanks who traditionally sold questionable investments of this kind got to eat our dust. What were the investors buying, I wondered? Why, they were buying videotape TV shows. The investor would pay the company $10,000 and own the copyright to something supposedly worth $100,000. They would write off $70,000 of income tax over the next few years (a 7–1 write off) and everyone lived happily ever after.

"But what kind of TV shows and who was going to produce them?" I asked. Good question. The parent company had acquired a bankrupt TV companies' library and aimed to re-purpose the material by re-editing the shows thus creating a bunch of new titles to copyright. "But who was going to do the work?" The fancy offices were filled with nice people who had no discernible talents and had no idea how to make TV shows. "I'm glad you asked that question, Steve," the bossman replied. "Seems to me that you have a background in editing so I'm putting you in charge of this."

So I got out of selling and started editing the 'new shows' together. I devised an ingenious plan to sit up all night in an edit bay and glue together a bunch of new TV shows from the old material. Throw on a new title card and away we went. These sessions would begin at 11 PM. The editor would pull into the edit bay carrying a shoebox under his arm and proceed to roll three of the largest doobies I'd ever seen and smoke them all by himself. (A wise decision on his part because God knows what the shows would have looked like if I had inhaled.) At midnight he would turn to me and say, "I'm ready!" His fingers moved faster than the computers could keep up with. We would edit six to eight half hour TV shows together before the sun came up. He would trot off to his day job cutting promos at ABC. He got about three hours of sleep at the end of his daytime shift and we would start the process all over again the following evening. This went on for 33 nights in a row. Some events in your life leave indelible impressions. The shows had to be in the can and registered in the Library of Congress before Dec. 31st in order for the tax deductions to be applicable that year.

These 'new shows' sold faster than I could turn them out because all the other tax shelters in town had dried up. Back at Whacko Central, I soon realized that Michael, the corporate lawyer, and I were the only two sane people in the company. He would sit in meetings like Leo Bloom from *The Producers* saying, "We're all going to jail. We're all going to jail." Michael had made headlines the year before in a unique way; "Lawyer Buys Baby Bigfoot!" He quit a promising law career, having argued in front of the Supreme Court in his early 30's, and had purchased a chimp named Oliver that looked like your ugly uncle Fred. Oliver had been found roaming around the jungles of South America and was discovered to have a questionable chromosome count. We have 48, monkeys have 46 and Oliver reportedly had 47. Hmmm?

Michael had taken the chimp to Japan the year before and made a quarter of a million dollars in a month of exhibitions. On the Japanese version of the Tonight Show, Oliver sat down, crossed his legs, popped open a can of beer and hobnobbed with the host. Apparently the Japanese went wild for him. Michael used to wrestle with Oliver playfully until the day the chimp wrapped him up tightly and wouldn't let go until the trainer forcefully persuaded him to do so. Michael decided it was time to sell the possible missing link and sat up in Laurel Canyon until the money ran low. About the same time I was reading the want ads in the newspaper, he read an ad in Variety that a TV Production company was looking for a head of Business Affairs. We both arrived within a few of days of each other. In hindsight, maybe I was the only sane person on the premises.

When I asked about the twenty other employees who seemed to sit around in their offices all day with nothing really to do, he let me in on the big secret — all of the occupiers of the offices with the fancy titles were members of Christos Religion. Apparently a woman in a condo in Marina Del Rey had convinced a group of folk that she was Christ reincarnate. They met on Sundays to worship together. I immediately blocked out the concept of these folks standing around naked, chanting and drinking blood from a chalice. Some things are better left unimagined.

Fearless Leader was one of her most faithful admirers, so it turned out that all of her followers needed jobs, hence the fancy titles and nice offices. I had fallen through the rabbit hole and landed in a parallel universe. I stuck around until the end of the year and had knocked out 200 shows in the editing room that had sold like hotcakes. There was nothing left for me to do, so in January I was let go. Me and Michael had lunch upon my departure and I remarked, "If somebody could produce new shows for under $5000 that would pass an IRS audit valuing them at $100,000 then this crazy idea could actually work."

"Eureka!" He says. "Do you think you can do it?" "Of course," I said not knowing what I was about to get myself into. So we shook hands. He quit the firm and we went off to make tax shelter TV shows together. I produced thirteen series over the next three years. From October to Mid December I had three stages pumping out five 1/2 hour TV shows a day ... each. Out of the investors $10,000 down payment; I received $4000 to produce an original 1/2-hour TV show that supposedly was worth ten times the purchase price. Somewhere down the road, the IRS would evaluate the finished product and disallow the deductions if these shows didn't make the grade.

There was no net. I produced 540 original half hour TV shows over a three-year period. If a show went over budget, it came out of my pocket. (Always thought this would be the best solution for out of control spending by producers working for the studios. Subsequently, I learned the more wildly profligate you are over in Studio land, the better your chances are to continue working.) In order to qualify, these new tax shelter shows had to be put in service during the calendar year. An arrangement was made so they all aired in late night marathons on a Wyoming TV station and were registered in the Library of Congress before December 31st.

I had no idea that what I was doing was impossible, but there was nobody around to stop me. If this hadn't happened to me, I'd think whoever wrote this had an overactive imagination. Having learned so much about how to make TV shows with virtually no money prepared me for when the big money finally did arrive.

How these 540 shows got made is another book unto itself. Let's just say I was having too much fun making way too much money. I was young and foolish and didn't know how to best to invest the windfall. My sister calls me an action junkie and I guess in a way, it's all her fault. I was 28 years old and had spent a couple of million dollars of other people's money, and now I was hooked. Bought a new house, ordered up a couple of new Volvos over the phone and things got even more interesting. In retrospect, my older self shakes his head in wonder... but whenever I find myself in Marina Del Rey, I look up at the buildings and wonder if Christos still there, still doing the water to wine trick.

I avoid the Sunday want ads because I never know what amazing opportunities might be lurking there.

What "It" is

The mysterious "it." She's got "it." Just do "it." What is "it" that separates an individual from the crowd, a great story from a mountain of mediocre ideas, a winner from a loser? A hundred smart people can read a script and all it takes is the right one to get "it." Then they have to get a lot of other people to notice that this one's worth doing and convince them to turn "it" into a reality. "It" is very subjective and everything depends on the eye of the beholder and their position in the pecking order.

Tens of millions of people all over the world are infatuated with this magical, mystical place called, "Hollywood." It's where ribbons of dreams become reality. Swimming pools, movie stars. Beautiful people living in Shangri–lala land. Unless you are born into "it" and have worked in a business all your life, as an outsider looking through the glass, you can never really know how that business works until you jump in and give it a go. As in most other businesses, the choice spots have been taken and most of the great innovations and ways of doing business are well defined. Out there in the real world, they're counting on you to pull the plow for thirty or forty years. After you retire or drop in your tracks, they remove your carcass from the harness and replace you with one or two young bucks that are willing to pull the plow for half the money you were making. Nothing personal — just business as usual.

There is hardly anything usual in the Reel World. Although it is true that all the prime real estate is currently occupied, ours is one of the few sustaining enterprises in the world where there is no rhyme or reason and everything can change in the blink of an eye. The executions at the top of the heap are very public affairs, occurring weekly on the front pages of *The Wall Street Journal*, *Daily Variety*, and *The Hollywood Reporter*.

In fact, there are several little murders taking place on a daily basis out of the public eye. A wannabe startlet submits to the rigors of the casting couch, usually at the hands of someone who has no real intention of helping them out of anything but their clothes. A good idea is "borrowed" by an unscrupulous producer, and yet another creative person is robbed of what they've rightfully earned by the standard forty-page definition of Net Profits that would take a fancy lawyer and high priced accountants big bucks to understand. Art Buchwald once quipped that he hadn't known that the studio he was suing for intellectual property infringement was a "non-profit organization."

Having spent a couple hundred millions of dollars of OPM (other people's money) I am one of the lucky ones. I've earned small fortunes and lost them. And during my tenure, I have witnessed numerous shooting stars that had meteoric rises to the top who then just as quickly faded into obscurity. The biggest question facing anyone contemplating this kind of life is: *How can I survive long enough to have a career and help create a body of work I can be proud of?* Once you're inside the machine, the real question becomes; *How can I keep going for months (years?) on end never knowing which end is up, or if I'll ever work in this town again?* That's what "it" is. It's a mysterious thing that has always been and will always be. So while searching for "it," you have to figure out how to stay alive and enjoy the journey or the process will bury you and your dreams in the blink of an eye.

CHAPTER 2

THE STARTING GATE

A Status Quo Prisoner Report

When I arrived in LaLa land over thirty years ago, a proverbial babe in the woods, I had three strikes against me and didn't even know it: 1) didn't know anybody, 2) didn't have a Rabbi, and 3) Dad forgot to give me a million to get started with. I was blissfully ignorant of the odds against me or anyone else in a comparable situation from ever accomplishing their dream of being successful in Showbiz. It was nothing personal. Long ago, I came to grips that Hollywood couldn't care less when I arrived or departed as my place will be filled in half a heartbeat when it's time to leave.

Like most baby boomers, I bought into the, "Work real hard and you can accomplish anything you want" philosophy. It, and a profound faith in a divine being who is looking out for me, has actually allowed me to raise a child to adulthood and keep a family together in this capricious climb up the slippery slope. If it weren't for a few lucky breaks along the way, I'd be long gone from the scene. The same could be said for most people who have accomplished anything resembling a "career in Show Business."

As an outsider, there's an unofficial five-year fistfight entrance exam in the foyer. This is followed by several barefoot trips across the Gobi Desert, punctuated by the occasional job at some oasis where your spirits and bank account get replenished before you blithely sign on for another journey, hoping this time to be treated well. Each job is an adventure and no two adventures the same. A life in Showbiz is a mother of a roller-coaster ride and unless you (or daddy) owns the company, fasten those seatbelts because you are in for a bumpy ride.

After the opening salvos, where most sane people flee back to the real world, you realize that your youth is gone and you've painted yourself into a corner. You look around, take stock and start to gaze at the rooftops of various buildings wondering if the jump will kill you, or only result in a broken leg. And when you least expect it, nothing you ever planned for actually happens. A chance meeting with a stranger you've met along the way, a scrap of paper blows by with a phone number on it, a cup of coffee at the right restaurant on the right day and your life suddenly changes. Somebody saw something in you, remembered your name, and gave you a chance to prove yourself. (Only later do you discover that nobody else in his or her right mind wanted this particular job but that doesn't really matter.) This is it! The moment you've waited for your whole life. A chance to succeed! A sliver of the back end profits is waved in your face to compensate for the lousy up front pay.

It's the highest high to pull off something against long odds. No drugs, booze or sexual encounter can match the feeling. It creates a hunger in you to duplicate the feat, relive the feeling. It gets a little easier each time. Your confidence grows. Amazing things are created in front of your very eyes that you had a hand in shaping, that you even get a credit on. Your name up in lights! Kilroy was here! Magic really does happen.

The lot of the independent producer, the unfathomable endurance contest that you are hoping to survive, is fraught with many such cycles. "Feast or famine" is not just some empty catch phrase. It becomes a way of life. Vacations are put off because there's a job in the offing. "If I miss this boat, I don't really know when the next one will come along." You look into the eyes of people who love you and realize that they think you're nuts. Family and friends call to you from some distant shore yelling, "Turn back before it's too late," "Get a job teaching," or "You're never going to make it so why be unhappy?" By the time they say these things it's already too late. The Showbiz tse-tse fly has already claimed another victim. You're a goner.

The status quo stinks. But, the handwriting is on the wall and it's only a matter of time until the Internet provides the artists of the world direct access to the paying public, and when it finally happens, it'll be a whole new ballgame.

WHAT'S YOUR HANDLE?

When attending any social gathering or cocktail party in Lala land, sooner or later someone standing nearby will invariably ask, "What do you do? Who are you?" They want to know what's your handle? We all appear to be different things to the outside world. In my case, I'm a; father, husband, brother, lover, friend, confidant, writer, producer, director, editor, but at the core I am an idea machine. A non-stop flow of ideas coming in all sizes, shapes and colors. If I like the person, I'll tell them what I do. If I want to shut them down, I'll say I write dog food commercials, watch them roll their eyes and quickly wander away.

One of the most difficult tasks facing any creative person is to be objective about their work. Nobody wants to kill his or her own children. "Hey, I created it so it must be good!" Michelangelo, Picasso,

DaVinci, Jack London and Shakespeare all came up with clunkers along the way. Nobody is absolutely brilliant all the time. A notion takes hold, is acted upon, and when held up to the light of day, it either sparkles like a gem or the fatal flaws become evident.

If you're the obsessive-compulsive type, you carry these flawed ideas around intending to fix them someday or at least make them better. I have quite a collection of notebooks, old computer disks, and yellow legal pads brimming with notes, ideas, half stories, poems, songs, short stories and screenplays. The voices inside my head demand an outlet, or they will someday be carting me off to the funny farm. There are stories to be told, people to talk to and sell these ideas to before they all dissipate in the wind. Producing TV shows and movies is my way to pay the rent, but all I really want to do is sit in front of the computer, open the floodgates and let it flow like any number of successful writers. Maybe then the voices will give me some respite or maybe, with a little financial encouragement, it'll just get worse.

"Millions for morons, why not me?" is my mantra. Never underestimate the value of cheap theatrics! A little yelling and speaking up for myself could've changed the course of my life. I wasn't raised to be a yeller. I was raised to be creative. I was ushered into this world by a pair of bohemians: an entertaining Lucille Ball type who was married to a witty Jack Paar type. They both loved ideas, words, art, and music. They didn't seem to have a clue as to how big business really worked and had their hands full raising eight kids, keeping a roof overhead, and staying a foot in front of the steamroller.

Got the drinking, smoking and gambling jones in my genes. I've just about learned to control them. It's simple really- don't drink, don't smoke and stay away from casinos. Oh sure, I've tried drinking and smoking myself into oblivion. Got too costly as I came precariously close to losing the most important people in my life. They made my choice to quit the excessive self-indulgences relatively easy.

Losing them would have been far too high a price to pay for a little mental recreation and self-medication

So now I pound away chasing these twenty-six letters around the keyboard, hoping to make people laugh or cry, but mostly to try to get the reader to think about things from a different perspective. My handle is being a working producer. My job is to get through this journey one TV show, movie, treatment, original screenplay, and essay at a time. I hope one day to enjoy the handle of being known as "a successful writer."

FREE FALL

A scene from *The Bank Dick*, written by and starring W.C. Fields features Fields trying to convince his future son-in-law, Og Oggleby, to buy some worthless shares of stock. It goes something like this:

Fields: Take a chance! My uncle took a chance. Jumped out of a hot air balloon at six thousand feet without a parachute. Took a chance he'd land in a haystack!
Og: Did he make it?
Fields: No, but had he been a younger man, he would've.

Although I've never been up in a hot air balloon or jumped out at six thousand feet without a parachute, I understand what motivates a person to take such a leap of faith. If you are fortunate to reach a lofty position in Showbiz when you're young, then everything is beautiful. If Dame Fortune intercedes on your behalf and propels you to a vantage point that few others achieve, you can't help but look at your neighbors clinging to their respective piece of the American dream and think, "I deserve this." The smart ones know they can try harder, do better and get even higher. A few lucky ones even get farther up the food chain. You dine where the elite meet to eat. You get to park your butt in preferred seating and enjoy the sights, sounds and sensory pleasures that the good life has to offer.

As a film school graduate trying to figure out my place in the world, while eating lunch with my young bride in a corner of the Boston Commons one day, I was attracted to a large crowd of people. They had gathered to watch the shooting of a TV movie of the week. There were a handful of C+ stars that were walking and talking in front of the cameras. A thin yellow rope restrained the spectators and I vividly remember standing four feet away from the director and thinking, "I'm a million miles away from where this person is in their Showbiz career." I resolved right there and then to put myself in harm's way and cut the distance in half by driving to that magical place, Hollywood.

When you finally reach the 101 Hollywood Freeway, there's a sign that reads "Hollywood - next eleven exits." We got off at the last exit that landed us in the middle of Studio City in the San Fernando Valley. *Hello, Hollywood! We're here! Could somebody please point me in the right direction?*

Just west of Coldwater Canyon on Ventura Boulevard is an old fleabag pit stop known as the Park Motel where we spent our first two weeks in LaLa land. On Day Two, I remember asking a stranger where Hollywood was. He looked at me, laughed and kept walking. Whenever I drive by the Park Motel today, I remember there was an old guy (probably all of 55) living in one of the rooms year round, which we thought a bit odd. His claim to fame was that at a young age he had written the song, *Rudolph, the Red Nosed Reindeer,* and arranged his life so that the Christmas royalty windfall sustained his existence for the entire year. He was within walking distance of The Sportsman's Lodge and the old Tail of the Cock. This guy was working on the ever-popular, slow self-embalming course. It's thirty years later and I wonder if he's still there.

It's very difficult to build a body of work that people appreciate. Fate awaits you at every turn, opening door number one, two or three, and gives you a shove. Early on, the elevators always seem to be going up. The destinations usually aren't what you were promised, but you learn to roll with the punches or you don't last very long. Can't keep track of the number of narrow minded, inflexible, extremely talented people I have known along the way who didn't make the cut.

The smart successful ones protect their turf surrounded by friends and relatives. If you don't hit it early, the elevators get fewer and farther between. It's like this in every business where power and money are concentrated. Saddam Hussein is only the latest example in a long line of power mad dogs who rose through the ranks, built an empire and held on for dear life before his statue got toppled.

When you are an outsider, building a career in Showbiz is almost impossible. Somewhere along the line you realize that you're too old to become a brain surgeon and weren't cut out to sell stocks or real estate in some small town. And so, while waiting for the next elevator, we take the stairs, one day at a time. Once you get started, it gets easier and as the climb continues, there are fewer folk in front of you than when you started. This knowledge doesn't pay the bills but it helps.

And if you're fortunate enough to be standing in the right place when that next elevator door opens, you will step in blindly, once again taking a leap of faith hoping that it's not the open shaft but rather the vehicle that will get you where you always wanted to go. If not, it'll get you closer to the end of the marathon, one way or another.

Take a chance!

WAITING FOR THE LIGHT

Having arrived once again at the old familiar intersection my life takes me to when I'm "in between films" (aka. unemployed), I paused yesterday to take stock of the situation. Showbiz is strange because we can expect that a third to half of our adult lives will be spent looking, praying and hoping for work. Normal people in the real world get a job somewhere along the line and stay there for years at a time figuring out their next big move. If you are employed in Showbiz for more than six months at any one job, you probably deserve a gold watch and a retirement (wrap?) party when it's over.

Each job that you throw yourself into taxes your mental and physical capabilities as it replenishes the bank account. You often finish up exhausted and in no shape to enjoy the "fruits of one's labors" before that flashing yellow light, the distant horn honking lets you know it's time to start looking for your next job, long before you need to have one.

As much as you've enjoyed your time off, resting on your laurels, feet up, sipping something cold, the fascination with the high wire act, the working without a net isn't quite finished with you. Out on the wire is when you feel most alive. You learn that all the rest of your life is spent anticipating your next trip or recuperating from your latest fall. Most of each day is spent waiting for the immediate future to take shape.

You're never quite prepared for the exact requirements of your next job, but a positive approach to life, belief in ones' self and a successful track record is the best preparation for "getting lucky." Having hired thousands of people, I can say a person with quiet confidence makes the most attractive candidate. Loud, braggadocio is usually a false bravado covering up some inadequacy. It's the people who meet your eye and have the answers to your questions long before they are asked, that you are willing to take the leap of faith with. In weighing comparable resumes, I'll usually hire the person who I believe is going to let me sleep at night. Every once in awhile, I'll gamble on an extremely talented stranger, someone who has the makings of greatness and brings something extra to the project.

Although this has sometimes resulted in the artist's personal life interfering with the project, the rewards are more often greater than the risk. I really don't mind the occasional phone call in the middle of the night from the local state troopers saying they've arrested my drunken Production Designer for speeding if he's otherwise done a spectacular job. We'll both live with the end results.

Upon returning to that old familiar intersection of my life where any one of six or seven lights could turn green, I rev the engine, impatient with my lack of progress but experience tells me something will happen. When the green light appears again, in that instant I realize that it's the joy of the hunt, the looking for that next job, the not knowing that turns me on. I am once again casting my fate to the wind. Anything you plan for usually doesn't happen. Every independent minded person has got a backpack full of dreams (scripts) that they'd love to do. We push ahead honing our pitch, greeting our fellow travelers along the way, wondering which of our projects is going to be our Pet Rock, our so-called "ticket out of the ghetto."

And then one day, as the fuel gets lower due to our idling engine, there is the inevitable phone-call out of the blue, an item in the newspaper, a chance meeting on an airplane and our lives again change in ways never planned for. As we step into the whirlwind of our next job, we hold on tight to our dreams because someday we might actually get our turn at the microphone and we better have something interesting to say. But as soon as that light changes, we will be consumed by the new challenge that fate has dropped on our doorstep. Soon enough, it will be time to go and show them once again what we can do.

As Roy Scheider says in *All That Jazz*, "It's Showtime!" Ladies and Gentlemen, start your engines!

BAD NEWS, GOOD NEWS

Think of something bad, i.e. car accident, kidnapping, death, illness, etc. Think of someone you love. Think of something bad happening to someone you love. It happens sooner or later to everyone you know.

You have a conversation with someone you know that turns your world upside down as they relate something will soon happen to someone you love. You stop what you're doing and re-evaluate the world armed with this new information. A child, a spouse, a parent, a best friend or loved one has been given The Word. The unlimited horizon suddenly becomes very close and very limited. You reorganize your life and try to do everything possible to help them through the crisis.

There's a knock on the door, a phone call in the middle of the night with news you weren't ready for. You open a letter, pick up the newspaper, turn on the radio or TV and there is a terrible surprise about someone you once knew, once loved, once shared many a good night with, ate with, drank with, laughed with who is simply gone.

You remember what they looked like. Once you've conjured up your favorite image, you try to recall their voice, how they spoke, how they yelled when angry, how they laughed when happy. You try to reconstruct how they walked or some of the things you shared together.

We are being so bombarded on a daily basis by new sights and sounds, new faces, that try as you might, unless you have one of those photographic memories, the dead soon become but a wisp of a dream. You keep their essence alive in your memory banks because that's all you have room for. As time goes on, there are more names on that chart you keep in your heart for the dearly departed.

Every once in awhile, a dream will bring them back to life so vividly that you can touch them, smell their particular brand of shampoo, feel their body hugging yours, see the twinkle in their eyes, hear their unique voice in all it's richness and peculiar cadence and you wake up happy for the opportunity to visit with them again and are sad that you can't be with them in your waking life.

We get on with our lives but we always carry them with us. The good news is that as we look around, we realize that we have been blessed with other people who populate our waking life who love us, care about us. We must try to make the time in our busy lives to say thank you, not only to those who wish us well on our daily journey, but to the big guy (or gal) upstairs who gave us this life in the first place.

Any day that bad news doesn't happen to you is a good day. Life is a daily miracle that happens to you. Enjoy each day as if it's your last, because one day, way too soon, you'll be right.

Gypsy Blood

I don't know if you've reached the fork in the road yet, but everyone traveling down this path that isn't independently wealthy eventually will. The signpost features two arrows pointing in opposite directions. The one pointing down a dark winding road reads, "Gypsy Blood." The other points towards the entrance ramp to the main highway reading, "Steady Eddy." Who you are and where you are on life's journey determines your choice.

If you find yourself married up, maybe a couple of rug rats underfoot and are carrying the world on your shoulders, you need a Steady Eddy paycheck in order to keep the wolf from the door. It's comforting to know that your time has been prescribed by a host of responsibilities that you have accepted and need to handle well. Because of its transitory nature, sinking down roots in Showbiz is difficult to do. Just as you settle in and become comfortable with a job, the world shifts on its axis and everything slides sideways. It is the nature of the business.

Inside the studio walls, months of rumors prove true and a bigger company buys the company you were working for or the corporate "downsizing" goes into effect. Musical execution chairs take place in the executive suites. One way or another, some people are going to land on the sidewalk. Maybe the last two or three projects didn't work out as planned and unfortunately you get caught up in the "last hired, first fired" revolving door. This usually happens before you were able to make any significant impact on the bottom line or stand out in your particular field.

In sports, when a new General Manager or Manager is hired, the team undergoes a transformation. A core group of players remain but everyone else is thrown under the bus. A new philosophy takes hold and hopefully results in a winning team. Oftentimes it's the chemistry in the clubhouse that determines what happens out on the field of battle. One player can make all the difference in leading the team to the winner's circle. Conversely, one rotten apple can spoil the whole bunch. As management, if you can't control or at least influence your bunch of millionaires, it soon becomes apparent and there will be want ads put up on the bulletin board looking for a new manager.

In Showbiz, a new regime takes over at a studio or network and changes direction. The old slate of projects gets gutted because nobody wants to be responsible for investing another dime in making the former slate work. Defenestration becomes the order of the day. After all, the only reason there is a new regime is because of the bad judgment exhibited by the previous one. If a great project from the old regime that is too far along to abort happens to strike gold, the new regime will happily take credit for it.

If you're lucky and tenacious, a good paying job will materialize that utilizes your talents. You hold on for dear life because the older you get, the more you realize how difficult these jobs happen to be. Occasionally, you will win the Survivor Series and hold onto your job through several regime changes. This is the exception to the rule, as you become the mortar that holds the brick wall together.

And then there is that winding dirt road that runs alongside the main highway. If you want a life full of adventure featuring the highest highs and the lowest lows, good and bad surprises awaiting you around every corner, then you, my friend, have Gypsy Blood in you. It is simultaneously a curse and a blessing. It's a curse because if they gave you a high paying job in the executive suites where you were expected to perform pretty much the same task day in and day out for years to come, they'd probably find you dead in the bathtub within a few months with your veins opened or your brains blown out. The combination of monotony, mendacity and settling for a comfortable life would sooner or later do you in. It's a blessing because you find the world to be endlessly interesting full of the most amazing array of talented people who want to live each day to it's fullest.

Like cats and dogs, a gypsy approaches life with an entirely different philosophy than a Steady Eddy. The gypsy is a curious, rootless type who embraces change as a good thing. They doff their tail and disappear when things aren't to their liking. A Steady Eddy needs constant stroking that they're doing a good job and their routines hardly ever change. They often are required to provide unrequited love. In return they get rewarded with a pat on the back and a weekly paycheck.

The gypsy life is too unpredictable for most people. Taking risks entails failing because most things don't work out as planned. Nobody wants to fail or be embarrassed in front of family and friends. The gypsy tries their hand at several things until they find something that they're really good at. It's a blessing to be one of the fortunate few who make a living doing something that you love. If that certain something happens to be successfully entertaining the masses in some way, it can become a very high paying job.

Although I've crossed over and under the main road and occasionally hitched a ride for a short distance, early on I chose the gypsy path in the hopes of finding an onramp to the highway somewhere down the road after the big traffic jam. It hasn't been easy and I wouldn't recommend it to most people. Feast or famine inevitably gets old as you envy the Steady Eddy's their comforts and predictability. Relying on serendipity often leads to disappointment. But when it works, it is exhilarating. You feel the blood coursing through you as your internal tuning fork throbs with excitement knowing that it doesn't get much better than this. The sights and sounds, the emotional wellspring that we passionately drink from confirms that we're still alive, still ticking and that this is what life's all about. Contrary to the current status quo, mankind wasn't designed to sit in front of a computer all day and talk on a cell phone.

I have a reoccurring dream that each leg is tied down on either side of the railroad tracks. One rail reads "Art" (Show) and the other reads, "Commerce" (Business.) Off in the distance I hear that train a'coming, and the thrill returns knowing I have to get free and dive one way or the other. Art usually wins in my dream because figuring out new ways to tell stories is what I've gotten good at.

CHAPTER 3

ADVENTURES IN MEDIALAND

DOUBLE FEATURE

There is a private circuit of bigwigs in Tinsletown who have 35mm or digital projection theaters in their mansions where current films or soon-to-be-released prints are screened. It's a very practical status symbol because big shots don't have time to stand in line with the hoi polloi and pay for tickets. In the relative safety and comfort of their homes, they can not only see what the competition is up to but make frank comments without fear of seeing their words in print the next day.

I was fortunate to attend several shows at the Arkoff Twin Cinemas over the years. It took place on Saturday nights at Sam and Hilda Arkoffs' home in the Hollywood Hills. Sandwiches and soda, bowls full of chocolates and nuts occupied every surface, as ten to twenty people would gather for another unique double feature. (Sam was the president of AIP and produced over five hundred B movies.)

The lights would dim. The screen would drop down from the ceiling and Sam would sit down in his oversized lounge chair, light up a foot long Cuban cigar and say, "Roll 'em." The 35 mm projector flickered to life and Sam's cigar smoke would curl up through the carbon arc beams as another celluloid "ribbon of dreams" would play out.

After the first ten or twenty minutes, if it was a real turkey, Sam would bark out to the projectionist, "Stop here!" or "Just put up the last reel." It was like a mercy killing. He'd been doing this long before they invented VCRs or DVDs with fast forward remotes. We'd jump ahead to see the film's big climax and when the lights would come up, Sam would stand up, brush the cigar ash from his polyester shirt and say, "Pippyshit!" or "What a load of crap!" or "I thought it was pretty good." With a devilish grin and twinkling eyes, Sam would walk around the room, trying to avoid stepping on one of the grandkids who were usually playing underfoot, and ask people what they thought. Hilda and he would argue about the merits of this or that and we were their audience for this unique theater in the round.

He listened to our interpretations and comments while the projectionist would set up the second picture. There was always a twin bill and the combos were always unique. One memorable evening featured the pairing of Martin Scorcese's *Last Temptation of Christ* followed by *Pom Pom Girls*, for probably the first and only time in cinema history.

In homage to Sam, I went to see Mel Gibson's, *The Passion of Christ* and afterwards immediately walked into the adjacent theater to catch *Starsky and Hutch*. Starsky is the funnier of the two. I kept thinking about how many hours per day James Claveizel had to sit in the makeup chair as they matched yesterday's horrific makeup. "Was that ninety five lash marks on his back or is that one hundred and four?"

The Passion was every bit as brutal as had been advertised. I don't think I'll rent the DVD to see Mel Gibson's uncut version.

That's the one he really wanted us to see, featuring more gruesome scenes he was forced to leave on the cutting room floor by the MPAA, the movie ratings board. I just kept thinking of poor Jim Claviezel in that makeup chair. The twenty minutes of Marquis DeSade footage was unnecessary, but it's Mel's money and he can do what he wants. Obviously there were a lot of people out there who enjoyed watching Jesus flayed within an inch of his life but I wasn't one of them.

Jesus' mother Mary was the emotional core we were supposed to relate to. Throughout the film, Mary managed to get a choice perch to witness the humiliation and physical abuse of her son. Oh, I won't spoil the big surprise ending. Maybe you've already heard about it. Suffice it to say, something else was needed to cleanse the palette and *Starsky* proved to be the perfect second feature. Never relating to the original TV show, I wasn't expecting to like it but was pleasantly surprised. It had heart and humor and the pre-requisite amount of action to keep an extremely thin plotline semi-interesting.

As I was watching the light comedy, I kept thinking of what Sam's review of *The Passion* would have been. Hilda would have hated the excessive screen violence. I have a feeling Sam might've skipped a few reels and gone right to the big finale. Don't think I would've blamed him.

WHEN WORLDS COLLIDE

Attended the annual NATPE convention in Las Vegas along with thousands of other people. NATPE, the National Association of Television Production Execs, is a chance to schmooze with people from all over the TV landscape. You meet up with old friends, listen to speakers, and ogle the pretty girls who are trying to lure you like sirens on the rocks into their booths promoting this or that new TV show. It's a cacophony of sensory overload as you are bombarded by slick promo trailers and glitzy graphics while trying to avoid being stepped on by oversized wrestlers and funny looking mascots.

The big boys occupy the nicest booths. The little guys are relegated to a rabbit-warren of 8'x 10' spaces on the fringes of the hall in a scene reminiscent of a Mideastern bazaar. Colorful posters, silicone babes, actors in odd outfits all designed to snag your eye and get you to buy something, please, please, puleeeze!

Some of the major conglomerates have consolidated their empires so one could find Viacom, Paramount, Kingworld, MTV and CBS in one temporarily walled-in city. Their 1/2-acre booth was populated by well-scrubbed suits scurrying around, currying favor, Because hundreds of millions of dollars are at stake and their performance will be judged afterwards, everybody tries to look good and are at their jocular best.

As far as Las Vegas conventions go, NATPE is just another three-day mid-week speed bump between the really big conventions, holiday traffic and championship fights. The world of first run syndicated TV programming has dramatically changed in recent years and NATPE has lost much of its oomph. 250–300 formerly independent TV stations around the country are now affiliated with the Fox network, the CW (formerly the WB/UPN) or the My TV networks. Each of these stations still has to buy shows for their fringe programming needs but their network overseers occupy their prime time real estate. Even if they all banded together, there aren't enough truly independent stations left over to have any real clout. Foreign buyers comprise half the crowd as they are always in need of new, entertaining, affordable programming from good old Hollywood.

This particular year's convention was situated on the second floor at the Mandalay Bay Resort Casino. There are always seminars talking about new, different and exciting ways to attract the key 18 – 39 year old demographic. The funny thing about this particular experience was that that very group was directly downstairs attending a much bigger Extreme Sports convention. Snowboarders, skiers, in-line skaters and surfer dudes had taken over a brightly lit hall and were holding a coming out party of their own.

It was fun to walk through the main tunnel that delivered thousands of folk per hour to their respective conventions. Strolling among the suits were kids with baggy pants, various piercings, tattoos and t-shirts: the cherished 18–39 year old demographic. The kids have got over *$30 billion* in disposable income and the boyos upstairs are trying desperately to get their attention and to steer a little bit of it in their direction. As these two very distinctive groups walked shoulder to shoulder, they were broken up into small clusters talking among themselves, eyeing each other warily. The establishment vs. the new young grungers.

Since the old guard still controls the airwaves, the feeling was let the kids downstairs have their fun because eventually they'll all be hooked up to the giant media milking machine. Just another batch of data to be studied and dissected by the boys upstairs who are way down the road plotting out the future, dividing cyberspace into easy-to-digest, bite-size pieces. Pay cable, PVR's (private video recorders), YouTube, cell phones, TIVO and VOD (video on demand) have the boys upstairs in a tizzy. What happens to them when the old TV ad supported business model is scrapped? The :30 and :60 spots that have kept the hot air balloons aloft all these years are being threatened with extinction. People are desperate to know what happens next.

At a seminar upstairs, one of the speakers pronounced the penultimate truth, "Content is king! You can have all of the fanciest, high tech delivery services in the world but if you don't have something that a significant and quantifiable number of people want to see, all is for naught!" I wondered if the NATPE convention floor gave way and suddenly dropped down into the Extreme Sports convention below, if both shows would be a lot more energized. Buyers, sellers and end users all under one tent. It certainly would have been a lot more exciting and provided keen insight as to how these two generations of business people could better work together. They were speaking slightly different languages and wearing different clothes, but basically doing the same thing; trying to divert a bit of commerce called, "capitalism" in their direction.

Whether it's the Rose Parade or The Golden Globes, it's always interesting to drop in on a "media event" that has been in the works for a whole year. Some producer(s), with the help of lots of smart people, have conquered a ton of logistical problems and put on a show that lasts a few hours, or in NATPE's case, a couple of days, and then it's over. All traces of its existence disappear as the space quickly returns to its original configuration — be it Colorado Boulevard, the Beverly Hilton ballroom or a convention floor at one of many Vegas Casinos. Blink your eyes and presto-change-o, it's gone! As though it never happened except in the minds of the attendees.

We are but humble storytellers, plying our wares, momentarily entertaining the masses in return for some food, shelter and financial reward. We're encouraged to keep doing what we're doing as we temporarily divert the crowd's attention from the bigger problems this world has to offer.

Have always enjoyed the spectacle of Las Vegas. Watching worlds collide was an extra-added attraction.

WHIP, CHAIR, PISTOL! *INSTEAD OF LIGHTS, CAMERA, ACTION!*

After the script has been chosen, the money committed, the actors cast, the crew hired, the equipment deals done, the sets built, the locations found, the lights, camera, and everything is in place, once production on a project actually commences and the electronic slate identifying the scene and take number for the editors has been pulled out of the way, there comes that briefest pause where the crew holds its collective breath, the actors try to remember their lines and what they are supposed to do, and finally the magic moment arrives when the director finally utters the all-important word — "Action!"

This is the moment of truth. If Showbiz were a religion, this would be the consecration of all that is held sacred. Time seems to stands still as the film silently whirs quietly through the camera. A foot of 35mm film costs about a dollar. That's approximately .52 to buy, .15 to develop and .33 to transfer the images to digital video for viewing and editing purposes. A foot of film is about a second and a half of viewing time. A thousand foot 35mm magazine load represents approximately ten minutes of film negative.

Big budget movies will shoot 8,000 to 15,000 ft. of film each day to be edited down to one or two minutes of usable film. Every shot is a Kodak moment. A dramatic prime time TV show might burn through 6,000 to 10,000 feet a film a day (60 to 100 minutes) in the hopes of getting five to seven minutes of usable footage. Smaller TV shows and low budget movies will shoot 16mm or super 16mm, which is a third off the price. 24p Hi Def video is quickly making big inroads into the movie and TV business because it's cheaper to use and nobody in Iowa can tell the difference.

Back in the old days, the producer was in charge and had the final word over how things went. Today, on most movies and sometimes on a TV show pilot, the director has more power on the set than the producer. Everyday after production, a "hot cost" report is generated that lets the studio or funding source know what was accomplished and how much it cost. Sometimes a studio exec calls wanting to know why we're going over budget. Besides obvious weather problems or other inevitable delays, the producer often points out that too much film is being burned and the scheduled number of scenes are not being completed. The execs, who usually kowtow to the director, get flummoxed and tell the producer to, "Just fix it". So you have a private chat with the powerful director who nods "uh huh" and watch any cautionary advice goes in one ear and out the other. They simply return to what they were doing before you got in their face. If you get too vocal, they'll often call your boss, the same studio exec that yelled at you for being profligate and try to have you replaced because you're not being "collaborative."

The producer must try to avoid getting caught up in the tug of war between art and commerce. The production arm of the studio yells at you for spending too much money. The creative arm wants you to give the directing geniuses their way, meaning it's okay to spend more money than is in the budget. In this pissing contest between the Studio creative and production arms, the creative folk have at least 51% of the power because every once in awhile they're right and a winning show they championed means tens of millions of dollars to the bottom line and keeps them off the unemployment line. The producer is often rendered powerless and watches helplessly as money is wasted because of some artistic whim on the part of the director. In the final analysis, this particular shot that is taking way too long to produce isn't going to make a whit of difference whether or not this show gets picked up or the movie is a success. For the uninitiated, it is shocking to learn that this is a world of spoiled, privileged children. When push comes to shove, the director doesn't have to hold his or her breath and turn blue in order to get his way because he or she can make a phone call and knows the studio creative team is on their side.

I knew a producer who was offered the job of handling the fifth season of a top ten TV series where the stars were literally fighting with each other off screen. He asked for a referee shirt, a whistle and $40,000 per week in cash. The powers that be were willing to provide the shirt the whistle and meet his financial requirements, except for the part about the money being delivered in cash. They felt it would set a dangerous precedent and looked elsewhere for a less demanding producer.

... AND ACTION!

I once produced a TV pilot where a "connected" director drove me crazy. At the end of the show, I wanted to give this director, who insisted on shooting from the hip (no preparation – just making it up as he went along), a copy of a full-length documentary film that he had inadvertently directed called, ... *And Action!* It could have been entered into some film festival and given serious consideration as a new form of artistic expression — and probably earned more money for the parent company than the pilot did to boot.

... *And Action!* would have been a 90 minute film consisting of a sequence of shots in all kinds of locations where nothing happens. There would be a series of empty frames as the slate was clapped in front of the camera and Herr Director off camera would say, "And Action!" Then he would suddenly start giving last minute instructions to the off screen actors. Some directors will shout out a short reminder to the actors as the film is rolling through the camera before the take begins, but this guy suddenly became engaged in long, rambling narratives. He was a former actor who had made it to the director's chair. It was as if he were saying, "Now that I have everyone's undivided attention, I just wanted to remind all of you that I'm in charge and I've just figured out what we're supposed to be doing with this scene. And besides, I like to hear myself talk."

It would be insightful stuff like, "Remember when you walk through the door, you need to look around and wonder where the dog is. And when you don't see her, you go over to the piano and look around some more and then you play a couple of notes but not a whole song and then walk over here to the couch and pick up the newspaper with a puzzled look on your face ... but not too puzzled." All of this direction should have been given to the actor before the camera was turning. Since I was being held accountable for the bottom line, I would occasionally mention this unnecessary burning of film to Herr Director. He would simply grin at me like, "tough shit."

Because he knew it bothered me and understood that I was helpless to stop him, he would get into longer involved conversations with the actors or the DP or one of the other crewmembers as the cameras continued to roll. The embarrassed first Assistant Director would sometimes interrupt after awhile and ask if we should cut. The Director would respond, "No", and then think up one or two more things to say, often countermanding a previous direction with some new inspiration, thus thoroughly confusing the actors who would occasionally poke their heads into frame to clarify something and then step back out of frame awaiting a replay of the fateful words " ... *And Action!*" His monologue would sometimes go on for minutes. Would've been laughable if it wasn't so flagrantly wasteful.

Under normal conditions, producers keep their fingers crossed that the actors hit their marks, know their lines and say them well. We are ready to rip off heads if somebody steps in an actors' eye-line or in any way disrupts their concentration. We hope the lighting guy hits his cue and turns on the lights at just the right instant. We pray that the expensive aquarium that has been rigged with explosives implodes properly because we've got four cameras rolling and only one shot at it. We silently will the Boom Man to keep the goddamn microphone from causing a shadow on each take. We mentally help the dolly grip stop the camera at exactly the right place. We're ready to adopt the first assistant cameraman if they hit their focus marks on a complex camera move. We wince at the sound of the approaching airplane in the distance and hope the soundman doesn't cut this perfect take in the middle. We keep our eyes on the second assistant director who signals the extras to move around in the background at just the right moment. God forbid anyone coughs in the middle of a take or the idiot producer's cell phone rings. (Had that happen more than once. Nothing the crew loves better than to have the producer screw up a take.)

And then there was the smiling jackal, the director, laughing in my face. I should've cut " ... *And Action!*" together and sent it to the president of the company with a note reading, "By way of explaining why we're $90,000 over budget on this project, do you notice anything wrong with this picture?"

My fear, of course, would be that they couldn't acknowledge their complicity in a system that supports such profligacy. My greater fear was that they wouldn't understand what ... *And Action!* was all about.

GOING FOR THE GOLD

Occasionally there's sad news coming out of Tinsletown. Today's headlines featured Pam Anderson's decision to quit her acting career and devote full time to her kids. She said in her E interview, "I never wanted to be an actress", and she got her wish. She never really was. Calling this half blown-up Barbie doll an "actress" was an insult to the profession. Pam came to town with the big dream of fame and fortune with little or no discernible talents other than wanting to get in front of the cameras. She met the right plastic surgeon, enjoyed a career that spun off a couple of hundred million dollars and now, like Sandy Koufax, is apparently leaving at the top of her game. Her publicist, agent, manager, attorney, hairdresser are aghast. The gravy train stops here.

We won't have Pam to kick around anymore. Not until they offer her a lot of money to make a comeback and show off her assets one more time. Don't worry. There are a hundred (thousand? a hundred thousand?) other starlets out there hoping to fill her void (cup size?) Just like baseball's need to have a batting or home run champ, Showbiz requires a reigning sex queen and king. After all, sex is one of the major pistons driving this machine. Producers get paid a lot of money to remind the audience that they're here to go forth and pleasure themselves and procreate.

Money is the other half of the one-two punch. It's the green juice that keeps the wheels from falling off and the primary thing that fuels our cinematic juggernaught. There's public cash, such as announcements telling us who makes how much and what a movie took in on the opening weekend. And then there's private cash, the kind being thrown over the transom, under the table, behind closed doors, sent off to Swiss bank accounts that really keeps this baby trundling along. There's so much cash traveling around the alternative routes away from prying eyes, especially the IRS, that it's hard to comprehend and virtually impossible to keep track of.

The happy confluence of sex and money arrives once a year in the form of The Academy Awards. The Oscars are Tinsletown's version of the World Series, Super Bowl, Miss America Contest, and Nobel Prize all rolled into one extravagant evening. Which actress is wearing what? Designers have been working madly for months trying to figure out how to cover up the naughty parts with as little fabric as possible. The guys look very stiff in their penguin outfits as they'd be much more comfortable in a t-shirt, shorts and backwards baseball hat like they wore the night before to the Independent Spirit Awards.

I, along with a billion other people around the world, watch this totally manufactured evening where all of the waiting, hoping, hyping and praying comes to a head. There's singing and dancing as extroverts get to strut their stuff. The envelopes are opened. Lots of shrieking and crying as a very small piece of history is recorded. Afterwards, the TV audience gets to tag along outside the big parties where gushing reporters announce arrivals and stick microphones in peoples' faces clutching their golden trophies. The winners were relative unknowns a year ago or five years ago and now the world holds its collective breath wondering what they will answer when asked, "How do you feel?"

It is more blather to get all lathered up about than a fella can take. In the end, as the last limos deposit their celebrities home after the biggest prom night of the year, after all the hoopla dies down and the little old Oscar statue is used as a paper weight or rests on the mantle, it all boils down to the following equation; Show Business=Sex & Money. Art? Art's is a deli on Ventura Boulevard.

Producers are simply the middlemen who take people's dreams, craft them, reshape them and sell them back to them for a profit.

I heard a story about a bright young hustler who wanted to be a millionaire before he was thirty. He tried his hand at producing and failed. He tried selling life insurance and failed. He got into the

Internet game early before anybody knew what it was and struck it rich. He understood people and set himself up as the guy to go to if you wanted to secretly buy porn. In other words, if you wanted porn but didn't want it to be on any public record, you'd order from him and he'd become the purchaser of record and buy the porn for you, mark up the price and mail it off in a brown paper wrapper.

This particular middleman, however, nets $200,000 per day. Seven days a week. 365 days a year. You do the math. Sex and money. Jack and Jill. Oh, what a game we're all in.

9/11/01

I was once again reminded of the power of television last night. Every TV station had prepared special programs about the horror and aftermath of 9/11/01. They did a good job of tying it all up into neat little packages – pretty montages using the same visual material. New interviews with both the victims and survivors. President Bush attending the three principal memorial services – Pentagon, Pennsylvania and New York. Hopefully you've seen the remarkably powerful documentary on CBS by the French filmmakers who happened to be following around a NYC fire company on that fateful day. They were able to put a human face on the tragedy. We got to know the firefighters before they answered the call that claimed so many of their lives. I cried.

We saw the story of the lone trumpeter in NYC who arrived late one night and wished to pay his last respects by playing Taps for the fallen. We watched as he was brought to the center of Ground Zero, how the clean-up crew stopped what they were doing to remember the significance of what had happened there as the sad notes echoed throughout the concrete jungle. I cried for the families that weren't as fortunate as I have been.

It was a very vivid reminder of the power that our business has to reach inside, past color, age, status, the trappings of the modern world and touch something primal inside each of us. The right combination of sights, sounds and music can make us all weep, make us laugh, make us feel for strangers; make us think about our lives from a new perspective. We are the storytellers. We are the chosen people – people who have chosen to entertain the rest of the world. It is incumbent upon us to aspire to touch peoples' hearts and minds and temporarily lighten the load of our fellow man.

Fast-paced, slick visuals full of bigger, better, flashier effects with little to say other than "go here", "buy that", "watch this" are raining down on us in a daily sensory bombardment. Instead of adding to that bombardment, it's important that when we get our chances to tell our stories, they need to be good ones because it's how we will be remembered.

And one day we'll be gone. As our parents have departed or are heading for that door, someday we'll be seeing them again and I, for one, want to be able to look them in the eye, thank them and the Creator for this great gift of life knowing that I had done the best with the time that I had.

We owe it to those who preceded us to tell the stories about this amazing country that we are so fortunate to live in. Our job is to bring simple laughter and joy to our fellow man, put a face on the human experience as we struggle to not only exist but to excel in a very complicated world. We can never lose sight of the amazing forest we have wandered into. We find some friends, people who love us, band together and try as best as we can to get where we're going. It's an awesome challenge and once we've proven ourselves, it's an even greater responsibility.

I wake up everyday thinking, "the best is yet to come, and won't it be grand?"

CHAPTER 4

LEARNING HOW TO TREAD WATER

THE FIVE-YEAR PLAN

I'm not sure where the concept originated, Stalin, Marx, or Mao, but the Five Year Plan was one of the cornerstones of Communism. With concerted effort on the part of everyone in the commune, things were supposed to dramatically improve for everyone involved. Five years was a doable stretch of time to keep an idea alive. Initially, until the resources were depleted and not replenished, most of the Five Year Plan communal efforts were successful. It was enough time to work out the bugs and turn an idea into a smooth running machine.

Upon arriving in LaLa Land as a bright-eyed 22 year-old dreamer I convinced my wife, (who I am nominating for Sainthood) that all I needed was five years. If we didn't put a dent in the side of the battleship, I would return to the real world and sell stocks or real estate in some lovely little burg back east. Those five years were fraught with peril as our little dinghy just plain ran out of provisions and was almost swamped on many occasions.

In hindsight, I was the proverbial babe in the woods, wet-behind-the-ears, fish out of water, who arrived with stars in my eyes and hope in my heart. It is amazing how utterly naïve a college grad can be about the profession they think they are ready to conquer. Up to that point, it had all been book knowledge and I soon discovered a reality I wasn't prepared for. For future reference, looking at the Want Ads in Daily Variety doesn't necessarily mean you are in Showbiz.

There were enough adventures along the way to keep hope alive but financially speaking, swimming against the current as hard as I could, I wasn't getting any closer to shore. Some of the memorable early moments included being an assistant editor on a "kill whitey" movie for Gene and Roger Corman, retiring from Showbiz to sell pens and tape recorders to nuns across the country for a year and a half of early morning phone sales, returning to showbiz on a fluke and working as Orson Welles' film editor for two and a half years. I received credit for directing "Orson Welles at the Magic Castle" for a fledgling cable concern called HBO. (Naturally, he did most of the directing as I made a few suggestions along the way.) Driving my battered car to Bel Aire or a cottage in back of the Beverly Hills Hotel everyday to edit with the Great Man was too great a disparity to contend with while living in a cramped $150 a month cottage in LA's red light district (Hollywood & Western Ave.) Romantic as it all seemed, I just wasn't cutting it. Oh, in hindsight it all sounds exotic and provided me with a good look at how this business really operated, but in four years and eight months I had earned a grand total of $30,000 in Showbiz. I'm not talking per year. I'm talking cumulative. With a college degree, a wife and new baby boy, you do the math.

And as the five-year expiration date approached, it seemed like we had merely succeeded in surviving.

As I mentally began to pack my bags, *it happened*. An opportunity arose and I caught a wave that permanently ruined my return to the real world. I produced 540 half hour TV shows over the next three years for a tax shelter group. Doctors, airline pilots and lawyers were legally able to take a 7-1 write off before the IRS closed the loophole. I made a small fortune in a short time period. It was all downhill from here or so I thought. I remember calling up a Volvo dealer and buying a brand new station wagon for the missus and a new sedan for moi over the phone. Bought a new house with four times the floor space in Studio City and the world was my oyster. Oh, to be so wonderfully young and stupid.

How I spent all that money and almost ruined my life is another story for another time. Let's just say that I've got a fond place in my heart for Five Year Plans.

FOR BETTER OR WORSER

Somewhere back in the dim recesses of our mind, it's difficult to remember exactly the moment because so much has happened since then, all of us who arrived in Lala land made a choice to give ourselves over to an uncaring beast named Show Business. We ran away from the real life that awaited us and joined the modern day equivalent of the circus. It was done by some of us in the cold clear calculating light of day, others in the flash of a moment, still others accidentally wandered into the big top and just never left.

A lot of us made the decision when we were young and impressionable. The big magnet of fame, fun, money and power passed thru town and picked up all the loose screws and nuts lying around that hadn't yet found their place in the square-pegged world out there.

Waking up with this affliction is akin to a guy who discovers he is a woman trapped inside a man's body or vice versa. It usually requires dramatic steps, a completely new wardrobe and sometimes a lot of plastic surgery to rectify the situation (did somebody say actors?). Realizing you've married the beast is half the problem. Figuring out what to do about it is how we spend our time.

Seems you just weren't destined for that job at the DMV or gas station or behind that desk at the insurance company. No matter how hard you tried to please your parents, loved ones and friends, you answered to some little voice inside who naively threw caution to the wind and without all the facts, got you to take the biggest leap of your life.

Falling through the looking glass is the journey each of us has to take. It is the door we all have to pass through if we are truly going to "make it" in Showbiz. One of these days somebody will hopefully explain what "making it" means. Some people "have it made" and then disappear off the radar screens in a blink of an eye. (Quick, who won "Best Supporting Actor" or "Best Director" Oscars two years ago? .... time's up.) A whole lot of people who "make it" appear to be unhappy, chemically imbalanced, unstable types.

It's important to understand the Seven Ground Rules (vows) of this unspoken marriage that you have knowingly or unknowingly consented to:

1. This is a really hard truth for the spouse to take, especially if they are non-coms (non- industry pros); *the Beast comes first.* You are married to Showbiz and your spouse is your mistress. It actually can be a lot of fun if you have an understanding spouse. There'll be hell to pay if you don't.

2. "It's not fair!" is tattooed on the inside of your eyelids. This is not a reason or justification for your lack of success. It just is. Accept it and move on. It's up to you to make it fairer for you. Getting the right agent, knowing who the players are, doing your homework before a meeting, finding out what people are buying, etc. That's all part of the job and helps determine if you get lucky.

3. The good fairy ain't coming to your house, unless, of course, you happen to live in West Hollywood. Then there's a chance.

4. Whatever happens, it's your own damn fault. Nobody stuck a gun in your ribs and forced you to enlist. If it's such a big pain in the ass, either quit complaining or get out. Nobody loves a whiner. Everybody loves a winner.

5. Find your pleasures along the way. It is the friends you make, the love you give and take and the quality of the projects you stick your name on that really counts. If it's all about the toys, notches on the bedpost and number of zeros in the bank account, you've missed the most satisfying part of the ride.

6. The tide goes in, the tide goes out. How we ride the waves determines how we are perceived in the world and establishes our character. Abe Lincoln said, "A man makes up his mind to be as happy as a man makes up his mind to be."

7. Do something for yourself today. Not the Beast. Not the boss. Not the spouse. Not the kids. Just you. Carve out a little time each day to allow yourself to do something fun. Remind yourself that it's good to be alive. Hit some golf balls, read a magazine, get the car washed, talk to some strangers. Someday these will be those rocking chair moments that make you smile as you reflect back.

For Better or Worser, these are the good old days so you better learn to enjoy them.

CHANGING TIMES

I found myself standing in a hallway over at Paramount, waiting to see an old friend. She had become a big shot in the Home Video Division. My mind drifted back to the time when we would sit around on patio furniture outside of the Castlerock Maple Drive offices, compare notes, have a bite to eat, laugh about this crazy business, looking for clues as to how to advance our careers. I was a neophyte producer and she was a talent manager handling one client who was starring in a TV series.

Way back then everything seemed like fun. Kids in a candy store full of rich and powerful people. Somewhere along the line, she breached the studio walls and got a gig as a second assistant, assistant to some executive. Through talent and attrition, she arrived in this plum job just as the marketplace was exploding. Home Video is one of the most important arms of any major studio. Just to put it in perspective, theatrical US box office in 2006 was $9.4 Billion. Home video was $22.5 Billion.

So we try to get together once a year to say hello but things have definitely changed between us. She's up there traveling in the jet stream of power lunches and corporate concerns and I'm still prowling the trenches, looking for my next project.

If you're around the game for any length of time, you'll have similar experiences. A couple of people you started the race with will zoom ahead. Most others will fall behind, some right off the face of the earth. Power and money are a heady brew. They do strange things to ordinary people. That big magnifying glass in the sky keeps turning over the rocks and feeding talented people into the white-hot fire of the public eye. It's very tough to get the important jobs in the first place. Tougher still to hold onto them.

So I stand there in that hallway watching the bevy of well-scrubbed twenty-somethings answering the phones, trying to look busy. They eat lunch everyday in the same room with famous and powerful people. They go to splashy parties and get invited to movie premieres to help fill up the empty seats. They certainly don't want to be somebody's assistant, assistant forever but if they play their cards right and hang in there, who knows where the corporate ladder will take them? They have jobs inside the walls and life is infinitely more interesting than reading the want ads in the Hollywood Reporter while standing in the unemployment line.

After a wait, I'm admitted to the sanctum sanctorum. It's always a little bit awkward at first but she's polite and haggard looking. Says this is the first weekend she'll spend at home this year. Busy, busy, one film festival after another. She oversees a couple hundred million dollars of cash flow for the parent corporation. I look for a piece of humor or story about someone we both knew from the old days. We're interrupted by a spate of phone calls. It's slow roasting over the spit sitting there as she tells somebody that the boyos love this or that idea and want to proceed. It means another fortune to the person on the other end of the phone line and then she returns to me with, "Now, where were we?"

Where we were was we used to be friends. I realize I'm still in her good graces but she's now comfortable traveling in rarefied air. What elements are attached to your project is how they judge the value of a property. Is it from a cult comic book or best selling novelist? What big time director or stars do you have attached? How much money is lined up from outside investors? These are the only types of deals she's interested in these days. A very commercial idea or great script isn't enough. It's simply a good starting point. "Go get all of these bankable or semi-bankable elements attached and then we'll talk."

I keep my fingers crossed hoping that inspiration hits and she'll be reminded that I could be the best person in the world for this or that job. In the end, I thank her for carving out a little bit of time in her endlessly busy schedule. And as I leave the twenty-somethings behind, I pray they learn survival skills because this business will break your heart a thousand times if you let it. I put mine away for safekeeping awhile back and don't fall in love so easily anymore. I'm too old to become a brain surgeon. Time keeps moving along and the only constant is change. Adapt or risk becoming obsolete.

INCUBATION

"The slow development of something, especially through thought and planning."

We're all enmeshed in the slow development of something called "our careers." Inevitably, there are long periods of thinking and planning. In my case, it's been running hot and cold for over thirty years now and you'd think you'd get used to it but you never do. The Chinese have one word that means both "disaster" and "opportunity." Being an independent producer is like you're an ER doctor on call, waiting for the next "disaster/ opportunity" to prove to anyone paying attention that you have mastered your craft.

The good news is that they have to keep building new programming to feed the audience's insatiable appetite for more, more, more. If you have a reputation, your name eventually comes up in the chamber as a producer who has survived this or that type of project before. It may not be a project you want to do but the necessities of staying alive periodically dictate your choices. Can't remember how many times I tried to avoid a backbreaking project that somehow I was destined to do. Being resigned to my fate, I would jump in, make a few new friends and learn a whole lot of interesting things that served me well the next time I got a job I really wanted.

In between our nightly sleep blackouts, our life force is being used up each day. Sooner or later the question is how to best use your day when it's not prescribed by having a job. Being a journeyman producer, it's a lot harder looking for work than when you actually find it. Once the new job arrives, life falls into a predictable schedule of going to an office and beginning the whole process again. Schedules, budgets, pre-production meetings, location scouts, casting, hiring crew, renting equipment, starting production, post production and then it's over and pretty soon you're back on the sidewalk again looking for your next gig.

You think to yourself that there has to be a better way to skin this cat. Maybe it's time to get one of those Steady Eddie jobs and become a suit in an executive office somewhere. Naw, that would be too predictable. Those folk don't understand the thrill of walking out on the high wire without a net. They're far too smart and conservative for that. "Hell, what if I try and fail?" Much safer to stay put in this job and hold on for dear life. So you periodically mull over all of the brilliant ideas you've heard lately and decide which ones are the best ones to pursue.

You replay all of your recent job interviews and try to figure out what you did right or wrong. You get fantastic feedback from a meeting thinking you've made a new friend inside the walls and then absolutely nothing happens. Phone calls aren't returned. Letters or e-mail goes unanswered. What happened? Is my tuning fork so out of whack that I missed all of the obvious signs? The silence becomes deafening. If you are prone to being discouraged, there is no lack of negative reinforcement readily available to help point you to the nearest ledge.

One of my early breaks was becoming the Associate Producer (AP) in charge of Post Production on *The Paper Chase*, an idea that had started as a novel, became an award winning film. The subsequent TV series moved from CBS prime time after one season to reruns on PBS. A few years later, Showtime produced three more seasons. The series had lost its steam primarily because the aging star was pre-dementia and other leads were going bald from having been in TV law school for seven or eight years.

I'll never forget going to the producer's office on the studio lot and watching a man practice his putting all day. By the fourth or fifth season, a TV series gets into a smooth rhythm and there are very few surprises. At six o'clock, he would go down to the set and at six thirty would pull the plug so he could be home in time for dinner. I thought, "Gee, producing looks easy enough. I think I can handle it."

Waking up now a quarter of a century later, I somehow feel like there's a big face outside the glass aquarium looking in on a tiny baby hooked up to life support. I tap on the glass and try to get the younger me, the very fragile me's attention. I want to wave and say encouraging things like, "You're okay, hang in there kiddo. You're going to make it. Help is on the way. You're just a phone call away from getting the job you've been waiting for" and the be-all, end-all, best ever catch-all lie, "Everything is going to be all right."

It's about the time you hear that phrase that you'd really better start worrying.

Sometimes these clichés from the older me have a hollow ring to them and sometimes I can say them with absolute conviction. Feast or famine. You have to get used to the fact that your entire life can turn on a dime. Of the five or ten projects you are waiting for somebody to make a damned decision about, it usually turns out to be a phone call from left field inquiring about your availability and could you come by this afternoon to meet so-and so? Once again, everything is in Fate's hands.

So you jump on board a moving train that is often careening downhill sans brakes and get right to work. You try to keep as many of your options alive because you know this current gig won't last forever. Never does in this business (unless you happen to be producing *Jeopardy* or *Wheel of Fortune.*)

The search continues to find that ultimate producing gig where I collect a big paycheck every week, work on perfecting my office putting, and get home at a regular hour in time for dinner.

CROSSING THE CHANNEL

You've been told that this is the best place to get a glimpse. You drop a few coins into the mini-telescope, point it across the water until you can make out a shimmering island on the horizon where fame and fortune are rumored to dwell. Yep, that's for me. You glance around to see scads of fellow dreamers blithely running headlong over the cliff. Looks like a pretty steep drop. You don't want to be labeled, "chicken." After all, you've told everyone you know you were going to do it. So you remove most vestiges of your previous life and take the plunge.

After the initial smack wears off, you have to struggle to the surface for that all-important next lung-full of air. You congratulate yourself for having survived. Peels of laughter and splashing all around momentarily allows you to ignore a couple of dead bodies bobbing to the surface. Strangers who didn't make the initial cut. Too bad for them. Now that you're in the water, where do we go from here?

You get your bearings and spot the island an impossible distance away. All you have to do is somehow figure out a way to get there. A few others head for the safety of shore because they quickly realize they're not going to make it. Maybe those are the smart people, you think to yourself, and maybe you should follow their lead. They came, they saw and they got out fast before their fate was sealed. You ignore all that because you have a date with destiny. The journey of a thousand nautical miles beginning with the first breaststroke? backstroke? etc.

The weather is deceptive out here in LaLa Land. You calculate how many years you're willing to invest in this process of getting where you want to go. You decide you're still young enough and strong enough to make the crossing intacto. There are lots of other heads in front of you swimming towards the same destination and there are still people jumping off the cliff behind you so the survival instinct kicks in and you begin moving in the right direction.

You continue to churn through the water with strong, powerful strokes. You try to avoid bumping into people who stop without warning. They decide to rest because swimming is tiring. It's hard work. After many hours, you wonder if you're in one of those exercise tanks where a steady stream of water shoots past as you swim in place because whenever you look up, that damn island doesn't seem to be getting any closer. You don't seem to be making very much headway.

Occasionally you have to rest. You stop, go underwater and enjoy that otherworldly silence. It's as though time is standing still in some liquefied reality. There is a faint buzzing sound off in the distance that you don't recognize but as you pop up for air and tread water for awhile, you wonder if you have what it takes. Rested and refreshed, you begin swimming again with renewed vigor. That annoying buzz seems to be getting a little louder.

You are startled by the occasional shark swimming by from time to time feeding off those who have decided to make treading water a way of life. They stayed too long in one place. There is usually a yelp or a gurgle, a wave goodbye as they disappear from sight. Yes, it's discouraging but at the same time motivating. Survival of the fittest. After all, the pod is thinning out in front of you. You're at the halfway point so you're damned if you do and damned if you try to go back. "Miles to go before you sleep" and all that poetic rot. As W.C. Fields said about drinking, "Quitting's easy. Why I've done it a thousand times." It's much easier to quit than to continue expending precious time and energy in pursuit of a dream that you have no idea if it will ever pay off.

So you decide to keep pounding away, learning your craft, measuring yourself against all the others who also decided to continue on. There is a camaraderie among the hearty band of souls who pursue a mutual dream. They recognize a fellow survivor when they meet one. You share war stories and shake your head wondering, "What was I thinking when I jumped off that cliff? Shoulda had my head examined."

The buzzing noise gets louder. A tiny speck approaches from an oblique angle to where you are. As the shapes come into focus you recognize the speedboat. A rescue boat? The lift you've been waiting for? As it gets closer you can make out the details of the expensive craft. It's seems to be skimming across the surface of the water kicking up a rooster tail and it's heading right for you. You start waving your hands to let them know you are there. Surely they'll see you and stop to help?

They barrel along and you suddenly realize that you're about to become chum in their propellers unless you take evasive action. Just at the last second before you dive out of harms way, you catch a glimpse of the boat's passengers. It's those grinning kids in daddy's boat, out joyriding. With their perfect teeth, beautiful babes in skimpy bathing suits, sipping their mai tais, out for a lark. Not a care in the world.

Hell, they own the island and we are but the newest crop of interlopers who are always trying to find a way in. Good help is still hard to find and god knows they're not going to get their hands dirty if they don't have to.

If given the chance, you'd like to think you'll be different from them but you won't really know 'til you get there, will you?

Oh, what a sight we must be when we finally drag ourselves up on that beach. Tattered clothing, half-starving, exhausted, desperately in need of a shave. Now that we're here, now that we understand how this game is played, a whole new set of challenges awaits us but at least we're among the lucky few who made it across that damn channel. You can't help but look back across the expanse and way off in the distance you think you see the place where you started from. You can't believe it but people are still jumping off that damned cliff.

You shake your head in wonder and think, "This channel crossing is a bitch, ain't it? " Suddenly a boat horn goes off in your ear. An announcer's voice booms out over the PA system out on the beach, "Now that you've arrived, you've qualified as a contestant on Fame or Fortune? where no two games are exactly alike. Pay attention as we explain the rules ... there are no rules! The clock has started ticking and good luck!"

A HISTORY LESSON

What do I have to do to succeed in this business?
Be standing in the right pace at the right time, have a relative in high places who will usher you in the back door, marry someone who has relatives in high places, be the son or daughter of someone famous, date someone famous, be the college roommate of someone who becomes famous, write (or option) a best selling novel, make a low budget movie that gets a theatrical release and earns a fortune. These are the easiest ways to reach the top of the heap.

Very few people find this mountain to be an easy climb. Some lucky few are deposited halfway up the hill via chopper, but because Showbiz is essentially a meritocracy, they also have to struggle to reach the top. Their cushion is that whenever the going gets too tough, they can always call in the chopper again to deposit them elsewhere while the rest of us continue the climb because there is no cushion and we're too old to turn back. We willingly pay our dues and are often required to contribute the extra pound of flesh.

When does a person stop paying their dues?
Not until you're clutching your gold statue, are ensconced in Bel Air or entombed in Forest Lawn.

It gets increasingly harder as one gets older in a youth obsessed culture. Unless you've made it to the other side of the ravine where the winners dwell, it seems the more you know, the less valuable you become.

To go above and beyond the call of duty is expected of you. Mediocre ideas and half-assed efforts are reserved for those who have it made and don't have to try so hard anymore. From you, the un-rich, the un-powerful or un-famous, they want cartwheels on the front lawn, 24/7/365 and occasionally blood. If you are mildly amusing and play the fawning sycophant really well, you're allowed to stick around, suck up their excess oxygen and enjoy a few scraps from the banquet table. If you're great at your job, you will be allowed to stick around as long as it pleases the court. The minute they find a younger person with great ambition at half your salary, they'll unhitch your broken carcass from the plow you've been pulling because you, my friend, are "history."

Discouraging? Depressing? Frustrating? Despair? These words don't begin to cover the depth of emotional outrage at the injustice of it all. Welcome to The School of Hard Knocks. Let's see if you have what it takes. The tram departs every fifteen minutes, brimming with hopefuls and wannabes. All aboard!

Through this dark assessment emerges the truth. We are here because we want to be. We are trying to do something special with our lives as opposed to consigning ourselves to some mind-numbing career in the corporate jungle, leading quiet but boring lives of desperation. We're taking a chance on us. Practically nobody else in the world believes we will succeed in this very tough business.

Somewhere along the line you will realize that simply taking the journey is the joy. Never knowing what lies ahead is terrifically exciting. Making friends with fellow gamblers along the way is exhilarating as no two stories are alike. Everybody in Showbiz has lotto fever, the gambling jones that makes people put up with an incredible amount of bullshit and disappointment on their way to accomplishing amazing things.

You have to keep one eye on the foreground and one eye on the horizon, never losing sight of where you want to go. The goal is to get where you want to go retaining some semblance of the ethics and morals you started with, while stepping on as few warm bodies along the way. To accomplish this, you have to learn how to enjoy the daily climb or you, my friend, will soon be history.

THE MAYBE DANCE

Been to the "Maybe Dance" more than I care to admit. At last count, I'm involved with no less than a dozen possible productions of all different sizes and budgets. They are all floating around the "Maybe Dance" looking for a) the rest of the money - which usually means all or half of the required dough, b) the right talent in front of and/ or behind the camera, c) a distribution outlet that will provide assurances to the financiers that they have a fighting chance of getting their money back, d) a script rewrite that will satisfy the star who will trigger the distribution deal that will trigger the bank loan or venture capitalist to start the engine, e) the business affairs people to complete the deal with the talent's lawyers, agent, business manager, partner so that they are officially on board so that all of the above can be triggered.

There's a growing list of folk I'd like to see triggered.

Nobody seems to want to make a definitive decision anymore.

"What if I'm wrong? What if I make a mistake and cost somebody some money? I'll be so embarrassed and worse, I might lose face!" If nobody makes a decision, everything twirls around in place until the clock is about to strike midnight and suddenly, at the very last minute, just when the train is about to leave to leave the station, somebody finally comes down from the mountaintop carrying the tablets that say, "Yes, we go", "No, we stop" or "Hold on while we procrastinate some more!"

It is nothing short of maddening. Those in power say, "Let 'em wait while I eat a little more cake and think about things," or don't think about things as is usually the case. "Let everybody cool their jets until I feel like making this decision. I need to consult with my advisors, manager, handler, agent, bookie, spouse, shrink, and astrologer because god forbid, I make a decision by myself! Rest assured, if things turn out right, I'll take all the credit and make most of the dough, but if they don't, I want to see blood on a lot of other people's hands so I'm not the only schmuck standing there holding the bag."

My theory has always been to go ahead and make the damn decision and if it's wrong, do your best to rectify it before too many other people notice.

The so-called decision makers simply procrastinate you to death. In fact, it often takes somebody they know dying before they feel their mortality and realize that time's awasting. At any given moment, there are hundreds of projects trapped in the Showbiz limbo known as Development Hell. And finally, when the various corporate department prognosticators (home video, foreign sales, TV sales) chime in and the company is theoretically in the black, then maybe they'll decide to take a chance on your project. By then, you usually want to tie them all up in a hefty bag and drop them off a pier someplace.

Where the hell are the true gamblers anymore? Where are the people who bet with their guts and more importantly, their own money without waiting for Market Research to confirm their decisions? Seems like most people in the corporate upper echelons are wedded to the concept of "plausible deniability." If something should go awry, they can always point to the blue chippers involved with any project and the Market Research report that supported their decision. "How was I to know that everything would go in the crapper? Look at all this data. How could it be wrong?" What they really mean is, "Please, please, don't blame me and send me back to the sidewalk! It's awfully cold out there and I don't function well in an unpaid, unstructured environment where anything can happen to poor little me!"

Goddamn cowards! CYA (cover your ass) should be tattooed on their foreheads. I stopped blaming them individually but rather the system that fostered them. Looking back on the Golden Age of Hollywood, Adolph Zukor, Louie Mayer, Sam Goldwyn, Carl Laemmle, Harry Cohn, David O. Selznick, Thomas Ince, the Warner Brothers, these guys would be turning over in their graves at 2500 rpms if they knew what happened to their amazing baby. Each of these moguls began in some other business that dealt directly with the public. They developed a sense of what was needed to build a relationship with a satisfied customer before they got the itch and brought their street smarts to the Showbiz game. They had hunches about people and projects and bet the ranch on them. Hell, Sid Graumann lost the world famous Chinese Theater in a card game!

Now the Executive branch is filled with wunderkinds who land right out of Harvard or Stanford Business Schools into the rarefied air inside the studio vacuum. No real world experience to start with. Not knowing which end of the camera to look through and yet making decisions by committee about which projects get the green light and which ones die in the cradle. And this is only after every possible excuse has been used up about why nobody wants to make a f*@!#ing decision.

Here's a news flash! – the Executive Branch doesn't trust the artistic types. The feeling is mutual as the artistic types don't appreciate the creative bookkeeping that keeps the Executive Branch functioning. The decision makers are schooled in "risk avoidance." They avoid even going to the "Maybe Dance" unless the semblance of the sure thing comes along. In case anybody's looking at the big picture, after all their Market Research and hemming and hawing, they're perpetuating a system that guesses wrong most of the time

I've been to the "Maybe Dance" with a wide variety of projects featuring a myriad of colorful partners. I got to hang around famous big shots and some absolutely charming snake oil salesmen. "Pie in the sky! Rich beyond your wildest dreams! This is a can't-miss proposition! I'll buy you a big house in Beverly Hills if you make this work!" are all phrases I've heard tossed around like confetti. Some of the best experiences and coolest people are alive and well down there. You just have to learn how to separate the truth from the BS.

Once you get away from the Studio system and are looking for independent financing, you will learn that there are a thousand reasons not to write the check to finance a project. Sometimes it's bad timing. A few years back, the SARS epidemic in Hong Kong knocked out financing for a $10 million "go" movie I was supposed to produce. California earthquakes, fires or mudslides in Malibu and any other natural disaster have stopped or altered many a financing scheme. Seems that on the day when the contract is supposed to be signed or the check delivered, a variety of things can go wrong. Usually it is a (fill in the blank) _____ wife, lawyer, accountant or business manager who says, "Stop the Bus! What are you, crazy? I'm not letting you invest in this or that project."

Unfortunately, this last minute kibitzing usually takes place after a lot of hope, spit, chewing gum, smoke and mirrors have been applied to keep the proposition alive. Why do we keep hope alive? Because every once in awhile, the stars align themselves just so, somebody got lucky in bed last night, somebody won the lottery, somebody died, somebody had a revelation in a dream or that tiny voice inside finally screamed, "Let's do something, damnit!"

There's only two reasons to write the check – hope for a gain and fear of a loss. Hope for a gain is for the suckers outside the tent. Fear of a loss is what mostly drives those inside the tent. Nothing means nothing until somebody is able to cash a check at the bank and actually turn on the ignition switch. So you wanna be a producer? Welcome to the "Maybe Dance."

CHAPTER 5

HOPE, SMOKE, CHEWING GUM & MIRRORS

ON THE BUBBLE

I went in for a job interview at Paramount on Monday afternoon. Got dressed up, even wore a tie for the occasion. I had done my homework and read the script, came up with a bunch of questions and comments to demonstrate that I knew how to put this very difficult project together and that I was interested in the task. Having hired thousands of people during my career, there is a delicate balance between seeming too eager and letting the person on the other side of the table know you'd really like the job. It's a quick judgment call to appear confident but not cocky. Part of my homework is to look up the credits (if they have any) of the person you're being interviewed by on IMDB.Com. (International Movie Database) If they're a recent Stamford graduate or Bryn Mawr Girl, chances are they aren't listed. In this case, it was an old war dog with a lot of credits. It always helps if you can throw a reference or two into the conversation just to let them know you cared enough to check them out.

You have a scant thirty minutes to make a good impression because other candidates are in the waiting room, stacked up like airplanes waiting to land. You always want to be the first interviewee for a project because they measure what follows against you. If you can't be first, try to go last when all of the other candidates have turned into oatmeal and you suddenly seem like the breath of fresh air that will rescue them from the abyss. You try to make them laugh to demonstrate a sense of humor. You try to be interactive and make eye contact with everyone in the room while you're speaking. Pick out the most important person and focus on them but don't totally ignore anybody else who happens to be there because oftentimes they influence the decision that determines your fate.

I once witnessed a million dollar job go out the window for a director because the secretary told her boss that she used to work for the guy and he just chased her around the desk. A young secretary took down a very qualified candidate who happened to have a problem with his zipper. Hint: always be nice to the secretaries and assistants because they can knock you out of the box with comments like, "What's with that guys hair or bad breath?" The other important thing to remember is the assistants often end up with the interviewers job somewhere down the road and everyone has long memories, especially for bad first impressions.

In the one-hour episodic dramatic pilot business, which happens to be one of my strengths, the opportunities are few and far between these days because of the cheaper, faster reality waves that keep pounding the shore. Dull-eyed, pretty young people prancing around, saying stupid things in their underwear about their shallow unlived lives. You'd think there's an IQ limit for all of these contestants. Anybody in triple digits need not apply, unless of course it was *The Apprentice.*

And after you leave any job interview, you kick yourself and say, "Why didn't I mention this credit or that person we have in common or that show you loved ten years ago?" Hindsight with 20/20. You can't worry about it because you know the odds are against you from the gitgo. There's always a candidate of equal value out there who has worked for this studio or company before, has photos of someone in action, any number of reasons that when push comes to shove, they get the nod. Not being pessimistic, just realistic.

I once had to choose between two blonde female Art Directors for a six episode half-hour comedy for Castlerock. They had equivalent resumes and checked out equally well. I went with the gal who interviewed with a bird in her hair. She had a collection of different headbands and clip-ons that all featured a different little bird sitting atop her head. She was absolutely terrific and went on to do some very big features. Saw her mug in the trades standing between two recognizable stars at the Sundance Film Festival promoting the film she had directed that was getting a lot of attention. The birds had been replaced by a reggae hairdo and granny glasses, but I definitely gave her the job because of the birds. After all, the person doing the choosing usually picks someone they'll be comfortable inviting into their lives for the next couple of months. Regardless of the credits, most of the decision making simply boils down to personal chemistry.

After a great interview, you occupy your time ignoring the potentially great new job that will make your better half very happy and take care of your finances for the next couple of years. You yearn to find out if you got the job. My agent called with some follow-up news that I'm in the running. It's between me and one other guy. The fact that this other guy's brother is one of the biggest power brokers in show business is not good news. One phone call from big brother promising favors in the future and my goose is cooked. I didn't do anything wrong other than not having a powerful brother, (or other well-placed relative) to grease the runway for my arrival.

I tell the little man inside who wants to jump up and down like Rocky Balboa to go back and sit on the bench. Maybe next time. Having had my hopes dashed on the rocks on so many other occasions, I've learned to be cautiously optimistic and firmly believe that if the job and I were destined for each other, it'll happen. In the meantime, every time the phone rings the little man jumps up, comes running up to forefront with an expectant grin awaiting the word. [†]

Hell, if this doesn't work, maybe I'll hitch a ride with one of those reality shows surrounded by the dull-eyed scantily clad kids. Maybe next job interview I'll go buy a stuffed bird and put it on my shoulder. Gotta have a story to go along with it. "That's Artie. He goes with me to every job interview. Got me to give up smoking and I owe him my life. My lucky charm. Say hello to my little friend, Artie". Then you throw your voice and Artie starts talking to them and pretty soon they're laughing their asses off and if you don't get the job, at least you'll have made a lasting first impression.

THE AGE THING

Another birthday has snuck up. Oh, you see them coming from miles away and your heart is either filled with dread or glee. You blink your eyes a few times and it suddenly arrives. After a while, it's not as if reaching one of these minor milestones significantly rocks your world. In the ancient history department, hitting 16 or 21, that was something special. Youth was like the Oklahoma Land Rush! Every day began with a starters pistol, running, tumbling, pitching headlong into the great unknown of your adult life. Couldn't wait for it to arrive.

I landed in LaLa Land at the tender age of 22, stars in my eyes, clutching my film school diploma like some kind of magic talisman used to ward off evil spirits and not knowing a blessed thing about

---

[†]The word arrived and unfortunately my realistic side was correctamundo. Tough luck. Their loss. Better luck next time.

PS. The pilot failed. $6m down the drain. Too, too bad.

how to get into the game. I was totally unprepared to be in this marathon, so I just started running.

Hitting the big Three-O with a wife, child, and two mortgages was a bucket of cold water in the face. The herd I had started with thinned to a pack. Most had wised up, pulled up stakes and returned to the real world. At 30 you've still got youth, vitality, and enough experience to convince yourself that you actually know something. Older people would say, "Let the kid do it." Hitting 40 was looking around at the handful of friends I knew from the old days and wondering what happened. Lots more experience under the old belt, a belt that no longer fits the pants one is currently wearing. Cops and doctors are suddenly ten years younger than you. Production execs making decisions about your life look like somebody's younger brother, barely old enough to shave.

Just when I'd discovered how to make a decent living producing one-hour action dramas, they changed the rules. Forty percent of the TV dramas in Hollywood evaporated and relocated to other states or countries. Believe me, after you've moved 36 times in 33 years, glamorous new settings become less than alluring. The gypsy blood still answers the call but with a little less enthusiasm each time. It's nice sleeping in your own bed.

Hitting 50 was an Arctic blast. You take stock and are amazed to still be sitting at life's big blackjack table saying, "Hit me!" A bunch of fellow crazy people have turned up along the way but only one or two remain from the original gang. Long ago you learned there's no rhyme or reason to it. We are but talented leafs blowing around in a mysterious wind, always hoping to get lucky. The most important thing is to hold on tight to the ones you love and respect those who make you laugh and cry. They are the treasure chests of knowledge and surprises who every day teach you new things about this life and make it all worth living.

At dawn, you hope today is the day you get the call or have that chance meeting that will send you back into the fray. You're mentally prepared for just about anything. You push forward on any number of fronts, taking meetings, making phone calls, creating budgets and writing scripts. At the end of that special day, a loved one plunks a birthday card or cake in front of you. You stop; grab a quick look in the mirror to see if anything significant has changed since yesterday. Will anybody notice you've hung another year on the line? Nope. Still here. Still ticking ... " Hit me!"

BECAUSE YOU NEVER KNOW

My sister in-law works in the art world in Santa Fe, New Mexico, a small town of 60,000 people that features over two hundred art galleries. She said that the employees are instructed to treat everyone who crosses the threshold well. The reason is that more often than not, the person with the ill-fitting clothes, bad haircut and body odor who checks out the inventory will often step up to the cash register and plunk down a check for five or six figures to buy something that has caught their fancy.

"Because you never know!" is my standard reply when my better half asks why I am meeting with this or that person. Opportunities come in a wide variety of packages, no two exactly alike. I wish there was a fast, easy way to determine if what the stranger across the table says is true, half true, almost true or they just hope will soon be true.

Usually these initial meetings take place over a cup of java or a meal. It would be nice if you could carry around a "Bullshit-ometer" that measured other people's brain waves, heart rates, and auras before the check arrived. That way you would know whether: A) to be magnanimous and pick up the check because you definitely want to see this person again, B) let the check sit on the table for as long as possible because it's bad enough you stayed here for this amount of time but now you want I should pay for it too? C) go "dutch" which is a polite way of saying, "I'll take care of mine and you yours and let's do this again sometime." Hint: when somebody is talking about a multi-million dollar deal and doesn't, can't, won't pick up the tab, run, don't walk to the nearest exit. Another great tip-off is when they ask about the local bus schedule.

Everybody in Showbiz has a piece or a couple of pieces of the puzzle. Do you immediately hit it off with somebody like two peas in some reincarnation pod or is it instant dislike? The interesting thing is that if you've hung around this betting parlor for any amount of time, you've been screwed over by your new best friend at least once and the person you didn't instantly click with has become a good friend. You never know.

What you will quickly discover is that sitting at home by the phone, waiting for opportunity to call, isn't a great game plan. It usually ends up with a skeleton covered in cobwebs with one bony hand resting on the receiver. Waiting sucks. Quality thinking time, reading (or writing) a good book and hanging around with loved ones is a good use of time. You never know what brand spanking new opportunities are out there with your name on it unless you step on the gas and get yourself into traffic.

On several occasions in the past, someone would look at me and say, "You have to meet so-and-so." I would say, "They sound very interesting" and then immediately get caught up in other things. Six months later, somebody entirely different would arrive and say, "You have to meet so-and-so!" It would be the same so-and-so but it was two different messengers. I would immediately stop whatever I was doing and make arrangements to meet so-and-so because more often than not, they had a piece of the puzzle I needed or we were destined to become good friends.

I no longer need to be hit up the side of the head with a 2'x 4'. When somebody says I really ought to meet so-and-so, I try to make it happen ASAP. Naturally, every meeting doesn't turn out great. You don't hit a home run every time at bat.

The wonderful, exciting, energizing, amazing thing about this business is you never know. I was sitting next to a young guy in the audience at a NATPE seminar (National Association of Television Production Executives) whose convention is held annually in Las

Vegas. The seminar was about the future of branding and creating alternative revenue sources. I mentioned that a certain panelist looked drunk. We laughed about this and eventually he told me that it was his boss I was dissing. They had been out drinking until 2am. Turned out the big law firm in LA that he worked for was sponsoring the panel. We continued to chat and got together back in LA. After a few meetings, one of his VC (venture capital) associates agreed to help arrange for their investment group to throw eight figures at the production company I was the President of. I'll get a sliver of the deal, if and when it goes through, and finally be able to buy the missus that new house.

It just goes to show that – you never know.

THE BEST ANGLE OF APPROACH

If you don't happen to be one of the fortunate few who arrive in Hollywood with a reservoir of money and get to buy their way to the front of the line, you'll have to figure out the best angle of approach if you want to get into the game. As with any attempt to succeed with the opposite sex, your charm and good looks will only take you so far. If this isn't just a fleeting series of one night stands and you really, really intend to stick around and make a go of it, there needs to be an overarching plan that is flexible enough to take advantage of the opportunities when they materialize, learn from your mistakes and believe in yourself more than anything or anybody else.

When you don't know anyone, driving around Los Angeles the first time, scoping out the impenetrable fortresses known as The Studios, figuring out how to scale the walls is a daunting task. Perseverance separates those who realize their dreams from those who don't. For the independent producer, getting paid half a year to work on one big project or taking on a variety of little projects is regarded as being successful. The other half of the year is spent moving around from vineyard to vineyard, hustling up the next gig, working your butt off in short spurts, "taking lots of lunches", chasing rumors, learning as much as you can about that elusive thing called "success", and literally praying for work.

The birth of any project is a painful process. The producer usually assumes the roles of mother, mid-wife and expectant father. One of the most fascinating aspects of the game is that nobody is ever quite sure how the baby is going to turn out. Often the race-horse that was originally envisioned goes through many filters and gets transformed into the proverbial camel, leaving the marketing folk to figure out what to do with it. It's hard to comprehend a business where a small independent $35,000 black and white, home-videoish *Blair Witch Project* out-grosses a whole passel of $100 million, star-studded extravaganzas produced by the best and brightest talents in the business. Who'd a thunk it possible? It's Hollywood, baby, where anything can happen!

Tens of millions of people bask in the nightly glow of *E.T.*, *Access Hollywood*, *Extra*, *Extra*, *Celebrity Justice*, *The Insider*, *The Tonight Show*, etc., etc. Stars are modern day royalty or, in some cases, Olympian gods. At least that's what their publicity machines would have you believe. Hollywood is Shangri-lala land and if nothing else, the spin-doctors and plastic surgeons have done a fantastic job of erecting terrific looking façades. It's the greatest smoke-and-mirrors act in the world. The glamour, excitement and glittery magnet that is Hollywood attracts 14,000,000 tourists to Tinseltown each year. Countless magazines and specialty publications about Showbiz life attest to a growing audience interest in everything Hollywood. Entertainment is one of America's top exports. It's not only the filter of how we look at ourselves but it influences how the rest of the world sees us as well.

Once you've embarked on this journey, you'll meet all kinds of dreamers and schemers who populate an Alice Through The Looking Glass world. You'll definitely learn the painful truth about most of the 'geniuses' that make the decisions as to what is seen down at your local theater or on TV tonight. As it has been repeatedly proven, they are all just guessing and keeping their fingers crossed that something hits the target before their time at their current job is over. And these are the lucky people inside the studio walls who control the major media outlets to the sea.

Nobody tells the next wave of young producers, writers, actors, directors, and cinematographers how hard it is to have a career. There are the obvious and not-so-obvious pitfalls awaiting anyone who thinks it's all a lot of fun and one quick leap to the podium to pick up their gold statue. Chances are, if you're not connected, are impatient or short on diplomatic skills, you won't make it as a producer. There are, of course, some well-known exceptions with gold statues on their mantelpieces who have that "go-for-the-jugular" mentality that it often takes to reach the top of any business. It's not the only way to succeed but it still works.

Regardless, a successful producer has to grow a thick hide because the slings and arrows are coming. You learn to listen to that little voice inside that is actually making the decisions. It got you this far. You have to be daring and try things you didn't think you ever could. You need to really learn how to read people correctly. Understand that everyone has an agenda and you are being judged on your ability to help them, not vice versa. You'll have to develop various skill-sets that'll see you through the hard times because the hard times are coming.

Most people who get to plant their flag atop this mountain have gotten there through hard work, perseverance, getting lucky and an unshakeable belief in themselves. For my money, it is the best angle of approach.

Good News, Bad News

No matter what position you've attained in the showbiz pecking order, sometimes the phrase, "You got the job!" can be both good news and bad news. You've opened your mouth during the interview process and said things like, "No problem. I can handle that. Piece of cake." Someone on the receiving end took comfort in your assurances, actually believed you and gave you the job you were auditioning for.

The good news is that you are going to make some money. People in showbiz get paid well for working hard. The average work week is 60 hours. The higher up the food chain, the greater the pressure to perform. When you compare what some people get paid for what appears to be hardly working at all to what people earn in the outside world, it truly can be deceiving. The top of the pyramid in any business is filled with rich people. They that have the money make the rules. Not surprisingly, the rules are usually slanted in their favor.

A Japanese shoe company wanted to shoot a commercial with a particular superstar whom they were willing to pay a million dollars to for one morning's work. They wanted to make things as easy as possible so they pitched the following idea: the crew would show up at the superstar's home, shoot one shot and be gone in less than two hours. The shot consisted of a close up of their shoes and the camera would pan up to find the grinning superstar leaning against his garage door, giving the thumbs up sign. The superstar turned them down.

It was unfathomable that someone who had started in the chorus line would turn down more money than most people earn in their lifetime for one mornings "work", if you could really call it that. I couldn't understand it at the time but I came to realize that a) he didn't really need the money, b) he simply didn't want to dilute his value in some foreign market by endorsing just another pair of shoes. If they had been the Rolls Royce of shoes, maybe. If he was doing somebody a favor, fine. He couldn't be any more famous than he already was and besides, why take a chance of being associated with a pair of shoes that could possibly fall apart in the first rainstorm?

A lot of Hollywood celebrities and international sports stars pick up extra money doing liquor commercials or other ads for the foreign markets with the stipulation that they will never be shown in the U.S. It's a little perk that goes with fame.

For every one of the hard-working showbiz survivors who made it through the shoals and actually figured out a way to make a living in this feast or famine world, there are thousands of talented ship-wrecked dreamers who couldn't or wouldn't adapt to this strange new environment. Oh, they're still out there pumping gas in San Bernadino, back working in daddy's store or maybe lost themselves in a bottle along life's highway but things just didn't work out the way they had hoped for.

The bad news in this equation often takes the form of some incompetent asshole telling you how to do your job. In Vietnam, newly minted junior officers who didn't adapt quickly to the jungle, were occasionally fragged by their own men. In Showbiz, do you punch the jerk or grab their throat when they say or do the next stupid thing or do you grin and bear it? It usually depends on how badly you need the job.

The scariest part of the bad news is that since you opened your big mouth and got the job, you have to go out and prove it or eat your words. This is a very unforgiving game. Although your work isn't in the everyday public eye like a ballplayer might be, Hollywood is a small town and the word gets around pretty quickly when you're a liar, an asshole or a thief.

It takes physical stamina to succeed in this business. Long hours are the norm. People in the 9-5 world don't have a clue what is asked of the crew nor should they. Many of them think the actors make up the words as they go along. They don't care about the millions of dollars, the thousands upon thousands of decisions that went into the making of their favorite movie or TV show. They turn on their TV or go to the movies because they want to be temporarily enter-tained.

In a game full of smoke and mirrors, princes and posers, the person who earns a reputation for living up to their word and exceeding the expectations of the people who hire them becomes valuable. If they can consistently tell a good story that entertains the target audience, they become invaluable. If you can't adapt, have an inflated opinion of yourself or don't perform when under the gun, you will be shown the exit door in a hurry.

That's the good news and the bad news in a nutshell.

CHAPTER 6

WHIMSY

OVER THE FALLS

Almost everyone in Showbiz has had some non-com ask what it's like to be in "The Biz!" It took awhile to determine up from down, right from left and sort of figure out how to make a living but when I reflect back on my journey, it's best to begin at the beginning. Here's my humble attempt to answer the aforementioned question.

An adventurous trip has been promised, so you climb aboard an oversized cruise ship, eyes wide, cheeks flushed with excitement and the journey begins. You stroll the decks exchanging pleasantries with anyone who will talk with you and the low rumbling noise in the distance is dismissed as thunder. You read the trades and find out who is getting some award at what gala festival, who is going to what fancy dinner party that you weren't invited to, who sold what idea for how much, who is suing whom, etc.

You're generally feeling buoyant about being on the fringes, one day soon to be included in all that fame, fortune and fun you've heard about. The ominous noise in the background grows louder as your bank account grows slimmer. The sound of gnashing rocks can be heard. You try to ignore it as long as you can but eventually your reverie is disrupted. "What the hell is that?"

As you head for the front of the boat, others stream past with a wild look in their eyes going in the opposite direction. Common sense dictates that you should turn around and join in the retreat and yet you continue forward like a moth drawn to the flame. Having passed the security of the cabins and the stately staterooms, that you are fully confident to someday soon be occupying, you finally reach the bow of the boat and step out into the glorious sunshine where you are immediately engulfed by a liquid cacophony of noise.

Your view is obscured by the giant churning water immediately ahead. As you reach the railing, all thoughts of running away depart, your fear replaced by fascination as the waters temporarily part and the most beautiful sight you can ever imagine overwhelms the senses. There before you is your glorious future, hobnobbing with the swells, millions of dollars being tossed around like confetti, handsome men and beautiful women running around like hot and cold water, your name up in lights, the envy of all the small-minded rubes back home who didn't recognize your genius early on. And just as you're getting comfortable with this picture ... the bottom drops out!

The boat ride has taken a decidedly wicked turn going vertical instead of horizontal and you find yourself plunging headfirst into the icy waters below. Self-preservation takes over and you realize you have to get clear of that damn boat because if it crashes down on top of you, you will be a goner. And so you push off with all your strength leaping into the watery void. There is the most terrible gut-wrenching sound ever heard, the air punctuated by yells and screams ... and then nothing.

As you sink into the watery grave that awaits you, a decision gets made and you fight like hell to reach the surface one more time. The dream is shattered, the illusion replaced with the only thing that matters, getting one more lung full of air. As you struggle to reach the surface, you are dodging a variety of objects sinking to the bottom, steel beams bent in half, shattered wood and broken dreams. Lucky for you, one last gasp of the dying engine envelopes your body and propels you toward the light.

You explode to the surface, look around at the other people gasping for air, and then, (just like in *Titanic*) they begin disappearing all around you ... and then nothing. Temporarily deaf, dumb and blind, you spit the water out of your lungs. The loud churning of the falls you have just plunged over recedes into the distance as you float downstream, a limp dishrag that barely resembles the person you once were such a short time ago. Every now and then you see another head bobbing up and down. Other survivors swept along by the same strong current. You call out to them and wave. They respond and slowly you all head for shore.

Upon arriving in Lala land, you drag your broken carcass out of the water and check for damage. Miraculously the body has survived the fall but the mind has forever been altered. Nothing is as before. The world has been turned upside down. Right is wrong and vice versa. A couple of hand-painted signs are posted on trees reading, "Justice is for those who can afford it!" and "Signing a contract is the first step to any lawsuit".

Until you become a power to be reckoned with, you learn that your guaranteed percentage of hard earned, back end profits is akin to buying swampland in Florida during hurricane season. You either make the adjustment to this new set of rules or you die. As has previously been noted, there is no boat to rock. It's sink or swim. Nobody loves ya, baby! Then you begin to search for people of a like mind. Sometimes it's a wink or a nod, sometimes it's reading between the lines but you find them. Fellow survivors who aren't happy about the status quo and wish to do something about it. There must be a better way to achieve the dream.

And so the conspirators gather ...

WELCOME TO THE NUTHOUSE

I dreamed last night about an aging philanthropist (John Cleese type) with a crazy but beautiful 20 year old daughter, Magda (young Audrey Hepburn-type), who wants more than anything in the world to be a movie star. A sanitarium on the outskirts of Los Angeles is purchased and overhauled to look like a movie studio. Oasis Pictures is born. They advertise in the trade papers for out of work actors and other wannabes to fill in the rest of the parts. Actors from the Old Actors Home are bussed in each day to play different roles.

This phony studio comes to life and pretty soon the actors all believe that they really are the roles that they have been hired to play. Magda waltzes around and fulfills her leading lady dreams. There are makeup and wardrobe people flitting about, acting coaches with foreign accents, tap dancing lessons, gymnastics, fencing lessons. She is taught how to ride a horse, swing on vines, and perform her own stunts. Magda is preparing herself for future stardom until the day she falls in love with Johnny, a handsome newcomer, whom she reads with at an audition.

Johnny is mightily attracted to the boss' beautiful daughter but knows she's crazy and that Oasis Pictures is all a sham. When he confesses that he can't keep playing his part because it's unfortunately the closest he'll come to realizing his own dream, he tearfully quits and returns to his job as a waiter in a fancy Beverly Hills restaurant. Magda is heartbroken and everyone at the studio goes into a mini-depression with her. It's as if some great tragedy has befallen them all.

It's the original sanitarium superintendent, Dr. Moe Howard, who had agreed to the conversion if he got to play a Lew Wasserman type mogul, who comes up with the bright idea that Oasis Pictures really ought to make a movie. Magda picks the script that will reunite her with Johnny and convinces daddy to finance the film. Johnny quits his lousy waiter job in grand style and returns the conquering hero. The studio/ sanitarium kicks into life and a great *Wuthering Heights* type epic gets filmed. The pretenders all get their moments to shine. An out-of-work taxi driver cum Eric Von Stroheim gets to direct the movie he always wanted to, jodhpurs, riding crop, et al.

Their Victorian drama made by whacky people turns out like *Airplane!* The finished film, of course, can't find distribution because it was made outside of the real studio system by a bunch of has-beens and nuts. Naturally, it gets selected for a little festival, wins the prize, is acclaimed by the critics and becomes an overnight success. Without asking anyone, Dr. Howard gushingly reveals a slate of upcoming pictures, *Wuthering Heights 2, 3 and 4*, at a news conference starring Magda and Johnny. The real studios all want in and offer financing.

Other moguls and rich people with crazy children send them over to Oasis Pictures for therapy. They make a bunch of movies and whether the films are any good or not, it doesn't really matter because the kids are having fun playing pretend.

I awoke and realized there really is a very thin line between Showbiz and the sanitarium. And, yes, *Harvey* is one of my favorite films.

FEAST OR FAMINE

In the San Fernando Valley, a little burg just over the hill from Hollywood, home to seven or eight million people, an ebb and flow of wind cuts through the mountain pass late in the afternoon and if you're standing in just the right place, the enervating heat melts away as you're once again caught up in God's good graces. It is a release from the internal tensions of the day. A gentle voice inside whispers, "Calm down. Don't be so anxious. Everything is going to be okay."

You have to slow down your racing heart, blink your eyes a few times and try to determine if this is a dream or has part of your dream come true. We are all so used to being bandied about wherever, whenever there is the hint of work that when a good job finally arrives, it's a genuine surprise. Someone out there has recognized your genius and is willing to validate your parking, both literally and figuratively. Oh frabjous day! Kaloo, kallay!

The famine portion of your odyssey is over ... for now. Wondering about next months' bills or that overdue payment suddenly becomes a trivial inconvenience. Not only are the bills taken care of for the foreseeable future but the best news is that, "work has arrived." What work really means is "action". Most independent-minded people in Showbiz are action junkies looking for their next fix.

We are people who thrive on impossible tasks, tight deadlines and shorter money than is reasonably required to do a great job. And a great job we must do in order to find more action. Our work requires adherence to a well-defined, unstated set of rules. Try your best. Communicate well. You can look at the other person's rice bowl but don't touch. The truth is always the easiest way to go because sooner or later, lying, cheating or stealing will get you thrown out of the game. Down here, beneath the jet stream, we have to treat our fellow galley slaves with respect. Nobody conscripted us for this life. So what holds us here? Inertia? Centrifugal force? Fear? There's always that exit sign leading back to the real world. Once you've been corrupted by this business, it's very difficult to ever return.

I've known several people who've saved up a nest egg, doffed their tails, left town to follow a dream they always harbored to open that restaurant or Mom and Pop camera store. It usually takes them two or three years to run through the money and return, often on their knees, begging for another chance. "What was I thinking? I couldn't make it out there! I was so foolish. Please take me back!" (For you fellow cinefiles, think of John Torturro begging for his life in *Miller's Crossing*.)

And after a good long run of work or, better yet, a miracle has occurred and somebody has bought your script and wants to make it into a movie, the famine is over. The knee (or the knife) gets pulled back from the throat. It's time to get back on your feet, straighten up your dignity and do what you came here to do. To do good work is the goal. Hitting the Trifecta is nearly impossible but every once in a great while, it happens. To work with people you want to on projects you want to and get paid what you ought to being the ultimate dream. Any of these three developments will keep the boat afloat a little while longer. It's why we're here.

The magic wand in the sky has dropped on your forehead saying, "Here's a chance to shine up like a new penny. Let's see what you can really do!" The voice inside whispers, "If you pull this one off, there'll be more chances, bigger opportunities. Who knows, if you play these cards right, maybe, just maybe, they'll unhitch that plow and really see how far and how fast you can go!" When looking in the mirror, I see a racehorse. Unfortunately, most everyone else sees a plow horse. (I'll lose the weight, promise)

Feasting is the easy part. Don't need a lot of instruction on how to spend it once you've got it because you've already done it a thousand times in your head. It's how you handle adversity that is the true test of character. Enough with the tests, already! Let me just enjoy the respite for a change. The knowledge that there's money in the bank and more coming is a sweet treat for the part of the mind that carries the burden of your continuing existence on the planet.

A project you've diligently helped develop finally materializes on your doorstep. Or, an impossible project dropped in your lap and it's too good to turn down. Sure, it's going to be a lot of hard work and paying attention to details but after the most recent barefoot trip across the Gobi desert, pulling this off will be a piece of cake. There are going to be problems. If there weren't, why would they need you? If just anybody could handle the task at hand, then surely there's some half-wit relative who needs a job where they can't get into too much trouble. Nope, there are problems aplenty a coming and you're exactly the right person to solve them. You've been selected for better or worser. Time to put up or shut up. Show us what you've got.

It's a strange world navigating between the very real extremes of feast or famine. We work so hard to get our shot and then one day, it arrives. You say a prayer, step up to bat and do your best. Don Sutton, the baseball Hall of Fame pitcher, once said, "Every pitch makes somebody happy." Feast or famine. Oh, frabjous day!

[Lewis Carroll, the writer of Alice in Wonderland, was reputed to have been a heroin user. Instead of being regarded as a creative genius, maybe he was just loaded, had bad penmanship or just couldn't really spell all that well.]

THE WALK-IN CLOSET

It seems like but a blink of a sleepy eye but almost fifty years ago I discovered a terrible family secret in our walk-in closet that shook my belief system to it's very core. I grew up in a very religious household led by a mother whose answer to any problem would be solved through the power of prayer. It always seemed that God was alive and resting in our attic, awaiting her next request. Christmas time was the best time of year because we were going to be visited by St. Nicholas, who apparently had been watching over our shoulders all year and keeping track of who had been naughty or nice. Our individual stack of presents under the tree was a direct reflection of the balance sheet. Kind of like a childhood "end-of-the-year bonus."

After a two successive Christmas mornings where I actually unwrapped a box of sticks and stones, I figured it was time to right my ship and try harder to get on the positive side of Santa's ledger. I worked hard to be a good paperboy because the final collection of the year usually included a few extra dollars in recognition of the stellar service I had provided all year. This bonanza paid for all of my Christmas purchases and then some. Two weeks off from school without homework. Sleigh rides, snow forts, eggnog and hot chocolate, carolers on the radio all day, etc. Serving Midnight Mass as an altar boy is heady stuff when you're eight years old, staying up past midnight, incense and candles burning brightly, the Monsignor decked out in his finest robes along with all of the other priests and nuns, the church choir belting out God's greatest hits from the balcony. Proud family and friends dressed to the nines in the jam-packed church. An ethereal experience. My little heart racing with anticipation about the new toys about to be discovered a few scant hours later under the tree with my name on it provided by the ultimate old scorekeeper, St. Nick himself! Life don't get much better than that.

Santa was inextricably entwined with the whole Baby Jesus story. He had the church's Good Housekeeping seal of approval. He was a European dude who apparently achieved Sainthood by delivering presents to all the kids of the world. He certainly had my vote if anyone had asked. He employed an army of elves making presents all year long. What's not to like? Kind of like the guardian angels that everybody had sitting on their shoulders to help answer correctly when faced with an ethical or moral dilemma. The secular and religious worlds peacefully co-existed until one fateful day.

Oh, there had been nasty rumors of some massive conspiracy in the air about the validity of Santa but they were always met with vehement denials by our parents, the people we trusted most in the world. After all, these were the same people who seared, "Thou shalt not tell a lie" into our souls. Heck, I'd actually seen a nun wash Petey McDonald's mouth out with a bar of soap the year before for telling a lie. Lying was against God's laws. Eternal damnation and hell-fires awaited those who broke any of the ten big ones.

It all began innocently enough. I entered the walk-in closet on the third floor of our house to get a winter coat and discovered a stash of wrapped Christmas presents tucked away on an upper shelf. They were addressed to several of my seven brothers and sisters, "From: Santa!" How could this be? I carefully un-scotch taped the end flaps and checked out who was getting what when the truth dawned on me. The label looked remarkably like my mother's distinctive handwriting.

I had to sit down because the world as I knew it was spinning out of control. Holy mackerel, the adults of the world were lying to kids! These overseers of our health and well-being were nothing but a big pack of liars. If they lied about the jolly old man who was God's pal, of all things, what other falsehoods were they capable of? In a moment of quiet reflection, all of my mythological touchstones were shattered. The Easter Bunny, the Tooth Fairy, Smokey the Bear, Rudolph the Red Nosed reindeer- all shimmered for a second and were gone. Devastating because I somehow knew that I would have to shoulder the burden of the rest of my life without them. The scales had fallen from this innocents eyes and nothing would ever be the same.

Around Christmas time, quiet conversations being held by my parents with my older brother and sisters would suddenly cease when I walked into the room. I didn't want to let on that I knew the horrible truth. A few days later my five year old brother, Johnny, in first grade came to me and wanted to know the truth about Santa. I made a decision to become one of the liars and kept the myth alive for at least another couple of years.

I happily foisted this myth on my own kid because there is nothing in the world like seeing those twinkling lights and squeals of delight as wrapping paper is ripped off and the retreating jingle of bells can be heard as St. Nick disappears into the night and all is right with the world for a little while.

AT THE 3/4 TURN

Psychologically speaking, everyone starts out of the gate each new year with a clean slate. We're all going to the gym more often, lose that extra weight, find that perfect job, be a better mate, lover, friend, caretaker, etc. etc. After the first few months of getting used to writing a new number in the upper right hand corner on your checks, you come to realize that the "new you" is a whole lot like the "old you" who magically reinvented themselves at the stroke of midnight on December 31st.

Those early months of the new year feature a bounce in your step, maybe some new clothes or hairdo. You look maaahhvelous! The world is full of infinite possibilities. Big dreams require big plans and look out world, here I come. Nothing is going to stop me from getting where I want to go. "Give me a hand or get out of my way" is the battle cry.

Then Spring hits and those new threads are splattered with a little mud. You're hanging in there but the going has been tougher than the last time around the track. There are a couple of unexpected bumps along the way. You settle into the middle of the pack waiting for one of those guys in front to give you half an opening so you can shoot out in front like greased lightning. You keep pacing yourself, looking for a chance to show everybody in the stands who is betting on you that you've still got what it takes to - Go! All! The! Way!

The good news is the TV Executive branch has finally made up their minds as to who is looking for what for the fall season and either you're on board or scrambling for your next mount. Producing is a lot like trying to get a horse around the track. Either you're in that envious position to choose the best horse to ride or its any horse that's still available will do. The nag with the greatest pedigree doesn't assure your place in the winner's circle. It still has to be ridden (written?) well, the conditions need to be conducive to your little mudder, i.e. right time slot, right network, and right night. And in the end, you just have to get lucky. That's all. Easy peasey.

Then summertime, the halfway point of the year arrives, and your heart is still racing along fast and furiously. Pounding the sidewalk on a hot humid day without a cloud of relief in sight can be just as exhausting as running flat out all the time. And there's always a couple of shoves out of the way and a few elbows to the face. Oops! Please overlook the occasional misplaced whip from your fellow combatants, all jockeying for position. Nothing personal. Everyone still loves you. But the curses and mutterings under the breath become noticeably louder.

If you happen to be in one of the parts of the country where deciduous trees still exist, fall arrives in all of its glory. You've been running the race for nine or ten months and it looks like you're somehow going to make it to the finish line. Landing in the money is uppermost in your mind. You still have a shot if a couple of the boyos in front would just drop dead but right now, you don't really know how much more gas there is in the tank and you're afraid to look. Just finishing this year in one piece will be quite an accomplishment.

There've been some pleasant surprises along the way. Friendships forged. Projects advanced. It hasn't all been mud in your eye but it's very tiring getting knocked off your high horse and keeping from getting trampled underfoot.

So as we take the 3/4 turn, it's still anybody's call. Daylight streaks into what was once darkness and hopefully some insights have been gained. We gather up what's left of our reserves to give it our best shot as we all head down this year's homestretch. The crowd is on it's feet yelling, encouraging you to make everything work out. Expectations are high. The noise is roaring. The juices are flowing. You know you've still got what it takes and if opportunity strikes, you'll show everyone out there what you can do, what you had hoped to do at the beginning of this race.

We'll keep you posted as to how it all turns out.

Always appreciated W.C. Fields definition of Horse Sense: "It's what keeps horses from betting on people."

REALITY SOUP

A glib Host flips around the channels with his remote and intros us to the newest crop of Reality Shows.

Ms. Personality – A middle-aged dork gets to fall in love with a bevy of beauties wearing masks trying to woo him. The hook is that they're all transvestites and he just can't tell. The kicker is the first one to seduce him gets the bonus money.

Meet the Parent – Two scenes in each half hour show. One features an overprotective single parent father with a beautiful daughter and three guys trying to score. His lie detector machine has an electrical shock component. The second half hour features a single poor white trash mother who competes with her pretty daughter to see who can get the luckiest the fastest with a trio of potential hillbilly suitors.

Anything Goes – half a dozen certifiable sex addicts assisted by booze, weed, thong bikinis, Speedos, lap dances and a hot tub. You do the math.

Stick Up – Ordinary folk get to play heiress Patty Hearst for a day. They're in on some kind of hidden camera heist with professional robbers and thieves recently paroled from prison. They get to experience that adrenaline high that comes from sticking up a liquor store or local bank. It's all rubber bullets, car chases and lots of laughs.

Blonde Date – We puncture the myth about stupid blondes as we ask a quartet of beauties to accomplish some everyday tasks. We get to tag along as they try to work the washing machines at the local laundromat, balance their checkbooks on the Internet, and pick up their phone messages from a remote location. Bonus points are awarded if they can program their VCR's to record a particular TV program.

Down With That – A group of Jackass style pyrotechnics guys have to figure out how to topple a statue and blow up a building each week without killing anyone or getting caught.

Rich vs. Poor – A group of Ivy Leaguers challenges an underprivileged, unemployed team from the inner city in friendly games of lacrosse, cricket, rugby, and golf. Alternate weeks find the Ivy

Leaguers playing street basketball, stickball, drag racing for pink slips and break dancing.

Art Fair – A Bob Barker type entices ordinary people visiting County Fairs to enjoy the experience of getting tattoos and body piercings. The more extreme the pain, the higher the dollar amount they get paid.

Blink your eyes and we'll be seeing more fine quality reality TV shows like these in the future.

CHAPTER 7

THE BOTTOM LINE

Paying Your Dues

In Showbiz, "paying your dues" covers a myriad of sins. Usually it takes the form of some kind of indentured servitude. Back in the good old days, that's what passage to America often cost the freshly arrived immigrant. Two to four years of slavery working for a family that could use an extra pair of hands around the house. Things have changed but the basic premise is alive and well in Showbiz.

Newcomers who want to get a toehold in Showbiz should expect to work 60 – 80 hour weeks for little or no money just to see if they have what it takes. This opportunity usually takes the form of an intern position (traditionally unpaid), a job in the mailroom or as a production assistant (think minimum wage.) From this vantage point, the individual gets to wander around inside the belly of the beast and hopefully picks out a career path they wish to pursue. After that choice is made, the next task is to become a sponge of information. Eat, sleep and drink in as much knowledge about the subject as possible so that you can hold your own in a conversation whenever the chance arrives to impress someone in a position of power. Dick Cavett, a very smart former late night talk show host from an Ivy League school, said he always tried to have something witty to say whenever he had a chance to meet a guest lecturer. It made him stand out from the crowd and shot him up the ladder.

Unfortunately for the applicants wanting to get into Showbiz, there is no open audition like they have in professional sports from time to time where you get to strut your stuff. All throughout the journey, it is a series of chance encounters with people whom you either hit it off with or you don't. It all boils down to timing, chemistry, who you know and being able to survive the slow roasting over the spit, unless you have some special talent that somebody else can use right away.

If you achieve success early, God help you. Met a fellow who at 23 won an Academy Award for his "Best Short Film." A few years later he was sitting in my office looking for an Associate Producer Job, an Assistant to the producer job, any job. He was still in a daze as to what happened after all the hoopla died down and there was no seat at the banquet table with his name on it. Felt badly when I sent him on his way. He could've easily handled an assistant job but deserved a better spot on the roster.

Once gave a lecture on the backlot at Universal to a class of USC film school students. All they wanted to know was how long it took to be successful because they had it all plotted out. They were going to write, produce, direct, and edit their short films so as to showcase their talents at various big time film festivals. Next, the talent agencies and/ or major studios would be swarming over each other to sign them up and give them an E-ticket on the gravy train.

I told them one secret to being successful is to find a good agent who loves you. "How long is that going to take?" they clamored to know. When I said it only took me ten years and four agents to find mine, there was a collective groan. "Man, you must've been some kind of loser if it took that long," was their unstated response. After all, these were the elite, mostly sons and daughters of the rich and powerful. They were accustomed to taking shortcuts. Why pay your dues when you can get in the back door for free?

In explaining about the harsh realities of trying to make a living in Showbiz, you could see their little faces scrunch up with anger if half, if a third of what this geezer was saying were really true. Why hadn't anybody told them? I asked them to look around at their fellow classmates who shared the same dream of fame and fortune and told them that five years after college two thirds of them would be in some other line of work. "Hey, screw this old guy!"

All of the biographical selections down at the cinema bookstore are about lucky luminaries from the world of Showbiz who had started from scratch and conquered the world or about people who got famous and flamed out. Most of this film school's guest lecturers were successful people who had made it into the pantheon of the gods and encouraged the kids to join the party. Who the hell was this asshole to tell us that things might not work out?

In a perverse way, I rather enjoyed the experience. Not so much in puncturing the kiddies balloons but in hopefully planting a seed of doubt in their brains about what to expect and how to prepare for a business that doesn't really want or need them. Got a nice letter from their professor the next week inquiring as to my availability to come and speak to a few other classes. It was tempting but I was too busy trying to stay ahead of my own personal steamroller.

It's been over thirty years since I began this journey and in spite of over 700 credits, I oftentimes feel as if I'm still paying my dues. You get to stop when you die or when they give you one of them little gold statues that admits you to the club.

SQUEEZE THE BUFFALO

In 1986, I was the second American producer of a TV series in Vancouver, B.C. My Executive Producer (EP) would arrive at our distant location in a chauffer driven limousine having just deplaned from L.A. in his Lear jet with gold dripping from every orifice. He would tell corny jokes and rah-rah his way through the day. His visits every other week were usually disruptive because our job was to produce a very ambitious action TV series, *Airwolf,* for very little money. Pleading poverty was my middle name and instilling esprit de corps the solution. Later on, I, and all of the other producers who worked for Disney, faced a similar challenge, which was made a little bit tougher because the top dog was making headlines for collecting his annual $500,000,000 payday.

One day I told our visiting EP/ Grand Poobah that our Prop Master was giving up his weekends to be prepared for the next episode that began shooting the following Monday and was asking for a $50 raise. "Fire him!" was the knee-jerk response followed immediately by, "How do you like my new watch? Cost me $37,000, has 18 diamonds and can tell time in six different countries." This was the same guy who laughingly told me, "You do all the work, and I'll take all the credit and make all the money." In jest we find the truth.

His motto in relationship to a nickel was, "Squeeze the buffalo, see the Indian cry." He would climb back into his limo and return to L.A. in time for dinner. It usually took two days to smooth out all the ruffled feathers but we continued to figure out how to make it work. I gave the Prop Master the raise under the table as we produced 24 one-hour action adventure shows in 24 weeks and two days.

The EP conveniently forgot to buy me that house in Beverly Hills he had promised me (in front of witnesses) if I pulled this off. I guess I should've gotten it in writing or at least screamed and yelled and made a big stink about it. I probably could've shamed him into actually keeping his promise. Hell, he gave his daughter a big house for a wedding present. A couple of months after her divorce he showed up on the doorstep of his former son-in-law and demanded the house back. The guy shut the door in his face. Would've liked to have had a camera rolling on that scene.

Just came up with an idea for a TV show with the politically incorrect title of, "Indian Giver!" You win something fabulous and then we get to see the look on your face when we come to take it back. Anyway, my "do unto others" attitude explains my inability thusfar to accumulate that elusive mountain of money. The actor, Robert Hayes, tells how he turned down a million dollars to star in the second sequel of *Airplane*. "Somebody just kick me, will you?"

There are other ways to get where you want to go that don't leave dead bodies or your self-respect in your wake. They just take a little longer to reach but in the end are hopefully more satisfying. It's that qualitative judgment where nobody's right or wrong and the only one who really gets to decide anything is you.

Recently met a couple that bought a house in Beverly Hills for $150,000 in the 1960's. Today it's worth $14,000,000. Screaming and yelling to get what I want wasn't the way I was raised. In hindsight, I could've really used a small house in Beverly Hills.

Never underestimate the value of cheap theatrics!

EXIT STRATEGY

I was amazed during a negotiation for my services to-be-rendered on a studio production that one of the clauses in the contract dealt with whom I could be fired by. We had to actually agree who could fire me. "These three people can fire your ass and boot you out on the street. However, these other four people can't." I felt like arguing for one more person who could fire me in return for a better parking space and a smaller back end royalty that I will never see anyway.

I guess I was supposed to be ass-kissing these three folk who could fire me and treat everyone else like crap? It didn't make any sense. You do the job you're hired for. You do the best you can within the time and money parameters and you move on to the next job, right? Why hire somebody in the first place if you need a clause in a contract to agree who can fire you when you don't live up to this contract? It was an entirely new concept to me. This myopic thinking certainly didn't bode well for my future dealings with the overseers.

Seems they've got some Business Affairs lawyers with too much time on their hands. What's next, who we can eat with and who we can't? Who we can be seen talking to on the set and who is off limits? My brother-in-law is a Key Grip who told me of a production he worked where on stage, the Producers sat in a section roped off by that Police: Do Not Cross yellow tape so the Producers (all six or eight of them) didn't have to mix with the hoi polloi. Yet another new concept.

The whole idea of setting up a company and building in golden parachutes for the inner circle seems foreign to me. What ever happened to starting a business that grows and prospers that you nurture along to give to your kids? I guess those bumper stickers proclaiming, "I'm spending my children's inheritance" apply to many of our current crop of business leaders.

According to the Executive Pay Box Office reports, the arbitrage mentality appears to be winning. What my inquiring mind wants to know is, "How do you get these jobs?" The president of the E! Channel is forced out after two whole years because of some misdeeds and she walks away with a $20 million severance package? Hell, Mike Ovitz fought with Michael Eisner for one whole year and left with $100 million plus change in his pocket. I guess up in that rarified polo field where they whack people's balls around for sport, you have to have brass *juevos* and a "let's-rob-the-widows-and-orphans-fund" kind of jugular mentality to survive.

I was brought up to believe that you earned an honest days pay for an honest days work. You don't set up a new company primarily to loot the treasury at some point in the not-too-distant future. It's myopic thinking. So why do all of those myopic thinkers seem to have a second house down in Newport Beach? Hey, who's the dummy in this picture? Where's my IPO? "What's in it for me?"

should be tattooed inside the eyelids of every young business major, wannabe stockbroker or future corporate mergers and acquisitions folk.

Now, if I could figure out how to get one of those jobs where nobody can fire me but me and I earned every cent the old fashioned way — by the sweat of my brow — that's the only exit strategy I'm interested in and I would die a most happy camper. Otherwise, if I'm supposed to jump aboard the arbitrage bandwagon in order to survive, you might as well take this old dinosaur out and shoot me now.

Half the Money

A familiar cliché in Hollywood is, "I've got half the money and I'm just looking for the other half." Upon closer inspection it usually means that an arms dealer in Syria is putting up a guarantee that a Lebanese bank will honor. This gets married up with an Irish post production tax shelter deal and all of this gets bundled together into an official looking letter that says if you can attract the other half of the budget, we got a deal. One small caveat being that the arms dealer has a son who wants to be a producer or a girlfriend who will be the leading lady. The longer you stick around, the crazier the financing schemes get.

Whatever happened to the good old days when a patron of the arts (often inspired by the proximity of beautiful young women) simply took a flyer? Nowadays it's all corporate money and they traditionally need to see someone else's head, besides the Syrian arms dealer, out on the chopping block. The typical well-heeled investor is absolutely ready to take the plunge predicated on having foreign distribution, domestic pre-sales, contracts that guarantee his money back and a handsome profit. Once those are in place, it's a green light. Thanks for nothing! (If you have all those things, you no longer need the investor as any entertainment banker will loan you the money.)

Today's would-be high roller still wants to take meetings and talk the talk about being in Showbiz but after the first meeting a-go-go, there is a lawyer, a wife or business manager who usually says, "no-no." They politely explain to you that Charley is off his rocker and didn't really mean it. And old money, fugetaboutit! The blue chippers have all their equity tied up before they're born and long after they're dead. It's a lovely ride over to the country club for drinks and a game of tennis but the bottom line is they ain't paying for anything other than their next party (a tax write-off), their next Hummer (another tax write-off), or going out to play with their polo ponies or new girlfriends. Very rarely do you encounter the blue chipper who's determined to burn through the family fortune during their lifetime. It's very bad form and just not done.

You're not a true independent filmmaker in Hollywood until you've taken a meeting or three with somebody who represents a mysterious Asian connection who has at least $100 million looking for the right project. There probably is such an individual who gets his jollies by sending out a myriad of emissaries just to stir the pot and see how many free dinners and hot babes they can score before wearing out the welcome mat. The would-be mogul has no intention of really parting with his money and his agents just like to talk about it. They like to say, "yes, yes, yes" to all the various deal points until the day the contract is to be signed or the money deposited and then it's, "No, so sorry. Didn't know that you really thought we were going to do the deal!"

Had a Korean man appear in my life one time with a suitcase full of hundreds. ($500,000 to be exact.) He said, "Numerology says I need to make a movie beginning in three weeks or else I buy condominium in Marina Del Rey." I asked, "Have you got a script?" He says, "No, but wife write treatment, two pages." I looked at the money and back at the guy and said, "Let's make a movie." We ended up shooting a rip-off of, "The Karate Kid goes to College" for 20 days up in San Jose. The movie behind the scenes was ten times better than what landed in front of the camera. The Korean hopefully got his money's worth and I paid the rent for the next couple of months. (He probably would have made more money buying the Marina Del Rey condo but that's beside the point.)

The real home run these days is finding the true gambler — a person who started with nothing more than a good idea and made their fortune by following their gut instincts. After several successes in the computer business, stock market or real estate they finally arrive at what has always been the true gamblers Mecca – Showbiz! Where hope springs eternal, millions are won or lost every weekend and busloads of future starlets keep arriving from the hinterlands.

This is such an amazing game. Now if you can just find someone who actually has the other half of the money, let's do lunch.

CHAPTER 8

LESSONS LEARNED THE HARD WAY

I Have a Lamp

We all have keepsakes from the past to remind us of special events in our lives. They are stored in boxes in the garage or attic, stashed in photo albums or adorn the walls of our domicile. Every once in awhile, we pull them out to gaze at or touch and try to remember the day, the hour, the moment of the rapidly retreating past from whence they came. They make us smile, laugh, cry at how young we all once were, how fast it all goes. Me, I have a lamp sitting by my computer that illuminates my keyboard in the dark of night. It's the most expensive lamp I will ever own.

If you have priced lamps lately in a store, you can get a decent upright table lamp for under a hundred bucks. If you want to make a splash in the den and buy a chrome job that bends this way and that, has tinted frosted glass and three levels of brightness, it'll set you back several hundred. If you really want to go wild and replace the ratty antique over the dining room table with a splashy carved glass chandelier, announcing to the world that you've arrived, you can spend a little under ten thousand. Hah! Pikers!

One of the perks of being a producer is you often get to choose your own office furniture. I've set up shop in over thirty offices. These have been in everything from fancy-schmantzy digs behind the studio walls to portable Acco trailers in a VFW parking lot – wherever the job has taken me. A few years ago I found myself ensconced in a great corner office at some new sound stages. I picked out some stuff from a catalogue and lo and behold, they delivered it the next day. Presto, change-o, empty room gets filled with spanking new furniture after a single phone call from the production coordinator. Part of the deal was a new desk lamp pulled out of its original packing box; purchase price of $20.

To make a painfully long story short, I had fallen in with a nest of whackaderos. These are people who look good on the outside, have obvious talents, are colorful characters, even charismatics, but underneath it all, they are basically flawed human beings. Show business is full of these folk — attracts them like a magnet. Once you've committed yourself to the project and get to examine them more carefully, you realize that these interesting cats don't really have their shit together and more often than not, they're somebody in a position to make your life miserable. While you are trying to make sense out of the rapidly changing set of "facts," they're just screwing with you because they can. It's bad enough when you're around one of these people but try a six-pack sometime and see how crazy life can get.

A $20 lamp has thus far cost me $40,000. This little beauty is a daily reminder of my own folly and a cautionary tale for you.

The movie was to be my big break taking me to the next level. It was a well-written, true story about a troubled boxer turned hit man. He was one of the writers and liked to hang around the production offices. Short, ethnic, powerfully built, with sharks' eyes that reeked of alarm bells and danger signals. He was always polite to me because I was helping to facilitate his life story being told in all of its sordid glory.

Pre-production was underway. Crew hired. Sets being built on the sound stages. The final money was circling the field. The first traunch was paying for pre-production. The fact that a superstar was going to play a pivotal cameo role and be a fellow producer had convinced me to leap into the vortex. The fact that the original budget had doubled since the script was rewritten to include over a dozen different boxing scenes all over the country was troubling but when an established foreign distributor stepped up to the plate with pre-sale commitments equal to 90% of the budget with North American rights yet to be sold, I thought we were off to the races.

I should have been alarmed when said superstar had to change his available dates on us, truncating our prep period by half because a big payday had just arrived on his horizon that happened to conflict with our shooting schedule and our little payday. We didn't pull the plug and get out while the getting was good. We decided that destiny was simply making our lives a little more interesting on the way to the big time. The financial partners said, don't worry, we can get the rest of the money together by pre-selling North America or finding an investor to cover the gap. The next few weeks were excruciating as the first monies ran out ($650,000 doesn't go as far as it used to.) The distribution money was going to be triggered by our having a Completion Bond in place. This is an insurance policy meaning there's another neck on the chopping block if things go terribly wrong, i.e. key actors get sick, sets get destroyed by a hurricane, acts of God happen that upset the best laid plans, etc. etc. The Bond Company is on the hook to help get your leaky ship back to port, one way or another.

We had no Completion Bond yet because the writers refused to change one word of the script that slandered several people still living who for some reason had refused to sign their release forms. The real life boxing trainer legend to be played by our superstar was suddenly asking for a quarter of a million for allowing us to use his name. Our once docile pussycat director had recently transformed into a maniac, having daily screaming matches with his superstar pal who would quit the picture one day and they would kiss and make up the next. He refused to cut out a couple of short expensive scenes because this was going to be his moment in the sun and he wasn't about to let anybody change one word. As time was running out, we needed to slash the budget by ten percent, edit the script of the offending material, get the Completion Bond and make our deadlines. The creative whackaderos wouldn't budge and called our bluff.

Three days before the start of principal photography, things got ugly as I experienced the worst day of my professional career having to tell everyone to pack up and go home. As the dispirited crew trashed the sets, the office staff pulled up stakes, the movers returned to repossess the rented furniture, I took my desk lamp home. Six months on the roller coaster was over and I wanted something to remember it by. Don't do that again! Then the lawsuits arrived. Things finally wound down after five years and $40,000 in legal bills.

Beware the whackaderos! Beware going out into the field of battle without the necessary ammo. Beware of getting caught up in the future you so desperately desire that you override your own best judgement as to what makes sense and what doesn't. Trust your internal compass that got you this far. Believe me, there is nothing in the world that would make you want to pay this much for a lamp.

GOING IN FOR THE CLOSE

Did you ever walk out of a meeting and five minutes later you come up with the perfect response to a question you'd been asked? You want to run back in and re-answer the question with something better, more witty, more original but alas, the moment has passed. I always say, "Beware the innocent question." The interviewer tosses out something and you either flub it or field it beautifully. Every question they have is a good sign. Means they're interested enough to keep asking.

Sometimes when I'm interviewing someone, I make a determination in the first ten seconds that they're not the right person for this particular gig but there is something intriguing enough about the person to keep me asking questions. I'll pick their brain and see how they might approach a particular problem. Sometimes they have half a good idea. Every once in awhile, they'll surprise me and have a whole different take on things and I appreciate the original thinker who isn't afraid to voice their opinion. I hold onto their resumes for future reference.

It's often the little things that determine whether you get the job or if you sell the project. Obviously, you have to sell yourself first before somebody is going to buy an idea from you. One of the best sales experiences I ever had was a year and a half on the phones in the wee hours of the morning selling a bunch of audio-visual supplies primarily to nuns around the country. I'd average thirty calls an hour and in retrospect, getting hung up on ten times an hour is good training for a life in Showbiz. Ten people weren't available and of the remaining ten who had a little time on their hands and would talk, all sorts of info could be gleaned by the innocent question. I'd find out how many kids were in their school, average class size and most importantly, when their budget was being replenished. I'd make a date to call them back in two, three weeks, two months, whenever.

I'd call them up on the appointed day, remind them of our earlier conversation and often end up with a small order around $100. When they paid up, the guy in the next room, Karly the Hungarian, would immediately get them back on the phone and deliver his pitch that went something like this:

"Hallo, Sister. I'm calling for Steve, ju know de guy ju bought de overhead projection marking pens from (or Bic Pens or, or, or)…

Yes, dat guy. Well, he fell down and broke his leg. Ju know, we recently had an inventory sales tax out here in California and all de prices went up but ju know Steve, he set aside two more gross with your name on it at de same low price…Dat's right! Now Sister, Steve asked me to send along a little something special for ju, a glow-in-the-dark picture of de Last Supper (or a small black and white TV dat you can watch in bed after lights out.) If ju would give me de address of de nunnery where ju live, I'll send it right along because all de other sisters are gonna to be jealous when dey see this so it should just be between ju and him… Okay, I'll send it along and de two gross of de marking pens (or whatever he was pushing that week.) Thank ju, Steve thanks ju and I'll have him give ju a call when he's feeling better."

Now, it sometimes took me three to ten phone calls to get this nun to pry open her purse strings and buy $100 of stuff with me receiving a whopping 10% commission. In a few entertaining minutes, Karly would get her to spend $500 - $1000 and he took home about $1500 a week. Not bad for a part time job way back in 1975.

I realized that you have to tell people a story when you want to sell them something. Give them a reason to buy. After the story-telling is over, you ever so gently put the knife up to their throat and ask for what you want. It's called, " going in for the close." It is the point of all sales pitches. It is a vastly underrated art form mastered by a few talented salespeople. We see their handiwork everyday in movie theaters and on TV screens. They are called Producers.

GETTING LUCKY

We spend the better part of our childhoods learning survival skills. In Showbiz, we spend most of our adulthood looking for the best way to express ourselves. We try a variety of approaches: music, art, writing, singing, dancing, acting, producing, deal making, promoting until we ultimately find the one we are good at and then improve upon it over time. The big trick is to figure out a way to make a living at something you truly love so you can get great at it. Most people in the world never have that opportunity.

I don't believe anyone in the real world willingly asks for this affliction known as a love of Showbiz. Most people certainly love the show. In the darkness of night, man has always gathered in groups to talk about the day, compare notes, grumble and grouse, play cards, share a pint. Sooner or later the music breaks out, a joke teller, maybe a story teller or flickering image appears and everything else quiets down to listen as the audience is temporarily transported to another place where they will laugh or cry, do or die, and simply think about the world in a different light.

Don't know about you but I was never really groomed for a role in the real world. I had no glib answer for the eternal question asked of every child, "What do you want to be when you grow up?" Somehow, "Cowboy, fireman or President" didn't ring true. You might as well have asked me what planet I wanted to visit and why? I had no idea. Most children daydream about how they're going to be rich and famous and enjoy the rest of their lives. Then the terrible reality of life intrudes and they have to go out and make a living. Don't think most kids dream about being an insurance salesman, working at the DMV or driving a cab and yet that's what they end up doing. Life just sorta happens that way. A chance meeting, somebody knew somebody, and *boom!*, in the blink of an eye they have a wife, two kids, two cars, two mortgages, two week vacations and the rest of their lives meted out in weekly paychecks doing something they never, ever saw themselves doing.

Being the offspring of two free lance writers, I thought a person only had to sit down in front of a typewriter with a blank piece of paper, conjure up an idea, capture it on paper, send it out and a couple of weeks later, a check arrived in the mail. Great! In hindsight it's damn near impossible to sit in front of a typewriter or computer and earn a living by writing up ideas, let alone keep a roof overhead and feed eight hungry children. I am amazed at the miracle my parents pulled off in just surviving.

My parents were word lovers. They loved to laugh. My mother broke her leg at a party demonstrating how a friend broke her leg skiing. My father wrote a little book, "How Not To Make A Million in Mail Order", based upon his thirty-five year side business that he kept alive in the basement. The Wry Idea Company in Rye, New York sold a variety of knick-knacks, wall plaques, bumper stickers and cocktail napkins with original funny sayings on them. Pop was always in search of the next Pet Rock. All of us kids had our first job working for him licking envelopes or stuffing the first self-watching golf ball into a shipping container. I didn't know it at the time but it was the perfect training ground for a career in Showbiz where everything starts with an idea that gets run up the flagpole to see if anyone is going to salute.

Everyone can look back and shake their heads in wonder at the twists and turns that got them here. Once you determine that Showbiz holds your destiny, it is a ton and a half of hard work and heartache to stay here. Many are called but only a few actually figure out how to make a living at it. Unfortunately, ambition and hard work alone aren't the determining factors. Ultimately, you have to be in the right place at the right time and get lucky.

To Fame or Not to Fame

Anybody out there interested in fame, fortune, hanging out with beautiful young men and women all over the place? Your face on the cover of magazines? Power lunches at elite restaurants? A private box at major sporting events? Six and seven figure paychecks arriving frequently in your mailbox? Maids, butlers, security guards, accountants, business managers, agents, attorneys, a great view of the Pacific ocean from your Malibu Colony sun deck? People kissing your ass, telling you how wonderful you are wherever you go? Anybody ... ? Raise your hands!

A couple million (billion?) hands just shot up in the air not really knowing what they're volunteering for but it sure sounds better than the life they have.

It's a bit much for an ordinary person to deal with. A lot of famous folk spend an inordinate amount of time and money trying to make us forget the fact that once upon a time they were mere mortals who got real lucky. Their "Spin Doctor"/ press agents/ managers change their names and alter their past as busy plastic surgeons reshape their bodies and remove any imperfections. Often, the newly minted famous person conveniently eradicates memories of their earlier, un-famous time. You wonder if they pinch themselves or even remember how they got to be famous. (see *The Oscar* if you haven't screened it lately.)

Once upon a time, I supported a likeable enough actor for a few years. Had breakfast with him on the day he got his lucky break. He hit the right button and took that fateful elevator ride up into that rarefied air called, "stardom." I believed in him, enjoyed his company and was happy to see him succeed. But on this day, he stepped out of the elevator, hit the down button and I was unpleasantly surprised as the doors closed in my face. You awake from this dream back where you came from. Now, however, I was on the other side of some great divide. A half a million miles down, a half a million back up between me and my former pal who had been transformed into one of them newly minted famous people. It was a hard lesson to learn.

Oh, they'll wave at you from the back of the limo or from their lofty new perch. They got theirs. You'll have to get your own. At chance encounters, they'll come over, all smiles and sincerity, pat you on the back, say something meaningful like, "I love this guy", and one of my favorites, "Call me", but they conveniently forget to give you their private number. And if you do track them down, their secretary checks with the big guy and then sweetly says, "Oh, he just stepped into a meeting" or, "He's in with someone, can he get back to you?", which translates into, "You'll get a call back when hell freezes over, when the cows come home, or maybe if he's drunk or drugged (just like the good ole days) and feeling nostalgic." Thanks for the memories!

Hey, ten thousand love letters a week from strangers telling you that you're great, that women around the world want to have your baby would have a tendency to obscure the vision of the sanest among us. A lot of people would trade everything they have for a "put" three-picture deal at Paramount. Could you, in good conscience, say for sure that you wouldn't hit the down button in the elevator of the world you currently enjoy in exchange for that rarefied air? If leaving your current world behind is the price you had to pay for fame and fortune, would you? "In a heartbeat", many people just answered.

Being famous is an interesting dilemma that most of us will never have to face. You haven't drastically changed from a few days, weeks or months ago but suddenly your opinions carry more weight. Your appearance causes a stir wherever you go. Your private life suddenly merges with your public life and nothing seems off limits anymore. People want your attention, an autograph, or just to be near you. Once again, there is no manual on "How To Be Famous" to refer to. You can only rely on those people you decide to trust to be honest with you. Don't know what the percentage of famous folk who hold onto friends from the past versus surrounding themselves with a new cadre of fawning sycophants. Appears to be split down the middle.

And there will of course be a lot of new friends at your beck and call. Legal consultants and financial managers suddenly appear at your elbow with new ideas how to shelter your huge income and help you live happily ever after. Of course, a couple of times a year, some unscrupulous money manager to the stars is carted off to jail for having stolen a ton of dough from their clients. It's really amazing that it doesn't happen more often because what ordinary person really knows what to do with those excess millions?

Of those who do become famous, some are too young to appreciate it or too old to really enjoy it. Royalty and offspring of the rich and famous are groomed from the start to handle life in the fishbowl. So few of the ordinary people who achieve fame seem prepared for it, which is why so few handle it gracefully. It's white hot under that intense media spotlight. Not many people's private lives can stand up very long to the scrutiny of the big magnifying glass in the sky and the horde of paparazzi waiting outside to capture your every move.

Don't know about you but I don't want that thing coming anywhere near my closet. Too many skeletons rattling around in there.

NOT A CLUE

I can honestly say after thirty-five years of watching this business from inside the belly of the beast that I have no idea of what works and why. My job as a producer is to put a frame around an idea with facts, figures, schedules and budgets. Once the parameters have been defined, then we get to paint by numbers all the areas that the script has called for. When you step back at the end of the day and look at your handiwork, it is in the eye of the beholder that determines whether it's a work of art or a piece of crap.

The producer traditionally gives everybody their marching orders. It is a perfunctory exercise of marshalling the forces within the budget limitations, putting the best people available into the right places and moving forward. I've been on shows where everyday the crew gathered at lunchtime to watch dailies (yesterday's work) and laugh their asses off only to have the results be an unfunny show that didn't work. I've seen flat, poorly written scripts spring to life and become memorable TV shows or movies in the right people's hands.

There is something ineffable, indefinable, unquantifiable that happens once a production is underway. The original concept is transformed from words on a piece of paper into a three dimensional, tangible asset you can see and hear that actually causes the audience to feel some visceral emotion. If it's really good, the work is transformed into a kind of celluloid immortality. A well-told story wrapped up in a nice package will last forever.

On the production side, we have to fly by the seat of our pants everyday and hope to land this baby safely. The combination of experience and intuition points us towards the best solution for any particular situation. You make your choices and hold your breath. Often the goal is just to get through the day while achieving some semblance of what was originally planned without killing anyone.

And every once in a great while, the magic happens.

The right people are in the right place both in front of and behind the camera. The weather and other lucky breaks go your way. There's enough money in the budget to get it right the first time. God smiles down from the heavens as a lump of coal is transformed into a glittering diamond. It happens often enough to make one believe in the power of prayer. Why it happens and how it happens is still a mystery. If you had the answer, you'd be a billionaire and the world would await your next pronouncement. It's important to remember, it's a totally subjective business where nobody is right all the time.

Oh, and don't worry, the audience will let you know one way or the other. Unlike an umpires' bad call that gets an immediate response, after your project hits the big or little screen, the crowd out there is not shy. They will shower you with applause or total neglect over the next several months to let you know whether you guessed right or wrong.

Being a producer is not unlike being a baseball manager or football coach. Instead of fifty thousand armchair quarterbacks in the stands, we will be judged by the great, unwashed masses out there. It just takes a little longer for the yeas or the boos to reach our ears.

Like a manager or coach, you have to understand the players on your team, inspire them, providing them with the best possible chance of realizing their full potential and create an environment where magic can happen. In doing so, you are giving the enterprise the best post possible chance to get lucky.

And if you look back at most games, most teams, most movies or TV shows, you'll find that their success or failure boils down to a few key decisions that were or weren't made in time to influence the outcome. A baseball manager doesn't take a poll of everybody in the stands as to what he should do in a given situation. I can see it now - "Hey everybody, should the runner on first base steal second base on the next pitch or not? " gets posted on the scoreboard. The crowd locks in their answer using their armrest computer or their text message instant cell phone survey. (If corporate America has anything to say about it, I'm sure it's on the drawing boards but hopefully won't be adopted until I'm gone.) In the meantime, the manager just goes ahead, pulls the trigger and lets the chips fall where they may.

A happy confluence of good people occasionally exceeds all expectations, like the Boston Red Sox in the 2004 and 2007 World Series. It's magical and memorable because beating the odds happens so rarely.

If you are afraid to make a decision without the committee or market research to back you up, do everybody a favor and head for the nearest exit. If you are afraid of seeing your shadow on the hot sidewalk in the middle of the day looking for work instead of living in the vacuum of some cushy air-conditioned office, get out now. This is a business built by risk takers and if there's one thing I've learned in thirty-five years of trying, it's that things don't usually work out as planned. Sometimes they're better, sometimes they're worse but when the dust settles, there stands something different than what was originally envisioned.

You gussy up your latest effort, put on your game face and hope for the best. Either way, you live with the results.

I always try to look for patterns and rhythms that run just beneath the surface. It's like an undertow unseen by the unsuspecting bather. Everything looks great so you jump on in. You're about to be drowned if you're not careful. There's always another set of circumstances working in the background, often at odds with whatever the task at hand is. It's only by delving into the facts, usually in retrospect, can it be determined why so few things arrive better than expected and why most things fall into the "just okay" or "uh-oh" category. "Just okay", means you get to live another day. Many people spend their entire careers working on "just okay" projects, playing on so-so teams, wallowing safely in mediocrity.

Risk takers often land in the "uh-oh" category because they didn't figure on that last S.O.B. who had the power to wreck everything. Sometimes it turns out that they bet on a flawed horse in a key position or believed in some crackpot idea before their wallets could get out of the way. Regardless, it's all about being in the right place at the right time when the alchemists do their thing. Where, when and why it happens, there is no way to accurately predict the outcome. I haven't a clue. How 'bout you?

WAR DOG

I look in the mirror and wonder, "Who is this middle aged guy staring back at me?" In my minds eye, I'm still 25, a lean mean fighting machine who is going to conquer the world. A lot of adventures have happened since my arrival and I've been one of the fortunate few allowed to stick around long enough to have helped create "a body of work". At this point in my life, I'm simply glad to have a body that works.

The first celebrity I ever saw was Raymond Burr, (*Perry Mason, Godzilla*) hulking down Hollywood Blvd. in a blue polyester leisure suit. I was excited when Bob Hope drove by in an old Chrysler in

Toluca Lake. And hey, aren't you Charles Durning sitting in front of me at a movie theater?

Thinking back on these early celebrity encounters, I have to laugh about how naive, how much the tourist rube I was. Having a college diploma in Mass Communications, reading Showbiz insider books and subscribing to Daily Variety doesn't mean you know anything. I was totally smitten and couldn't wait to get into the game. Klieg lights in the night on Hollywood Boulevard meant there was a movie premiering and stars were in evidence. I'd go late to celebrity funerals and position myself just outside the church or synagogue knowing there would be a lot of famous people walking by. At John Ford's funeral it was "rug city", Duke Wayne, Jimmy Stewart, Bing Crosby, Henry Fonda, Richard Widmark, all my heroes, all within touching distance of this wide-eyed innocent. I had enough good sense not to ask for autographs. Never really saw any use for illegible names scrawled onto some piece of paper.

We lived on Western Avenue for four years in a bungalow built in the 1920's by the old United Artists (Chaplin, Pickford, Fairbanks) to house talent they imported from New York. The bungalows were next door to a very large hotel that rented by the hour. Walking down the street back then featured several encounters with scantily clad women sitting in windows or on doorsteps looking for "a date." Pimps drove by in loud Cadillacs and there was the occasional bloodletting at the local Laundromat. Hollywood and Western Avenue was the place to shoot if a production required a sleazy part of town. Lucky us, we lived right there.

Oh, I was going all the way to the top of the mountain and nothing was going to stop me. After a couple of false starts, I was in the right place at the right time and started mass-producing TV shows. There were country western music shows, singing shows where every college chorale, barbershop quartet, black gospel group and choir within a hundred miles got a chance to perform their repertoire, Masters of the Martial Arts, kid shows. I produced comedies featuring people who went on to become rich and famous, travel show documentaries featuring a pair of stoned out whackaderos, one of whom has straightened out his life and became a big movie and TV star. One of my funny writers went on to make millions writing big time, crazy feature film comedies and now lives in a castle in Minnesota. Another hosted the bird show on Paradise Island in Disneyworld for the past decade. Fate is a cruel and indifferent mistress as I am constantly being reminded of missed opportunities. Regrettable mistakes. On the other hand, I also enjoyed myself enormously and nobody can ever erase that from the old memory banks. It's an exhilarating feeling of freedom knowing that your destiny is in your own hands and anything can happen.

I would knock out 140 or 250 half hour shows in a three month period because these were tax shelter shows that had to be produced and aired by December 30 and registered with the Library of Congress by year's end in order to lock in the tax benefits for the "executive producers". What insanity. I've never met or heard of anyone else who ever produced 15 half hour shows on three different sound stages a day, five days a week. I didn't know what I was doing was impossible so I just did it. I directed a couple hundred of them as well and got that out of my system.

I hadn't been told one minor detail. Other than the one late night showing on a Montana UHF station, these shows were never intended to air because if, god forbid, they became successful then the owners would have a capital gain and that would defeat the purpose of the tax shelter. A wizened old pro who produced the other 350 shows knew the truth and pocketed most of the cash and built himself a post production empire that he recently sold for several million dollars.

Take it from this old war dog, listen to the advice given by people who have survived the war and care about you. Things would have been so different if I only had been a better listener.

Going South

In Showbiz, it's funny how quickly you fall in love with a project you only heard about a short time ago. You immediately embrace the possibilities, sketch in the next couple of months in your head, get the engines warmed up and prepare yourself mentally for the challenges to be overcome in order to make this baby work. You start making calls to good people to find out their availability and your team of gypsies starts to smell a meal. And then, just as suddenly, the vision evaporates, usually through no fault of your own.

I don' t know the last time you had a sure thing blow up in your face but it's always a surprise. How you roll with the punches in Showbiz determines your longevity. Until you've crossed that invisible line where you migrate from being "valuable" to "invaluable", you will continue to suffer the vicissitudes this game has to offer.

It's an unusual business in that projects fall apart for no apparent reason. More often than not, it's because the money didn't come together quickly enough, or the star or some other key component who was committed to the project suddenly had to drop out. In a recent encounter, my Exec Producers were spending money, had Academy Award winners lined up to work for scale, it was going to be great, yadda, yadda, yadda.

Bottom line is they'll postpone the project until next spring. Because the average studio movie takes several years to reach the screen, it probably means it's going away for a while, if not forever. As the Executive Producer was telling me this news last night over a drink at a fancy bar, I was reminded of Yogi Berra's, "It's dejavu all over again." The disappearing project has happened to me a hundred times over the last thirty years. I did the math the other day and was chagrined to realize that I'd been standing out on the sidewalk for ten years, pounding the pavement, "in-between films," paying my dues, making the calls, taking lunches, not really knowing when or where the next gig was coming from. It's a lot more stressful in-between gigs than when you're actually working.

I stopped by Carney's in the San Fernando Valley for a hotdog mid-afternoon and in walked a guy I'd known for twenty years; beard, long hair, Wizard basketball t-shirt, wearing what appeared to be pajama bottoms. It was shocking in that he had been the head of TV production at a major studio for 25 years and was always meticulous in his appearance. In between his chili cheese fries, he said he enjoyed the first year and a half of his early retirement, but the second year and a half off had been an eye opener. Old members of the fraternity wouldn't return his calls. Nobody would give him a break to show them what he can do. Although he walked away with a tidy severance package, I was talking to a shadow of his former self.

He had a TV pilot that was fully financed by a major car company earlier in the year, set up offices on a studio lot, everything rolling along, was a month into pre-production when they got cold feet and pulled out. He got a new car out of it but missed TV pilot season. Shook his head at, "Close but no cigar!" As an independent producer, you come to know that feeling well. Yes, it's been a series of disappointments but hopefully, you have learned something invaluable from the experiences, even if it's only not to trust this or that person's word again. When things finally do work out, you learn not go jumping for joy and shouting about it until you've made it safely across the wire and the film is in the can.

Even though I had a job until last night, I already had two job interviews lined up the next week because I got out of the "counting-my-chickens-before-they-hatched-business" a while ago. Execs make dates with you on their calendars weeks or months in advance. When they finally get around to seeing you, you're ten times more attractive to them if you have gotten a job in the interim. You're not sitting there hat in hand and they're relieved that they don't have to tell you why they can't hire you. By actually having a job elsewhere, they'll either try to hire you away or move you up the charts to take advantage of your next availability.

So the ultimate truth in Showbiz is that nothing means nothing until the check clears your bank. As a friend once said, "It's all happy crap until it happens." Better get some sleep. Another day on the roller coaster awaits me. Oh, and I've finally learned my lesson; in the future, when asked to a fancy restaurant for drinks with the Exec Producer on a project I'm about to start, I just won't go.

CHAPTER 9

THE GIFT
OF OVERVIEW

The Salesman Cometh

Any good Producer is nothing more than a glorified salesman with a unique skill set. The same can be said for most of the important jobs in this world.

What is a salesman? A salesman is a catalyst that has an idea that they need to impart to you so that you will take some action that you probably otherwise wouldn't take. A salesman goes into every business meeting, luncheon, or casual conversation with the idea that he is the seller and you are a potential buyer. A good salesman is a great storyteller who gets you to commit your hard earned money today by painting a rosy picture about your tomorrow. Every good salesman has a plan for just about everyone they meet. They are never at rest while there are sheep to be shorn, people to meet and miles to go before they sleep.

They have a compulsion to knock on that door, get that foot in position, steel themselves to deliver the pitch, be prepared for the familiar two letter word, "no" in it's myriad forms and be ready to give it the old college to try to turn it into a "yes". They also have to be smart enough to recognize a "yes" whey they hear it. Good salesmen are always ready to take advantage of the slightest hesitation, the desire for interaction, information, entertainment and ultimately, in order to stay alive, they have to close the deal.

Many people who think of themselves as salesmen are really ticket takers. Their degree of salesmanship is on a par with, "Would like fries with that hamburger?" People are naturally lazy. Gravity makes their choices easy. Lie down or sit down whenever possible. What's difficult is the daily resurrection as you get up to face the world, light the fire and give it another try. A lot of us take the easiest possible path to our Laz-e-boy chairs, frittering away our time, being hypnotized by the tube. *Being There's* writer, Jerzy Kozinski, called TV "moving wallpaper". It's the best description I've yet heard.

Most people plane off somewhere and settle into a steady paycheck that lulls them into some false sense of security. From my vantage point, security starts internally. No amount of trappings or zeroes in your bank account can cover up your insecurity. Madison Avenue is built upon identifying our insecurities and selling us all kinds of things we don't necessarily need but are somehow convinced we absolutely have to have, the sooner the better. That's the lob ball, the easy stuff, piece of cake – like shooting fish in a barrel with an AK 47.

A good salesman learns how to dig in the corner for the puck when the easy shot on goal isn't available. They instinctively learn how to get off their shot and avoid getting smashed by their opponent who is bearing down from behind like a freight train. They get to hang around and live to fight another day because when you are a survivor, a "playa", the playing field evens out a bit because almost everyone wants the same thing; an outlet to the sea for something that they are responsible for creating.

Great Salesmen are alchemists who turn strangers into customers and customers into extended family and friends. They all look forward to the next story. The great Producer picks a few spare bucks from your pocket and you don't really mind.

Remember this one truism: *If you hate imposing on people to do what you want them to do, you won't make a good producer — period.* Conversely, *If you enjoy getting people to do what you want them to do and can get them to do it, you already are a producer.*

KEEPING THINGS IN PERSPECTIVE

The truth about Hollywood is that there isn't much truth in Hollywood. Truth in Hollywood is carefully crafted by publicity handlers, highly-paid executives and market researchers. The "varnished truth" is easier to accommodate and therefore more important than the real truth. "This ship can't be sinking because the band is still playing." Show Business is a series of large corporate fiefdoms producing the number one export of the U.S. For the most part, it appears to be run by greedy people hell-bent on wringing every last cent from an insatiable public. Everybody in Showbiz is vying for the unwashed masses' billions of "disposable dollars."

Like professional sports, Show Business is primarily diversion for the masses. No matter how hard the "Spin Doctors" attempt to make the public care who is currently in First Place, whether it's Weekend Box Office Grosses, Network TV Ratings or standings in the pennant race, the reality is, and I know this will be controversial in some quarters, that, with the exception of a few unlucky gamblers and racehorses who literally and figuratively "broke a leg", none of these end results are vital for anyone's continued existence on the planet. Somebody might lose a couple of million bucks on some screwed up business deal, but they're still on the right side of the river where one can only fail upwards for awhile. These are the lucky few who beat the odds and are going to milk their ride for every last dollar.

The producer's job is to consistently try to fool the public into thinking they are getting their money's worth. If one succeeds, one is paid handsomely and becomes famous for a while. Just about everyone is susceptible to flattering portraits and large transfusions of capital into their bank account. Underlying these material demonstrations of self-worth is the basic human desire to leave ones mark on the world — the "Kilroy Was Here" syndrome. While all of these high-minded and ennobling experiences were happening in front of the curtain, behind the curtain, most members of the creative community have to forgo the lion's share of their profit participation that isn't covered by the various guild residual agreements. These profits are used to pay for the mistakes of others in order to helpp keep the "mother ships" afloat. These include NBC/ Universal, Viacom/ Paramount, Time-Warner, Sony/Columbia, 20th Century Fox, Disney and BMG (Bertlesman Music Group).

If any of us cogs in the wheel cause trouble, we are quickly reminded that there's thousands more out there who will happily take our place in half a heartbeat.

No matter what they may say, outside of your immediate family and the temporary help who attach themselves to any rising career (agents, attorneys, managers), just about everyone else is rooting for you to fail. Success is not by design but rather a happy accident, a triumph over failure.

After watching the game from the fringe and subsequently inside the bowels, the only common denominator between those who make it from those who are defeated is one simple word, "perseverance." Black/ white, old/ young, saint/ sinner, male/ female, stupid/ smart, Jewish/ Christian/ Agnostic, it doesn't matter how many categories you fall into but rather it is in believing that you are one of the lucky ones and comprehending what it means in having to make your own luck. Perseverance, more often than not, is the ticket. Most sane, rational people leave abusive relationships at the first sign of trouble. How long you stay in this game is determined by what your definition of "quit" and, "success" happens to be.

After a hundred years of trying to define it absolutely, there is no clear-cut formula for guaranteed success in Showbiz. Eventually everything boils down to risk. This is the basic conundrum facing the bean counters that run Show Business. They have been trained in risk avoidance and everyday they are forced to risk great sums of money on flighty, artistic types with the "next sure thing, can't miss, great idea". The truth of the matter is that the public won't pay to watch someone count beans or they'd have no need of us at all.

The public is looking at Showbiz to provide them with the daily narcotizing escape from their own bean-counting type of lives.

In other businesses, you buy a product and it's guaranteed to work or you get your money back. If you pay to see something purporting to be entertainment that turns out to be a piece of crap, most people won't go back to the box office to ask for their money back because they are too embarrassed to admit that they were suckered in to see this show in the first place. Believe me, the producers, distributors and theater owners are counting on this fear of being embarrassed. You can only imagine the number of failures and executives jumping out of windows if, like in the restaurant business, you paid for your movie after seeing it and only if you liked it. Most of the studios would be bankrupt in a year.

We live in times when mediocre is still a passing grade. Each year there seems to be a handful of artists who discover new ways to pick up the edge and advance the art of storytelling. Making a TV Show or movie isn't brain surgery, but the components of what works and why is every bit as complicated.

One of television's early pioneers, Ernie Kovaks wry observation about most TV shows still holds true today, "They call television a medium because it is never rare and hardly ever well done."

The Fun Factory

Hollywood Studios are missing a bet.

Take a short but long overdue overview of how studios function today versus the Golden Age of Hollywood. Free Agency is the order of the day, as it has become every producer, director, man, woman and child actor for themselves. There is little or no "esprit de corps." Not so long ago there was a system that worked well for only about half a century (1920-1970). Free agency hit the marketplace and control of the medium was wrested away from the hands of a few moguls by some very big corporations. While the names of the studios mostly remain the same, the system that spawned them has been discarded.

An updated version of the old Hollywood system could really work today.

The goal would be to set up a Fun Factory, attract good people, teach them what they don't know, secure adequate funding and create an environment where they can perform their best work. The studios used to sign up talent both in front of and behind the camera for seven years. During that time their financial worries, along with half their time spent hustling their next gig, were replaced by having a steady job to go to each morning with the prerequisite of becoming the best artist, executive, writer, director, producer one could be. If you did well during that time period, you got additional perks and a better contract.

Nobody doubts the plethora of talent is out there. Why not incorporate the same basic "Golden Age" philosophy on a smaller scale and see what happens? The Fun Factory would provide the talent with a two (or three) year contract. In today's environment, many great young and old filmmakers would bang down the doors to get in. How do you pay for this? Convince a major Studio to real-locate the money spent on *one B movie* and create *fifteen* smaller movies, each with a clearly defined target audience and a fighting chance to score big, i.e. *Napoleon Dynamite, My Big Fat Greek Wedding, The Blair Witch Project, American Graffiti, Halloween, Easy Rider, Blood Simple, The Evil Dead, Badlands, The Groove Tube, Mean Streets, Friday the 13th, American Pie, Night of the Living Dead, Nightmare on Elm Street.* These films (and many more) were made outside of the studio system for very little money, spawned big careers and have proven to be enormously profitable.

Instead of ignoring this rich vein of talented filmmakers whose projects often don't fit into whatever the current blockbuster studio mentality happens to be, create a space for them to grow. The enlightened Studio who tries this approach will harvest a bumper crop for years to come.

The average studio B movie – two big stars rob a bank - costs $50 million to produce. Why not reallocate the money over a two-year period thusly:

Five $5 million dollar films – A team
Five $3 million dollar films – B team
Five $1.5 million dollar films - C team

$2.5 million would be allocated to set up the production offices and afford two year contracts for as many key personnel as possible.

This game plan calls for at least one movie a year to get a theatrical release through the parent company distribution arm. The other films will have to earn their way into the theaters and justify the marketing expenses or be sold off to the exploding home video, foreign and VOD marketplaces. The titles will help satisfy the voracious appetite of the Internet, cable TV, network TV and foreign TV for any new genre-driven studio movies. Every one of the filmmakers in the Fun Factory will bust their butts to become one of the theatrical releases by the parent studio. It's a tremendous carrot stick to hold out to proud, hungry filmmakers.

Another great reason for a major studio to get behind an idea like the Fun Factory is to be able to announce, "We're making a bunch of new movies right here in L.A." to help counteract the negative publicity caused by increasing runaway productions. Besides efficiently amortizing the overhead in an off-the-lot production over the 15 new titles, an additional benefit will be the availability of famous faces working on little films with low money and confirmed start dates. There are a lot of famous actors in-between big movie projects that really like to work. Some of them appear in small films they really wanted to make — *Pulp Fiction, Rocky, The Apostle, Sling Blade, Tender Mercies, Reservoir Dogs, In the Bedroom, The Straight Story, Barton Fink* to name but a few. If the right structure were created, the Fun Factory would become the cool place to produce them.

The Fun Factory could become an in-house minor league system for the Studio that takes the plunge. As talent wills out, as it always does, they move up the ladder. The director of a C Team feature gets a shot at a B Team film in the second year. Talented B Teamers will move up to an A Team slot in the second year. Amazing talent is bound to be discovered both in front of and behind the camera. The parent Studio would enjoy a first option to put the talent under contract and use them in bigger projects within a certain time frame at pre-negotiated rates (ala TV holding deals.) While nurturing undiscovered talent, the Fun Factory would provide a home for some of the great older talent that isn't being properly utilized in the X-Gen's version of Hollywood.

The Fun Factory would become the premiere hands-on Showbiz teaching lab not only for those who directly benefit from it but as a working model for how film productions can be run efficiently in the future. It's marrying up TV methodology with feature film sensibilities.

If any one of the new titles is a breakout winner, it'll pay for the entire investment and then some.

Today's Studios are missing a bet.

SPRING TRAINING

As any sports fan knows, spring training is where high-priced athletes get put through a series of drills and conditioning to prepare them for the upcoming season. They first learned these skills when they were children playing Little League, Pop Warner football or intramural sports. How to slide into a base without breaking your leg or twisting an ankle. How to properly catch, throw, hit or kick a ball. The rudimentary basics of their chosen profession. If you are management, you have to ask yourself if this is really necessary? The answer is, "yes", because every time one of those players dives for a ball or has a collision at home plate, millions of dollars are at risk.

Regardless of our profession, everybody occasionally needs to take that refresher course to remove the off-season rust, get into shape, remind us why we're here and fine-tune our mechanical skills.

I was a guest lecturer at a UCLA film school adult education course. The classroom held forty people who shared the notion that they'd like to become film directors. Having lectured before, the dialogue falls into a rhythm. The challenge is how to splash cold water in their faces without dousing the ember that got them there.

Lecturing young people who are paying for information is a lot like spring training. It's a wonderful opportunity to look back down the road you started on and revisit the first mountain you ever climbed, that life-altering decision when you took those first baby steps in pursuit of the dream. You hear yourself answering questions you asked somebody else eons ago. Although it's self-evident information to you now, it's a drink at the fountain of experience for those who are just beginning their journey. I can't explain how it feels but everyone should take advantage of the opportunity if and when it comes along.

In going back to basics you have to hit all the familiar notes.

Imagine yourself at a crossroad. Your first decision is; where do you see yourself fitting in — film or TV? There's ten times more work in TV and a much better chance for paying your bills. If movies are your decision, the approaching fork in the road will force you to make another choice: low budget independent films or mainstream, multiplex flicks? What kind of stories do you really want to tell? If you are truly lucky and all the stars align just so, at the end of a year or two, you will have a DVD copy of something you have been responsible for ushering into the world to proudly show others and hopefully secure more work.

Young people rarely think about or have any idea about what happens next. In their fantasy world, they just arrive full-blown rich and famous and enjoy the fruits of their labor. Standing in line and paying ones dues is for suckers! Someone will undoubtedly see their short film and give them a three-picture deal at Paramount. They are surprised to learn that it just doesn't quite work out that way.

Oh, how their faces fall when you mention that the Sundance Film Festival receives 800 submissions each year and only chooses 40 films. The rival Slamdance Film Festival will pick 20 more leaving a whole bunch of dead dreams littering the roadside. "Oh no! How am I going to pay back Mom, Dad and Uncle Fred?" In spite of the developing new revenue streams like the Internet and VOD, these tyro directors and producers will be lucky if they can sell the results for pennies on the dollar that was spent to make them. "How am I going to live with the friends or relatives who financed my self indulgent/ piece of crap/ shattered dream?"

Should've thought about that a year ago, pal.

Back in the classroom, in dashing some of their hopes on the rocks, maybe I planted a seed or two of doubt and saved a few of them years of trying to make it in a business that will chew them up and spit them out for breakfast. A third of the class mentally checks out at this point because they don't want to hear it. But a few take the bad news as a challenge. They have this vague idea of some story they need to tell, come hell or high water. Eating, sleeping and drinking show business isn't enough. If it's what they think about in-between heartbeats, there's half a chance they'll succeed.

I ever so gently remind them that there are a lot of other career opportunities within show business besides being a director. Many of those who do stick around will have to find another niche besides directing to pay the bills.

Back to the basics: passion sells.

Your passion for a project occasionally turns on the people on the other side of the desk. This entails you having a vision and a coherent plan how to achieve it. Having confidence in your own ability is great but you have to do your homework - another third of the class just checked out. "Too much work, man!" Your plan has to be flexible enough to accommodate the inevitable curveballs and other people's great ideas. It is a collaborative effort. It's a people business. The quickest way to the directors' chair is to find or write a great story and hold on for dear life. If you can turn on the right star, DP, or a little film production company, and you're really lucky, you'll get your shot. (Fifteen percent more slip away into the icy waters.) The real challenge is to rise above the mediocrity out there and show the talent scouts that you've got something uniquely special going on.

By this point, their eyelids began to droop. Most have a day job or other classes to go to the next morning, Some of them walk out looking for another career. Afterwards, one or two come up and you can see that glint in their eye, that touch of madness that is required to fuel the singular dream that nobody else believes in right now but you. They have been turned on. They have tossed aside your admonitions because none of that precautionary crap applies to them. They are the lucky ones or unlucky ones, depending on your point of view. They have the desire and necessary zeal to take the journey. Whether they have the stamina, can figure out how to make a living so they can hang around the tables and maybe get lucky is anybody's guess.

The initial five-year fistfight in the foyer will thin out the ranks of the young hopefuls, but these few have a chance and deserve to be encouraged. Because one day, thirty or forty years up the road, when the older generation's fingers are finally pried off the steering wheel, they will get their chance to drive, and by then, we'll all be dirt napping or along for what's left of the ride.

In closing out the Spring Training metaphor, sharing your knowledge and experiences, filling in some of the blind spots, pointing out the dead ends and quicksand pits, it's all part of paying back, putting something in the collection plate. You're helping to prepare the next generation of filmmakers and storytellers. You don't have to do it. It just makes you feel good when you can.

GIMME A HAND

Friendship is the best thing that can happen between two people. Some might argue that the short-lived intersection of private parts tops the list of meaningful human interaction but because the same experience can almost be replicated with a healthy imagination as a singular pursuit, it comes in second place in my book. Others might say that "love" is the pinnacle of what two people can achieve in this lifetime but love is also a transitory expression of feelings. Don't get me wrong — love is great but ... it is one of the most abused concepts out there. We are all in love all the time because love takes many forms: we love our spouse(s) or significant other, ourselves, our pets, our new car, that movie star, this flavor ice cream, our favorite sports team, etc., etc. Like the ocean tide, love comes and goes, ebbs and flows as things change. But the real glue that binds two people together is friendship.

Sometimes it happens instantly like two peas in a pod. The best anyone can hope for is when it's like reincarnated souls who were destined to meet again. Long lost brothers or sisters. Somewhere along the line a bolt of lightning fused these two souls together from now 'til the end of time. It only happens a couple of times in your lifetime and you better hold onto those folk for dear life.

Sometimes it takes a lifetime to solidify an understanding between two people. Sometimes they never quite achieve friendship and the closest they come to it is a grudging admiration. I'm always amazed by the instinctive ritual of shaking hands. Two strangers who have decided not to kill each other, (at least not yet) meet and shake hands. You know pretty quickly whether you've met somebody you could be friends with or should be wary of. Back in the old days, people shook hands to show they weren't carrying any obvious weapons. Shaking hands was an act of faith. Kind of an informal declaration of intent that, "I won't harm you right away if you won't harm me. Let's at least wait until we get to know each other a little better."

We all come in contact with thousands of people over the course of a lifetime. It is a mystery why these two people connect where the other thousands didn't. Mostly it's because we don't have endless hours of free time on our hands to explore each other's minds and discover all the things we have in common. But it's much more than that. Great friendships result from a chemical reaction in the brainpan.

Underneath our thin coat of civility lurks the animal within. Every relationship is evaluated on some primal level. What do I want from you? What do you want from me? Will it be an even swap of goods and services or will one have the advantage? And if one does have the upper hand, is this a relationship I really need, want or would like to have?

Trust issues. Shrinks have made a nice living off those two words because anyone who has lived has trust issues. If you make a friend and they let you down, do you never trust that person again? Do you ever trust any other person again?

Most of your friends have or will at some point in time let you down. They don't measure up to your expectations. Some forget to call or miss an appointment or even bounce a check on you. The animal inside determines what is acceptable behavior and where we draw the invisible lines that we all live within. You live and learn. Friendship is a kind of love. And like love, it's elastic. You make exceptions to whatever rules you have because of friendship. You choose to see people in a different light. You give your friends the benefit of the doubt.

And when you have a great friend, even if you haven't seen each other for weeks, months, decades, you slip right back into that familiar pattern of talking or thinking that attracted you in the first place. It's that chemical reaction that gladdens the heart and rejuvenates the spirit. Having true friends is the greatest thing one can have. Greater than love, power, fame and fortune. It is the greatest treasure available here on earth. Value it. Respect it. Nurture it because it is rare indeed.

Because, as some great philosophers pointed out once upon a time, you get high with a little help from your friends.

CHAPTER 10

REVELATIONS

GOD ONLY KNOWS

On the first day of a production, before the first shot of the day is taken, I usually arrange for a local holy man to come to the set and in return for a small donation, conduct a short service where they bless the show. There have been the traditional priests, ministers and rabbis but on a couple of occasions, I've opted for the exotic.

This is after the budget has been funded, the locations found, the sets dressed, the crew hired. The heads of the various departments have met with the director and producers and understand the game plan. They have prepared as best as they can to make this as good a show as possible because part of their future is riding on the outcome of this project. If it's a hit, it enhances their status in the marketplace. On this first day of battle, there's wide-eyed excitement in the air, even by the most jaded crewmembers as we collectively step off the plank and hope there's water in the pool.

If time and the budget permits, I always try to arrange for a Prep Party the night before production begins. We are all about to be submerged together for a trip into the unknown. The cast and crew can renew old friendships and possibly make a few new ones before diving into the fray.

A couple of days before commencement, there is a Technical Scout where the department heads are taken to as many locations as possible. The Director and DP (Director of Photography) decide what the best camera angles are to shoot each scene and determine their lighting requirements. The transportation captain determines the best place to park The Circus at each location that offers the greatest accessibility out of camera range. The location generator and crew also need to park nearby, etc. The Key Grip and Gaffer figure out what extra manpower, lighting and rigging equipment will be needed each day.

After the Tech Scout comes the Final Production Meeting. After everyone introduces themselves, the 1st AD (Assistant Director) traditionally chairs the meeting and the gang walks through the script page-by-page, scene-by-scene and any last minute questions or concerns get addressed. Everybody is supposed to get on the same page. This often proves to be an extremely productive exercise because maybe somebody from wardrobe has a problem, and somebody from the transportation or camera department who had to solve the very same problem on a previous show offers a solution. There are usually hundreds of years of collective production experience in attendance, and most of the major obstacles have been previously encountered and overcome by someone in the room.

And so, on the first day, the holy man arrives. A few prayers get said to the heavens asking for good weather and a safe and successful journey. In the exotic arena, I've arranged for a Cherokee Indian Shaman in North Carolina to bless our production. After a big drum ceremony pounded on by half a dozen young warriors, the Shaman spoke for fifteen minutes in his native Cherokee language as the crew stood around respectfully and everyone hoped for the best. The shoot went off with only a few minor bumps in the road, the most memorable of which happened when a pair of dogs owned by crew members went off into the hills and killed someone's pet goat. The poor local man practically ran over half a dozen crew-members in his pickup truck yelling about his prize goat getting killed. I believe $200 soothed the outraged fellow's ruffled feathers.

The shoot in North Carolina film was a true collaboration as first time Director, Timothy Hutton, ended up in the capable hands of DP, Jorgen Persson (*My Life As A Dog, Pele, The Conqueror*). The end result was a neat little movie called, *Digging To China* that introduced the world to eleven year old Rachel Evan Woods.

My other favorite first day ceremony occurred at dawn one morning in a downtown LA parking lot where a Buddhist Monk blessed a pig that was roasting on a spit and then lit off a brick of firecrackers that were thrown to the north, south, east and west. Everybody had a bite of pork and then went to work on a totally forgettable Korean martial arts picture with the unfortunate title, *A Touch Of Wing*.

After all the plotting, planning, pre-thinking and preparation, an experienced crew knows that anything can happen during a shoot. There are traditionally a few fender benders, sprained ankles, various scrapes and bruises. A few things of value get lost, stolen or broken along the way. Unfavorable weather can totally wreck the best-laid plans and wreak havoc on the budget so it's a good thing to have the man upstairs on your side.

With the fate of the production and all of our careers are up in the air, I believe it's worth a little insurance policy to have one of His emissaries present as we launch the ship because God only knows how it's all going to turn out.

GREATNESS

Buried beneath the layers of clothing, under the scars of dashed hopes and chards of broken dreams, deep down inside there is a special item that we keep hidden from the prying eyes of the outside world. It's locked away in that hope chest near our hearts. Every once in awhile, in the stillness of the night, when no one is watching, we'll carve out a few moments of quiet introspection and pull out the hidden package, dust it off, unwrap it gently, and take a look. It is the portrait of our younger self. It is the person who dared to be different. Who wanted something better out of this life. The little kid who wanted to be great at something.

This is America after all, a place where paupers can become millionaires. Where nobodies are allowed to become somebodies. Where dreams can come true and it can happen to you, if you're young at heart. Libraries, magazine racks and video stores are full of other people's stories. Why not yours? Too many stories, not enough shelf space. The public appears to have an inexhaustible, insatiable appetite for more, more, more.

When you rent three movie videos in the hopes that one of them delivers on the promises made on the jacket cover, once in a great while you'll be pleasantly surprised, sometimes astonished, by a little jewel of a movie that didn't make it to the top of the heap. The discovery is encouraging, just knowing that somebody else got their dream made.

They didn't blow it when they finally got their chance,. They fought off the entropy that surrounds any original enterprise and beat back the committee that wanted them to play it safe and water down their vision, thus making it more palatable to the masses. With danger and failure awaiting at every turn in the road, the great ones manage to speed by, avoid trite storytelling pitfalls and reach the finish line to deliver on the promises that were made.

It is the potential for greatness that lies within each of us that we need to try harder to get in touch with. It's not trying to please everybody else — it's really about pleasing yourself. Not in that self-indulgent petulant spoiled brat kind of way. Not in the getting high too often that causes a wonderful paralytic stupor. No, the quest for greatness is all about doing the work, hitting the heights you once aimed for, and realizing your dreams.

Too many people settle for being average. Unfortunately, there are a lot of folk wandering around without any kind of philosophy of life. They exist, buy things, eat, sleep and screw. They have no clue how to get from here to there. They're in love with the idea of being rich and famous but don't want to do the hard work required to get there.

Only a lucky few make it through unscathed. Most veterans have taken their fair share of torpedoes along the way and somehow manage to keep going. The flame still burns brightly within the hope chest. A slightly older version of ourselves has to duke it out everyday. Rolling with the punches isn't as much fun as it used to be when we were kids.

People who aspire to greatness are the only ones who have a chance of getting there. Sooner or later, everyone else gets caught on the flypaper (pest control strips?) of mediocrity. Each of us has our own definition of greatness. The world will let us know when we've succeeded but it's definitely something to shoot for.

FRIENDSHIP

Who goes there? Friend or foe? For every lone sentry at every lonely outpost down through history, this was the first and most important question. It often had a very lethal answer. Instinctively, we all ask this question of everyone we meet along the way. You can tell within less than a minute if the new stranger you just met is someone you need to be wary of or possibly want to get to know better. Rarely is that first impression wrong.

Every once in awhile, you're surprised by someone but for the most part, the internal divining rod that got you this far in these shark infested waters is a pretty accurate barometer when it comes to divining friend or foe. Wouldn't it be great if there was an infallible, FDA approved mechanical device down at K-Mart that could predetermine if every new person you meet has the potential to be someone you can trust, rely upon, become a good fiend, or even a great friend.

"C'mon down! There's a sale this week on the new Pal-Ometer. Why waste time with people who are going to disappoint you? Why waste money on phony clubs, dating services, etc? Get the new Pal-Ometer and find out instantly if you have found a true friend. Hell, if the Pal-Ometer spikes out, this could be someone to love."

The Pal-Ometer would be a palm-size black box with mini-jumper cables that you could attach to each other's earlobes. Three seconds later you would say "Thanks, but no thanks" or "Lets grab a cup of java and swap stories." There is no such device on the market today that measures friendship, one of the most important human relationships any of us ever embraces during our lives. (And if any of you invent it, I want a royalty. "Pal-Ometer" is a now a registered trademark with fifteen patents pending.)

No matter how much we love our computers, they don't love us back. They don't have a drink with you, laugh at your jokes, and make you hot soup when you're sick and tired. Don't loan you money when you need it. Don't offer a shoulder to cry on or rub your sore, tired feet. Don't read your screenplay and give you honest criticism. Don't grab a lunch and listen to your latest scheme. They don't walk around the block with you and help put things in perspective. They don't pick you up when you fall.

That's what friends do. They are there when you need them. They go out of their way to do something nice for you. They are important parts of your personal orchestra as you are a part of theirs. Don't know about you but I want a lot of people at my funeral. I want them to come together for the final sendoff, say what a wonderful guy I was, have a nice schmoozefest at the wake, laugh and cry and feel enriched by the experience of having known me.

You have to recruit that crowd one person at a time. You have a responsibility to make your friends feel good about themselves. It's all part of life's unwritten rules. Unfortunately for all of us, relationships are not readily available at the FRIENDS "R" US drive-thru window. It would be a place where you could pull in and order – "I'd like to find the love of my life, a sexy little something on the side, and a bunch of pals to hang out with."

Friendship cannot be bought or sold. It must be earned the old fashioned way. The neat thing about Showbiz is that one of these days you, or one of your friends, are going to pull the lever and it's going to come up cherries and then there'll be a lot of new friends to celebrate with.

THE LONG VIEW

It's important to take stock one in awhile. Pull off to the side of the road, drink in the scenery while listening to your favorite music, take a deep breath and try to put this whole thing in perspective.

If you lead a productive work life for forty years and average $50k a year, you'll have earned $2 million dollars. It would be nice to get it in one lump sum but not too shabby on the overall scheme of things. Most people in show business have a pretty good shot of at least making a million during their lifetime.

Q. Hey, what are you going to do with all that loot?
A. Try to survive.

If you live to be a hundred, you'll have witnessed a little over 36,500 sunrises and sunsets. You'll have eaten approximately 100,000 meals. A little fewer if you believe in dieting. A little more if you believe in indulging yourself. If you were born after 1950 and have seen your average of 6 hours of TV a day, you're looking at over

200,000 hrs of TV and film watching (or 25 years of solid tube watching- no sleep) Twenty five :30 second TV ads per hour x 200,000 hrs translates into 5,000,000 ad hits. No wonder your head is spinning. When you throw in the billboards, radio spots and magazine ads we're exposed to every day, you're heading into some really scary numbers.

"Sensory overload" is too neat a phrase. We're talking professional brainwashing on a huge scale not seen since Mao Tse Tung grabbed the soapbox and the microphone over there in China. Madison Avenue makes Mao Baby look like a piker – a speed bump in the history of mass manipulation. We are a nation of consumers. It's what we were programmed for.

I always had this image of Judgment Day where you were ushered into a large white cove cyclorama stage and a final accounting was done. All the books you ever read were stacked up. All the clothes you ever wore were in a pile. All the candy bars, cookies and treats in another pile. All the drinks, plates with food you've eaten, everything that has entered your body is stacked high.

Everything that has passed out of your body is kept in separate odor-contained vats. The people you slept with are lined up. The children you spawned appear. Everything you were responsible for creating from book reports to Income Tax returns was brought in by forklifts. There will be some giant scale that you stand on one end of and all these things are loaded onto the other. St. Peter has this giant 10 feet high computer report that all gets fed into the database. After a few seconds of sorting, the toaster bell rings and you either get a green light or a red light.

This experience would determine the direction of your eternal soul. Green means north. Red means south. No appeals. No saying a few words in your own defense. Upon reaching your final destination, hopefully all the talking will be over by then and everyone will just get a chance to enjoy each other's spirit for who they really are. One thing's for sure — we will have finally escaped Madison Avenue. From all reports, there are no billboards or TV spots in the afterlife ... yet.

THE GOLDEN HOUR

An old man, unsteady gait, approaches a headstone in a cemetery. He kneels, puts a quarter into a slot, pushes a button on the side of the headstone and an index card sized LCD TV monitor flickers to life featuring a short film about his late wife. He gets to watch her through the years, a photo montage, underscored by her favorite music, grainy home movies of a few distant moments captured in time; her pulling the Thanksgiving turkey from the old oven, blowing out some birthday candles or there she is all gussied up for one of the kids weddings. A super 8 movie of her younger self in an old fashioned bathing suit and a bathing cap, laughing, smiling, and waving as she runs into the water.

The old man's eyes well up with tears. He laughs, cries and shakes his head at how beautiful his bride, his partner in life once was. He has done this a thousand times before and never tires of it. She was the love of his life and now, outside of his dimming memories; this is the closest he can be to her.

A cemetery that provided this extra-added attraction would become a huge success. Imagine a place the size of Forest Lawn where each headstone had a mini TV monitor. Imagine the friends and relatives wandering around throwing a quarter into a slot to watch a five-minute biography about their dearly departed loved ones. The crowds on the weekends would be SRO. Strangers would find their favorite people and return with other friends to show off their discoveries. Sort of a living museum paying tribute to wonderful people who they once shared the planet with. It would be a way of physically bridging the chasm between where we are and where each of us will one day be.

I admit that I am fascinated with the end of the line. Most people live their lives in denial that death will ever happen to them.

They fritter away their time and opportunities as though there is a never-ending stream of tomorrows on their horizon. Early on, having gone head first through my windshield and bouncing off another car's windshield one rainy afternoon in Laurel Canyon thirty years ago, I learned the value of life. Every day since then has been a miracle. It's not as though I feel like I'm living on borrowed time, but rather that I got lucky. We all got lucky and not enough people truly appreciate it. Every day above ground is a good day.

One evening, I found myself sitting in the back of a Jet Ranger helicopter flying through the canyons of downtown L.A. The back doors had been removed so that the stuntman could lean out and fire a phony bazooka at a flying car. There was another helicopter flying alongside with the camera crew. After the shot was completed, our pilot suddenly banked the chopper and peeled away in order to get back in position for another take. However the stuntman wasn't properly tethered in, and I had to grab his belt as he was sliding by and hold on for dear life because his legs were dangling out the open door. I was yelling into the headsets at the pilot and after awhile he righted the ship. It was one of the scarier experiences of my life and I thank my lucky stars that it ended well. No filmmaking experience should ever cost someone their life. It's far too high a price to pay for a little piece of make-believe.

As a producer of different sized stories designed for mass consumption on a film or TV screen, part of my job is to look ahead to what the finished product is supposed to look like. I have to make a hundred little choices everyday to help translate the project from the written word to a moving image for the viewing pleasure of the audience. I look at my life's work as one long continuous production challenge waiting to be solved. Where do I want to be at the end? What do I want to have accomplished? If you never think about this, you are a wandering nomad with no great goals on your horizon, happy to survive another day in the howling wind that engulfs us all. If, however, this realistic line of thinking can be incorporated into your daily lives, decisions get easier and life can be a hell of a lot more fun.

I always try to project a piece of myself into the future to act as my own scout. Leaving little signs along the trail, especially at the many forks in the road – go this way, not that. The scout has already been to the end of the line, the near death experience. It reminds me of what's important on this journey and what's not.

Every moment of every day, several people around the world are having what doctors call "their golden hour" - the last hour of their lives. It's idyllic to think that in the final hour of our lives, we have all of our marbles, we're not in great pain, have family, friends or people around and we get a chance to put things in order one last time. Why wait? Try to find a golden hour every day for yourself. Clear your mind of the debris and enjoy the sensation of just being alive. Get ready for that golden hour because look out, just when you least expect it – here comes that windshield!

I SUSPECT

As children, we are ignorant of most things. As we get older, we learn a ton about the world we have landed in. Sometimes we learn too much too soon. For instance, the rumors going around that one day all this will end are apparently true. As part of the crowd that believes the glass is always at least half full, one has to learn to ignore a lot of things that could spoil each day. The evening news has pretty much turned into a nightly compendium of natural disasters or man-made incidents that resulted in the untimely demises of some of our fellow men and women, captured for posterity on video.

I've been told that one day my own body will give out and so will yours. Sad but true. This amazing machine that does my bidding each day will either stop dead in its tracks or become so broken down that it'll take some very expensive machinery to keep me ticking a little while longer. I suspect this will happen to the majority of us and yet, nobody wants to talk about it or really think about it. We're so caught up in the "here and now" that we're in denial about the "over and out" part.

When we do focus on our upcoming release from this mortal coil, we all have this idyllic picture in our heads like a scene from an old movie. Family and friends are gathered around a four-corner post bed to see us off. We hope to be able to recognize the faces and tell each of them something witty or pithy like, "I never did like your hairdo or choice of boyfriends." Or maybe something helpful like, "Take that trip you've been putting off" or "Stop talking about it and just do whatever it is you've been procrastinating about. Enough already."

And maybe you'll even get a chance to right the wrongs, say the things that you should've said long ago; "I've always hated your cooking", "Your idea of romance is sorely lacking", "Try shutting up once in awhile", "Let's talk about your breath, choice of careers or total lack of ambition." I suspect nobody wants to hear these things, especially when you're at the end of the line and there's no time to argue about it. Much better if you get these things off your chest now and live with the consequences.

Peaceful departures don't make the news unless you're someone worth noting. Most people have to earn their way onto the nightly news the bloody hard way. Any departure leaves aching holes in the hearts of friends and loved ones who didn't get a chance to say, "Goodbye, have a nice afterlife, see you on the other side, save me a good seat."

You'd think we'd all be a whole lot more sympathetic to each other if we ever faced the fact that we all share the same daily challenges; to keep moving forward with our heads held high, to fight the gravity that keeps trying to return us to the sender, to enjoy the time we spend together, to live, laugh and love as much as possible.

It will get sad, dark and gloomy soon enough. Until they prove that reincarnation really works, it'll apparently stay that way for quite awhile. Enjoy each day, hour and moment. They are gifts from on high. Whatever is happening to you, good, bad or indifferent, I suspect it's far more interesting than when it's no longer happening to you.

And finally, here's an article written by my father that was published in Reader's Digest. Long ago, Pop mastered the written word and reading his work always humbles me. It is reprinted here without his permission because he is no longer here to ask but I'm sure he would approve. Thanks, Pop.

THE LIGHT TOUCH
by Joseph Ecclesine

The light touch in writing flows automatically from the not-too-widely held premise that readers, in return for the demands that reading makes on their time, are entitled to some reward beyond the bald information the writing contains.

What, as a reward, is the light touch?

In music, it would be the obbligato — the accompaniment that exists outside the melody, runs along with it as the counter-point or accent, never interferes with it, yet is so integral to the total effect that the music would be a lot poorer without it.

In art, it would be the chiaroscuro — the interplay of light and shadow as a vital element of the total picture.

In the daily newspaper, it would be the editorial page cartoon that brings a smile. In advertising, the TV commercial starring a little girl happily mimicking the side-by-side waddling walk of a penguin.

In writing it appears to be hard to come by — and far too often an accidental or unintentional ingredient.

The light touch is a personality, a frame of mind — a likeable brightness and warmth that filters through the words like sun through the clouds. A quality that says the words weren't written by a machine. An adult spirit abroad in an adult world, with power to charm — and charm to burn. A colorful, vibrant gypsy piedpipering you down a coolly-calculated road to understanding and acceptance.

But the light touch is not merely an end to be sought for it's own sake. Rather, it's a catalytic agent that lifts writing to higher levels of interest without distorting or diffusing its message.

With it, writing is warm, alive. Without it, cold, factually correct — and no more or less interesting than the cold facts themselves.

The light touch thrives on the fact that many words have more than one meaning — yet it shuns puns for puns' sake. It weighs nuances coldly, as if they had weight. It uses those that delight, discards those that distract, or worse, detract.

It knows that words are music — and arranges them so they supply the restful subordinate joys of harmony while carrying the melody.

It knows that words are lights and shadows — and plays them against each other to give writing the sparkle anything so public and expensive deserves.

It treasures precision, yet enjoys surprise, when it can be found. It distrusts formality, follows no rules — or if pressed, blithely rolls its own. It has an ill-concealed eagerness, the joy of conscious communication. It has a four-track mind, yet never moves freight over all four at the same time. It has balance, speed and control. It talks to everybody — and to very many it sings.

The light touch is not a string of gags masquerading as humor wistfully courting applause. Often it is not humor at all — but, always, it is esthetically, intellectually amusing.

It is a quality that can sometimes be infused *post facto* — the way blood is transfused into an accident victim. But usually it is as indigenous to the copy it graces as fragrance to flowers, oxygen to air. And it seems to come naturally to the people who own and operate it — people who are seldom pompous, not often neurotic (they've learned to employ, rather than exploit, their emotions). They are mature, yet understand the child in all of us. They are rarely egotistical as they have a right to be, yet they know, better than most, what they can do — and what they can't. They love to write — but put writing where it belongs — at the far end of the essential preliminary processes of analysis and thought. They bubble — but with ideas. And, above all, they laugh at themselves — rather than others.

Writing — any writing except that designed for tombstone carving — stands only to gain from the light touch.

It is at once an insulation against boredom and a recognition that if the reader's interest is as important as the writer's own, if not indeed more so, it has the joy of living, but subordinates it to the joy of communication, the joy of persuading, the joy of entertaining. And more often than not it leaves the reader not only better informed but happier for just having read it.

AFTERWORD

I hope these essays have provided you with some pleasure, some valuable information and something to think about in case you really are contemplating a career in Showbiz. I wish it, or something like it, had been available to me earlier on in my career. I would've better understood the challenges I faced and wouldn't have had to find out about everything the hard way.

In retrospect, as I re-read some of these missives, I have tried to balance my advice to the neophytes with hopefully some helpful suggestions on how to improve things and level the playing field. New technology will continue to provide new opportunities to the next bumper crop of wannabe filmmakers.

I've had a chance to do a lot of things that most other people will never get to do and for those opportunities, I am eternally grateful. It really is true – *There's No Business Like Show Business.*

GENERIC HORROR FILM

Producers : TBD
Director: TBD
2 Cameras - 35mm
20 DAYS on Location- NEW MEXICO
DELIVER VIDEO MASTER

SAG, WGA, IA, TEAMSTER, DGA
12-HOUR WORK DAYS FOR CREW
IATSE TIER ONE BA RATES
AGENCY COMMISSION
PREPARED BY S. ECCLESINE
DATE (2008)

Acct No	Category Description	Page	Total
1100	WRITER	1	95,152
1200	PRODUCERS UNIT	1	336,678
1300	DIRECTORS UNIT	2	95,108
1400	CAST	2	276,792
1500	STUNTS	4	27,828
1600	CASTING	5	38,346
1700	TRAVEL & LIVING COSTS	5	73,332
1800	DEVELOPMENT	8	7,000
	TOTAL ABOVE-THE-LINE		**950,236**
2000	PRODUCTION STAFF	10	236,938
2100	EXTRAS	12	39,839
2200	DESIGN	13	71,161
2300	SET CONSTRUCTION	15	153,647
2400	SET STRIKING	17	1,755
2500	SET OPERATIONS	17	108,383
2600	EFFECTS	19	56,379
2700	SET DRESSING	21	80,728
2800	PROPERTY	22	32,732
2900	WARDROBE	23	77,588
3000	GRIP	25	77,912
3100	MAKEUP & HAIR	27	126,452
3200	ELECTRIC	28	102,905
3300	CAMERA	30	215,557
3400	PRODUCTION SOUND	32	40,398
3500	TRANSPORTATION	33	302,730
3600	LOCATION	38	129,107
3700	PROD / FILM & LAB	41	97,165
3800	TRAVEL & LIVING COSTS	41	76,472
	TOTAL PRODUCTION		**2,027,847**
4500	EDITORIAL	44	291,558
4600	MUSIC	44	41,278
4700	POST SOUND	45	77,100
4800	STOCK SHOTS	45	5,000
4900	MAIN & END TITLES	45	9,000
5000	POST HD/FILM & LABORATORY	45	36,475
5100	POST MANAGEMENT	46	9,067
	TOTAL POST PRODUCTION		**469,477**
6600	LEGAL	47	35,018
6700	INSURANCE	47	64,500
6800	AGENCY PACKAGING FEE : 1.0%		35,471
6900	COMPLETION BOND : 1.75%		62,074
	CONTINGENCY : 10.0%		354,708
	TOTAL OTHER		**551,770**

Acct No	Category Description	Page	Total
	Grand Total		3,999,330

Producers : TBD
Director: TBD
2 Cameras - 35mm
20 DAYS on Location- NEW MEXICO
DELIVER VIDEO MASTER

SAG, WGA, IA, TEAMSTER, DGA
12-HOUR WORK DAYS FOR CREW
IATSE TIER ONE BA RATES
AGENCY COMMISSION
PREPARED BY S. ECCLESINE
DATE (2008)

Acct No	Description	Amount	Units	X	Curr	Rate	Subtotal	Total
1100 WRITER								
1101	WRITER							
	Screenplay	1	ALLOW	1		80,000	80,000	
	Total							80,000
1102	RESEARCH							
	SCRIPT CLEARANCE							
	PA Certificate of Copyright	1	Fee	1		60.0	60	
	Certificate of Authorship	1	Fee	1		150	150	
	Title/Copyright Search	1	Fee	1		1,200	1,200	
	Hollywood Screen / Other)							
	Script Clearance	1	Fee	1		1,300	1,300	
	Total							2,710
1108	SCRIPT COPIES							
	Photocopy Allowance	1		1		250	250	
	Total							250
1199	Total Fringes							
	WCOMP-(CA) CLER	1.69%				80,000	1,352	
	PR FEE (Chks)	0.05%				80,000	40	
	WGA-P&H	13.5%				80,000	10,800	12,192
Account Total for 1100								95,152
1200 PRODUCERS UNIT								
1201	EXEC PRODUCER							
	Company Fee (Contract)	1	ALLOW	1		150,000	150,000	
	Total							150,000
1202	PRODUCER							
	PRODUCER	1	ALLOW	1		100,000	100,000	
	LINE PRODUCER	10	WEEKS	1		7,500	75,000	
	Total							175,000
1205	ASSISTANT TO PRODUCER							
	Assistant	10	WEEKS	1		750	7,500	
	Total							7,500
1206	GIFTS/ENTERTAINMENT							
	CAST GIFT BASKETS	4	CAST	1		75.0	300	
	ENTERTAINAMENT COSTS							
	Producer's Discretionary	1	ALLOW	1		2,000	2,000	
	Total							2,300
1299	Total Fringes							
	PR FEE (Chks)	0.05%				325,000	162	
	FICA (NM/CA/NY)	6.2%				7,500	465	
	MED (NM/CA/NY)	1.45%				7,500	109	
	FUTA (NM/CA/NY)	0.8%				7,000	56	
	SUTA (NM)	5.4%				7,500	405	
	SUTA (CA/NY)	6.2%				7,000	434	
	W-COMP (NM)	2.85%				7,500	214	

Acct No	Description	Amount	Units	X	Curr	Rate	Subtotal	Total
	ETT (NM)	0.1%				7,000	7	
	PAYROLL FEE	0.35%				7,500	26	1,878
Account Total for 1200								336,678
1300 DIRECTORS UNIT								
1301	DIRECTOR							
	(DGA Min +10% Agency)	1	CONTRACT	1		80,000	80,000	
	Total							80,000
1310	MEDICAL							
	Director Medical Exam	1	EXAM	1		100.0	100	
	Total							100
1399	Total Fringes							
	PR FEE (Chks)	0.05%				80,000	40	
	W-COMP (CA/NY)	4.71%				80,000	3,768	
	DGA-ATL P&H	14%				80,000	11,200	15,008
Account Total for 1300								95,108
1400 CAST								
1401	STAR #1							
	Production	4	WEEKS	1		20,000	80,000	
	Incl. Rehearsal/Travel included)							
	Total							80,000
1402	STAR #2							
	Production	4	WEEKS	1		7,500	30,000	
	Overtime Allowance							
	48 hrs wk /2x @ $250 hr)	20	DAYS	2		250	10,000	
	Total							40,000
1403	STAR #3							
	Production	2	WEEKS	1		7,500	15,000	
	Overtime Allowance							
	(48 hrs week / 2x = $250 hr)	10	DAYS	2		250	5,000	
	Total							20,000
1404	STAR #4							
	Production	1	WEEK	1		6,500	6,500	
	Overtime Allowance							
	(48 hrs week / 2x @ $250 hr)	5	DAYS	2		250	2,500	
	(Average 12 hr day)							
	Travel	2	DAYS	1		496.6	993	
	Total							9,993
1405	SUPPORTING STAR #1							
	Production	1	WEEK	1		2,483	2,483	
	44 hrs wk/ 1.5x @ $84.646 hr)	4	HOURS	1		84.646	338	
	8 hrs day/2x @ $112.86 hr)	8	HOURS	1		112.86	902	
	Agent Fee -10%	1		0.1		3,724	372	
	Total							4,097
1406	SUPPORTING STAR # 2							
	Production	2	WEEKS	1		2,483	4,966	
	44 hrs wk/ 1.5x @ $84.646 hr)	8	HOURS	1		84.646	677	
	8 hrs day / 2x @ $112.86 hr)	16	HOURS	1		112.86	1,805	
	Agent Fee - 10%	1		0.1		7,449	744	
	Total							8,194
1407	SUPPORTING STAR #3							

Acct No	Description	Amount	Units	X	Curr	Rate	Subtotal	Total
	Production (12 hr day)	1	DAY	1		1,343	1,343	
	Schedule B - Wkly Scale							
	Production	1	WEEK	1		2,483	2,483	
	44 hrs wk/ 1.5x @ $84.646 hr)	6	HOURS	1		84.646	507	
	8 hrs day / 2x @ $112.86 hr)	12	HOURS	1		112.86	1,354	
	Agent Fee - 10%	1		0.1		5,688	568	
	Meal Penalty Allowance	1	ALLOW	1		25.0	25	
	Total							6,282
1408	SUPPORTING STAR # 4							
	Production (12 hr day)	1	DAY	1		1,343	1,343	
	Schedule B - Weekly Scale							
	Production	1.4	WEEKS	1		2,483	3,476	
	(44 hrs week / 1.5x @ $84.646 h	4	HOURS	1		84.646	338	
	(8 hrs day / 2x @ $112.86 hr)	8	HOURS	1		112.86	902	
	Agent Fee	1		0.1		6,061	606	
	Meal Penalty Allowance	1	ALLOW	1		25.0	25	
	Total							6,692
1410	BIT PART #1							
	BIT PART #1 - KID							
	Production	2.2	WEEKS	1		2,483	5,462	
	Agent Fee	1		0.1		5,463	546	
	Meal Penalty Allowance							
	Total							6,009
1411	BIT PART # 2							
	Production	1.6	WEEKS	1		2,483	3,972	
	44 hrs wk/ 1.5x @ $84.646 hr)	4	HOURS	1		84.646	338	
	8 hrs day / 2x @ $112.86 hr)	8	HOURS	1		112.86	902	
	Agent Fee	1		0.1		5,212	521	
	Meal Penalty Allowance	1	ALLOW	1		50.0	50	
	Total							5,785
1412	BIT PART #3							
	Production	1.2	WEEKS	1		2,483	2,979	
	44 hrs wk/ 1.5x @ $84.646 hr)	5	HOURS	1		84.646	423	
	8 hrs day / 2x @ $112.86 hr)	10	HOURS	1		112.86	1,128	
	Agent Fee	1		0.1		4,531	453	
	Meal Penalty Allowance	1	ALLOW	1		25.0	25	
	Total							5,010
1413	BIT PART #4							
	Production	1.2	WEEKS	1		2,483	2,979	
	44 hrs wk/ 1.5x @ $84.646 hr)	4	HOURS	1		84.646	338	
	8 hrs day / 2x @ $112.86 hr)	8	HOURS	1		112.86	902	
	Agent Fee	1		0.1		4,221	422	
	Meal Penalty Allowance	1	ALLOW	1		25.0	25	
	Total							4,668
1414	BIT PART #5							
	Production	1	WEEK	1		2,483	2,483	
	44 hrs wk/ 1.5x @ $84.646 hr)	4	HOURS	1		84.646	338	
	8 hrs day / 2x @ $112.86 hr)	8	HOURS	1		112.86	902	
	Agent Fee	1		0.1		3,724	372	
	Meal Penalty Allowance	1	ALLOW	1		25.0	25	
	Total							4,122
1496	LOOPING/WALLA							
	CAST LOOPING - PRINCIPALS	4	DAYS	1		716	2,864	

Acct No	Description	Amount	Units	X	Curr	Rate	Subtotal	Total
	WALLA GROUP	5	ALLOW	2		716	7,160	
	COORDINATOR	1	ALLOW	1		500	500	
	Total							10,524
1497	STUDIO TEACHER							
	STUDIO TEACHER							
	Production	5	DAYS	1		250	1,250	
	Supplies/Other	1	ALLOW	1		50.0	50	
	Total							1,300
1498	CAST CONTRACTUAL							
	Cast Medical Exams	6	EXAMS	1		100.0	600	
	Total							600
1499	Total Fringes							
	FICA (NM/CA/NY)	6.2%				212,450.56	13,172	
	MED (NM/CA/NY)	1.45%				212,450.56	3,081	
	FUTA (NM/CA/NY)	0.8%				105,290.56	842	
	SUTA (NM)	5.4%				51,560.96	2,784	
	SUTA (CA/NY)	6.2%				53,357.2	3,308	
	W-COMP (NM)	2.85%				51,933.36	1,480	
	W-COMP (CA/NY)	4.71%				161,576.4	7,610	
	ETT (NM)	0.1%				50,683.36	51	
	SAG-P&H	14.8%				205,700.56	30,444	
	PAYROLL FEE	0.35%				212,450.56	744	63,516
Account Total for 1400								**276,792**

1500 STUNTS

Acct No	Description	Amount	Units	X	Curr	Rate	Subtotal	Total
1501	STUNT COORDINATOR							
	STUNT COORDINATOR							
	Production (includes Travel/Prep	1	WEEK	1		2,908.36	2,908	
	44 hrs wk/ 1.5x @ $90.885 hr)	3	HOURS	1		90.885	272	
	8 hrs day / 2x @ $121.18 hr)	6	HOURS	1		121.18	727	
	Total							3,908
1511	STUNT PLAYER-DBL							
	STUNT DOUBLE							
	Production (12 hr day)	2	DAYS	1		1,343	2,686	
	Agent Fee	1		0.1		4,386	438	
	Total							3,125
1514	STUNT PLAYERS							
	Production (10 hr day)	2	DAYS	5		985	9,850	
	Agent Fee	1		0.1		4,925	492	
	Total							10,343
1580	STUNT ADJUSTMENTS							
	Adjustment Allowance	1	ALLOW	1		2,500	2,500	
	Total							2,500
1582	FITTINGS/TESTS/MU							
	WARDROBE FITTINGS							
	Fitting Allowance	10	HOURS	1		89.5	895	
	Total							895
1585	STUNT EQUIP RENTAL							
	Pads/Equip Rental	1		1		1,000	1,000	
	Total							1,000
1599	Total Fringes							
	PR FEE (Chks)	0.05%				3,908.1	2	

Acct No	Description	Amount	Units	X	Curr	Rate	Subtotal	Total
	FICA (NM/CA/NY)	6.2%				16,862.1	1,045	
	MED (NM/CA/NY)	1.45%				16,862.1	245	
	FUTA (NM/CA/NY)	0.8%				14,012.1	112	
	SUTA (NM)	5.4%				16,862.1	911	
	W-COMP (NM)	2.85%				20,770.2	592	
	ETT (NM)	0.1%				14,012.1	14	
	SAG-P&H	14.8%				20,770.2	3,074	
	PAYROLL FEE	0.35%				17,861.84	63	6,057
Account Total for 1500								**27,828**

1600 CASTING

Acct No	Description	Amount	Units	X	Curr	Rate	Subtotal	Total
1601	CASTING DIRECTOR							
	Casting Fee (Payroll)	1	Fee	1		12,500	12,500	
	NEW MEXICO CASTING							
	Casting Fee (split for two)	1	CONTRACT	1		11,250	11,250	
	Total							23,750
1602	CASTING ASSISTANTS							
	LA Assistant (Payroll)	6	WEEKS	1		700	4,200	
	NM Assistant (Payroll)	6	WEEKS	1		700	4,200	
	Total							8,400
1620	CASTING EXPENSES							
	KIT RENTAL							
	Assistants	6	WEEKS	1		50.0	300	
	MISC EXPENSES							
	Video Tape/Photos/Phone/Ship	1	ALLOW	1		1,500	1,500	
	Advertising	1	ALLOW	1		250	250	
	Computer/Printer/Ink	1	ALLOW	1		450	450	
	Total							2,500
1699	Total Fringes							
	WCOMP-(CA) CLER	1.69%				15,450	261	
	PR FEE (Chks)	0.05%				11,250	6	
	FICA (NM/CA/NY)	6.2%				20,900	1,296	
	MED (NM/CA/NY)	1.45%				20,900	303	
	FUTA (NM/CA/NY)	0.8%				15,400	123	
	SUTA (NM)	5.4%				4,200	227	
	SUTA (CA/NY)	6.2%				11,200	694	
	W-COMP (NM)	2.85%				4,200	120	
	W-COMP (CA/NY)	4.71%				12,500	589	
	ETT (NM)	0.1%				4,200	4	
	PAYROLL FEE	0.35%				20,900	73	3,696
Account Total for 1600								**38,346**

1700 TRAVEL & LIVING COSTS

Acct No	Description	Amount	Units	X	Curr	Rate	Subtotal	Total
1701	AIRFARE							
	PRODUCER'S UNIT							
	EXEC PRODUCER							
	LA/NM	2	RT	1		450	900	
	PRODUCER							
	LA/NM	2	RT	1		450	900	
	LINE PRODUCER							
	LA/NM	2	RT	1		450	900	

Acct No	Description	Amount	Units	X	Curr	Rate	Subtotal	Total
							2,700	
	DIRECTOR							
	LA/NM	2	RT	1		450	900	
							900	
	STAR # 1							
	LA/NM	2	RT	1		450	900	
	STAR #2							
	LA/NM	2	RT	1		450	900	
	STAR #3							
	LA/NM	2	RT	1		450	900	
	STAR # 4							
	LA/NM	1	RT	1		450	450	
							3,150	
	STUNTS							
	LA/NM	1	RT	1		450	450	
							450	
	CASTING							
	LA/NM (2)	1	RT	2		450	900	
							900	
	ADDITIONAL							
	Allowance for added Distant Cast	1	ALLOW	4		450	1,800	
	Total							9,900
1702	**LODGING**							
	PRODUCER'S UNIT							
	EP Lodging	2	WEEKS	1		875	1,750	
	Prod -Lodging							
	Prep	3	WEEKS	1		751.87	2,255	
	Shoot	4	WEEKS	1		751.87	3,007	
	Line Prod - Lodging							
	Prep	3	WEEKS	1		751.87	2,255	
	Shoot	4	WEEKS	1		751.87	3,007	
							12,276	
	Director Lodging							
	Prep	4	WEEKS	1		800	3,200	
	Shoot	4	WEEKS	1		800	3,200	
							6,400	
	STAR # 1							
	Lodging	4	WEEKS	1		800	3,200	
	STAR #2							
	Lodging	4	WEEKS	1		800	3,200	
	STAR # 3							
	Lodging	2	WEEKS	1		800	1,600	
	STAR #4							
	Lodging	1	WEEK	1		800	800	
							8,800	
	STUNTS							
	Lodging	1	WEEK	1		560	560	
							560	
	CASTING							

Acct No	Description	Amount	Units	X	Curr	Rate	Subtotal	Total
	Lodging							
	Prep	2	WEEKS	1		560	1,120	
	Shoot	4	WEEKS	1		560	2,240	
							3,360	
	ADDITIONAL							
	Allowance Lodging Distant Cast/S	3	DAYS	1		80.0	240	
	Allowance Lodging Local Cast	6	DAYS	1		70.0	420	
	Total							32,056
1703	PER DIEM							
	EXEC PRODUCER							
	Per Diem	2	WEEKS	1		450	900	
	PRODUCER							
	Per Diem	7	WEEKS	1		450	3,150	
	LINE PRODUCER							
	Per Diem	7	WEEKS	1		450	3,150	
							7,200	
	Director's Per Diem							
	Prep	4	WEEKS	1		450	1,800	
	Shoot	4	WEEKS	1		450	1,800	
							3,600	
	STAR # 1							
	Per Diem (Location)	4.2	WEEKS	1		420	1,764	
	Per Diem (Travel)	4	DAYS	1		75.0	300	
	STAR # 2							
	Per Diem (Location)	4.2	WEEKS	1		420	1,764	
	Per Diem (Travel)	4	DAYS	1		75.0	300	
	STAR # 3							
	Per Diem (Location)	2	WEEKS	1		420	840	
	Per Diem (Travel)	4	DAYS	1		75.0	300	
	STAR #4							
	Per Diem (Location)	1	WEEK	1		420	420	
	Per Diem (Travel)	2	DAYS	1		75.0	150	
							5,838	
	STUNTS							
	COORDINATOR							
	Per Diem (Location)	3	DAYS	1		60.0	180	
	Per Diem (Travel)	2	DAYS	1		75.0	150	
							330	
	CASTING							
	Per Diem	6	WEEKS	1		350	2,100	
							2,100	
	ADDITIONAL							
	Allowance Per Diem Distant Cast	1	WEEK	1		420	420	
	Total							19,488
1704	GROUND TRAVEL							
	EXEC PRODUCER							
	Vehicle Rental	2	WEEKS	1		250	500	
	Airport Transport	2	PU	1		60.0	120	
	PRODUCER							
	Vehicle Rental	7	WEEKS	1		250	1,750	

Continuation of Account 1704

Acct No	Description	Amount	Units	X	Curr	Rate	Subtotal	Total
	Airport Transport	2	PU	1		60.0	120	
	LINE PRODUCER							
	Vehicle Rental	7	WEEKS	1		250	1,750	
	Airport Transport	2	PU	1		60.0	120	
							4,360	
	DIRECTOR'S UNIT							
	Prep	4	WEEKS	1		250	1,000	
	Shoot	4	WEEKS	1		250	1,000	
	Airport Transport	2	PU	1		60.0	120	
							2,120	
	STAR # 1							
	Vehicle Rental	4.6	WEEKS	1		250	1,150	
	Airport Transport	2	PU	1		100.0	200	
	STAR #2							
	Vehicle Rental	4.6	WEEKS	1		250	1,150	
	Airport Transport	2	PU	1		100.0	200	
	STAR #3							
	Vehicle Rental	3	WEEKS	1		250	750	
	Airport Transport	4	PU	1		100.0	400	
	STAR # 4							
	Vehicle Rental	1	WEEK	1		250	250	
	Airport Transport	2	PU	1		100.0	200	
							4,300	
	STUNTS COORD.							
	Vehicle Rental	1	WEEK	1		250	250	
	Airport Transport	2	PU	1		100.0	200	
							450	
	ADDITIONAL							
	Allowance Additional Vehicles/Pic	1	ALLOW	1		408	408	
	Total							11,638
1706	OTHER/L&D							
	EXCESS BAGGAGE							
	Allowance	1	ALLOW	1		250	250	
	Total							250
1799	Total Fringes							0
Account Total for 1700								**73,332**
1800 DEVELOPMENT								
1801	SCOUT							
	SCOUT/SURVEY COSTS							
	Airfare							
	Allowance	1	ALLOW	1		1,250	1,250	
	Lodging							
	Allowance	1	ALLOW	1		1,000	1,000	
	Ground Transport							
	Allowance	1	ALLOW	1		1,000	1,000	
	Fuel							
	Allowance	1	ALLOW	1		500	500	
	Per Diem							
	Allowance	1	ALLOW	1		1,000	1,000	

Continuation of Account 1801

Acct No	Description	Amount	Units	X	Curr	Rate	Subtotal	Total
	Meals/Snacks							
	Allowance	1	ALLOW	1		650	650	
	Location Scout Contracts							
	Allowance	1	ALLOW	1		1,100	1,100	
	Fees/Misc							
	Allowance	1	ALLOW	1		500	500	
	Total							7,000
1802	OTHER							
	DEVELOPMENT FEES							
	Entertainment	1	ALLOW	1		5,000	5,000	
	Festival Costs	1	ALLOW	1		25,000	25,000	
	Finance Costs	1	ALLOW	1		7,500	7,500	
	Other	1	ALLOW	1		2,500	2,500	
	*not include in budget	1	ALLOW	1		-40000.0	-40,000	
	Total							0
1899	Total Fringes							0
Account Total for 1800								7,000
	TOTAL ABOVE-THE-LINE							950,236

Acct No	Description	Amount	Units	X	Curr	Rate	Subtotal	Total
2000 PRODUCTION STAFF								
2001	PRODUCTION MANAGER							
	Prep	4	WEEKS	0.6		3,928	9,427	
	Shoot	4	WEEKS	0.6		3,928	9,427	
	Wrap	2	WEEKS	0.6		3,928	4,713	
	Production Fee (Prep/Shoot/Wrap)	8	WEEKS	0.6		850	4,080	
	Completion of Assignment	1	WEEK	0.6		3,928	2,356	
							30,005	
	Total							30,005
2002	1ST ASST. DIRECTOR							
	Prep (above scale)	3	WEEKS	1		2,800	8,400	
	Shoot	4	WEEKS	1		2,435	9,740	
	Wrap	0	WEEKS	1		2,435	0	
	Production Fee	4	WEEKS	0.6		691	1,658	
	Completion of Assignment (above :	1	WEEK	0.6		3,734	2,240	
	Total							22,039
2003	KEY 2ND ASST. DIRECTOR							
	Prep	1	WEEK	0.6		3,497	2,098	
	Shoot	4	WEEKS	0.6		3,497	8,392	
	Wrap	0	WEEKS	0.6		3,497	0	
	Production Fee	4	WEEKS	0.6		691	1,658	
	Completion of Assignment	1	WEEK	0.6		3,497	2,098	
	Total							14,248
2004	2ND 2ND AD							
	Prep	0.6	WEEKS	0.6		2,362	850	
	Shoot	4	WEEKS	0.6		2,362	5,668	
	Wrap	0.2	WEEKS	0.6		2,362	283	
	Production Fee	4	WEEKS	0.6		0.0	0	
	Completion of Assignment	1	WEEK	0.6		2,362	1,417	
	Total							8,220
2005	SCRIPT SUPERVISOR							
	Prep	1	WEEK	8		25.0	200	
	Production (12 hr day)	4	WEEKS	70		25.0	7,000	
	Wrap	1	DAY	8		25.0	200	
	B Camera (additional allowance	20	DAYS	1		40.0	800	
	Total							8,200
2009	PRODUCTION COORDINATOR							
	Prep	4	WEEKS	1		2,000	8,000	
	Production (12 hr day)	4	WEEKS	1		2,000	8,000	
	Wrap	1	WEEK	1		2,000	2,000	
	Total							18,000
2010	ASST PROD COORDINATOR							
	Prep	3	WEEKS	1		1,200	3,600	
	Production (12 hr day)	4	WEEKS	1		1,200	4,800	
	Wrap	0.6	WEEKS	1		1,200	720	
	Total							9,120
2011	TRAVEL MGR/SECRETARY							
	Prep	3	WEEKS	1		750	2,250	
	Production (12 hr day)	4	WEEKS	1		750	3,000	
	Wrap	1	WEEK	1		750	750	
	Total							6,000
2012	OFFICE PROD ASSISTS							

Acct No	Description	Amount	Units	X	Curr	Rate	Subtotal	Total
	Key Office Production Assist							
	Prep	4	WEEKS	1		625	2,500	
	Production	4	WEEKS	1		625	2,500	
	Wrap	1	WEEK	1		625	625	
	Office Runner							
	Prep	3	WEEKS	1		500	1,500	
	Production	4	WEEKS	1		500	2,000	
	Wrap	1	WEEK	1		500	500	
	Overtime Allowance/Added Day Pl	1	ALLOW	1		500	500	
	Total							10,125
2013	SET PROD ASSISTS							
	Key Set Production Assist							
	Prep	1.6	WEEKS	1		625	1,000	
	Production	4	WEEKS	1		625	2,500	
	Set Prod Asst #1							
	Prep	0.6	WEEKS	1		500	300	
	Production	4	WEEKS	1		500	2,000	
	Set Prod Asst #2							
	Prep	0.2	WEEKS	1		500	100	
	Production	4	WEEKS	1		500	2,000	
	Overtime Allowance/Added Day Pl	1	ALLOW	1		500	500	
	Total							8,400
2014	PRODUCTION ACCOUNTANT							
	Prep	4	WEEKS	1		2,046	8,184	
	Production (12 hr day)	4	WEEKS	1		2,046	8,184	
	Wrap	2	WEEKS	1		2,046	4,092	
	POST WRAP	10	WEEKS	1		1,000	10,000	
	Total							30,460
2015	PAYROLL ACCOUNTANT							
	Prep	3	WEEKS	1		1,250	3,750	
	Production	4	WEEKS	1		1,250	5,000	
	Wrap	1	WEEK	1		1,250	1,250	
	Total							10,000
2016	ACCOUNTANT CLERK							
	Prep	2	WEEKS	1		625	1,250	
	Production	4	WEEKS	1		625	2,500	
	Wrap	1	WEEK	1		625	625	
	Total							4,375
2020	MISC. EXPENSES							
	Miscellaneous Added Costs	1	ALLOW	1		500	500	
	Total							500
2025	COMPUTER BOX RENTALS							
	UPM							
	Prep	4	WEEKS	1		50.0	200	
	Shoot	4	WEEKS	1		50.0	200	
	1st AD							
	Prep	3	WEEKS	1		50.0	150	
	Shoot	4	WEEKS	1		50.0	200	
	2nd AD							
	Prep	2	WEEKS	1		50.0	100	
	Shoot	4	WEEKS	1		50.0	200	
	2nd 2nd AD							
	Prep	1	WEEK	1		50.0	50	

Acct No	Description	Amount	Units	X	Curr	Rate	Subtotal	Total
	Shoot	4	WEEKS	1		50.0	200	
	Prod Coord							
	Prep	4	WEEKS	1		75.0	300	
	Shoot	4	WEEKS	1		75.0	300	
	Asst. Prod. Coord							
	Prep	3	WEEKS	1		50.0	150	
	Shoot	4	WEEKS	1		50.0	200	
	Travel Mgr							
	Prep	3	WEEKS	1		50.0	150	
	Shoot	4	WEEKS	1		50.0	200	
	Accountant							
	Prep	4	WEEKS	1		100.0	400	
	Shoot	4	WEEKS	1		100.0	400	
	Payroll Accountant							
	Prep	3	WEEKS	1		50.0	150	
	Shoot	4	WEEKS	1		50.0	200	
	Payroll Clerk							
	Prep	2	WEEKS	1		25.0	50	
	Shoot	4	WEEKS	1		25.0	100	
	Key Office PA							
	Prep	4	WEEKS	1		25.0	100	
	Shoot	4	WEEKS	1		25.0	100	
	Total							4,100
2099	Total Fringes							
	FICA #1	6.2%				30,460	1,889	
	FICA #2	1.45%				30,460	442	
	WCOMP-(CA) CLER	1.69%				50,835	859	
	FUI	0.8%				30,460	244	
	SUI (CA)	5.4%				30,460	1,645	
	PR FEE (Chks)	0.05%				56,384.8	28	
	IA/TEAMSTER	13.5%				44,835	6,051	
	FICA (NM/CA/NY)	6.2%				115,909.36	7,186	
	MED (NM/CA/NY)	1.45%				115,909.36	1,681	
	FUTA (NM/CA/NY)	0.8%				108,376.56	867	
	SUTA (NM)	5.4%				95,534.36	5,159	
	SUTA (CA/NY)	6.2%				20,375	1,263	
	W-COMP (NM)	2.85%				121,459.16	3,462	
	W-COMP (CA/NY)	4.71%				30,460	1,435	
	ETT (NM)	0.1%				88,001.56	88	
	DGA-BTL P&H	20.34%				67,114.16	13,654	
	IATSE-%	12.22%				21,600	2,639	
	PAYROLL FEE	0.35%				115,909.36	406	
	IATSE-P&H	50	DAYS			4,150	4,150	53,146
Account Total for 2000								236,938
2100 EXTRAS								
2101	EXTRAS							
	Extras (8 hrs)	20	Extras	8		7.5	1,200	
	Extras (9 hrs)	30	Extras	9.5		7.5	2,137	
	Extras (10 hrs)	100	Extras	11		7.5	8,250	
	Extras (11 hrs)	0	Extras	12.5		7.5	0	
	Extras (12 hrs)	100	Extras	14		7.5	10,500	

Acct No	Description	Amount	Units	X	Curr	Rate	Subtotal	Total
	Total							22,088
2105	FEATURED EXTRAS							
	Allowance for Special Skills	1	ALLOW	1		2,000	2,000	
	Total							2,000
2110	STAND-INS							
	A. Stand In #1							
	Production	20	DAYS	14		9.0	2,520	
	B. Stand In #2							
	Production	20	DAYS	14		9.0	2,520	
	Total							5,040
2130	EXTRA CASTING CONTRACT							
	Coordinator (Additional)							
	Prep	2	WEEKS	1		225	450	
	Shoot	4	WEEKS	1		225	900	
	Casting Expenses							
	Prep/Shoot	1	ALLOW	1		500	500	
	Total							1,850
2141	EXTRAS WRANGLER							
	Prep (assist w/ Casting)	4	DAYS	1		125	500	
	Production	10	DAYS	1		125	1,250	
	Wrap	1	DAY	1		125	125	
	Total							1,875
2142	ASST EXTRAS WRANGLER #1							
	Extras Assistant Wrangler #1							
	Prep (assist w/ Casting)	1	DAY	1		125	125	
	Production	2	DAYS	1		125	250	
	Wrap	0	DAYS	1		125	0	
	Total							375
2185	OTHER COSTS							
	Wardrobe Allowance & Other	1	ALLOW	1		500	500	
	Total							500
2199	Total Fringes							
	PR FEE (Chks)	0.05%				1,350	1	
	FICA (NM/CA/NY)	6.2%				31,377.5	1,945	
	MED (NM/CA/NY)	1.45%				31,377.5	455	
	FUTA (NM/CA/NY)	0.8%				26,627.5	213	
	SUTA (NM)	5.4%				31,377.5	1,694	
	W-COMP (NM)	2.85%				31,377.5	894	
	ETT (NM)	0.1%				26,627.5	27	
	EXTRA	3%				29,127.5	874	
	PAYROLL FEE	0.35%				2,250	8	6,111
Account Total for 2100								**39,839**
2200 DESIGN								
2201	PRODUCTION DESIGNER							
	Prep	4	WEEKS	1		2,750	11,000	
	Production	4	WEEKS	1		2,750	11,000	
	Wrap	0.2	WEEKS	1		2,750	550	
	Total							22,550
2202	ART DIRECTOR							
	Prep	3	WEEKS	1		2,000	6,000	
	Production (12 hr day)	4	WEEKS	1		2,000	8,000	

Acct No	Description	Amount	Units	X	Curr	Rate	Subtotal	Total
	Wrap	0.6	WEEKS	1		2,000	1,200	
	Total							15,200
2205	ART DEPT COORD							
	Prep (10 hrs)	2	WEEKS	55		18.0	1,980	
	Production (12 hr day)	4	WEEKS	70		18.0	5,040	
	Wrap (10 hrs)	0.2	WEEKS	55		18.0	198	
	Total							7,218
2220	STORYBOARD ARTIST							
	Prep	2	WEEKS	1		1,500	3,000	
	Total							3,000
2225	PURCHASES							
	Prep	1	ALLOW	1		250	250	
	Production	1	ALLOW	1		250	250	
	Total							500
2230	RENTALS							
	Prep	2	WEEKS	1		150	300	
	Production	4	WEEKS	1		150	600	
	Total							900
2235	BOX RENTALS							
	Prep	4	WEEKS	1		150	600	
	Production	4	WEEKS	1		150	600	
	Art Director							
	Prep	3	WEEKS	1		100.0	300	
	Production	4	WEEKS	1		100.0	400	
	Art Dept Coordinator							
	Prep	3	WEEKS	1		50.0	150	
	Production	4	WEEKS	1		50.0	200	
	Total							2,250
2240	EXPENDABLES							
	Paper/Folders/Binders/Other	1	ALLOW	1		500	500	
	Printer Cartridges	1	ALLOW	1		150	150	
	Design Supplies							
	Drawing Paper	1	ALLOW	1		75.0	75	
	Other	1	ALLOW	1		40.0	40	
	Total							765
2245	PHOTOCOPY & REPRODUCTION							
	Blue Prints							
	Prep/Production	1	ALLOW	1		1,000	1,000	
	Photocopy							
	Prep/Production	1	ALLOW	1		500	500	
	Total							1,500
2250	FILM & PROCESSING							
	Prep/Production	1	ALLOW	1		500	500	
	Total							500
2272	CAR ALLOWANCES							
	Production Designer							
	Prep	4	WEEKS	1		125	500	
	Production	4	WEEKS	1		125	500	
	Total							1,000
2285	OTHER COSTS							
	Miscellaneous Charges	1	ALLOW	1		500	500	
	Total							500
2299	Total Fringes							

Acct No	Description	Amount	Units	X	Curr	Rate	Subtotal	Total
	IA/TEAMSTER	13.5%				11,000	1,485	
	FICA (NM/CA/NY)	6.2%				44,968	2,788	
	MED (NM/CA/NY)	1.45%				44,968	652	
	FUTA (NM/CA/NY)	0.8%				35,968	288	
	SUTA (NM)	5.4%				44,968	2,428	
	W-COMP (NM)	2.85%				44,968	1,282	
	ETT (NM)	0.1%				35,968	36	
	IATSE-%	12.22%				37,750	4,613	
	PAYROLL FEE	0.35%				44,968	157	
	IATSE-P&H	50	DAYS			1,550	1,550	15,278
Account Total for 2200								**71,161**

2300 SET CONSTRUCTION

Acct No	Description	Amount	Units	X	Curr	Rate	Subtotal	Total
2301	CONSTRUCTION COORDINATOR							
	Prep (10 hrs)	2	WEEKS	1		1,750	3,500	
	Production (10 hr day)	4	WEEKS	1		1,750	7,000	
	Total							10,500
2302	CONSTRUCTION FOREMAN							
	Prep (10 hrs)	2	WEEKS	55		21.0	2,310	
	Production (10 hr day)	4	WEEKS	55		21.0	4,620	
	Total							6,930
2311	GANG BOSS							
	Prep (10 hrs)	2	WEEKS	55		21.0	2,310	
	Production (10 hr day)	4	WEEKS	55		21.0	4,620	
	Total							6,930
2315	CARPENTER LABOR							
	Prep	2	WEEKS	55		18.0	1,980	
	Production	4	WEEKS	55		18.0	3,960	
	Additional Man Days to equal 60							
	Prep/Production/Wrap	4	Added Days	1		5,940	23,760	
	Total							29,700
2320	LABOR FOREMAN							
	Prep (10 hrs)	2	WEEKS	55		17.0	1,870	
	Production (10 hr day)	4	WEEKS	55		17.0	3,740	
	Total							5,610
2325	LABOR HIRE							
	Prep	1	WEEK	55		15.6	858	
	Production	1	WEEK	55		15.6	858	
	Additional Man days to equal 20							
	Prep/Production/Wrap	3	Added Days	1		1,716	5,148	
	Total							6,864
2330	KEY SCENIC							
	Prep (10 hrs)	2	WEEKS	1		1,600	3,200	
	Production (10 hr day)	4	WEEKS	1		1,600	6,400	
	Total							9,600
2333	PAINT FOREMAN							
	Prep (10 hrs)	2	WEEKS	55		21.0	2,310	
	Production (10 hr day)	4	WEEKS	55		21.0	4,620	
	Total							6,930
2335	PAINT LABOR							
	Prep	2	WEEKS	55		18.0	1,980	
	Production	4	WEEKS	55		18.0	3,960	

Acct No	Description	Amount	Units	X	Curr	Rate	Subtotal	Total
	Additional Man Days to equal 45							
	Prep/Production/Wrap	1	Added Days	0.5		5,940	2,970	
	Total							8,910
2351	CONSTRUCTION OFFICE PA							
	Prep	1	WEEK	1		500	500	
	Production-NM	4	WEEKS	1		500	2,000	
	Total							2,500
2360	CONSTRUCTION MATERIALS							
	Location Sets							
	Allowance	1	ALLOW	1		20,000	20,000	
	Total							20,000
2361	CONSTRUCTION SERVICES							
	Cleaning/Restoration	1	ALLOW	1		750	750	
	Garbage Haul	1	ALLOW	1		400	400	
	Other	1	ALLOW	1		250	250	
	Total							1,400
2362	EXPENDABLES							
	(nails, tape, etc)							
	Prep/Production	1	ALLOW	1		750	750	
	Total							750
2365	CONSTRUCTION RENTALS							
	Tool Rental							
	Prep	2	WEEKS	1		500	1,000	
	Production	4	WEEKS	1		500	2,000	
	Compressers/Painters Kit							
	Prep	2	WEEKS	1		425	850	
	Production	4	WEEKS	1		425	1,700	
	Total							5,550
2366	BOX RENTALS							
	Prep	2	WEEKS	1		50.0	100	
	Production	4	WEEKS	1		50.0	200	
	Additional	1	ALLOW	1		250	250	
	Total							550
2367	SCAFFOLDING							
	Scaffolding/Wall Jacks	1	ALLOW	1		200	200	
	Total							200
2370	SPECIAL EQUIPMENT							
	Condors/Lifts/Other	1	ALLOW	1		750	750	
	Total							750
2375	SHOP RENTAL							
	(Doors/Locks/Dividers/Other)							
	Prep	1	ALLOW	1		500	500	
	Total							500
2376	CONTRACTS							
	Signage Contract	1	ALLOW	1		2,000	2,000	
	Total							2,000
2385	L&D/OTHER COSTS							
	L&D/Miscellaneous Charges	1	ALLOW	1		500	500	
	Total							500
2399	Total Fringes							
	FICA (NM/CA/NY)	6.2%				94,474	5,857	
	MED (NM/CA/NY)	1.45%				94,474	1,370	
	FUTA (NM/CA/NY)	0.8%				77,714	622	

Acct No	Description	Amount	Units	X	Curr	Rate	Subtotal	Total
	SUTA (NM)	5.4%				88,614	4,785	
	W-COMP (NM)	2.85%				94,474	2,693	
	ETT (NM)	0.1%				77,714	78	
	IATSE-%	12.22%				91,974	11,238	
	PAYROLL FEE	0.35%				94,474	331	26,973
Account Total for 2300								**153,647**

2400 SET STRIKING

Acct No	Description	Amount	Units	X	Curr	Rate	Subtotal	Total
2401	STRIKING - LABOR							
	Wrap	1	WEEK	55		15.6	858	
	Total							858
2402	STRIKING - MATERIALS							
	Set Strike Materials	1	ALLOW	1		500	500	
	Total							500
2403	OTHER COSTS							
	Grounds Repair/Other	1	ALLOW	1		250	250	
	Total							250
2499	Total Fringes							
	FICA (NM/CA/NY)	6.2%				858	53	
	MED (NM/CA/NY)	1.45%				858	12	
	FUTA (NM/CA/NY)	0.8%				858	7	
	SUTA (NM)	5.4%				858	46	
	W-COMP (NM)	2.85%				858	24	
	ETT (NM)	0.1%				858	1	
	PAYROLL FEE	0.35%				858	3	147
Account Total for 2400								**1,755**

2500 SET OPERATIONS

Acct No	Description	Amount	Units	X	Curr	Rate	Subtotal	Total
2501	SET/LOCATION SECURITY							
	Guard Manager							
	Prep/Production	6	WEEKS	1		400	2,400	
	Security Guard #1							
	Prep (construction + wkend)	14	DAYS	12		15.0	2,520	
	Production (wkends)	8	DAYS	12		15.0	1,440	
	Production (shoot days)	20	DAYS	12		15.0	3,600	
	Security Guard #2							
	Prep (construction + wkend)	14	Nights	12		15.0	2,520	
	Production (wkends)	8	Nights	12		15.0	1,440	
	Production (shoot days)	20	Nights	12		15.0	3,600	
	Location Sec. Guard #3							
	Prep (w/ weekends)	10	DAYS	14		10.0	1,400	
	Production (w/ weekends)	10	DAYS	14		10.0	1,400	
	Location Sec. Guard #4							
	Prep (w/ weekends)	7	DAYS	14		10.0	980	
	Production (w/ weekends)	7	DAYS	14		10.0	980	
	Contract - Location Security							
	Prep	24	HOURS	7		3.0	504	
	Production	24	HOURS	7		3.0	504	
	Total							23,288
2510	KEY GREENSMAN							
	Prep (10 hrs)	0	WEEKS	55		18.0	0	
	Production (12 hr day)	1	WEEK	70		18.0	1,260	

Acct No	Description	Amount	Units	X	Curr	Rate	Subtotal	Total
	Total							1,260
2515	GREENS MATERIALS							
	New Mexico Allowance	1	ALLOW	1		1,000	1,000	
	Total							1,000
2530	LOCATION CATERING FOOD							
	Crew size = 90							
	Cast size = 6 (average)							
	Production	20	DAYS	96		12.0	23,040	
	Extras	1	ALLOW	250		9.5	2,375	
	Total							25,415
2535	LOCATION CATERING CHEF							
	Prep (10 hrs)	1	DAY	8		22.3	178	
	Production (10 hr day)	4	WEEKS	55		22.3	4,906	
	Wrap (8 hrs)	1	DAY	8		22.3	178	
	Total							5,263
2536	LOCATION CATERING ASST #1							
	Prep	1	DAY	1		150	150	
	Production	4	WEEKS	5		150	3,000	
	Wrap	1	DAY	1		150	150	
	Total							3,300
2537	LOCATION CATERING ASST #2							
	Prep	1	DAY	1		125	125	
	Production	4	WEEKS	5		125	2,500	
	Wrap	1	DAY	1		125	125	
	Total							2,750
2539	LOCATION CATERING VEHICLES							
	NM Catering Vehicle #1							
	Production	4	WEEKS	1		500	2,000	
	NM Catering Vehicle #2							
	Production	4	WEEKS	1		100.0	400	
	Total							2,400
2540	SUPPLIES & MATERIALS							
	Propane	1	ALLOW	1		600	600	
	Gasoline/Oil/Diesel							
	Production	1	ALLOW	1		250	250	
	Total							850
2542	CRAFT SERVICE FOOD							
	Crew size = 90							
	Snacks/Coffee/Other	20	DAYS	96		3.0	5,760	
	(250 Extra Man Days)							
	Production	1	ALLOW	250		2.0	500	
	Water (reimbursable)	1	ALLOW	1		1,000	1,000	
	Ice (reimbursable)	1	ALLOW	1		100.0	100	
	Total							7,360
2545	CRAFT SERVICE MANAGER							
	Prep (10 hrs)	1	DAY	55		20.0	1,100	
	Production (12 hr day)	4	WEEKS	70		20.0	5,600	
	Total							6,700
2546	CRAFT SERVICE ASST							
	Prep (10 hrs)	1	DAY	55		15.6	858	
	Production (12 hr day)	4	WEEKS	70		15.6	4,368	
	Total							5,226
2550	CRAFT SERVICE VEHICLES							

Continuation of Account 2550

Acct No	Description	Amount	Units	X	Curr	Rate	Subtotal	Total
	Prep	1	DAY	1		60.0	60	
	Production	4	WEEKS	1		300	1,200	
	Total							1,260
2560	EMERGENCY MEDICAL TECH							
	Prep (10 hrs)	2	WEEKS	40		19.0	1,520	
	Production (12 hr day)	4	WEEKS	70		19.0	5,320	
	Total							6,840
2565	EXPENDABLE SUPPLIES							
	Prep/Production	1	ALLOW	1		400	400	
	Prep/Production	1	ALLOW	1		200	200	
	Touch Up/Filler/Other	1	ALLOW	1		175	175	
	Misc Set Supplies	1	ALLOW	1		150	150	
	Medical Supplies (Expendable)	1	ALLOW	1		100.0	100	
	Total							1,025
2566	EQUIPMENT RENTALS							
	Catering							
	Prep/Production	4	WEEKS	110		1.0	440	
	Craft Service							
	Prep/Production	1	ALLOW	1		50.0	50	
	Greens Equipment							
	Prep/Production	1	ALLOW	1		50.0	50	
	Total							540
2568	BOX RENTALS							
	Medical Tech (On-Set)							
	Prep	2	WEEKS	1		50.0	100	
	Production	4	WEEKS	1		50.0	200	
	Total							300
2575	LOSS & DAMAGE							
	Loss & Damage Allowance	1	ALLOW	1		500	500	
	Total							500
2585	OTHER COSTS							
	Miscellaneous Other Costs	1	ALLOW	1		100.0	100	
	Total							100
2599	Total Fringes							
	PR FEE (Chks)	0.05%				3,408	2	
	FICA (NM/CA/NY)	6.2%				36,098.8	2,238	
	MED (NM/CA/NY)	1.45%				36,098.8	523	
	FUTA (NM/CA/NY)	0.8%				36,098.8	289	
	SUTA (NM)	5.4%				36,098.8	1,949	
	W-COMP (NM)	2.85%				36,098.8	1,029	
	ETT (NM)	0.1%				36,098.8	36	
	IATSE-%	12.22%				20,026	2,447	
	TEAMSTER-%	11.72%				27,328.8	3,203	
	PAYROLL FEE	0.35%				39,758.8	139	
	TEAMSTER-Hr	4	HOURS			1,151.04	1,151	13,006
Account Total for 2500								108,383

2600 EFFECTS								
2601	SFX COORDINATOR							
	Prep	3	WEEKS	1		1,850	5,550	
	Production (12 hr day)	4	WEEKS	1		1,850	7,400	
	Total							12,950

Acct No	Description	Amount	Units	X	Curr	Rate	Subtotal	Total
2602	SFX KEY ASSISTANT							
	Prep	2	WEEKS	1		1,500	3,000	
	Production (12 hr day)	4	WEEKS	1		1,500	6,000	
	Total							9,000
2605	SFX ASSISTANT #1							
	Prep	0.4	WEEKS	1		1,200	480	
	Production (12 hr day)	2	WEEKS	1		1,200	2,400	
	Total							2,880
2620	SFX ARMORY HANDLER							
	Prep (10 hrs)	1	DAY	11		24.0	264	
	Production (12 hr day)	3	DAYS	14		24.0	1,008	
	Total							1,272
2625	CONTRACTS							
	Special Effects Contracts							
	Tendrils & Monkey	1	ALLOW	1		5,000	5,000	
	Total							5,000
2630	SUPPLIES & MATERIALS							
	Misc	1	ALLOW	1		1,600	1,600	
	Misc Rigging Supplies/Other	1	ALLOW	1		750	750	
	Total							2,350
2635	EXPENDABLE SUPPLIES							
	Blood	1	ALLOW	1		700	700	
	Blank Loads/Squibs	1	ALLOW	1		1,000	1,000	
	Other	1	ALLOW	1		500	500	
	Total							2,200
2650	RENTALS							
	Rentals	1	ALLOW	1		1,000	1,000	
	Dummies/Body Parts/Prostetics	1	ALLOW	1		3,000	3,000	
	Total							4,000
2655	BOX RENTALS							
	Prep	1	WEEK	1		500	500	
	Production	4	WEEKS	1		500	2,000	
	Other Box Rentals	1	ALLOW	1		500	500	
	Total							3,000
2660	ARMORY RENTALS							
	Weapons/Armory Rentals	1	ALLOW	1		2,500	2,500	
	Total							2,500
2675	LOSS AND DAMAGES							
	Loss & Damage Allowance	1	ALLOW	1		250	250	
	Total							250
2685	OTHER COSTS							
	Misc Other Expenses	1	ALLOW	1		50.0	50	
	Total							50
2699	Total Fringes							
	FICA (NM/CA/NY)	6.2%				26,102	1,618	
	MED (NM/CA/NY)	1.45%				26,102	378	
	FUTA (NM/CA/NY)	0.8%				25,702	206	
	SUTA (NM)	5.4%				17,102	924	
	SUTA (CA/NY)	6.2%				9,000	558	
	W-COMP (NM)	2.85%				17,102	487	
	W-COMP (CA/NY)	4.71%				9,000	424	
	ETT (NM)	0.1%				16,702	17	
	IATSE-%	12.22%				26,102	3,189	

Acct No	Description	Amount	Units	X	Curr	Rate	Subtotal	Total
	PAYROLL FEE	0.35%				26,102	91	
	LA-IATSE-%	12.22%				24,830	3,034	10,927
Account Total for 2600								**56,379**
2700 SET DRESSING								
2701	SET DECORATOR							
	Prep (10 hrs)	3	WEEKS	1		1,600	4,800	
	Production (10 hr day)	4	WEEKS	1		1,600	6,400	
	Total							11,200
2702	LEAD SET DRESSER							
	Prep (10 hrs)	3	WEEKS	55		23.0	3,795	
	Production (11 hr day)	4	WEEKS	62.5		23.0	5,750	
	Wrap (10 hrs)	1	DAY	11		23.0	253	
	Total							9,798
2703	ON-SET DRESSER							
	Prep (10 hrs)	2	DAYS	11		21.0	462	
	Production (12 hr day)	4	WEEKS	70		21.0	5,880	
	Wrap (10 hrs)	1	DAY	11		21.0	231	
	Total							6,573
2704	SWING DRESSER #1							
	Prep	2	WEEKS	55		19.0	2,090	
	Production	4	WEEKS	55		19.0	4,180	
	Total							6,270
2705	SWING DRESSER #2							
	Prep	2	WEEKS	55		19.0	2,090	
	Production	4	WEEKS	55		19.0	4,180	
	Total							6,270
2706	SWING DRESSER #3							
	Prep	2	WEEKS	55		19.0	2,090	
	Production	4	WEEKS	55		19.0	4,180	
	Total							6,270
2708	BUYER							
	Prep	1	WEEK	55		18.0	990	
	Total							990
2709	ADDITIONAL LABOR							
	Prep	1	WEEK	55		18.0	990	
	Production	1	WEEK	55		18.0	990	
	Total							1,980
2710	DRESSING SHOP LABOR							
	Prep	2	DAYS	8		15.6	249	
	Total							250
2720	SET DRESSING MATERIALS							
	Allowance	1	ALLOW	1		10,000	10,000	
	Total							10,000
2730	RENTALS							
	Ladders/Lifts/Other	1	ALLOW	1		500	500	
	Total							500
2732	COMPUTER BOX RENTALS							
	Set Decorator							
	Prep	3	WEEKS	1		150	450	
	Production	4	WEEKS	1		150	600	
	Lead Dresser							

Acct No	Description	Amount	Units	X	Curr	Rate	Subtotal	Total
	Prep	2	WEEKS	1		100.0	200	
	Production	4	WEEKS	1		100.0	400	
	On-Set Dresser							
	Prep	2	DAYS	1		20.0	40	
	Production	4	WEEKS	1		100.0	400	
	Swing Dresser #1							
	Prep	2	WEEKS	1		100.0	200	
	Production	4	WEEKS	1		100.0	400	
	Total							2,690
2735	EXPENDABLE SUPPLIES							
	Brooms/Brushes/Other	1	ALLOW	1		1,000	1,000	
	Total							1,000
2736	ASSET PURCHASES							
	Allowance	1	Purchases	1		1,000	1,000	
	Total							1,000
2740	CONTRACTS/LICENSES/MANUFAC							
	Local Contracts (Location Labor	1	ALLOW	1		300	300	
	Manfacture							
	Manufacture	1	ALLOW	1		300	300	
	Total							600
2745	FILM & PROCESSING							
	Film/Processing/Prints	1	ALLOW	1		200	200	
	Total							200
2775	LOSS AND DAMAGES							
	Loss & Damage Allowance	1	ALLOW	1		500	500	
	Total							500
2785	OTHER COSTS							
	Misc. Other Charges	1	ALLOW	1		100.0	100	
	Total							100
2799	Total Fringes							
	FICA (NM/CA/NY)	6.2%				49,600.6	3,075	
	MED (NM/CA/NY)	1.45%				49,600.6	719	
	FUTA (NM/CA/NY)	0.8%				49,600.6	397	
	SUTA (NM)	5.4%				49,600.6	2,678	
	W-COMP (NM)	2.85%				49,600.6	1,414	
	ETT (NM)	0.1%				49,600.6	50	
	IATSE-%	12.22%				49,351	6,030	
	PAYROLL FEE	0.35%				49,600.6	174	14,537
Account Total for 2700								80,728
2800 PROPERTY								
2801	PROP MASTER							
	Prep (10 hrs)	3	WEEKS	55		24.0	3,960	
	Production (12 hr day)	4	WEEKS	70		24.0	6,720	
	Wrap (10 hrs)	1	DAY	11		24.0	264	
	Total							10,944
2802	ASSISTANT PROPS							
	Prep (10 hrs)	2	WEEKS	11		21.0	462	
	Production (10 hr day)	4	WEEKS	55		21.0	4,620	
	Wrap (10 hrs)	1	DAY	11		21.0	231	
	Total							5,313
2810	RENTALS/PURCHASES							

Acct No	Description	Amount	Units	X	Curr	Rate	Subtotal	Total
	Prop Rentals	1	ALLOW	1		4,000	4,000	
	Total							4,000
2811	ASSET PURCHASES							
	Allowance	1	ALLOW	1		2,000	2,000	
	Total							2,000
2815	CONTRACTS							
	Prop Const. & Contract							
	Allowance	1	ALLOW	1		1,500	1,500	
	Total							1,500
2825	EQUIPMENT RENTAL							
	Containers/Ladders/Other	1	ALLOW	1		1,500	1,500	
	Total							1,500
2830	BOX RENTAL							
	Production	4	WEEKS	1		150	600	
	Asst Prop Master	4	WEEKS	1		75.0	300	
	Total							900
2840	EXPENDABLE SUPPLIES							
	Misc. Expendables	1	ALLOW	1		1,000	1,000	
	Total							1,000
2845	FILM & PROCESSING							
	Prep/Production	1	ALLOW	1		150	150	
	Total							150
2850	LOSS/DAMAGE/REPAIR							
	Loss & Damage	1	ALLOW	1		500	500	
	Total							500
2885	OTHER COSTS							
	Miscellaneous Other Costs	1	ALLOW	1		150	150	
	Total							150
2899	Total Fringes							
	FICA (NM/CA/NY)	6.2%				16,257	1,008	
	MED (NM/CA/NY)	1.45%				16,257	236	
	FUTA (NM/CA/NY)	0.8%				16,257	130	
	SUTA (NM)	5.4%				16,257	878	
	W-COMP (NM)	2.85%				16,257	463	
	ETT (NM)	0.1%				16,257	16	
	IATSE-%	12.22%				16,257	1,986	
	PAYROLL FEE	0.35%				16,257	57	4,775
Account Total for 2800								**32,732**
2900 WARDROBE								
2901	COSTUME DESIGNER							
	Prep	3	WEEKS	1		2,000	6,000	
	Production (12 hr day)	4	WEEKS	1		2,000	8,000	
	Total							14,000
2902	COSTUME SUPERVISOR							
	Prep (10 hrs)	2	WEEKS	55		22.0	2,420	
	Production (12 hr day)	4	WEEKS	70		22.0	6,160	
	Wrap (10 hrs)	1	DAY	11		22.0	242	
	Total							8,822
2903	KEY SET COSTUMER							
	Prep (10 hrs)	1	WEEK	55		21.0	1,155	
	Production (12 hr day)	4	WEEKS	70		21.0	5,880	

Acct No	Description	Amount	Units	X	Curr	Rate	Subtotal	Total
	Wrap (10 hrs)	1	DAY	11		21.0	231	
	Total							7,266
2904	COSTUMER							
	Prep	1	WEEK	55		18.0	990	
	Production (12 hrs)	4	WEEKS	70		18.0	5,040	
	Total							6,030
2906	ADDITIONAL DRESSER							
	Production (12 hrs)	1	WEEK	70		18.0	1,260	
	Total							1,260
2920	PURCHASES/RENTALS							
	Wardrobe	1	ALLOW	1		15,000	15,000	
	Total							15,000
2924	PURCHASES/RENTALS-EXTRAS							
	Allowance for Extras Wardrobe	1	ALLOW	1		1,000	1,000	
	Double/Stunt Wardrobe Allowanc	1	ALLOW	1		750	750	
	Total							1,750
2925	ADDITIONAL PURCHASES							
	Additional Purchases	1	ALLOW	1		300	300	
	Total							300
2930	JEWELRY							
	Wardrobe jewelry	1	ALLOW	1		100.0	100	
	Total							100
2935	EXPENDABLES							
	Hangers/Cleaning Supplies/Pins/C	1	ALLOW	1		300	300	
	Packing Boxes	1	ALLOW	1		100.0	100	
	Total							400
2940	EQUIPMENT RENTAL							
	Sewing Magchine	3	WEEKS	1		75.0	225	
	Racks -Prep/Production	1	ALLOW	1		500	500	
	Washer/dryer Prep/Production	1	ALLOW	1		250	250	
	Storage Prep/Production	1	ALLOW	1		100.0	100	
	Total							1,075
2945	BOX RENTAL							
	Kit Rental-Designer							
	Prep	3	WEEKS	1		150	450	
	Production	4	WEEKS	1		150	600	
	Supervisor							
	Prep	2	WEEKS	1		100.0	200	
	Production	4	WEEKS	1		100.0	400	
	Key Costumer							
	Production	4	WEEKS	1		50.0	200	
	Costumer							
	Production	4	WEEKS	1		50.0	200	
	Other Box Rentals	1	ALLOW	1		400	400	
	Total							2,450
2950	FACILITY/CONTRACTS							
	Install Washer/Dryer	1	ALLOW	1		100.0	100	
	Renovation-Fitting/Dressing Are	1	ALLOW	1		250	250	
	Total							350
2955	CLEANING/DYEING							
	Cleaning (Washing & Dry Cleaning)							
	Prep/Production/Wrap	4	WEEKS	1		400	1,600	
	Dying/Aging							

Continuation of Account 2955

Acct No	Description	Amount	Units	X	Curr	Rate	Subtotal	Total
	Contract Dying	1	ALLOW	1		600	600	
	Total							2,200
2960	ALTERATION CONTRACTS							
	Prep	2	WEEKS	55		18.0	1,980	
	Production (12 hrs)	1	WEEK	70		18.0	1,260	
	Total							3,240
2975	FILM & PROCESSING							
	Allowance	1	ALLOW	1		200	200	
	Total							200
2980	LOSS & DAMAGES							
	Damage/Loss/Repair	1	ALLOW	1		250	250	
	Total							250
2982	CAR ALLOWANCES							
	Prep	3	WEEKS	1		125	375	
	Production	4	WEEKS	1		125	500	
	Total							875
2985	OTHER COSTS							
	Miscellaneous Other Costs	1	ALLOW	1		100.0	100	
	Total							100
2999	Total Fringes							
	FICA (NM/CA/NY)	6.2%				40,618	2,518	
	MED (NM/CA/NY)	1.45%				40,618	589	
	FUTA (NM/CA/NY)	0.8%				39,618	317	
	SUTA (NM)	5.4%				40,618	2,193	
	W-COMP (NM)	2.85%				40,618	1,158	
	ETT (NM)	0.1%				39,618	40	
	IATSE-%	12.22%				40,618	4,963	
	PAYROLL FEE	0.35%				40,618	142	11,920
Account Total for 2900								**77,588**
3000 GRIP								
3001	KEY GRIP							
	Prep (10 hrs)	4	DAYS	11		24.0	1,056	
	Production (12 hr day)	4	WEEKS	70		24.0	6,720	
	Wrap (10 hrs)	1	DAY	11		24.0	264	
	Total							8,040
3002	BEST BOY							
	Prep (10 hrs)	3	DAYS	11		21.0	693	
	Production (12 hr day)	4	WEEKS	70		21.0	5,880	
	Wrap (10 hrs)	1	DAY	11		21.0	231	
	Total							6,804
3005	DOLLY GRIP							
	Prep (10 hrs)	0	DAYS	11		21.0	0	
	Production (12 hr day)	4	WEEKS	70		21.0	5,880	
	Total							5,880
3010	GRIP #1							
	Prep (10 hrs)	1	DAY	11		19.0	209	
	Production (12 hr day)	4	WEEKS	70		19.0	5,320	
	Wrap (10 hrs)	1	DAY	11		19.0	209	
	Total							5,738
3011	GRIP #2							
	Prep (10 hrs)	1	DAY	11		19.0	209	

Continuation of Account 3011

Acct No	Description	Amount	Units	X	Curr	Rate	Subtotal	Total
	Production (12 hr day)	4	WEEKS	70		19.0	5,320	
	Wrap (10 hrs)	1	DAY	11		19.0	209	
	Total							5,738
3012	GRIP #3							
	Prep (10 hrs)	1	DAY	11		19.0	209	
	Production (12 hr day)	4	WEEKS	70		19.0	5,320	
	Wrap (10 hrs)	1	DAY	11		19.0	209	
	Total							5,738
3035	PRE-RIG GRIP #1							
	IATSE-Thr Rate + $3.40							
	Production (11 hr day)	2	WEEKS	62.5		19.0	2,375	
	Total							2,375
3036	PRE-RIG GRIP #2							
	Production (11 hr day)	2	WEEKS	62.5		19.0	2,375	
	Total							2,375
3038	ADDITIONAL GRIP LABOR							
	Production (11 hr day)	1	WEEK	62.5		19.0	1,187	
	Total							1,188
3045	PURCHASES							
	Lumber/Duv/Other							
	Prep/Production	1	ALLOW	1		1,000	1,000	
	Total							1,000
3046	EXPENDABLES							
	Tape/Board/Other	4	WEEKS	1		300	1,200	
	Total							1,200
3050	BASIC PKG RENTAL							
	Production	4	WEEKS	1		2,000	8,000	
	Total							8,000
3051	DOLLY RENTAL							
	Dolly & Track Package	4	WEEKS	1		1,400	5,600	
	Total							5,600
3052	SPECIAL EQUIP RENTAL							
	Mount & Rig (Day Play)	1	ALLOW	1		1,000	1,000	
	Total							1,000
3055	GRIP BOX RENTAL							
	Key Grip	4	WEEKS	1		150	600	
	Best Boy	4	WEEKS	1		50.0	200	
	Total							800
3056	CRANE/JIB RENTAL							
	Crane/Jib	2	DAYS	1		1,200	2,400	
	Total							2,400
3070	MAINTENANCE & REPAIR							
	Production	1	ALLOW	1		250	250	
	Total							250
3075	LOSS & DAMAGES							
	Loss & Damage Allowance	1	ALLOW	1		800	800	
	Total							800
3085	OTHER GRIP COSTS							
	Other Costs	1	ALLOW	1		100.0	100	
	Total							100
3099	Total Fringes							
	FICA (NM/CA/NY)	6.2%				43,875.5	2,720	
	MED (NM/CA/NY)	1.45%				43,875.5	636	

Acct No	Description	Amount	Units	X	Curr	Rate	Subtotal	Total
	FUTA (NM/CA/NY)	0.8%				43,875.5	351	
	SUTA (NM)	5.4%				43,875.5	2,369	
	W-COMP (NM)	2.85%				43,875.5	1,250	
	ETT (NM)	0.1%				43,875.5	44	
	IATSE-%	12.22%				43,875.5	5,361	
	PAYROLL FEE	0.35%				43,875.5	154	12,886
Account Total for 3000								**77,912**
3100 MAKEUP & HAIR								
3101	KEY MAKE-UP							
	Prep (10 hrs)	1	WEEK	1		1,750	1,750	
	Production (10 hr day)	4	WEEKS	1		1,750	7,000	
	Force Call/OT Allowance	1	ALLOW	1		150	150	
	Total							8,900
3102	KEY HAIR							
	Prep (10 hrs)	0.6	WEEKS	1		1,750	1,050	
	Production (10 hr day)	4	WEEKS	1		1,750	7,000	
	Total							8,050
3104	MAKE-UP/HAIR ASST #1							
	Prep (10 hrs)	1	DAY	11		21.0	231	
	Production (12 hr day)	4	WEEKS	70		21.0	5,880	
	Wrap (10 hrs)	1	DAY	11		21.0	231	
	Total							6,342
3105	MAKE-UP/HAIR ASST #2							
	Prep (10 hrs)	1	DAY	11		21.0	231	
	Production (12 hr day)	4	WEEKS	70		21.0	5,880	
	Wrap (10 hrs)	1	DAY	11		21.0	231	
	Total							6,342
3108	ADDITIONAL LABOR							
	Production (12 hr day)	1	WEEK	70		21.0	1,470	
	Total							1,470
3110	SPECIAL MAKE-UP							
	Prep	2	WEEKS	1		9,000	18,000	
	Production	4	WEEKS	1		15,000	60,000	
	Total							78,000
3115	WIGS							
	Wigs	1	ALLOW	1		1,000	1,000	
	Total							1,000
3118	EXPENDABLES							
	Tissues/Towels/Pads/Other	1	ALLOW	1		300	300	
	Total							300
3120	SUPPLY PURCHASE							
	Make-Up Supplies	1	ALLOW	1		500	500	
	Hair Supplies	1	ALLOW	1		350	350	
	Total							850
3125	RENTALS							
	(mirror, lights, misc)	1	ALLOW	1		600	600	
	Total							600
3126	BOX RENTALS							
	Kit Rental-Key Make Up	4	WEEKS	1		100.0	400	
	Kit Rental-Key Hair	4	WEEKS	1		100.0	400	
	Kit Rental-MU/Hair On Set	4	WEEKS	1		75.0	300	

Continuation of Account 3126

Acct No	Description	Amount	Units	X	Curr	Rate	Subtotal	Total
	Kit Rental-MU/Hair On Set	4	WEEKS	1		75.0	300	
	Kit Rental-Day Play Assists	1	ALLOW	1		100.0	100	
	Total							1,500
3130	FILM & PROCESSING							
	Allow	1	ALLOW	1		150	150	
	Total							150
3180	LOSS & DAMAGES							
	Damage/Loss/Repair	1	ALLOW	1		100.0	100	
	Total							100
3199	Total Fringes							
	PR FEE (Chks)	0.05%				78,000	39	
	FICA (NM/CA/NY)	6.2%				31,104	1,928	
	MED (NM/CA/NY)	1.45%				31,104	451	
	FUTA (NM/CA/NY)	0.8%				31,104	249	
	SUTA (NM)	5.4%				31,104	1,680	
	W-COMP (NM)	2.85%				31,104	886	
	W-COMP (CA/NY)	4.71%				78,000	3,674	
	ETT (NM)	0.1%				31,104	31	
	IATSE-%	12.22%				31,104	3,801	
	PAYROLL FEE	0.35%				31,104	109	12,848
Account Total for 3100								126,452

3200 ELECTRIC

Acct No	Description	Amount	Units	X	Curr	Rate	Subtotal	Total
3201	GAFFER/LIGHTING DIRECTOR							
	Prep (10 hrs)	4	DAYS	11		24.0	1,056	
	Production (12 hr day)	4	WEEKS	70		24.0	6,720	
	Wrap (10 hrs)	1	DAY	11		24.0	264	
	Total							8,040
3205	BEST BOY							
	Prep (10 hrs)	3	DAYS	11		21.0	693	
	Production (12 hr day)	4	WEEKS	70		21.0	5,880	
	Wrap (10 hrs)	1	DAY	11		21.0	231	
	Total							6,804
3210	ELECTRICIAN #1							
	Prep (10 hrs)	1	DAY	11		19.0	209	
	Production (12 hr day)	4	WEEKS	70		19.0	5,320	
	Wrap (10 hrs)	1	DAY	11		19.0	209	
	Total							5,738
3211	ELECTRICIAN #2							
	Prep (10 hrs)	1	DAY	11		19.0	209	
	Production (12 hr day)	4	WEEKS	70		19.0	5,320	
	Wrap (10 hrs)	1	DAY	11		19.0	209	
	Total							5,738
3212	ELECTRICIAN #3							
	Prep (10 hrs)	1	DAY	11		19.0	209	
	Production (12 hr day)	4	WEEKS	70		19.0	5,320	
	Wrap (10 hrs)	1	DAY	11		19.0	209	
	Total							5,738
3235	PRE-RIG ELECTRIC #1							
	Prep (10 hrs)	0	WEEKS	55		19.0	0	
	Production (11 hr day)	2	WEEKS	62.5		19.0	2,375	
	Total							2,375

Acct No	Description	Amount	Units	X	Curr	Rate	Subtotal	Total
3236	PRE-RIG ELECTRIC #2							
	Production (11 hr day)	2	WEEKS	62.5		19.0	2,375	
	Total							2,375
3238	ADDITIONAL ELECTRIC LABOR							
	Production (11 hr day)	1	WEEK	62.5		19.0	1,187	
	Force Call Allowance	1	ALLOW	1		50.0	50	
	Total							1,238
3240	PURCHASES							
	Lamps/Cable/Practicals/Other	1	ALLOW	1		500	500	
	Total							500
3245	EXPENDABLES							
	Gel @ $90 per roll	30	Rolls	1		90.0	2,700	
	Tape/Connectors/Specials	1	ALLOW	1		400	400	
	Total							3,100
3250	ELECTRICAL PKG RENTAL							
	Production Package	4	WEEKS	1		8,000	32,000	
	Pre-Rig & Cable Pkg	4	WEEKS	1		1,000	4,000	
	Allowance for Prep/Travel	1	ALLOW	1		400	400	
	Total							36,400
3251	SPECIAL EQUIP RENTAL							
	Specials (Day Play)	1	ALLOW	1		600	600	
	Night Lights (Day Play)	1	ALLOW	1		800	800	
	Total							1,400
3252	SPECIAL RIGGING							
	Night Shoot (Pettibone/Lifts/Moun	1	ALLOW	1		600	600	
	Total							600
3255	ELECTRIC BOX RENTAL							
	Gaffer	4	WEEKS	1		150	600	
	Best Boy	4	WEEKS	1		50.0	200	
	Total							800
3260	GENERATOR RENTAL							
	Production Tow Plant (Small 500an	4	WEEKS	1		500	2,000	
	Production (750Amp)	4	WEEKS	1		750	3,000	
	Circus Basic Package	4	WEEKS	1		800	3,200	
	Allowance for Prep/Travel	1	ALLOW	1		100.0	100	
	Total							8,300
3265	GAS & OIL FOR GENERATOR							
	Production	1	ALLOW	1		1,000	1,000	
	Total							1,000
3270	MAINTENANCE & REPAIR							
	Production	1	ALLOW	1		250	250	
	Total							250
3275	LOSS & DAMAGES							
	Loss & Damage Allowance	1	ALLOW	1		1,000	1,000	
	Total							1,000
3280	GLOBE BURN							
	Burn Charges	1	ALLOW	1		250	250	
	Total							250
3285	OTHER COSTS							
	Miscellaneous Other Costs	1	ALLOW	1		100.0	100	
	Total							100
3299	Total Fringes							
	FICA (NM/CA/NY)	6.2%				38,045.5	2,359	

Acct No	Description	Amount	Units	X	Curr	Rate	Subtotal	Total
	MED (NM/CA/NY)	1.45%				38,045.5	552	
	FUTA (NM/CA/NY)	0.8%				38,045.5	304	
	SUTA (NM)	5.4%				38,045.5	2,054	
	W-COMP (NM)	2.85%				38,045.5	1,084	
	ETT (NM)	0.1%				38,045.5	38	
	IATSE-%	12.22%				37,995.5	4,643	
	PAYROLL FEE	0.35%				35,670.5	125	11,159
Account Total for 3200								**102,905**
3300 CAMERA								
3301	DIRECTOR OF PHOTOGRAPHY							
	Prep	3	WEEKS	1		3,000	9,000	
	Production	4	WEEKS	1		4,000	16,000	
	Travel	2	DAYS	1		800	1,600	
	Total							26,600
3310	OPERATOR A							
	Production	4	WEEKS	70		35.82	10,029	
	Total							10,030
3311	OPERATOR B (STEADI-CAM)							
	Production (Operator)	4	WEEKS	70		35.38	9,906	
	Total							9,906
3315	FIRST ASST CAMERA							
	Prep (LA Prep)	1	WEEK	55		31.09	1,709	
	Production	4	WEEKS	70		31.09	8,705	
	Travel (Local & LA Prep)	2	DAYS	9		31.09	559	
	Total							10,975
3316	FIRST ASST CAMERA B							
	Prep	0.2	WEEKS	55		31.09	341	
	Production	4	WEEKS	70		31.09	8,705	
	Total							9,047
3320	SECOND ASST CAMERA							
	Prep (LA Prep)	1	WEEK	55		23.82	1,310	
	Production	4	WEEKS	70		23.82	6,669	
	Total							7,980
3321	SECOND ASST CAMERA B							
	Prep	0.4	WEEKS	55		23.82	524	
	Production	4	WEEKS	70		23.82	6,669	
	Total							7,194
3325	LOADER							
	Prep	0.2	WEEKS	55		20.36	223	
	Production	4	WEEKS	70		20.36	5,700	
	Total							5,925
3340	STILL PHOTOGRAPHER							
	Production (8 hr day only)	4	WEEKS	40		35.82	5,731	
	Total							5,731
3345	VIDEO ASST TECHNICIAN							
	Prep (10 hrs)	1	DAY	11		21.0	231	
	Production (12 hr day)	4	WEEKS	70		21.0	5,880	
	Total							6,111
3350	PURCHASES							
	Cmaera Purchase (connectors/other)	1	ALLOW	1		100.0	100	

Acct No	Description	Amount	Units	X	Curr	Rate	Subtotal	Total
	Video Assist	1	ALLOW	1		50.0	50	
	Total							150
3355	EXPENDABLES							
	Unit Camera (air/eyepads/tape)	1	ALLOW	1		200	200	
	Video Assist (batteries/other)	1	ALLOW	1		100.0	100	
	Still Camera	1	ALLOW	1		25.0	25	
	Total							325
3360	BASIC CAMERA PKG RENTAL							
	2-35mm Principal Camera Pkg	4	WEEKS	2		8,500	68,000	
	(tripods/heads/filters/etc)	4	WEEKS	2		500	4,000	
	Total							72,000
3361	ADDITIONAL EQUIP RENTAL							
	Special Lenses (cu & tele)	1	ALLOW	1		1,000	1,000	
	Other Special Equip	1	ALLOW	1		500	500	
	Total							1,500
3362	BOX RENTAL							
	Director of Photography Production	4	WEEKS	1		500	2,000	
	First Asst (w/ Cart) Production	4	WEEKS	1		150	600	
	First Asst B (w/ Cart) Production	4	WEEKS	1		150	600	
	2nd Asst (w/ Cart) Production	4	WEEKS	1		100.0	400	
	2nd Asst B (w/ Cart) Production	4	WEEKS	1		100.0	400	
	Still Photographer Production	4	WEEKS	1		350	1,400	
	Total							5,400
3363	VIDEO ASSIST EQUIP RENTAL							
	Video Assist/Tap System	4	WEEKS	1		500	2,000	
	Total							2,000
3370	CAR ALLOWANCES							
	Prep	2	WEEKS	1		250	500	
	Production	4	WEEKS	1		250	1,000	
	Total							1,500
3380	LOSS & DAMAGES							
	Loss & Damage Allowance	1	ALLOW	1		1,000	1,000	
	Total							1,000
3385	OTHER COSTS							
	Miscellaneous Other Costs	1	ALLOW	1		200	200	
	Total							200
3399	Total Fringes							
	PR FEE (Chks)	0.05%				25,000	12	
	FICA (NM/CA/NY)	6.2%				72,898.26	4,520	
	MED (NM/CA/NY)	1.45%				72,898.26	1,057	
	FUTA (NM/CA/NY)	0.8%				63,551.86	508	
	SUTA (NM)	5.4%				72,898.26	3,937	
	W-COMP (NM)	2.85%				52,962.26	1,509	
	W-COMP (CA/NY)	4.71%				46,536	2,192	
	ETT (NM)	0.1%				63,551.86	64	

Acct No	Description	Amount	Units	X	Curr	Rate	Subtotal	Total
	IATSE-%	12.22%				99,498.26	12,158	
	PAYROLL FEE	0.35%				99,498.26	348	
	600-Hr	2	HOURS			5,678.15	5,678	31,983
Account Total for 3300								**215,557**
3400 PRODUCTION SOUND								
3401	LOCATION SOUND MIXER							
	Prep (10 hrs)	0.2	WEEKS	1		1,850	370	
	Production (12 hr day)	4	WEEKS	1		1,850	7,400	
	Total							7,770
3402	BOOM OPERATOR							
	Prep (10 hrs)	1	DAY	8		21.0	168	
	Production (12 hr day)	4	WEEKS	70		21.0	5,880	
	Total							6,048
3403	CABLE PERSON							
	Production (12 hr day)	4	WEEKS	70		18.0	5,040	
	Total							5,040
3410	PURCHASES							
	Sound Dept	1	ALLOW	1		200	200	
	Total							200
3421	EXPENDABLES							
	Expendable Supplies							
	Batteries (basic equip & headphor	20	DAYS	1		30.0	600	
	Total							600
3422	STOCK PURCHASES							
	DAT Stock - 30 min	20	DAYS	3		25.0	1,500	
	Back-Up (CD/DVD Stock)	1	ALLOW	1		200	200	
	Total							1,700
3431	RENTAL-SOUND EQUIP							
	Production	4	WEEKS	1		2,000	8,000	
	Total							8,000
3432	RENTAL-RADIO MIKES							
	Production	4	WEEKS	1		500	2,000	
	Total							2,000
3433	RENTAL-WALKIE-TALKIE							
	Production	4	WEEKS	50		10.0	2,000	
	Accessories	4	WEEKS	30		4.0	480	
	Total							2,480
3441	LOSS & DAMAGE							
	Loss & Damage Allowance	1	ALLOW	1		1,000	1,000	
	Total							1,000
3485	OTHER COSTS							
	Misc Additional Charges	1	ALLOW	1		25.0	25	
	Total							25
3499	Total Fringes							
	FICA (NM/CA/NY)	6.2%				18,858	1,169	
	MED (NM/CA/NY)	1.45%				18,858	273	
	FUTA (NM/CA/NY)	0.8%				18,458	148	
	SUTA (NM)	5.4%				18,858	1,018	
	W-COMP (NM)	2.85%				18,858	537	
	ETT (NM)	0.1%				18,458	18	
	IATSE-%	12.22%				18,858	2,304	

Acct No	Description	Amount	Units	X	Curr	Rate	Subtotal	Total
	PAYROLL FEE	0.35%				18,858	66	5,535
Account Total for 3400								40,398
3500 TRANSPORTATION								
3501	TRANSPO COORD							
	Prep	2	WEEKS	1		2,200	4,400	
	Production	4	WEEKS	1		2,200	8,800	
	Holidays (non worked)	1	DAY	10.25		42.31	433	
	Idle Days (4 wks)	8	DAYS	4		42.31	1,353	
	Meal Money ($20.00 per day)	20	DAYS	1		20.0	400	
	Total							15,388
3502	TRANSPO CAPTAIN							
	Prep w/ Scout (11 hr day)	2	WEEKS	62.5		27.67	3,458	
	Production (13 hr day)	4	WEEKS	80		27.67	8,854	
	Wrap (11 hr day)	1	WEEK	62.5		27.67	1,729	
	Holidays (non worked)	1	DAY	10.25		27.67	283	
	Idle Days (6 wks)	12	DAYS	4		27.67	1,328	
	Meal Money ($20.00 per day)	20	DAYS	1		20.0	400	
	Total							16,054
3503	TRANSPO CO-CAPTAIN							
	Prep (11 hr day)	2	WEEKS	62.5		25.19	3,148	
	Production (13 hr day)	4	WEEKS	80		25.19	8,060	
	Wrap (10 hr day)	1	WEEK	55		25.19	1,385	
	Meal Money	20	DAYS	1		20.0	400	
	Total							12,995
3504	FUELER DRIVER (MECHANIC)							
	Prep (11 hr day)	0.6	WEEKS	62.5		24.06	902	
	Production (13 hr day)	4	WEEKS	80		24.06	7,699	
	Meal Money	20	DAYS	1		20.0	400	
	Total							9,001
3505	CONST STAKEBED DRIVER							
	Prep (11 hr day)	2	WEEKS	62.5		20.45	2,556	
	Production (12 hr day)	2	WEEKS	70		20.45	2,863	
	Wrap (10 hr day)	0.4	WEEKS	55		20.45	449	
	Meal Money	10	DAYS	1		20.0	200	
	Total							6,069
3506	CREW CAB DRIVER (PAINT)							
	Prep (11 hr day)	2	WEEKS	62.5		20.45	2,556	
	Production (12 hr day)	2	WEEKS	70		20.45	2,863	
	Wrap (10 hr day)	0.4	WEEKS	55		20.45	449	
	Meal Money	10	DAYS	1		20.0	200	
	Total							6,069
3507	UTILITY STAKEBED DRIVER							
	Prep (11 hr day)	0.2	WEEKS	62.5		22.3	278	
	Production (13 hr day)	2	WEEKS	80		22.3	3,568	
	Wrap (10 hr day)	0.2	WEEKS	55		22.3	245	
	Meal Money	10	DAYS	1		20.0	200	
	Total							4,292
3508	PROP TRUCK DRIVER							
	Prep (11 hr day)	1	WEEK	62.5		20.45	1,278	
	Production (14 hr day)	1	WEEK	85		20.45	1,738	
	Wrap (10 hr day)	0.2	WEEKS	55		20.45	224	

411

Acct No	Description	Amount	Units	X	Curr	Rate	Subtotal	Total
	Meal Money	5	DAYS	1		20.0	100	
	Total							3,341
3509	SET DRESSING TRUCK DRIVER							
	Prep (11 hr day)	1	WEEK	62.5		20.45	1,278	
	Production (13 hr day)	4	WEEKS	80		20.45	6,544	
	Wrap (10 hr day)	0.4	WEEKS	55		20.45	449	
	Meal Money	20	DAYS	1		20.0	400	
	Total							8,672
3510	GRIP TRUCK DRIVER							
	Prep (10 hr day)	0.4	WEEKS	55		20.45	449	
	Production (13 hr day)	2	WEEKS	80		20.45	3,272	
	Wrap (10 hr day)	0.1	WEEKS	55		20.45	112	
	Meal Money	10	DAYS	1		20.0	200	
	Total							4,034
3511	GREENS/EFX DRIVER							
	Prep (11 hr day)	1	WEEK	62.5		20.45	1,278	
	Production (14 hr day)	2	WEEKS	85		20.45	3,476	
	Wrap (10 hr day)	0.2	WEEKS	55		20.45	224	
	Meal Money	10	DAYS	1		20.0	200	
	Total							5,180
3512	CAMERA TRUCK DRIVER							
	Prep (10 hr day)	0.2	WEEKS	55		20.45	224	
	Production (14 hr day)	2	WEEKS	85		20.45	3,476	
	Wrap (10 hr day)	2	WEEKS	55		20.45	2,249	
	Meal Money	10	DAYS	1		20.0	200	
	Total							6,151
3513	ELECTRIC TRUCK DRIVER							
	Prep (10 hr day) *LA Pick-Up/Re	0.4	WEEKS	55		28.25	621	
	Production (13 hr day)	4	WEEKS	80		28.25	9,040	
	Wrap (10 hr day)	0.2	WEEKS	55		28.25	310	
	Travel	2	DAYS	10.25		28.25	579	
	Idle Days (8 wks)	10	DAYS	4		28.25	1,130	
	Meal Money	20	DAYS	1		20.0	400	
	Total							12,081
3514	HONEYWAGON DRIVER							
	Prep	0	WEEKS	55		24.06	0	
	Production (13 hr day)	4	WEEKS	80		24.06	7,699	
	Wrap	0.2	WEEKS	55		24.06	264	
	Meal Money	20	DAYS	1		20.0	400	
	Total							8,364
3516	CAST DRIVER							
	Prep (12 hr day)	1	WEEK	70		17.0	1,190	
	Production (13 hr day)	4	WEEKS	80		17.0	5,440	
	Meal Money	20	DAYS	1		20.0	400	
	Total							7,030
3517	CREW VAN DRIVER #1							
	Prep (11 hr day) + scout	1	WEEK	62.5		22.3	1,393	
	Production (13 hr day)	4	WEEKS	80		22.3	7,136	
	Wrap (10 hr day)	0.2	WEEKS	55		22.3	245	
	Meal Money	20	DAYS	1		20.0	400	
	Total							9,175
3518	CREW VAN DRIVER #2							
	Production (13 hr day)	2	WEEKS	80		22.3	3,568	

Acct No	Description	Amount	Units	X	Curr	Rate	Subtotal	Total
	Meal Money	10	DAYS	1		20.0	200	
	Total							3,768
3520	RUNNER DRIVER							
	Production (13 hr day)	4	WEEKS	51.25		17.0	3,485	
	Meal Money	20	DAYS	1		20.0	400	
	Total							3,885
3521	DAY PLAY/OTHER DRIVERS							
	Production (14 hr day)	1	WEEK	85		22.3	1,895	
	Meal Money	5	DAYS	1		20.0	100	
	Total							1,996
3530	VAN RENTALS							
	Cast Transportation							
	Minivan # 1	1	WEEK	1		175	175	
	Production	4	WEEKS	1		175	700	
							875	
	Mini-Van #2							
	Production	4	WEEKS	1		175	700	
							700	
	15-Pass Van #1							
	Prep	2	WEEKS	1		375	750	
	Production	4	WEEKS	1		375	1,500	
	15-Pass Van #2 (as required)							
	Prep	1	WEEK	1		375	375	
	Production	2	WEEKS	1		375	750	
							3,375	
	Production Office							
	Prep	2	WEEKS	1		175	350	
	Production	4	WEEKS	1		175	700	
	Prop Department							
	Prep	1	WEEK	1		175	175	
	Production	4	WEEKS	1		175	700	
	Set Decorator/Dressing Dept							
	Prep	1	WEEK	1		175	175	
	Production	4	WEEKS	1		175	700	
	Wardrobe Department							
	Prep	1	WEEK	1		175	175	
	Production	4	WEEKS	1		175	700	
	Total							8,625
3535	TRUCK RENTALS							
	Transportation Coordinator							
	Pick-Up or Van							
	Prep	2	WEEKS	1		400	800	
	Production	4	WEEKS	1		400	1,600	
	Transportation Captain							
	Stakebed							
	Prep	2	WEEKS	1		500	1,000	
	Production	4	WEEKS	1		500	2,000	
	Transportation Co-Captain							
	Stakebed							
	Prep	1	WEEK	1		500	500	
	Production	4	WEEKS	1		500	2,000	
	Fueler/Mechanic							

Acct No	Description	Amount	Units	X	Curr	Rate	Subtotal	Total
	Prep	1	WEEK	1		600	600	
	Production	4	WEEKS	1		600	2,400	
	Construction Stake Bed							
	Prep	1	WEEK	1		500	500	
	Production	4	WEEKS	1		500	2,000	
	Crew Cab (Paint)							
	Prep	1	WEEK	1		550	550	
	Production	2	WEEKS	1		550	1,100	
	Stake Bed							
	Prep	1	WEEK	1		500	500	
	Production	2	WEEKS	1		500	1,000	
	Property Truck							
	5-Ton Prop Truck							
	Prep	1	WEEK	1		600	600	
	Production	4	WEEKS	1		600	2,400	
	Set Dressing Truck							
	5-Ton Dressing Truck							
	Prep	1	WEEK	1		600	600	
	Production	4	WEEKS	1		600	2,400	
	Grip Truck							
	5-Ton Grip Truck							
	Prep	0.4	WEEKS	1		750	300	
	Production	4	WEEKS	1		750	3,000	
	Greens/							
	5-Ton EFX Truck							
	Prep	1	WEEK	1		750	750	
	Production	4	WEEKS	1		750	3,000	
	Camera Truck							
	5-Ton Camera Truck							
	Prep	1	WEEK	1		600	600	
	Production	4	WEEKS	1		600	2,400	
	Electric Production Vehicle							
	10-Ton Electric Tractor/Box							
	Prep	1.2	WEEKS	1		1,100	1,320	
	Production	4	WEEKS	1		1,100	4,400	
	HoneyWagon							
	Prep	0.2	WEEKS	1		1,400	280	
	Production	4	WEEKS	1		1,400	5,600	
	Overflow 5-Ton							
	5-Ton Truck							
	Prep	0.2	WEEKS	1		600	120	
	Production	2	WEEKS	1		600	1,200	
	Total							45,520
3540	TRAILER RENTALS							
	Make-Up & Hair Trailer							
	Prep	1	WEEK	1		800	800	
	Production	4	WEEKS	1		800	3,200	
	Wrap	0	WEEKS	1		800	0	
	Wardrobe Trailer							
	Prep	1	WEEK	1		800	800	
	Production	4	WEEKS	1		800	3,200	
	Wrap	0	WEEKS	1		800	0	

Acct No	Description	Amount	Units	X	Curr	Rate	Subtotal	Total
							8,000	
	1. Cast-Leads							
	Prep	0.4	WEEKS	1		850	340	
	Production	4	WEEKS	1		850	3,400	
	2. Cast-Leads							
	Prep	0.4	WEEKS	1		850	340	
	Production	4	WEEKS	1		850	3,400	
	3. Production Trailer							
	Director/Producer/AD/Transpo							
	Production	2	WEEKS	1		750	1,500	
	Total							16,980
3555	PICTURE VEHICLE RENTAL							
	Picture Vehicles	1	ALLOW	1		10,000	10,000	
	Total							10,000
3556	OTHER VEHICLE RENTALS							
	(Mules/Gators/Special)							
	Prep	1	WEEK	2		200	400	
	Production	4	WEEKS	2		200	1,600	
	Total							2,000
3560	GENERATORS							
	Prep	1	WEEK	1		750	750	
	Production	4	WEEKS	1		750	3,000	
	Total							3,750
3565	VEHICLE TRANSPORT/MILEAGE							
	Production	2,000	Miles	1		0.42	840	
	Transport Charges	1	ALLOW	1		500	500	
	Picture Car Trailer	6	WEEKS	1		150	900	
	Total							2,240
3570	GAS/DIESEL							
	(cars/vans/trucks/other)	1	ALLOW	1		5,000	5,000	
	Total							5,000
3571	TRANSPORTATION PURCHASES							
	(cones/signs/barracades)	1	ALLOW	1		1,000	1,000	
	Total							1,000
3572	FITTING OUT RENTALS							
	Rigging	1	ALLOW	1		200	200	
	Shelving	1	ALLOW	1		150	150	
	Other Rentals	1	ALLOW	1		250	250	
	Total							600
3574	MAINTENANCE & SERVICE							
	Trailer/Vehicle Maintenance	0	ALLOW	1		500	0	
	Clean Outs- Honeywagon							
	Production	20	DAYS	0.5		200	2,000	
	Total							2,000
3575	PARKING & STORAGE							
	Production	1	ALLOW	1		250	250	
	Total							250
3576	EXPENDABLES/KEYS/SUPPLIES							
	Production	1	ALLOW	1		250	250	
	Key Duplication	1	ALLOW	1		100.0	100	
	Total							350
3580	REPAIRS & DAMAGES							

Continuation of Account 3580

Acct No	Description	Amount	Units	X	Curr	Rate	Subtotal	Total
	Damage & Loss Allowance	1	ALLOW	1		1,200	1,200	
	Total							1,200
3585	OTHER COSTS							
	Miscellaneous Charges	1	ALLOW	1		25.0	25	
	Total							25
3599	Total Fringes							
	PR FEE (Chks)	0.05%				12,595	6	
	FICA (NM/CA/NY)	6.2%				125,350.77	7,772	
	MED (NM/CA/NY)	1.45%				125,350.77	1,818	
	FUTA (NM/CA/NY)	0.8%				118,121.97	945	
	SUTA (NM)	5.4%				84,381.4	4,557	
	SUTA (CA/NY)	6.2%				35,274.97	2,187	
	W-COMP (NM)	2.85%				95,622.48	2,725	
	W-COMP (CA/NY)	4.71%				42,323.29	1,993	
	ETT (NM)	0.1%				82,847	83	
	TEAMSTER-%	11.72%				137,945.77	16,166	
	PAYROLL FEE	0.35%				125,350.77	439	
	TEAMSTER-Hr	4	HOURS			20,954.16	20,954	59,645
Account Total for 3500								302,730
3600 LOCATION								
3601	LOCATION MANAGER							
	Prep (10 hrs)	2	WEEKS	1		1,750	3,500	
	Production (10 hr day)	4	WEEKS	1		1,750	7,000	
	Total							10,500
3602	ASST LOCATION MGR							
	Prep	1	WEEK	1		1,000	1,000	
	Production (12 hr day)	4	WEEKS	1		1,000	4,000	
	Total							5,000
3608	LOCATION PA							
	Production	2	WEEKS	1		500	1,000	
	Total							1,000
3625	FACILITIES RENTAL							
	Production/Location Office	2	MONTHS	1		20,000	40,000	
	*Allowance (Distant Locations)	1	ALLOW	1		1,500	1,500	
	Total							41,500
3626	OFFICE EQUIP RENT/UTILITIES							
	Desks/Tables/Furniture	1	ALLOW	1		1,500	1,500	
	Electricity							
	Prep	1	WEEK	1		250	250	
	Production	4	WEEKS	1		250	1,000	
	Wrap	1	WEEK	1		250	250	
	Photocopy (rental)	8	WEEKS	1		400	3,200	
	Total							6,200
3628	PHOTOCOPY							
	Photocopy Machine Rental	7	WEEKS	1		275	1,925	
	Prep/Prod/Wrap	7	WEEKS	5,000		0.015	525	
	Total							2,450
3630	OFFICE SUPPLIES							
	Production Office Supplies	8	WEEKS	1		300	2,400	
	Total							2,400
3635	TELEPHONE/FAX/CELL/INTERNET							

Continuation of Account 3635

Acct No	Description	Amount	Units	X	Curr	Rate	Subtotal	Total
	Telephone/Internet Installation	1	Contract	1		2,000	2,000	
	Telephone System Rental							
	Prep	2	WEEKS	25		8.5	425	
	Production	4	WEEKS	25		8.5	850	
	Wrap	1	WEEK	25		8.5	212	
	Telephone Service							
	Prep	2	WEEKS	1		350	700	
	Production	4	WEEKS	1		500	2,000	
	Wrap	1	WEEK	1		500	500	
	Cell Phone Rental/Service							
	Prep	2	WEEKS	10		28.0	560	
	Production	4	WEEKS	15		28.0	1,680	
	Other Long Distance Reimbursal	1	ALLOW	1		250	250	
	Total							9,178
3640	SITE RENTAL FEES							
	Location Fees	10	ALLOW	1		1,500	15,000	
	Total							15,000
3641	LOCATION PERMITS/LICENSE							
	Park Service/BLM Permits							
	Landscapes/Parks/Desert	1	Permits	1		200	200	
	Other	1	ALLOW	1		150	150	
	Impact & Application Charges	1	ALLOW	1		100.0	100	
	Total							450
3642	HOLDING/PARKING							
	*Base Camp	1	ALLOW	1		1,000	1,000	
	*Holding Areas	1	ALLOW	1		800	800	
	*Crew Parking Areas	1	ALLOW	1		500	500	
	Total							2,300
3643	COURTESY/MONITOR PAYMENTS							
	Location Gratuities	1	ALLOW	1		1,000	1,000	
	Location Monitor Allowance	1	ALLOW	1		400	400	
	Total							1,400
3644	TRAFFIC/LOCATION CONTROL							
	Local Police Allowance							
	Production (Road ITC)	4	DAYS	20		30.0	2,400	
	Total							2,400
3645	TENTAGE LABOR/MATERIALS							
	Catering Tent Setup	10	DAYS	1		600	6,000	
	Production	4	WEEKS	1		100.0	400	
	Total							6,400
3648	EXPENDABLE SUPPLIES							
	Production	1	ALLOW	1		300	300	
	Total							300
3650	SHIPPING COSTS							
	Grip/Electric	1	ALLOW	1		500	500	
	Prop & Dressing Shipping	1	ALLOW	1		700	700	
	Camera Shipping (receive/return)	1	ALLOW	1		700	700	
	Sound Shipping	1	ALLOW	1		150	150	
	EFX Shipping	1	ALLOW	1		600	600	
	Wardrobe Shipping	1	ALLOW	1		500	500	
	Other Equipment	1	ALLOW	1		250	250	
	Exposed Stock & Dailies							
	Location to Lab	20	DAYS	1		100.0	2,000	

Acct No	Description	Amount	Units	X	Curr	Rate	Subtotal	Total
	Lab to Location	20	DAYS	1		18.0	360	
	Other	1	ALLOW	1		100.0	100	
	Messenger Service	20	DAYS	1		30.0	600	
	Production	1	ALLOW	1		1,000	1,000	
	Total							7,460
3655	LOCAL LABOR							
	Office Cleaning Service	6	WEEKS	1		300	1,800	
	Clean Up/Restoration	1	ALLOW	1		200	200	
	Other	1	ALLOW	1		250	250	
	Total							2,250
3660	SPECIAL EQUIPMENT							
	Heaters (portable)	1	ALLOW	1		2,000	2,000	
	Location							
	Dumpsters/Trash Removal	1	ALLOW	1		1,600	1,600	
	Misc Set Supplies	1	ALLOW	1		100.0	100	
	Total							3,700
3662	BOX RENTALS							
	Location Manager							
	Prep	2	WEEKS	1		100.0	200	
	Production	4	WEEKS	1		100.0	400	
	Total							600
3665	FILM & PROCESSING							
	Prep/Production Allowance	1	ALLOW	1		100.0	100	
	Total							100
3670	OFFICE CRAFT SERVICE							
	Production	8	WEEKS	1		150	1,200	
	Total							1,200
3672	CAR ALLOWANCES							
	Car Allowances							
	Prep	2	WEEKS	1		125	250	
	Production	4	WEEKS	1		125	500	
	Asst Locations							
	Prep	1	WEEK	1		75.0	75	
	Production	2	WEEKS	1		75.0	150	
	Total							975
3675	REPAIR & DAMAGE							
	Location Repair & Damage	1	ALLOW	1		1,000	1,000	
	Total							1,000
3685	OTHER COSTS							
	Miscellaneous Other Costs	1	ALLOW	1		100.0	100	
	Total							100
3699	Total Fringes							
	FICA (NM/CA/NY)	6.2%				19,300	1,197	
	MED (NM/CA/NY)	1.45%				19,300	280	
	FUTA (NM/CA/NY)	0.8%				19,300	154	
	SUTA (NM)	5.4%				19,300	1,042	
	W-COMP (NM)	2.85%				19,300	550	
	ETT (NM)	0.1%				19,300	19	
	TEAMSTER-%	11.72%				16,500	1,934	
	PAYROLL FEE	0.35%				19,300	68	5,244
Account Total for 3600								**129,107**

Acct No	Description	Amount	Units	X	Curr	Rate	Subtotal	Total
3700 PROD / FILM & LAB								
3701	35mm RAW STOCK							
	Neg. Raw Stock per Day	5,850	Feet	20		0.5	58,500	
	Total							58,500
3702	35mm PROCESS/DEVELOP							
	Develop 95% of Stock							
	Exposed Footage Process	111,150	Feet	1		0.1	11,115	
	Total							11,115
3703	35mm DAILIES							
	35mm Workprint	2,000	Feet	1		0.3	600	
	Total							600
3705	VIDEO TRANSFER							
	Film to Tape Transfer	3	HOURS	20		300	18,000	
	Dubbing Charges (VHS/DVD/DV Ca	160	Dubs	1		7.5	1,200	
	Negative Sonic Clean	1	ALLOW	1		200	200	
	Negative Assembly (for 35mm WP	1	ALLOW	1		100.0	100	
	DV Cam Tapes (2 copies)	35	Tapes	2		20.0	1,400	
	DVD Burn (2 copies)	35	DVD	2		2.0	140	
	Dub/Burn Fees	1	ALLOW	1		1,000	1,000	
	Multiple Deck-DVD Fees/Other	1	ALLOW	1		1,200	1,200	
	Total							23,240
3707	VIDEO DUBS & STOCK							
	Courtesy Dubs (3)	20	DAYS	2		25.0	1,000	
	Stock	1	ALLOW	1		250	250	
	Total							1,250
3745	STILL FILM							
	*3 rolls per day							
	Stock/Process/Proof	20	DAYS	3		30.0	1,800	
	Total							1,800
3750	POLAROID FILM							
	Polaroid Film	20	DAYS	2		9.0	360	
	Total							360
3760	STILL PRINTS							
	Printing	1	ALLOW	1		150	150	
	Total							150
3785	OTHER COSTS							
	Miscellaneous Other Costs	1	ALLOW	1		150	150	
	Total							150
3799	Total Fringes							0
Account Total for 3700								**97,165**
3800 TRAVEL & LIVING COSTS								
3801	AIRFARE							
	Prod Acct							
	LA/NM	2	RT	1		450	900	
	Payroll Acct							
	SC/NM	1	RT	1		650	650	
	Director of Photography							
	LA/NM	2	RT	1		450	900	
	Allowance for Unknown to date							
	LA/NM	3	RT	1		450	1,350	
	Total							3,800

419

Acct No	Description	Amount	Units	X	Curr	Rate	Subtotal	Total
3802	LODGING							
	2nd AD							
	Prep	2	WEEKS	1		354.27	708	
	Shoot	4	WEEKS	1		354.27	1,417	
	Prod Acct							
	Prep	2	WEEKS	1		560	1,120	
	Shoot	4	WEEKS	1		560	2,240	
	Payroll Acct							
	Prep	2	WEEKS	1		354.27	708	
	Shoot	4	WEEKS	1		354.27	1,417	
	Const. Paint/Crew							
	Lodging (share)	6	WEEKS	1		560	3,360	
	Chef/Asst 1/Asst 2							
	Lodging (share)	4	WEEKS	1		560	2,240	
	EFX CREW							
	Lodging (share)	5	WEEKS	1		1,000	5,000	
	Dressers							
	Lodging (share)	6	WEEKS	1		354.27	2,125	
	Costumers							
	Lodging (share)	6	WEEKS	1		354.27	2,125	
	MAKE-UP CREW							
	Lodging (share)	6	WEEKS	1		354.27	2,125	
	GRIP/ELECTRIC CREW							
	Lodging (share)	6	WEEKS	1		354.27	2,125	
	Director of Photography							
	Lodging	6	WEEKS	1		650	3,900	
	Camera Assts/Operators							
	Lodging (share)	6	WEEKS	1		354.27	2,125	
	Coordinator							
	Lodging	4	WEEKS	1		354.27	1,417	
	Captain							
	Lodging (payment/trailer)	6	WEEKS	1		354.27	2,125	
	Co-Captain							
	Lodging	6	WEEKS	1		354.27	2,125	
	ADDITIONAL							
	Allowance Lodging Distant Crew	1	WEEK	1		354.27	354	
	Total							38,762
3803	PER DIEM							
	2nd AD							
	Per Diem	6	WEEKS	1		350	2,100	
	Prod Acct							
	Per Diem	6	WEEKS	1		350	2,100	
	Payroll Acct							
	Per Diem	6	WEEKS	1		350	2,100	
	EFX CREW							
	Supervisor & Asst							
	Per Diem	6	WEEKS	2		350	4,200	
	Coordinator							
	Per Diem	4	WEEKS	1		350	1,400	
	Captain							
	Per Diem	6	WEEKS	1		350	2,100	
	Director of Photography							
	Per Diem (Location)	6	WEEKS	1		420	2,520	

Continuation of Account 3803

Acct No	Description	Amount	Units	X	Curr	Rate	Subtotal	Total
	Distant Crew							
	Per Diem (Location)	6	WEEKS	3		350	6,300	
	ADDITIONAL							
	Allowance Per Diem Distant Crew	1	WEEK	1		350	350	
	Total							23,170
3804	GROUND TRAVEL							
	Prod Acct							
	Vehicle Rental	6	WEEKS	1		250	1,500	
	Payroll Acct							
	Vehicle Rental	6	WEEKS	1		250	1,500	
	Mileage Allownace							
	Allowance	600	miles	1		0.4	240	
	Const. Coordinator							
	Vehicle Allowance	6	WEEKS	1		100.0	600	
	Key Scenic							
	Vehicle Allowance	6	WEEKS	1		100.0	600	
	Director of Photography							
	Vehicle Rental	6	WEEKS	1		250	1,500	
	ADDITIONAL							
	Allowance Additional Travel	1	ALLOW	1		250	250	
	LA Trips (Equip)	1	ALLOW	1		750	750	
	Mileage (Camera/Other)	1	ALLOW	1		250	250	
	EFX Crew	1	ALLOW	1		750	750	
	Total							7,940
3805	FUEL/MAINTENANCE							
	FUEL All Vehicles	1	ALLOW	1		2,000	2,000	
	Maintenance All Vehicles	1	ALLOW	1		200	200	
	Total							2,200
3806	OTHER							
	Loss & Damage	1	ALLOW	1		600	600	
	Total							600
3899	Total Fringes							0
Account Total for 3800								**76,472**
	TOTAL PRODUCTION							**2,027,847**

Acct No	Description	Amount	Units	X	Curr	Rate	Subtotal	Total
4500 EDITORIAL								
4501	POST SUPERVISOR							
	POST SUPERVISOR	1	ALLOW	1		20,000	20,000	
	Total							20,000
4502	EDITOR							
	Shoot	4	WEEKS	1		2,250	9,000	
	Post	12	WEEKS	1		2,250	27,000	
	Total							36,000
4503	ASST. EDITOR							
	Shoot	4	WEEKS	1		1,349	5,396	
	Post	16	WEEKS	1		1,349	21,584	
	Total							26,980
4504	EDITORIAL PURCHASE							
	Expendables	16	WEEKS	1		75.0	1,200	
	Tape Stock/Copies of Cut	1	ALLOW	1		1,000	1,000	
	Miscellaneous	20	WEEKS	1		100.0	2,000	
	Total							4,200
4506	EDITORIAL RENTALS							
	FINAL CUT PRO	1	ALLOW	0.7		11,000	7,700	
	MEDIA SHARE	16	WEEKS	1		500	8,000	
	OFFICES	16	WEEKS	1		200	3,200	
	TELEPHONE	20	MONTHS	1		100.0	2,000	
	MISC RENTAL	1		1		3,000	3,000	
	Total							23,900
4508	CONTINUITY SCRIPT							
	Dialogue Continuity & Spotting List	1	ALLOW	1		1,700	1,700	
	Total							1,700
4509	VISUAL EFFECTS							
	VFX PKG	1	ALLOW	1		150,000	150,000	
	TAPE STOCK	1	ALLOW	1		1,000	1,000	
	DUBS	1	ALLOW	1		1,000	1,000	
	Total							152,000
4520	DUBS							
	DELIVERY REQUIREMENTS	1	ALLOW	1		5,000	5,000	
	Total							5,000
4599	Total Fringes							
	FICA #1	6.2%				82,980	5,145	
	FICA #2	1.45%				82,980	1,203	
	WC - PROD	3.21%				20,000	642	
	WC - EDIT (CA)	1.75%				62,980	1,102	
	FUI	0.8%				82,980	664	
	SUI (CA)	5.4%				82,980	4,481	
	PR FEE (Chks)	0.05%				82,980	41	
	IA/TEAMSTER	13.5%				62,980	8,500	21,778
Account Total for 4500								291,558
4600 MUSIC								
4602	COMPOSER							
	Composer/Conductor	1	ALLOW	1		25,000	25,000	
	Total							25,000
4603	MUSIC EDITOR							
	Editor (Includes Pro Tools)	6	WEEKS	1		2,000	12,000	

Acct No	Description	Amount	Units	X	Curr	Rate	Subtotal	Total
	Total							12,000
4699	Total Fringes							
	FICA #1	6.2%				25,000	1,550	
	FICA #2	1.45%				25,000	362	
	WC - PROD	3.21%				25,000	802	
	FUI	0.8%				25,000	200	
	SUI (CA)	5.4%				25,000	1,350	
	PR FEE (Chks)	0.05%				25,000	12	4,278
Account Total for 4600								**41,278**

4700 POST SOUND

Acct No	Description	Amount	Units	X	Curr	Rate	Subtotal	Total
4704	SOUND PACKAGE							
	Pre-Dub/2 Mixers	10	DAYS	9		300	27,000	
	Final Dub/2 Mixers	12	DAYS	9		300	32,400	
	Print Master	2	DAYS	9		300	5,400	
	Stereo M&E	2	DAYS	9		300	5,400	
	Temp Layback	4	HOURS	1		300	1,200	
	Total							71,400
4789	MISC EXPENSES							
	CRAFT SERVICE	16	MONTHS	1		25.0	400	
	PARKING	5	ALLOW	1		200	1,000	
	MESSENGER	4	MONTHS	1		200	800	
	MISC. SOUND SUPPLIES	1		1		1,000	1,000	
	DOLBY LICENSE VIDEO ONLY	1		1		2,500	2,500	
	Total							5,700
4799	Total Fringes							0
Account Total for 4700								**77,100**

4800 STOCK SHOTS

Acct No	Description	Amount	Units	X	Curr	Rate	Subtotal	Total
4801	STOCK SHOTS							
	MISCELLANEOUS	1	ALLOW	1		5,000	5,000	
	Total							5,000
4899	Total Fringes							0
Account Total for 4800								**5,000**

4900 MAIN & END TITLES

Acct No	Description	Amount	Units	X	Curr	Rate	Subtotal	Total
4900	MAIN & END TITLES							
	MAIN TITLES	1	ALLOW	1		5,000	5,000	
	CLOSED CAPTIONING	1	ALLOW	1		1,500	1,500	
	END TITLE CRAWL	1	ALLOW	1		2,500	2,500	
	Total							9,000
4999	Total Fringes							0
Account Total for 4900								**9,000**

5000 POST HD/FILM & LABORATORY

Acct No	Description	Amount	Units	X	Curr	Rate	Subtotal	Total
5001	On Line Editing HD Cam SR 16x9							
	DIGITIZE SOURCE ELEMENTS	14	HOURS	1		350	4,900	
	ASSEMBLE to HD SR Segmented Re	10	HOURS	1		450	4,500	
	MISC. TITLING/OPTICALS	8	HOURS	1		450	3,600	
	HD CAM STOCK TAPE	6	TAPES	1		100.0	600	

Acct No	Description	Amount	Units	X	Curr	Rate	Subtotal	Total
	QC 100%	5	HOURS	1		175	875	
	TAPE TO TAPE COLOR CORRECTIC	1	ALLOW	1		22,000	22,000	
	Total							36,475
5099	Total Fringes							0
Account Total for 5000								36,475
5100 POST MANAGEMENT								
5101	POST ACCOUNTANT							
	Post Accountant	6	WEEKS	1		1,000	6,000	
	Total							6,000
5199	Total Fringes							
	FICA (NM/CA/NY)	6.2%				6,000	372	
	MED (NM/CA/NY)	1.45%				6,000	87	
	FUTA (NM/CA/NY)	0.8%				6,000	48	
	SUTA (CA/NY)	6.2%				6,000	372	
	W-COMP (CA/NY)	4.71%				6,000	283	
	IATSE-%	12.22%				6,000	733	
	PAYROLL FEE	0.35%				6,000	21	
	IATSE-Hr	3	HOURS			1,151.1	1,151	3,067
Account Total for 5100								9,067
	TOTAL POST PRODUCTION							469,477

Acct No	Description	Amount	Units	X	Curr	Rate	Subtotal	Total
6600 LEGAL								
6601	LEGAL							
	Legal Contract	1	ALLOW	35,000		1.0	35,000	
	Total							35,000
6699	Total Fringes							
	PR FEE (Chks)	0.05%				35,000	18	18
Account Total for 6600								35,018
6700 INSURANCE								
6703	INSURANCE							
	PRODUCTION INSURANCE	1.55	ALLOW	1		30,000	46,500	
	GENERAL LIABILITY	1	ALLOW	1		13,000	13,000	
	Total							59,500
6705	E&O PKG							
	Errors & OmissionPKG	1	ALLOW	1		5,000	5,000	
	Total							5,000
6799	Total Fringes							0
Account Total for 6700								64,500
	AGENCY PACKAGING FEE : 1.0%							35,471
	COMPLETION BOND : 1.75%							62,074
	CONTINGENCY : 10.0%							354,708
	TOTAL OTHER							551,770

Acct No	Description	Amount	Units	X	Curr	Rate	Subtotal	Total
	Grand Total							3,999,330

This book was designed by Lydia Marano for Menabrea Books, an imprint of Babbage Press, using a Macintosh G5 and Adobe FrameMaker 7. It was printed by LSI on sixty pound, offset cream-white acid-free stock. The text font is Minion, a Garalde Oldstyle typeface designed by Robert Slimbach in 1990 for Adobe Systems. Minion was inspired by the elegant and highly readable type designs of master printers Claude Garamond and Aldus Manutius in the late Renaissance. Created primarily for type-setting, Minion lends an aesthetic quality to the modern versatility of digital technology.